THE MEXICAN
ARISTOCRACY

An Expressive Ethnography,
1910–2000

HUGO G. NUTINI

UNIVERSITY OF TEXAS PRESS

AUSTIN

Requests for permission to reproduce material from this work should be
sent to Permissions, University of Texas Press, P.O. Box 7819, Austin,
TX 78713-7819.

♾ The paper used in this book meets the minimum requirements of
ANSI/NISO Z39.48-1992 (R1997) (Permanence of Paper).

Library of Congress Cataloging-in-Publication Data
Nutini, Hugo G.
The Mexican aristocracy : an expressive ethnography, 1910–2000 / Hugo G. Nutini.— 1st ed.
p.   cm.
Includes bibliographical references and index.
ISBN 0-292-70161-6 (cloth : alk. paper)
1. Aristocracy (Social class)—Mexico—History—20th century.   I. Title.
HT653.M6N877   2004
305.5′2′09720904—dc22
2003023946

CONTENTS

PREFACE

This ethnographic study is a sequel to *The Wages of Conquest: The Mexican Aristocracy in the Context of Western Aristocracies*, which deals with the inception, development, decline, and expressive culture of this vanishing social class in the superordinate stratification of Mexico. The ethnographic description and analysis were essentially completed by the spring of 1996; I then had a very difficult time with the expressive analysis and its integration into the ethnographic description. Having no model for the organization and presentation of an expressive ethnography, I had to tread carefully in developing the relationship between structure and expression and be equally careful in establishing the contexts in which the expression takes place. The problem revolved around what expression is, its structural sources, the contextual conditions of time and space, and the social and psychological factors that motivate expression. This led to several false starts, and I had to begin all over again. Finally, the various structural and expressive strands came together, and I was able to present an ethnographically consistent view of expression which accounted socially and psychologically for much of aristocratic behavior, particularly throughout this social class's precipitous decline during the past two generations.

This book presents the transformation of the Mexican aristocracy from the onset of the Revolution of 1910, when it was the undisputed social class of the country, until the end of the century, when the aristocracy was well on its way to disappearance as a functioning social group of superordinate stratification. From the inception of this study in 1978, the basic premise was that the aristocracy in the twentieth century could not be understood in isolation; rather, it had to be placed in the context of the superordinate stratification of Mexico City, where the aristocracy had concentrated since right after the 1934–1940 land reform during the presidency of Lázaro Cárdenas. The aristocracy had to be analyzed in close relationship with the plutocracy and the upper-middle class. (Given the highly centralized nature of the country, which from early colonial times until today has led to concentration of the political, economic, and social elites in Mexico City, it is quite proper to speak of a national superordinate class based in the capital.) Thus this study goes beyond the aristocracy and presents a fairly detailed picture of superordinate stratification.

Expressively, the ethnography extends beyond the superordinate class and includes a significant amount of information on the middle classes, the urban working classes, and rural Indian and mestizo society. This was a necessary strategy in order to analyze the expressive array of aristocrats in particular and several aspects of expressive culture in general. The aristocracy shares many domains with Indians and rural mestizos, and analysis of these groups was instrumental in exemplifying the distribution of expressive domains across the spectrum of stratification. It was important to say something about the expressive array of most classes of Mexican society in order to determine what belongs exclusively to the aristocracy and what the aristocracy shares with proximate and increasingly distant classes of society. (Unfortunately, the original manuscript came to more than 1,000 pages; no press would publish it, given the economic straits of university publishing today. I was therefore forced to make two books out of the original manuscript: the present volume and another on the Mexican stratification system co-authored by Barry L. Isaac, where I discuss the topics specified in this paragraph.)

The reasons that led me to the study of the Mexican aristocracy, the historical and ethnographic strategies employed, the social and stratificational context, the quantitative and qualitative data on which the overall study is based, and the methods and techniques involved are specified in the Preface to *The Wages of Conquest*. Suffice it to note here that the historical investigation had been completed by 1987, including the decline of the aristocracy since the Mexican Revolution of 1910. The collection of ethnographic data, however, continued until 1996, and a significant amount of this information is part of the present book. Thus, strictly speaking, the ethnographic present of this volume is 1990–2000; but the reader should be aware that some of the description and analysis extends to the turn of the twentieth century and more extensively to the period from the late 1940s to 1999.

Again I thank the National Endowment for the Humanities, the American Philosophical Society, the Wenner-Gren Foundation for Anthropological Research, the Pittsburgh Foundation, the University of Pittsburgh Center for Latin American Studies, and the University of Pittsburgh Faculty of Arts and Sciences Research Fund for the generous financial support that enabled me to gather the historical, ethnohistorical, and ethnographic data on which this book is based. I would also like to thank the Richard D. and Mary Jane Edwards Endowed Publication Fund for providing the necessary funds for preparation of the index.

It would be impossible to single out every individual or institution that in one way or another helped me in the fieldwork upon which the study is based, but I would like to express my appreciation to those that made the most significant contributions. I am grateful to the Academia Mexicana de Genealogía y Heráldica (Mexican Academy of Genealogy and Heraldry) for electing me to its membership and to its former president, Don Teodoro Amerlinck y Zirión, for discussions which bear directly on the present volume. I would like to thank the countless informants who provided ethnographic information in short interviews, extended interviews, questionnaires, and psychological and sociological tests and tasks for their openness and willingness to help and for the time and effort they devoted to these manifold data-gathering activities.

I am intellectually and professionally indebted to L. Keith Brown, Solange Alberro, María Teresa Cervantes, Rosa María Cervantes, Leonard Plotnicov, Guillermo Kreush, Jean F. Nutini, Harold D. Sims, the late Vinigi L. Grottanelli, and the late Italo Signorini, who read part of the manuscript, made constructive criticism, suggested changes in style and organization, or discussed theoretical and methodological matters with me. Among several dozen informants I particularly wish to thank José Luis Pérez de Salazar, Teodoro Amerlinck y Zirión, Fernando Cervantes Palomino, Peter Corsi Cabrera, Carlos Cervantes Escandón, the late Daniel Rábago Chávez, Gastón Mendoza Rul, María Concepción Amerlinck y Assereto, Juan Cervantes Palomino, Eduardo León de la Barra, Luis Ortiz Macedo, Marita Martínez del Río de Redo, Joaquín de la Borbolla, Carmen de Ovando de Cervantes, Isabel Cervantes de Ovando, Carlotta Mapelli Mozzi, the late Cucú Cabrera Ypiña de Corsi, and the late Landolfo Colonna di Stigliano. I am very grateful for their detailed information, comments, and suggestions, which were extremely valuable for the expressive analysis and greatly enriched the ethnographic description.

I dedicated *The Wages of Conquest* to the late Carlos de Ovando Gutie-rrez. He and his wife, Carmelita Pérez de Salazar de Ovando, were exceptional sources of information of inestimable significance. They were peerless informants and collaborators. The rich texture of their data (elicited in several hundred hours of conversation) constitutes my most important source; their precise, penetrating descriptions of the behavior and expression of the aristocracy contributed immeasurably to the realization of the present study. To them, I owe my greatest debt of gratitude.

To the late John M. Roberts, I owe many of the ideas concerning the expressive components of the aristocracy in particular and stratification in general. Indeed, the structural and expressive study of the Mexican aristocracy was a collaborative enterprise; John was instrumental in designing several domains of its implementation. Were he alive today, he would be the co-author of this book.

Last but not least, I am especially grateful to Doren L. Slade and Lisa J. Moskowitz for their intellectual generosity, readiness to discuss ideas, and willingness to offer exact and penetrating criticism. They read the entire manuscript and did an excellent editing job by making obscure passages readable, deleting personal biases, and toning down idiosyncratic proclivities. They were most effective in clarifying and expanding my psychological interpretations and helping me reach congruent socio-psychological conclusions.

H.G.N.

THE MEXICAN ARISTOCRACY

INTRODUCTION

This book is a continuation of *The Wages of Conquest* (Nutini 1995), which is concerned with the Mexican aristocracy, the superordinate class of the country since the Spanish Conquest. Together the two volumes constitute a comprehensive structural and expressive treatment of this social class, its evolution throughout nearly five centuries, and its place in the stratification system of Mexico. Although each is essentially a self-contained monograph, a certain amount of background information will help the reader. Therefore, in these introductory remarks I summarize the most salient points and themes discussed in the first volume. Since the methodological and theoretical framework on which the entire study is based is discussed in the Introduction to that monograph, here I confine myself to restating the basic components underlying the nature of social stratification as I have defined the term: its expressive aspect, upward and downward mobility, the new realignment of classes, aristocratic-plutocratic acculturation, and so on. This is necessary because the conceptual foundation of the study must be handled differently in diachronic and synchronic contexts.

In the balance of these introductory remarks, I address three sets of interrelated topics. First, I present a summary of the Mexican aristocracy which emphasizes the salient diachronic-synchronic junctures from the Spanish Conquest to the Revolution of 1910. Next, I discuss the differential efficacy of expressive behavior, social mobility, and class affiliation in terminal decline. Finally, I describe the aristocracy in the context of the new Mexican superordinate class as it coalesced during the second half of the twentieth century. Unless otherwise indicated, the ethnographic present of this monograph is 1990–2000.

Inception of the Study and Diachronic Background

The paucity of studies of upper-class stratification originally led me to investigate the aristocracy and how it had changed since the onset of the Mexican Revolution. As if by design, social scientists had ignored this social class. Few of the works written on Mexico and comparable areas of Latin America by social scientists are useful, but the works of historians on the nobility and various European aristocracies from the tenth century to the twentieth century are indeed useful for comparative purposes.

Historians, unencumbered by sociological concerns, have been able to ascertain, for example, that within the predominant capitalistic mode of production characteristic of European society during the last 250 years significant elements of the seigneurial period have survived as distinct categories. Thus historians and some gifted social critics analyze contemporary nobility or aristocracy in England, Spain, or France as significant groups, although most social scientists dismiss them as irrelevant by seeing them as spurious survivals from the past. Or these groups are indiscriminately seen as part of a contemporary bourgeois ruling class. Politically powerless and relatively insignificant economically as these social elites may be, they nonetheless exist in a distinctly organized fashion, and they have something that undoubtedly appeals to the real ruling class and/or political class. Explaining social elites and their persistence, once they have lost their status as ruling and political classes, is a central concern of this book.

Shortly after data collection began in 1978, I realized two things. First, a study of an upper class in the traditional mold would result in either another description of a classical aristocracy in the process of being replaced by a new plutocracy or just another urban ethnography in the usual anthropological style. Second, a historical or ethnographic account of the Mexican aristocracy based on structural considerations alone would not explain how this social class has survived without political power and most of its wealth and how it has managed to influence and shape a new upper class that is in the process of replacing it.

Being in this predicament, I turned to the expressive approach as a complementary analytical tool, both to generate some answers to questions of social mobility and persistence and to amplify the concept of social class, particularly at the higher echelons of the stratification system. Class position, mobility, and class consciousness are admittedly entailed by economic forces in action, are concomitantly discharged in a number of cultural domains (the most prominent being the social, the political, and the religious), and are supported by an ideological superstructure designed to perpetuate the status quo.

Thus to say that this study is first and foremost an expressive description and analysis of the Mexican aristocracy means that, based on a solid structural foundation, the expressive focus is the main analytical tool that generates explanations in domains that the traditional approach to social stratification has not explained. This approach may be characterized as one in which structural (economic, political, and other) variables constitute the necessary conditions for the conceptualization of social stratification, while expressive variables constitute the sufficient conditions that in specified settings and domains account for social mobility and the persistence of class ideology.

Although the Mexican aristocracy today does not have residential unity — nor does it constitute a community in the conventional sociological sense — the great majority of its members reside in circumscribed areas of Mexico City. This is not a rigidly bounded group; but by standard criteria of self-identification, the majority of married members know each other personally or by reference and individuals can always be placed genealogically by ancestral place of origin. The Mexican aristocracy today has an approximate membership of 5,500 at most, including roughly 800 households (nuclear family households with a sprinkling of extended family households). The adult population, including married couples and young and old single individuals (roughly 55 percent of the group), constituted the pool from which informants were drawn.

This study is primarily an exercise in expression. The attendant conceptual approach, which I have termed the expressive focus and strategy, serves as the guiding mechanism of description and analysis. This book and the previous volume demonstrate the fundamental proposition of the study: that expressive behavior and expressively derived considerations are at the heart of explaining social mobility. Two other conceptual approaches are complementary to the primary expressive thrust: network analysis and the renewal of elites. Network analysis has been previously employed in studies of ritual kinship (Nutini 1984; Nutini and White 1977). The network approach is used in the analysis of plutocratic upward mobility and the accommodations made by aristocrats in order to survive. The renewal or circulation of elites, as originally postulated by Vilfredo Pareto (1935), provides the main analytical stance in explaining the evolution of the Mexican aristocracy and organizing the diachronic description in the first volume.

Finally, a few words about the general organization of this book. I should reiterate that the standard ethnography and expressive ethnography of the Mexican aristocracy are treated as an undifferentiated whole, as this seems to be the most efficient method of presentation. It avoids repetition and lends itself better to the identification of expressive domains. Thus the organization by chapters follows traditional ethnographic presentation, albeit modified by an accompanying expressive analysis. In this framework the reader will experience an immediate vision of the unfolding expressive array and witness the origin and implications of expressive domains as emanating from social and cultural behavior. Moreover, this method entails optimal conditions for isolating exclusive and inclusive domains and associating the latter with the social classes of Mexican society that share them with the aristocracy.

Differential Efficacy of Expressive Behavior, Social Mobility, and Class Affiliation in Terminal Decline

The combined approach developed in the historical-evolutionary analysis of the Mexican aristocracy applies equally to the fundamental changes that this social class has experienced since the 1910 Revolution. But the sociocultural milieu in which the aristocracy was embedded until 1910 is radically different from the economic and political environment generated by the Revolution. Moreover, the four-century dominance of the aristocracy created structural and expressive constraints that made it virtually impossible for this social class to overcome the impending economic decline that never materialized during the three renewals before the Revolution. These two factors require modifications in the conceptual framework and its application to the contemporary analysis of the aristocracy in terminal decline. Thus this book explains the dynamics of total class renewal—as contrasted with the partial renewals characteristic of the aristocracy from its inception to the 1910 Revolution—when a plutocratic sector becomes the predominant social and ruling class.

Expressive Acculturation with and without Dominance

The ideology and *imago mundi* of the Mexican aristocracy are essentially those of the Spanish aristocracy but somewhat modified by the Conquest of Mexico and the new socioeconomic conditions that emerged during the sixteenth century. The founders of the colonial Creole aristocracy were an original nucleus of conquistador-*encomenderos* that, by right of conquest, came to control large numbers of Indians and, in time, vast landed estates. By ancient seigneurial rights, conquistadors considered themselves entitled to honors and dignities (commoners aspired to *hidalguía*—gentry status—and *hidalgos* aspired to titles of nobility) which the Crown was not willing to grant, as it did not want to perpetuate a seigneurial system that the Catholic kings had largely managed to dismantle in Spain. Nonetheless, despite the original refusal of the Crown and gradual granting of honors and dignities, conquistadors and *encomenderos* from the start regarded themselves as nobles and gentry. The possession of tributary Indians and (later in the century) landed and some mining wealth validated their pretensions; and it is in this environment that a Creole aristocracy came into being by the last quarter of the sixteenth century. Concomitantly, the Creole aristocracy created an expressive array that, although essentially Spanish in its fundamental tenets, was significantly modified by colonial resources and constraints.

By the turn of the seventeenth century the ideology and *imago mundi* of the Creole aristocracy had achieved a configuration that remained remarkably constant for 300 years. Not surprisingly, the exclusive expressive array of the aristocracy also remained constant, since the overall social and economic configuration of Mexico, even after Independence, did not change much. The hacienda system—which came into existence as the result of the virtual demise of the *encomienda* system during the first half of the seventeenth century—remained *de facto* essentially unchanged as a seigneurial system until 1910.

Throughout these centuries the aristocracy underwent three renewals during which large numbers of *nouveau riche* plutocratic magnates joined the ranks of the aristocracy. These renewals generated changes in the aristocratic expressive array, as plutocratic ideology in all three instances was able to influence the dominant aristocratic ideology. But given the overwhelming preponderance of the aristocracy, the changes provoked by the acculturative context did not substantially change the exclusive array created by the conquistador-*encomendero* class in the sixteenth century and perpetuated by the *hacendado* class in subsequent centuries. On the whole, plutocrats changed the expressive array and worldview of aristocrats only peripherally throughout these renewals, as in most ways they had to adapt to aristocratic ways.

The Mexican Revolution not only terminated the local political importance of the hacienda but radically altered the position of the aristocracy as a social class *vis-à-vis* the global stratification system of the country. Despite the fact that the aristocracy had never been a political class (at the national level), for more than 300 years its social and ruling predominance had been unchallenged, as befitted the *de facto* seigneurial system that pervaded several aspects of Mexican society. All structural and expressive changes had hitherto been unable to dislodge the aristocracy as a social class.

By the end of the second decade of the twentieth century, during which the armed phase of the Mexican Revolution took place, the aristocracy had been largely reduced to a social group, increasingly vanishing from the consciousness of the population at large but still a group to contend with at the top of the stratification system. The coup de grace, however, came a decade and a half later with the massive land reform of President Lázaro Cárdenas, which by 1940 had completely abolished the great landed estates, so that their aristocratic owners ceased to have any ruling functions. From this point onward, the aristocracy was a mere social class, and a precarious one at that, as it was perceived both by the upwardly mobile elements that were filling the vacuum and by the majority of aristocrats themselves.

By 1920 most of the great landed estates were still in the possession of aristocrats, but a thorough land reform was only a matter of time. This was realized by only a small number of aristocrats, who managed to parcel and sell most of their land to farmers and small proprietors. These forward-looking aristocrats invested in industry and banking, ultimately becoming aristocratic plutocrats and spearheading the terminal renewal of the aristocracy. The great majority of aristocrats, however, held onto their land, wishfully thinking that massive land reform would never come. More than 90 percent of aristocratic landowners fell into this category, and by 1940 they were left with little more than the manorial establishments of their once immense estates. The net result of this economic disaster was that the aristocrats had become impoverished in less than a generation, and only the sheer predominance that they had once enjoyed saved them from even greater economic downfall. The situation was mitigated by the fact that (to some extent as a hobby and to some extent for utilitarian reasons) by the turn of the century significant numbers of aristocrats had become lawyers, physicians, and members of other liberal professions. Thus perhaps most members of the class were able to survive economically, without even considering that many of them were still rich in terms of art, residences, and other heirlooms which they adamantly refused to convert into negotiable assets. Nonetheless, impoverished as the aristocracy had become by the early 1940s, it still thoroughly dominated the social scene of Mexico City. This milieu is poignantly captured in the words of an informant:

The Mexican Aristocracy

I remember well the years before and after the war [1940–1950], when we were in fact aristocrats and not in name only, and when the new rich still paid us homage and we dominated the social life of the city [Mexico City] as if the Revolution had not taken place. Many of the families were no longer rich as in the old days, but they spent money as if there were no tomorrow on celebrations and balls that were the admiration of the city. It seemed as if our world was coming to an end, and the ostentation and lavishness [were] the last gasps of something that was dying. Some years later our resources could not compete with the *nouveau riche* class with which we had nothing in common [1955–1960]. From then on our decline began, so that today [1990] we are aristocrats in name only.

The fundamental reality in the evolution of the Mexican aristocracy since the Spanish Conquest is the seigneurial system that pervaded much of Mexican society and survived even after Independence, when the country became a representative democracy *de jure* but not *de facto*, as it took more than a century to approach that ideal. This institutional state of affairs underlined nearly four centuries of aristocratic dominance, which (despite lack of national political functions) enabled this social class to retain undisputed social predominance. A concomitant aspect in the evolution of the aristocracy is that all the renewals it underwent throughout its history were basically acculturative transformations—that is, concentrated periods of interaction with relatively large numbers of upwardly mobile personnel. These plutocratic personnel, as I have termed them, had a different *imago mundi* and expressive array; in the process of upward mobility and incorporation into the aristocracy, they made themselves felt, thereby structuring an acculturative matrix that resulted in a new social and ruling milieu, usually after a generation or so. Thus, in the renewals undergone by the aristocracy before 1910, a plutocratic *imago mundi* and specific expressive domains modified the ideology and expressive culture of the aristocracy but always within tolerable boundaries. The exclusive array of this culture remained basically unchanged, as these ideational elements came to reinforce aristocratic wealth and power.

This situation came to an end with the Mexican Revolution of 1910. As the seigneurial system disappeared, society as a whole began to democratize, and eventually the social system acquired a modern fluidity. The aristocracy, however, did not *ipso facto* disappear; nor was it drastically curtailed. Rather, there was a slow decline marked by four rather well-delineated stages, which are detailed in the Conclusions.

Herein lies the crux of the explanation of the evolution and transformation of the Mexican aristocracy before and after the 1910 Revolution. Before 1910 the aristocracy, by virtue of its unchallenged social and ruling standing, prevailed expressively. Because of its social and economic decline since the Revolution, the aristocracy has been seriously challenged by the new plutocracy, which, for at least a generation, has been creating its own expressive array.

The diachronic context of stratification of the Mexican aristocracy means fundamentally its transformation throughout nearly four centuries of total predominance, punctuated by adaptations enhancing its perpetuation as a social and ruling class. In this dynamic of continuous preponderance, economic variables (the *encomienda* and hacienda systems and seigneurialism, accompanied by rather pronounced ethnic differences) were the necessary conditions for the maintenance of a worldview and expressive array that constituted the sufficient conditions of superordinate stratification. Throughout the three renewals, plutocratic personnel in significant numbers were always incorporated into the aristocracy, increasing its survival and strength. Thus the processes of acculturation that these renewals involved were limited and asymmetrical, as plutocratic inputs, no matter how strong, were never enough to upset aristocratic supremacy.

Western European aristocracies, beginning shortly after the inception of absolutism in the early sixteenth century, interacted with an increasingly powerful plutocracy that made the process of structural and expressive acculturation almost symmetrical; by shortly after the French Revolution, they had undergone a significant degree of *embourgeoisement*. This is the natural development of the European aristocracy's not having been able to compete economically with the industrial plutocracy, which was the main architect of the Industrial Revolution that continued to dominate the economic life of Europe until the twentieth century. Thus expressive acculturation was until recently symmetrical, while structural integration was greatly skewed toward the plutocratic side of the equation—mainly because landed wealth could not compete with industrial wealth, to say nothing of the natural process of democratization that Europe has been undergoing for more than two centuries. The Mexican aristocracy, however, began its decline in 1910 and the accompanying process of asymmetrical acculturation (that is, processes that the European aristocracy began to experience when the Mexican aristocracy was in its formative stage) nearly four decades later. This was the result of the confluence of a belated seigneurialism and basically different ethnic and demographic orders as compared to those of Western Europe. Given these considerations, and far away from the mother country, the Mexican aristocracy *de facto* represents the perpetuation of a stratification system that had begun to decline in Western Europe while forming anew in the New World.

The synchronic context of structural-expressive stratification, in contrast, is concerned with the terminal phase of the Mexican aristocracy as a super-ordinate class, triggered by the 1910 Revolution and now approaching its end. The main concern of this final renewal is not with the continuity of expression. Rather, the emphasis is on how the terminal phase of the aristocracy has been instrumental in creating a new superordinate class: a new plutocracy that has been acquiring ruling functions for more than sixty years and is on the verge of supplanting the aristocracy as the dominant social class of the country. Indeed, the new plutocracy (including increasing numbers of the political class who become plutocrats after their one term in high office) is already the ruling class of the country and probably achieved that status during the 1960s. As a social class, however, the process of expressive acculturation has been going on since the 1930s but has not yet run its course. In this process, the aristocracy predominated until the new plutocracy indisputably asserted itself as a ruling class. For the past twenty-five years or so, however, the plutocracy has been innovating on its own and has fashioned many domains in a new expressive array that is neither aristocratic nor new-plutocratic but a combination of both, increasingly colored by the ruling predominance of the plutocrats. Thus this volume chronicles not only the expressive ethnography of the aristocracy but, as an important aspect of it, the input of the new plutocracy, which has significantly affected the aristocracy as a social class. The main analytical aims addressed throughout this study may be outlined as follows.

The first goal is to establish the dynamics of asymmetrical acculturation in the context of the increasing and ultimate predominance of an upwardly mobile group that becomes a new ruling class. Most important in this endeavor is to delineate the developmental cycle of expressive acculturation in terms of specific stages to determine the give and take of aristocrats and plutocrats.

The second aim is to determine how and to what extent the *imago mundi* of aristocrats has been modified by increasing contact with plutocrats and by their own inability to create new wealth and thereby join the ranks of the new ruling class. This process is largely determined by expressive constraints, and it is of the utmost significance to determine the social and psychological profiles of aristocrats who are able to overcome them—thereby becoming upwardly mobile economically and active members of the new emerging social class—and of those who are not—thereby becoming downwardly mobile or static economically and ultimately dropping out of the system. Conversely, similar profiles of plutocrats must be determined in order to identify those who are creating the new expressive array of the emerging ruling class and those who—despite economic success—drop out of the system by their unwillingness to interact with plutocrats or independently of them create new expressive domains not consonant with their potential position in the ruling class.

Third, as a concomitant aspect of the first and second points, the dynamics of structural and expressive interaction strike at the heart of explaining superordinate stratification. Thus it is necessary to identify not only the economic and political conditions that structure the rise of a ruling class but also the extent to which its members are able to create a new *imago mundi* underlined by the original ideology that brought them economic power.

Configuration of the Social and Ruling Class in the Context of Final Renewal

It is useful to compare the decline and near extinction of the aristocracy as a class in Western Europe and Mexico and by extension in other situations in Latin America where so-called oligarchies survived until the second half of this century. The French Revolution initiated the decline of Western aristocracies as ruling and social classes; but, surprisingly, this event also represents a resurgence of political participation after the near obliteration of aristocracies as political classes with the onset of absolutism. Western aristocracies had lost their ruling predominance by the second half of the nineteenth century, as landed wealth could not compete with industrial wealth, and most aristocrats could not make the transition. As social classes, however, Western aristocracies managed to remain rather unchallenged for nearly another century, that is, until shortly after World War I. This discrepancy is an intriguing phenomenon that cannot entirely be explained; but it is perhaps related to the fact that Western European aristocracies were always numerous in relation to the total population.

The Mexican aristocracy, however, after having significant ruling functions and total social domination, declined drastically in three generations. This can be explained by the absence of factors that made the decline of Western European aristocracies significantly slower.

First, neither in colonial nor in republican times was the Mexican aristocracy the political class of the country, and it never had a firm control over the military (as most European aristocracies did until World War I). This was a serious mistake that made the aristocrats more vulnerable to and less salient among the urban masses, which no doubt feared their ruling power but did not relate to them in the wider social sense. To put it differently, the European aristocracy was always more in the social consciousness of the population at large than the Mexican aristocracy ever was.

Second, the Mexican aristocracy was an extremely small social class; even in the sixteenth and seventeenth centuries, when the ratio of *peninsulares* and Creoles to the entire population of Indians and mestizos was much smaller than in subsequent centuries, it never amounted to more than 2 percent. By the time of Independence the aristocracy represented roughly 0.5 percent of the country's population, and it was half that by the 1910 Revolution. Compared to the aristocracies of Western European countries, which ranged roughly from 5 to 9 percent of the population, the Mexican aristocracy was minuscule. Perhaps more powerful at the local level, where they reigned supreme over an ethnically different population, the aristocrats were never as visible and publicly salient at the national level as the European aristocracies were until well into the twentieth century.

Third, the abolition of titles of nobility shortly after Independence was another factor that diminished the visibility and integrity of the aristocracy as a social class. Significantly, such egalitarian developments right after Independence were due to an initial democratic fervor with a tinge of revolutionary zeal experienced by the Creole population, perhaps half of it racially mestizo. By the onset of the nineteenth century this Creole population numbered about a million and constituted the economic life of the cities; and in some rural environments it engaged in mercantile, trading, and manufacturing operations, including the hitherto underdeveloped liberal professions.

Because of the political inexperience of the aristocratic sector beyond the local and provincial levels throughout colonial times, the political vacuum left after Independence naturally was filled by Creoles, aided by the fact that aristocrats, so confident of their power, deemed it unnecessary actively to engage in politics. Thus ensued the tacit covenant that governed Mexico's political system throughout most of the nineteenth century: an increasingly mestizo political class which governed without undue interference as long as it respected the interests of the aristocratic and banking and industrial classes. This status quo was a double-edged sword for the aristocracy: on the one hand, it safeguarded its economic dominance, particularly after the 1857 Reforma Laws, when its landed power reached a zenith; on the other hand, it made the aristocracy vulnerable to political actions that it could not always control.

The net result of these factors and developments was that—predominant as the aristocracy was as a social class until 1910—it was a fragile institution that survived despite its weak mechanisms of control; the aristocracy endured mainly because the promise of democracy generated during the first decade after Independence did not materialize, and Mexico did not significantly evolve from its colonial situation. When Mexico experienced its first popular revolution in 1910, and the mestizo political leadership broke its traditional alliance with the ruling class, the aristocracy received a blow more severe than that dealt to its European counterparts by the French Revolution. Thus the aristocracy's inexperience with politics, its very small membership, and its lack of national visibility and limited vicarious appeal (except locally) are the main attributes that underline the precipitous decline of the aristocracy after 1910 and its inability to secure a stronger bargaining position *vis-à-vis* the rising plutocracy.

Concentrating on the second half of the twentieth century, what was the position of the aristocracy within the new superordinate sector of the country, which had not yet coalesced into a well-delineated class? The best way to characterize this sector is as an *haute bourgeoisie* composed of a social class, a ruling class, and a political class, all three in a state of disintegration or formation.

Briefly, the political class is composed of the heirs of the Mexican Revolution, that is, past high officials of the official party (Partido Revolucionario Institucional, PRI) at the federal, state, and occasionally local level. This is a rather small group that has wielded continuous political power and status since shortly after 1928, including past presidents, important cabinet members, some state governors, large-city mayors, and other assorted high-office holders. The political class of Mexico in the twentieth century at no time had more than 1,500 members, growing roughly at the rate of 150 for every six-year administration. One of the most significant results of the Mexican Revolution was to institutionalize the practice that high executive officers of state cannot be reelected. While this did not apply to nonelective officials, during more than sixty years politicians' careers culminated in a high office to which they could not be reelected: president of the republic, state governor, or mayor of the largest cities. After holding high office, members of this circle continued to have political influence; and over decades a fairly permanent nucleus emerged, fostering stability and enhancing the power of the political class.

The Mexican Aristocracy

In assessing the configuration and position of the political class of Mexico within the global stratification system, perhaps equally important is the universally acknowledged fact that high political office has always been a source of enrichment since colonial times. In the twentieth century some of the largest fortunes in Mexico had their origin in politics—that is, once in high office individuals amass hundreds of millions of dollars. The net result of this form of institutionalized corruption is that sooner or later politicians become plutocrats. As control of the ruling party is coming to an end, and the political system becomes more representative and democratic, politics as a source of wealth is being curtailed. But the role of the political class in the formation of the ruling class must not be underestimated. Moreover, constrained by the populist attitude and "revolutionary" image that went with the role of being members of the political class, politicians-turned-plutocrats were reluctant to engage in upward social mobility. This is changing rapidly, as more and more high-ranking politicians are being integrated into aristocratic-plutocratic circles.

The ruling class of Mexico today (2000) has been in the process of formation since the end of the armed phase of the Mexican Revolution (1910–1919), when the middle-class leadership that precipitated this momentous transformation became the political as well as the ruling class of Mexico, thus ushering in the last renewal of elites. By the late 1920s this plutocracy was in a vigorous process of formation, and by World War II it was already a significant force in the life of the nation.

The Mexican Revolution was the first popular revolution of the twentieth century; but even before the PRI was founded and established in the late 1920s and early 1930s, it was clear that its leadership was not modeling Mexico into a socialist or Communist state, despite occasional deviations from 1930 to 1950. By then the political ideology of the ruling class, the PRI, was a fuzzy combination of socialist ideas and capitalist enterprise.

Whether intentionally or not, the ruling party had become one of the breeding grounds for a capitalistic plutocracy, and many great fortunes were made by politicians in their one term in office. By 1940 the redistribution of land among the propertyless had been largely accomplished, fulfilling the socialistic claim of the Revolution. In other respects, a mixed economy was favored; and with the exception of the nationalization of railroads, the oil industry, and other basic services, the state interfered only moderately in the free-enterprise system. Given this state of affairs, and the fact that the mixed economy was fostered as a means for politicians-turned-plutocrats to invest their ill-gotten fortunes, this moderately laissez-faire type of economy was the breeding ground for a new plutocracy. Partly because of lack of entrepreneurial ability and partly because of government impediments, the traditional aristocracy-plutocracy of the era of Porfirio Díaz did not essentially participate in the formation of the new plutocracy; and today only a minimal number of aristocrats may also be said to be plutocratic magnates. The beginnings of the new plutocracy may be traced to the administration of President Plutarco Elías Calles (1924–1928); and by the last years of President Miguel Alemán's administration (1946–1952) it was exerting a mayor impact on the life of the nation. During the past forty years this new plutocracy has become a ruling class, not only by virtue of its great wealth but because it also includes many former high-ranking politicians.

The political class of Mexico today is directly or indirectly of revolutionary extraction: mostly of middle-class origin or more modest circumstances, once or twice removed from these milieux. More intimately relevant for the problem at hand, plutocrats of nonpolitical origin are mostly of middle-class extraction, considerable numbers are "self-made men," and many have training in the law and other professions. While some of the families of plutocratic magnates in the 1950s were already in control of certain entrepreneurial activity on the eve of the Revolution or shortly after, most of the great fortunes of Mexico today began to be made in the 1930s and 1940s and in a few instances during the years immediately following the armed phase of the Revolution. This period coincides with a significant migration of European, Near Eastern, and a few U.S. entrepreneurs. They came to Mexico with a certain amount of capital and almost invariably with a good deal of technical and financial expertise. All great fortunes were made in banking, industry, commerce, and services, as mining, transportation, and oil had become state enterprises. Most great fortunes were made during the administration of President Alemán and in the early 1970s, primarily in banking and industry.

The relationship between the political class (all high government officials of the administration in power, influential former officials, and the ruling clique of the PRI) and the plutocracy may be characterized as a delicate balancing act, in which the ostensibly socialistic aims and programs of the government are always pitted against the capitalist free-enterprise interests of the plutocracy. Policy and issues are decided so that government (actually the ruling party) is made to look "revolutionary" on behalf of the people's social welfare but without significantly altering or dislocating the free-enterprise system that ultimately serves the politicians' plutocratic interests. Most aspects of the private-public interaction (labor disputes, wage scales, labor-

The Mexican Aristocracy

management relations, and so on) are regulated by this unstated covenant; and the occasional drastic actions of the government that seriously affect the free-enterprise system are frequently determined by their effect on the economic interests of plutocratic politicians.

Finally, the aristocracy has perilously managed to maintain a foothold in the emerging social class. To put it in recent historical perspective, the plutocracy, with which the dying aristocracy has been increasingly interacting since the late 1940s, is coalescing into the new social class at the top of the Mexican stratification system. The interaction has been more intimate and sustained with the nonpolitical segment of the plutocracy. Plutocrats of political extraction have been more reticent to acquire the behavior and modes of expression of the traditional aristocracy (by now somewhat filtered and modified by plutocratic accommodations) and remain to a large extent marginal to the main aristocratic-plutocratic circles.

The coalescing of these rather disparate sectors at the top of the Mexican stratification system is largely governed by a process of expressive acculturation. Throughout this book, these strands are analyzed in the following manner. Expressive imperatives of aristocratic provenance—and plutocratic aspirations and the validation of social status—are in the process of coalescing into a single entity spanning the three basic sectors of the Mexican *haute bourgeoisie*. The final renewal in the upper reaches of the Mexican stratification system is not yet quite complete, but its basic form is evident: the political class is unmistakably embodied in the ruling political party but changing rapidly toward greater diversification; the ruling class is a mixture of politicians-turned-plutocrats and new plutocrats of nonpolitical extraction; while the social upper class is now in the process of rapid change, in which the old aristocracy is at the end of its existence and the new plutocracy is asserting itself.

Position of the Mexican Aristocracy in the Context of the *Haute Bourgeoisie*

Finally, let us substantively place the aristocracy in the context of the combined plutocracy described above and—with respect to its structural and expressive underpinnings—determine the domains and ambiances in which these sectors of the *haute bourgeoisie* are influencing each other, becoming homogenized, and innovating on their own. These concluding remarks offer a road map of what to expect and how the description will serve to generate analytical generalizations.

Structural Considerations: The Nature of Interaction, Acceptance, and Rejection

From 1940 onward the interaction between aristocrats (who have lost all ruling influence) and plutocratic upwardly mobile personnel has taken place in the context of expressive acculturation. Structurally, the plutocracy's interaction with the aristocracy was limited to the few aristocrats who had managed to amass fairly large fortunes and were being incorporated into the network of the evolving ruling class. The situation, however, is more complex; it has to be viewed as interaction in a position of equality or subordination of the aristocracy to the plutocracy but also in several domains configured largely by the realms of politics, economics, and the liberal professions.

Self-selectively and customarily, aristocrats did not participate in or were effectively barred from the political process; and from the onset of the Revolution until the late 1950s they did not hold political offices of any significance at the state or federal levels. The one exception to this generalization is that there were never any impediments to aristocrats' holding diplomatic posts. Indeed, because of behavioral and expressive considerations that were lacking among the political class that emerged after the Revolution, aristocrats in considerable numbers assumed diplomatic posts. The situation has become more fluid, and in 1994 there were a significant number of aristocrats who have been elected or nominated to important positions in the administration.

A related source of political rapprochement between aristocrats and members of the political class has been high school and university ties, which have been an increasingly important aspect of the socialization of the generation born immediately before and after World War II. Particularly since the mid-1960s the rapprochement has accelerated; and many political doors have been open to forward-looking aristocrats with low pretensions. Most importantly, these overtures on both sides of the equation have been instrumental in bringing increasing members of the political class into closer relationships with the entire spectrum of the plutocratic ruling class. It is equally significant, however, that the intransigence of many conservative aristocrats and members of the political class has diminished. There are roughly as many aristocrats and politicians in this diminishing intransigent category, who represent the most ideologically committed to remaining pristine aristocrats and true "revolutionaries" and constitute less than half of the social and political class.

In the economic domain, aristocrats play a minor role as primary movers, as so few of them are plutocratic magnates. Thus, in the domain of the ruling class, plutocratic aristocrats occupy subordinate positions; they are not players in economic policy and decision making. Aristocrats also occupy subordinate positions in the enterprises of plutocratic magnates. There are considerable numbers of aristocrats working in banking, industry, and manufacturing who occupy middle and high executive positions, which they achieved by working their way up the executive ladder or by virtue of long-standing family connections with plutocratic magnates. This is an important tie that— together with the few aristocratic plutocrats—has provided the most salient context of aristocratic-plutocratic interaction for more than a generation. It has constituted by far the most important milieu in which aristocratic-plutocratic expressive acculturation has taken place; more than in any other domain, there has been the kind of rapprochement that defines the impending coalescing of the new superordinate class. The effects of intermarriage between aristocrats and plutocrats should not be underestimated, however, as there is a noticeable tendency to enhance the egalitarian nature of aristocratic-plutocratic interaction in the process of ruling-class formation that has been going on in recent years.

In addition to the small minority of plutocratic aristocrats, roughly 30 percent of aristocrats are engaged in banking, manufacturing, and general business activities of medium to fairly large economic importance. Perhaps another 10 percent of aristocratic families engage in farming, cattle raising, and medium-size agribusiness. Altogether, then, the slight majority of aristocratic families are engaged in the liberal professions, most commonly the law, medicine, engineering, architecture, and accounting. Aristocrats have been particularly successful in law and medicine, and they have also distinguished themselves in the public administration of research, science, and art institutes. Thus the economic position of most aristocrats is in the upper-middle sector of the Mexican stratification system, overlapping to a significant extent with the world of business and trade that occupies that important niche below the ruling-class sphere of action in Mexico City. This upper-middle-class milieu is the structural, but not expressive, environment that most aristocrats have come to occupy. Practically every aristocratic family is associated with a small circle of individuals and families that may be regarded as the fringe boundaries of aristocratic involvement.

Until the 1910 Revolution the aristocracy was universally known and recognized by all sectors of the stratification system. By the late 1940s that degree of visibility had shrunk considerably, but it was still recognized as the preeminent social class of Mexico City. Thirty years later, however, the aristocracy's visibility had been drastically reduced to the upper-middle and upper classes, small segments of the population which were able to place the aristocracy as the social elite of the city and the former landed class of the country; and many aristocratic names still connoted their former exaltedness. The aristocracy also receives a modicum of mostly negative recognition from middle-class intellectuals and educated people, who regard it as a reactionary, uppity survival of the past with no functions in a modern democracy, undoubtedly implying that money and power are the only criteria of class recognition and vicarious identification. But despite the fact that the aristocracy today is so small a part of societal consciousness and has been reduced to such a restricted environment, it survives as a distinct social class that still commands expressive influence in the upper reaches of the stratification system.

Expressive Considerations: Symmetrical and Asymmetrical Transfer and Incorporation

Although Western aristocracies have survived many structural transformations throughout more than 2,000 years, their most constant attributes have been a common ideology and worldview discharged in an exclusive expressive array that has remained the model of upwardly mobile aspirations. That is also demonstrated in this book; the Mexican aristocracy, deprived of all political and ruling functions, is still a viable social class on exclusively expressive grounds. The aristocracy will come to an end as a distinct social class when it ceases to contribute to the expressive formation of a superseding social class. Thus this book deals with both the terminal expressive contributions of the aristocracy to a new superordinate class and how this contribution shapes the new structural-expressive order.

Intermarriage between aristocrats and new plutocrats has been taking place since the 1930s. The situation remained fairly constant until the early 1970s, when aristocratic-plutocratic marriages began to increase significantly; and by 1990 they had become common. In the earlier stage, most of the inter-marriages were unions between aristocratic males and plutocratic females, a situation characteristic of a class in superordinate social position. This has changed, and today there are as many aristocratic females marrying plutocratic males. The domain of marriage from 1960 onward defines all other expressive domains in interaction and reflects the extent to which these two social classes are coalescing. In this context plutocrats are internalizing many aristocratic traits and complexes, and aristocrats in turn are being influenced by the worldview of plutocrats, the *quid pro quo* of the process of expressive acculturation. In this respect intermarriage brings together not only the respective families of the bride and groom but widening circles of kin and not infrequently friends. This phenomenon does not affect the majority of aristocratic families; but the milieu of acceptance is there, and only the most conservative are unwilling to contemplate marital alliances with plutocratic families. Given the patrilateral tendency of Mexican society at this level of social integration, aristocratic males' marrying plutocratic females entails significantly more expressive and structural changes biased toward the aristocracy. Conversely, aristocratic females' marrying plutocratic males produces effects that integrate the couple more into the plutocratic milieu but also causes expressive changes that bring together widening circles of aristocrats and plutocrats.

By interaction I mean the contexts in which aristocrats and plutocrats come together due to social, economic, recreational, and political circumstances. Political circumstances have been limited, but economic and recreational environments have been increasingly important since the early 1950s in generating social ties. It was originally in the context of economic ties and interaction that aristocrats and plutocrats came together on an intermittent or fairly permanent basis: first among banking and manufacturing magnates and then in the context of aristocrats working for plutocrats in a wide range of business concerns. For probably two decades this milieu entailed social interaction confined to social clubs to which plutocrats increasingly gravitated, cocktail parties in the context of work, and occasional mutual invitations to dinner parties, balls, and weddings. From the early 1950s to the early 1970s plutocrats learned and began to internalize aristocratic patterns of personal behavior and public display: modes of entertainment ranging from weddings and balls to every occasion in the life cycle; and the niceties of display ranging from collecting and showing fine art to contributing and participating in exhibitions (art, crafts, furniture, pottery, and so on) and philanthropic work. Since the early 1970s all these patterns of expressive acculturation have intensified, and many plutocratic families have become undistinguishable from aristocratic families. These expressive changes have been asymmetric, signaling the thorough aristocratization of many plutocratic families. But aristocrats have not escaped expressive influences in related domains, mainly in the realignment of their inclusive array, signaling the extent to which aristocrats have undergone *embourgeoisement*.

In the category of personal behavior and demeanor fall contexts ranging from presentation of the self, personal attire, and adornment to body movement, language, and deportment in innumerable social situations. These are the most public attributes of aristocratic behavior, which Western aristocracies have always emphasized as an entry fee in social interaction with nonaristocratic personnel. The allure of the aristocratic mystique has been powerful, and plutocrats have invariably been willing to acquire these aristocratic traits in validating their status as aspiring members of the ruling class.

As plutocrats acquire these behavioral trappings, they become expressively more secure and independent, a factor as important as their power and wealth in acquiring social equality with aristocrats. Trivial as these expressive concerns may seem to outsiders, they are of capital importance in understanding mobility at the upper reaches of stratification. Conditions of the various periods of rapid transition have changed since classical times, but the principles have remained the same; and not even the democratization that society has undergone during the past 200 years has changed them appreciably, as new superordinate classes are presently being formed. Power and wealth, as the *sine qua non* of a ruling class, do not necessarily ensure continuity of social status: once they are secured, preservation of status becomes an overwhelming end that can only be achieved by expressive means.

The context of kinship and the household presents a different set of considerations, which may be characterized as the aspirations that those vying for superordinate status expect eventually to achieve from those who have had it for a long time. This is particularly the case with the denotation of kinship, which embodies the fundamental principle of Western superordinate stratification. Despite its original Greek etymology ("the rule of the best"), the concept of aristocracy has always denoted the rule of the best-born: that those who can boast of a distinguished lineage are entitled to be considered socially exalted. This is the principle that conditions social mobility in the upper reaches of stratification and in the present case what plutocrats desire as the ultimate validation of their achieved power and wealth—namely, an illustrious lineage that they can pass on to their descendants. Upwardly mobile plutocrats know that lineage, that most alluring and desirable attribute, cannot be learned or purchased—only time can confer it. Nonetheless, it can be symbolically enhanced and synchronically manipulated; hence the aspirations and often active efforts of Mexican plutocrats to marry aristocrats. Thus contracting marriage and kinship relations with aristocrats allows plutocrats to enhance the building of lineage in their own lifetime.

The household domain, however, although an intrinsic aspect of kinship, presents another set of considerations that entail more immediately achieved consequences. From the aristocratic viewpoint, the household remains the last bastion of aristocratic exclusivity. During the past forty years, since the aristocracy lost the last trappings of power and wealth and its visibility declined rapidly, the household is probably the only place where aristocrats can be themselves, vent their rejection of a world that they regard as essentially hostile, and seek comfort from the relics of the past. But even this last refuge of aristocratic exclusivity has changed during the past decade and a half, as aristocratic-plutocratic interaction becomes symmetrical, and economic constraints no longer permit the dichotomization of social life. Plutocrats have been very much aware of this last straw of aristocratic snobbishness, as expressed by many informants, and for them it represents another obstacle to overcome on the way to social predominance.

From the plutocratic viewpoint, the aristocratic household is something to emulate, and here again there has been a fairly high degree of expressive shift. The plutocratic household today is not exactly a replica of the aristocratic household, but it has incorporated many elements that depart from *nouveau riche* ostentation and often equals the understated elegance of aristocratic households in many respects (the arrangement of rooms, the combination of art and decoration, the subtle combination of colors and materials, the display of fine furniture and rugs, and so on). With respect to the household, but independently of it as well, plutocrats have become collectors of colonial art, contemporary art, pre-Hispanic art, furniture, and other valuables, a practice directly or indirectly learned from aristocrats. Many magnates hire advisors to help them collect and display fine art, including art imported from Europe and the United States. It should be noted that the expressive transformation that the new plutocrats have been undergoing for more than three decades also emanates from other sources, particularly from more established European plutocrats with whom they have extensive economic ties and through other international business connections.

Finally, patterns of entertainment and display are quite ramified contexts; they affect not only the social life of aristocrats and plutocrats but several aspects of the economic and religious life as well. Again, these contexts have been almost entirely asymmetrical in that aristocratic patterns have been incorporated by plutocrats, while there have been few inputs in the opposite direction. The most extensive domains of realization are social occasions in the life cycle, some aspects of the religious cycle, social occasions in the context of business and professional activities, and recreation in the conventional sense of the term. These entail manifold expressive domains that are inextricably interrelated with etiquette, contextual manners, personal behavior, and individual and collective display. Although the plutocrats were inexperienced two generations ago, they have been adept in learning, incorporating, and occasionally innovating. This has been done mostly by increasing contact with aristocrats but also independently in the context of the business and social networks that they have managed to establish abroad.

Throughout this section I have structurally and expressively placed the aristocracy within the context of the Mexican *haute bourgeoisie*. This road map, as it were, focuses on the regular and expressive ethnography of the aristocracy and its ramifications, which constitutes the substantive matrix in analyzing superordinate stratification.

An Operational Definition of Expressive Ethnography and Sources of Qualitative and Quantitative Data

If one asked ten anthropologists what an ethnography is, one would probably get as many different answers. Mine is the following. Ethnography, like history, is an end in itself: a deeply rooted proclivity, which in Western civilization goes back to the Greeks, to perpetuate the culture of a group—or, to put it more precisely, to preserve for the future the collective deeds and accomplishments of a social group. This syndrome has multiple variations in cultures and civilizations everywhere and has been embodied in written and oral traditions. Although the earliest ethnographies, in essentially the modern meaning of the term, go back to classical times (see Herodotus 1965; Tacitus 1948), ethnographic accounts in Western civilization until the sixteenth century were essentially written, sung, and told in the context of myth, legend, and epic literature. Systematic ethnography begins with the work of the Franciscan friar Bernardino de Sahagún (1956), who completed his investigation of the culture and society of central Mexico by about 1570. It remained the most complete ethnography until the onset of the twentieth century; and by the end of this period ethnography had become exclusively associated with the budding discipline of anthropology. Lest I be misunderstood, ethnography is an activity that has always been practiced exogenously and endogenously or both at the same time. Let me explain.

Herodotus wrote about his own culture but also about the practices and customs of several societies of the Mediterranean basin, whereas Tacitus wrote about Germanic peoples. This tradition of doing exogenous ethnography essentially disappeared in Western society until the Renaissance; from then on, due significantly to the expansion of Western European peoples throughout the world, it became the only kind of ethnography, as endogenous ethnography crystallized as various forms of literature. Endogenous ethnography did not disappear, but exogenous ethnography became the core of anthropology as a scientific discipline. Thus if Herodotus is our apical ancestor and something of a mythical figure, Sahagún is the legitimate father of modern ethnographers.

In the Anglo-Saxon world systematic ethnography begins with the work of Australian ethnographers shortly after the middle of the nineteenth century (Voget 1975), and more significantly in the United States with the foundation of the Bureau of American Ethnology (BAE) and the work of Major John Wesley Powell, Henry Schoolcraft, Lewis Henry Morgan, and several others. The specific aim of the BAE was to record the culture of American Indian tribes, which was rapidly disappearing. Indeed, much of the work of American anthropologists from Franz Boas and his students onward may be regarded as "salvage ethnography," which quickly extended to other parts of the world. For example, this is the case in Mexico, from the work of Manuel Gamio (1922) and Robert Redfield (1930) to the most recent work. This is what I consider the work that I have been doing in Mexico for nearly forty-five years. In a sense all ethnography, by its very nature of retrieving knowledge of culture for the future, is salvage ethnography. In the context of the hot (in the Lévi-Straussian sense), rapid context of change during the past century, however, salvage ethnography has acquired special meaning and urgency.

This motivational characterization of American anthropology also applies to the work of British and French functionalists. The work of Bronislaw Malinowski (1922) and Alfred Reginald Radcliffe-Brown (1933) was deeply concerned with ethnography, and the structural-functional approach of Radcliffe-Brown and his students is particularly relevant in assessing the descriptive integrational role of ethnography. It had two quite different components, however: on the one hand, the ideographic aim of extensive and in-depth description; on the other, the nomothetic aim of generalizing on a grand scale by the use of the comparative method. The former resulted in some of the best ethnographies in the anthropological literature, whereas the latter never materialized into Radcliffe-Brown's much vaunted sociological laws. Indeed, E. E. Evans-Pritchard (1949:65) proclaimed that "anthropology is history or nothing." The point is that—regardless of what the motivation to do ethnography has been—its uses and functions have an ideographic, diachronic as well as a nomothetic, synchronic aspect. Thus the ideographic, diachronic aspect of ethnography is an end in itself; and from this standpoint the work anthropologists do is a kind of specialized history.

Anthropology is also a science, however, and ethnography entails synchronic aspects. Although hitherto anthropology has not generated socio-logical laws, it does have a significant generalizing, ethnologic component in which ethnography plays a determinant role. There are two considerations that justify ethnography as the conceptual fulcrum of anthropology as a science. First is the synchronic testimony of organized bodies of sociocultural data for future testing, in the absence of adequate theories. This is the view of George Peter Murdock (1972), who, after a lifetime of formulating and testing hypothesis on kinship and social structure, came to the conclusion that the main achievement that would survive the labor of twentieth-century anthropology is ethnography. Second, although I share Murdock's position and the view of those who maintain that anthropology has not managed to generate genuine theories, there is no question that ethnography has both interpretive and explanatory roles to play.

Perhaps the best ethnographies in the anthropological literature are those written in the functionalist mold. The reason for this is that ethnography is fundamentally an exercise in descriptive integration: namely, the specification of a corpus of data whose parts are interrelated so that when alterations occur in one sector of the whole other sectors are affected in discernible ways. This, of course, is the classic functionalist position, most clearly specified by Radcliffe-Brown (1952), and a permanent contribution of ethnography as probably the most efficient method to describe a sociocultural system. It entails functional explanation (how a system is put together), but it does not entail linear explanation (how something causes something else). All my ethnographies have been structured on this premise.

From this standpoint, an ethnography is a synchronic construction—frozen in time, so to speak—whose component parts may be ascertained and placed in relation to each other. It is a system that provides actors with rules of behavior and action, which constitutes what anthropologists refer to as "cultural consensus" (see Boster 1986; Romney, Weller, and Bachelder 1986), which gives coherence to a system and characterizes it as a distinct, separate entity. But rules are broken—that is, the behavior and action specified by the rules conflict with those of other parts of the system and must be considered in order to give an account of the global system. Thus a descriptive ethnography is a statement of cultural consensus, a general statement of the rulers of behavior that "ought to be followed" in order to provide for the continuity of the system as a distinct social entity and how it is related to other systems. In other words, a descriptive ethnography is the equivalent of a history, a static account of the way in which the system is dynamically organized—namely, how its component parts are related to one another. Most ethnographies are of this type, and they constitute the basic blocks of data for the generalizations of ethnology.

But there is another type that I would like to call analytical or in-depth ethnography (roughly what Clifford Geertz called "thick description"), which contains endogenous and exogenous dynamic mechanisms that transcend purely descriptive integration. In addition to accomplishing what a descriptive ethnography does, an analytical ethnography accomplishes the following tasks. Endogenously, it specifies the relationship between the components of the sociocultural system—the links that obtain between them—and evaluates their significance in maintaining the system in a relative state of equilibrium, thereby suggesting likely avenues of change. Exogenously, it specifies how the system came into being at a given time, the social and cultural forces that configured it, and how it is embedded in a wider spatial, social, and cultural world. This book, in short, is an analytical ethnography of the Mexican aristocracy.

But why not simply entitle the book an ethnography of this social group? What is an expressive ethnography, and how is it different from an analytical ethnography? And what are the defining characteristics of expressive culture? I include only brief answers to these questions here, because I have dealt with them twice before (Nutini 1988, 1995).

In a nutshell, an expressive ethnography is a special kind of analytical ethnography focused on establishing the expressive culture of a social group. In the case of the Mexican aristocracy, the expressive ethnography was generated from the analytical ethnography; and the data-gathering process was centered on isolating the various kinds of expression. Although there is no model for structuring an expressive ethnography, the intent of the narrative is unquestionably expressive; to make the description more comprehensible, each of the chapters is accompanied by a short expressive analysis, where the most salient aspects of expression are considered. In any case, what has to be addressed in order to justify this approach to ethnography is the nature of expression.

Probably the most characteristic and universal attribute of expression is that it is intentionally noninstrumental—that is, it individually represents an end in itself. The motivation and discharge of expressive behavior are conditioned by the individual's reaction or adaptation to changing aspects of the social structure. It should be emphasized that although expressive behavior is psychologically motivated and individually manifested, it nonetheless has a collective, structured manifestation closely related to the social structure.

Thus expressive behavior may be nominally defined as the individual and collective choices that the members of a group can make. By themselves they do not necessarily alter the group, but they express whatever changing conditions the group is experiencing. The motivation of expressive behavior makes it noninstrumental. In functional terms, however, expressive behavior is an integral part of the social structure, as it manifests or exhibits certain diagnostic processes of the social system (see Roberts and Sutton-Smith 1962).

Just as the organization and constituent elements of the social structure vary in space and time, so also do the configuration and form of social expression. To pursue the analogy, social expression needs a technical vocabulary like the one that anthropologists have devised to analyze social structure. Thus far, students of expression (see Roberts and Golder 1970; Roberts and Sutton-Smith 1962) have formulated the concepts of expressive "array" and "domain" as the basic units in the analysis of expressive culture and behavior and isolated several types of expression.

The expressive array is the total of all patterns and contexts in a given group that entirely or partially realize expression. Every well-defined social group or class has an expressive array that is peculiar to itself, in terms of both intensity and the contexts in which expression is realized. Although every expressive array offers a unique organization of contexts, and no two arrays are exactly alike, total content and form show more overlap. Thus the French, Italian, Spanish, English, German, and perhaps even American expressive arrays manifest a degree of content and form that is exclusively their own while sharing the bulk of the array with Western society as a whole. Can one say something meaningful about the proportion of exclusive and inclusive content and form in this macrocontext? The answer is a tentative yes. Observations among Araucanian Indians, rural Tlaxcalans, and Mexican aristocrats suggest that the expressive array of any subculture is about 20 percent exclusive in content and form, while 80 percent of it is shared by all sister subcultures (Nutini 1988:379–382).

Class appears always to have been the compound variable most salient and efficacious in generating differential expressive arrays. The Mexican aristocracy displays an expressive array, for example, that more closely resembles the expressive array of the Spanish and Italian aristocracy than that of, say, Mexican plutocrats or members of the upper-middle classes, despite the fact that inclusively the aristocracy shares most of its expressive contexts in varying proportions with the entire Mexican stratification system. If one takes the expressive array of Mexican aristocrats, the exclusive array is that 20 percent identified above, while the remaining 80 percent is shared in various proportions with all other classes of Mexican society—for they have the same religion, are bound by many social customs, and are constrained by the same political, environmental, and ecological variables. But that 20 percent is what distinguishes Mexican aristocrats as an expressive class in Mexican society and secures their membership in the larger class of Western aristocrats.

One of the most characteristic attributes of expressive culture is that expressive behavior is contextual in the sense that the same content of social practice may sometimes be described structurally, at other times expressively. Therefore expression must be regarded as an individual's epistemological options within the social structure: expressive behavior represents the psychological and social alternatives, the available leeway between structural requirements and individual choices. Expression is realized in three basic contexts: those in which realized behavior is primarily expressive, those in which behavior is at times expressive and at times instrumental, and those in which behavior is primarily instrumental.

The expressive domain is the basic component of the expressive array. It may be defined as the cultural context in which expressive behavior is realized with some degree of semantic unity. The domain is not a fixed unit of expressive realization; it can aggregate to higher levels (broader domains) or decompose to lower levels (narrower domains) according to the needs of the analysis. For example, in all subcultures of Western society sports constitute a major expressive domain. This domain may be broken down into the subdomains of individual sports and team sports; and within these into sub-subdomains such as the individual sports of track and field, golf, and tennis and the team sports of football, basketball, and hockey. Some of these sports can be further decomposed into still narrower domains—track and field into sprints, middle-distance running, and field events, and even further into particular events such as the hundred-yard dash, the mile run, the shotput, and the high jump. Each event has its own expressive configuration, but it also shares some aspect of expression with the sport of track and field as a whole. This notion of a shared semantic field cannot be extended beyond the major domains of a given global system—that is, the expressive array of a well-defined culture, subculture, or permanently organized social segment such as a class.

The expressive array of the Mexican aristocracy includes more than 230 domains, many of which can be decomposed into subdomains. The array includes domains in all the usual ethnographic categories (kinship, religion, the life cycle, political life, economy and material culture, games and play) with different degrees of intensity and saliency. It contains many domains shared with plutocrats in what might be called the international set in Mexico City and with the upper-middle class. Aristocrats also share many expressive domains with all classes in the Mexican stratification system.

In summary, the expressive array of a social class, subculture, culture, or perhaps an entire culture area is the totality of expressive domains and their subdivisions configured in terms of inclusive and exclusive categories with reference to the three basic environments I have enumerated. The breakdown of exclusive and inclusive domains generally identifies the environments of greatest expressive realization and of most universal incidence in the social unit under consideration, for it is the 20 percent or so of exclusive domains of the global array that distinguishes the expressive behavior of the group.

No doubt many different kinds of expressive behavior exist, but so far it has been possible to distinguish five: the "natural" (or "inherent"), "conflictual," "terminal," "palliative," and "vicarious" types. They are more profitably discussed in the Conclusions after the data have been presented.

The adult population of the aristocracy, including married couples and young and old single individuals, is roughly 3,000. From this pool, informants were chosen on a voluntary and opportunity basis. A total of 157 male and female informants, ranging in age from the late teens to the early eighties, were interviewed at least once, and 35 of them at least ten times.

The basic ethnography was generated from twelve key informants who were interviewed at least ten hours each, three for more than one hundred hours. In the present ethnography, as in all my ethnographies of Indian and mestizo Mexico, key informants played the crucial role of providing the initial what-ought-to-be, cultural consensus model of the group under investigation. In this approach to generating a final product, the next step was to investigate how this to some extent idealized account was actually realized (why and when rules were broken), and how this affected the organization and structure of the system. In some domains the initial cultural consensus model corresponded to structural reality to a remarkable degree, that is, to what the average informant knows about a particular domain. In most domains, however, the structural reality departed from the cultural consensus model in various degrees, and the facts had to be ascertained by interviewing specifically knowledgeable informants. Moreover, quantitative data were a necessary complement to determine behavioral variation from the cultural consensus model elicited from key informants.

Group interviewing was another data-gathering technique that produced very good results. The groups were never larger than seven and included men and women of the same age set; they were always of the same sex, given that men and women by themselves were more likely to be spontaneous. Quite often group informants were given an open-ended questionnaire a few days in advance, so that they could think about the questions that were to be asked. As far as possible, I made sure that members of the group did not previously discuss among themselves the questions of the interview.

Interviewing children was another data-gathering technique in eliciting information on the ideational aspects of aristocratic life; I interviewed twenty-five boys and girls, ranging in age from nine to fourteen. Once the children's trust was gained, they became excellent spontaneous informants who often led me to interview adults on the same and related questions. Cultivating child-informants was not necessarily easy and occasionally took a long time, but the information they provided was highly instrumental in understanding the aristocratic worldview and how it is changing.

Quantitative data were gathered by the administration of questionnaires and several other fairly formal techniques. Questionnaires were administered to men and women ranging in age from twenty-five to eighty, who were asked from a dozen to as many as a hundred questions, some of which required short essays to answer. Depending on the task at hand, questionnaires were administered to opportunity samples of as few as twenty to as many as a hundred respondents. The subjects of investigation varied considerably, but the most common were expressive domains and the expressive array; expressive participation and withdrawal; expressive differentiation and clustering; voluntary association and membership rosters; dyadic and relational data on social, political, and economic interaction; career development and differentiation; status differentiation within the group; hierarchization of families and subgroup differentiation; strategies of relative upward and downward mobility; patterns of interaction and intermarriage; and genealogy. Male and/ or female respondents ranging from twenty-five to fifty years old were asked to complete short (fifteen to thirty minutes' duration) psychological tests, self-awareness tests, expressive participation tests, triad tests, attitudinal tests, card-sorting tasks, clustering tasks, and identification and correlation tasks.

CHAPTER 1

DEMOGRAPHIC COMPOSITION AND CONTEXTUAL DEFINITION OF THE ARISTOCRACY

Ideological Self-Identification and Structural Reality

Perhaps the most diagnostic characteristic of all variants of the Western aristocracy is its self-awareness and its consciousness of itself as a social class, or estate, from before the end of the eighteenth century. This self-conscious awareness is enhanced in Mexico and other New World aristocracies, where there is an important ethnic-racial component. There is an invariant component, reinforced by centuries of colonialism, that heightens self-identification, resulting in a high degree of consciousness of class, group belonging, and an ever-present milieu that emphasizes "we" and "others."

Formally speaking, Mexican aristocrats belong to a social class in the standard use of the term by U.S. sociologists (Davis and Moore 1945:242–245). But the aristocracy is a class in itself in the subjective, ideological sense (Laurin-Frenette 1976:252–257), since it is a historical reality, has a collective consciousness, and has a definite view of itself and the global society. In other words, the aristocracy no longer controls the agrarian sector of production; nor is it tied to a specific means of production, except that it is part of the *haute bourgeoisie.*

Individually and as a group, aristocrats are very much aware of who they are, where they came from, and their place in the history of the country. This translates into a high degree of shared identity as to what they once were, how they came to be, and what they think they were unjustly deprived of after 1910.

Endogamy, of course, has been a significant factor in maintaining the boundaries and integrity of the group. But this is a consequence of the unusual consciousness of kind that the members of the aristocracy have exhibited, even after they lost all power and most of their wealth. Probably more than any other factor, what has sustained their strong sense of identity is a deeply ingrained belief that, regardless of wealth and political power, their ancestors were the architects and rulers of Mexico for nearly 400 years.

The Mexican aristocracy today is in several ways an anachronism and a testimony to the persistence of social institutions. A social class is not only a self-defined entity; in order to be a significant category, it must be recognized by other social classes. By this statistical standard, the aristocracy exists only minimally, for it is doubtful that more than 2 percent of the total population of Mexico is aware of it, much less recognizes the highest status that its members attribute to themselves. This, of course, is the inescapable result of the overall democratization of Mexican society, the concentration of the aristocracy in the megalopolis, and the incredible demographic growth of the country. Whatever the case, the lower classes of Mexico today discriminate only between political power and wealth and accord status in terms of these two alternatives. The working and middle classes recognize degrees of status but based strictly on political power and wealth—and of the two wealth is undoubtedly the more important. The members of the upper-middle class (of Mexico City, unless otherwise indicated), composed of the highest professionals and the best-educated sector of the population, are aware of the aristocrats, know who they are historically, and can recognize them by aristocratic name association. It should be realized that the upper-middle class constitutes a very thin veneer of the Mexican stratification system. During the past generation and a half, however, it has been augmented significantly by foreign professionals, business leaders, and assorted personnel, with whom the aristocracy has established a fairly active network of social relations. Since members of the upper-middle class are well aware of their own position and can discriminate between social status and political power and wealth, they are quite often conscious of the subtle and not so subtle differences between aristocrats and the other sectors of the *haute bourgeoisie*. Finally, it is the plutocracy itself, including the upwardly mobile members of the political class, that is most aware of the aristocracy and accords it the highest degree of social recognition.

Ideological constraints and structural reality play an important role in the self-recognition of aristocrats and their perception by the proximate groups at the top of the Mexican stratification system. The ideological conception that aristocrats have of themselves—and the *imago mundi* that shapes their behavior and action—constitutes the model that upwardly mobile plutocrats have already acquired to a significant extent and are now in the process of internalizing. The model, of course, is an idealized construct cultivated by aristocrats based on undeniable historical facts that are validated in literally every aspect of aristocratic behavior. But the model is also a justification designed to enhance a once exalted position and inspire the continuation of their place in the emerging superordinate class. Aware of their vulnerability, aristocrats play this idealization to their advantage; but at the same time it serves to bolster their vanishing bargaining power and enhance their self-image. Thus aristocratic pride, refinement, and many kinds of behavior are expressive reactions designed to enhance interaction with plutocrats, without offending them but rather turning them into a mutually profitable interaction. Plutocrats, in turn, are attracted to this collusion, which permits them to acquire and internalize those aristocratic traits that will socially validate their power and wealth, without unduly giving up those attributes that made them powerful and wealthy.

Group Realignment and Concentration in Mexico City

Since early colonial times every aspect of the political, economic, religious, and even social system gravitated toward the capital, Mexico City. This has particularly been the case with the superordinate system embodying the social, ruling, and political classes of the country even after the great changes entailed by the 1910 Revolution. In one way or another, since its inception in the sixteenth century, the aristocracy has been closely associated and to a large extent enfranchised in Mexico City, even though its landed and local power base was always regional and provincial. Although the aristocracy had a somewhat diversified economy by the end of the Díaz dictatorship, landed wealth predominated. Thus, while the majority of the aristocracy was enfranchised in provincial cities by 1910, many families had secondary residences in Mexico City or periodically spent weeks and months in the capital every year.

By the onset of the Revolution in 1910, roughly 35 percent of aristocrats resided permanently in Mexico City—that is, they did not maintain manorial establishments in the provincial cities that were strongly associated with the hacienda system. The axis of existence of these aristocratic families oscillated

The Mexican Aristocracy

between the hacienda and Mexico City. Perhaps another 20 percent of aristocratic families were enfranchised in provincial cities, were more closely tied to the hacienda, but maintained a secondary residence in Mexico City. This leaves about 45 percent of aristocratic families that were in every respect residents of provincial cities: they perhaps visited Mexico City once or twice a year, but their lives were the most intimately tied to the hacienda, which was seldom more than 40 miles away. Basically, then, beginning in the early 1920s, concentration in Mexico City affected the last two groups in the following way and for the following reasons.

In 1910 Puebla, Guadalajara, Querétaro, Oaxaca, Morelia, Guanajuato, Mérida, Chihuahua, Jalapa, Durango, San Luis Potosí, Zacatecas, and Tampico were the *hacendado* cities *par excellence*. There were perhaps another four or five smaller cities that had aristocratic families but few in numbers. Altogether these cities harbored about two-thirds of the Mexican aristocracy. The average *hacendado* city had roughly 40 to 50 families, while cities such as Puebla and Guadalajara might have had twice as many. The total number of provincial families was about 700 to 750, with roughly 350 exclusively enfranchised in Mexico City. Concentration in Mexico City from the early 1920s to the late 1950s meant that the overwhelming majority of families of provincial origin became enfranchised in the capital. In 1993 probably less than 75 families that retained aristocratic standing remained in a handful of provincial cities, mainly Guadalajara, Querétaro, Morelia, and San Luis Potosí. This figure does not include perhaps another 75 families that did not migrate to Mexico City and today, after three generations, have become downwardly mobile, have lost their aristocratic affiliation, and are now members of plutocratic circles that have replaced the aristocracy as local social and ruling classes since World War II.

The Mexican aristocracy weathered the armed phase of the Mexican Revolution (1910–1919) and its aftermath (1919–1934) in Mexico City and the provincial cities mentioned above. Although some aristocrats were killed by local revolutionaries or as the result of mob action, mostly between 1914 and 1917, there were no revolutionary trials, organized persecutions, or outright ostracism of the aristocracy. Nonetheless, the effects of the Mexican Revolution were extremely serious and were felt most strongly at the local and provincial levels.

The first ten years after the fall of Porfirio Díaz witnessed the demise of the traditional hacienda system: the destruction of most of the manorial establishments, the disintegration of the landed labor force, the great loss of income, and above all the end of the seigneurial system that had been the hallmark of the landed estate and its environs. The situation, of course, varied throughout the country; but economic, social, and demographic reasons account for the aristocracy's ultimate concentration in Mexico City. Migration to Mexico City began in the early 1920s and involved mostly two kinds of aristocratic families. Some were families whose haciendas had suffered the greatest destruction and whose land either had been given legally to peasants—the earliest government efforts at land reform—or had been taken over illegally. Others were families who had been steadily losing their landed base throughout the Díaz regime and whose economy was by then mainly urban—that is, commercial or manufacturing.

From the onset of the Revolution, the provincial aristocracy was socially and economically more vulnerable than the aristocracy permanently enfranchised in Mexico City. The capital's aristocracy was more diversified economically and socially constituted a fairly solid block of more than 350 families, buttressed by a fringe of European families and a budding domestic "upper-middle" class. Under such conditions, this aristocracy was relatively undisturbed during the armed conflict and subsequent period until the mid-1930s. The members of the provincial aristocracy, however, did not fare so well, given their smaller numbers in the cities that they once thoroughly controlled, and were more susceptible to revolutionary activities. Closer to the rural environment of the haciendas, they experienced more directly the destruction of the manorial establishments, the banditry, and the obliteration of the traditional landed estate. With a less diversified economy than that of their counterparts in Mexico City, provincial aristocrats during the Revolution felt heavily the economic loss of hacienda income; and many, having no other source of wealth, fell into dire straits. As a result of all these adverse factors, provincial aristocrats did not feel safe. They sensed that control of their ancestral cities was slipping away and were unable to counteract the increasing political power of "revolutionaries" and those who profited from the political awareness engendered by the Revolution.

In this general ambiance, provincial aristocrats took nearly four decades (1920–1960) to migrate permanently to Mexico City. In the early 1920s aristocratic families began trickling into Mexico City from all *hacendado* cities of the country. The massive land reform of 1934–1940 greatly accelerated migration, when provincial aristocrats finally realized that the hacienda system was finished. By 1950 about 80 percent of the provincial aristocracy had made the transition to Mexico City; and by 1960 only handfuls of aristocratic families remained in a few cities. No aristocratic families remained in such prominent *hacendado* cities as Puebla, Oaxaca, and Jalapa by the mid-1950s, although a decade earlier all aristocratic families had migrated to Mexico City from such far-away cities as Mérida, Chihuahua, Durango, and Tampico.

Concentration in Mexico City meant a degree of downward mobility, and by 1950–1960 a significant number of those aristocratic families that remained in provincial cities could not maintain their aristocratic ties. They blended with the often rich plutocracies that had developed in many former *hacendado* cities, which had become large, diversified, and occasionally important manufacturing centers by the late 1950s. In Mexico City, however, migrating aristocratic families found a propitious environment with respect to both the new possibilities offered by the city at large and the cordial and helpful reception accorded to them by the capital's aristocracy. Opportunities opened up in business and in the liberal professions, in addition to a more diversified social environment entailed by the cosmopolitan ambiance that Mexico City had begun to acquire since World War II. Provincial aristocratic families were fully recognized by the capital's aristocracy by virtue of old genealogical ties, by their pedigree as *hacendados,* and primarily by virtue of marriage alliances that to one degree or another even peripheral provincial aristocrats had maintained with the core. The blending of provincial and local aristocrats happened quickly and smoothly; from the early arrivals of the 1920s to the massive migration from the late 1930s to the late 1940s, the different waves of aristocrats became integrated into the various sectors of what was by then a united superordinate social class. Indeed, during the period between the massive land reform and the early 1950s, the aristocracy in the capital experienced a veritable renaissance, dominating the life of the city. This terminal period of social prominence, despite waning economic prosperity, was significantly triggered by the concentration of the aristocracy in Mexico City but conditioned by the inexperience of the new plutocracy and its groping for social validation.

Briefly and in order of importance, the following main variables conditioned the concentration of the aristocracy in Mexico City and its development from 1920 to 1960. First, distance to Mexico City played a determinant role in the exodus, to the extent that almost all aristocratic families from the most faraway *hacendado* cities migrated to the capital, whereas a few families remained behind in those cities close or relatively close to the capital. As far as the date of migration, the earliest families to come to the capital were from the most distant cities, and vice versa.

Second, those aristocratic families that in their ancestral cities had economic interests and activities other than haciendas were the last to migrate, irrespective of distance to the capital. Many of these families stayed and retained a residual aristocratic connection, but they are *de facto* no longer part of the Mexican aristocracy.

Third, although the great majority of the most distinguished aristocratic families resided in Mexico City throughout four centuries, there were always a few equally distinguished families enfranchised in provincial cities, primarily in Puebla and Guadalajara. These families were the best connected with the aristocracy of Mexico City but were not among the most affluent of the provincial aristocracy and were among the first to migrate to the capital. By the late 1930s most of them had made the transition and quickly and easily joined the most aristocratic and prominent circles of the capital.

Fourth, throughout the centuries the most significant factor that had kept the Mexican aristocracy a fairly homogeneous and undifferentiated social class was the web of the matrimonial alliances that linked provincial and capital aristocrats. This factor operated throughout the entire spectrum of the aristocracy, from the highest circles in Mexico City to peripheral groups of aristocrats in the provinces. As far as the concentration of aristocrats in Mexico City, provincial families with the most extensive matrimonial alliances with families in the capital were the first to migrate.

Fifth, degree of wealth also played a role in aristocratic migration to Mexico City but in conjunction with other variables, mainly economic diversification and distance to the capital. Rich provincial aristocratic families with a diversified economy tended to remain in their ancestral cities, particularly when these were distant from Mexico City. Rich families residing in cities close to the capital made the transition late, but almost invariably they ultimately settled in Mexico City.

The foregoing generalization is sufficient to understand the general configuration of the concentration of the provincial aristocracy in Mexico City. This indicates that the transition to the capital was gradual and that the main causes were the total loss of haciendas, inability to continue to dominate ancestral cities socially, and political pressures that for the most part indirectly made it impossible to survive.

Mexico City aristocrats played a crucial role in the realignment and survival of the traditional superordinate class of Mexico from the onset of the Revolution until the new plutocracy coalesced as an independent social force in the late 1970s. Mexico City aristocrats performed an invaluable service by hosting the relocation of provincial aristocrats, helping them to find their social bearings, and consolidating the entire group into a fairly cohesive social class. This was due mainly to the Mexican aristocracy's high consciousness of kind and perhaps no less significantly to its ability to discharge its traditional social functions with distinction and panache, despite its economic decline.

Strength and Demographic Configuration of the Aristocracy Today

In 1910 the strength of the Mexican aristocracy in provincial cities and the capital was approximately 1,100 families and about 12,000 adults and children. By the mid-1950s it had been reduced to about 900 families. This drop in strength may be largely explained by economic factors and by their having remained in provincial cities after the massive land reform that began in 1934. By 1975 the aristocracy had been further reduced, and it stands today at about 800 families and roughly 5,500 adults and children. Although the aristocracy as a group is not a fixed community, its boundaries are rather well defined. The main demographic parameters can be established fairly accurately, particularly since the mid-1970s, as the aristocracy has remained basically stable until today. Thus the aristocracy in 1993 was constituted by about 750 households, about 20 of them harboring extended families. These nuclear and extended families are denoted by some 150 patronymics, which the overwhelming majority of aristocrats recognize as aristocratic names. Most of them, of course, are shared by thousands—some of them by tens of thousands—of Mexicans in all social classes.

Having accounted for downward mobility in most of the twentieth century in terms of lineage and tradition, we might ask: who are aristocrats today? Essentially they represent the following four categories:

1. Descendants of conquistadors, *encomenderos*, and settlers (quite often founders of cities and towns), the original nucleus of the Creole aristocracy that by 1560 was the budding social and ruling class of New Spain. This group of aristocratic families is very small, numbering less than 10 percent that can genealogically substantiate this claim with documentary evidence. Most of these families were always enfranchised in Mexico City, but several were found in formerly important cities of the viceroyalty, such as Puebla and Guadalajara, before migrating to Mexico City.

2. Descendants of plutocrats of various extractions that achieved aristocratic

rank by the end of the first renewal (1630), most of whom by then or shortly after had become great *hacendados* engaged in mining and various commercial operations. Perhaps 25 percent of all aristocratic families can substantiate this claim, and they are among the most prominent families today. These families by 1910 were found in Mexico City and most provincial *hacendado* cities, particularly those within a radius of 300 miles of the capital.

3. Descendants of plutocrats who achieved aristocratic status during the second renewal (1730-1810), that is, the great *hacendado*, mining, and trading plutocracy that dominated New Spain from the middle of the eighteenth century until the end of colonial times. Slightly over half of aristocratic families fall into this category and by 1910 were found in Mexico City and all provincial cities.

4. Descendants of plutocrats who achieved aristocratic status during the third renewal (1850-1910)—although a significant number of families in this category did not achieve this status until the late 1940s. They were mainly bankers, manufacturers, and assorted business leaders of domestic and foreign extraction who amassed great fortunes during the second half of the nineteenth century. Perhaps 15 percent of aristocratic families fall into this category, and by the time of the great exodus to Mexico City they were found in the capital and in all *hacendado* cities of the country.

These are the recognized segments of the aristocracy today, at least among its most traditional members. The genealogical, social, and expressive implications they entail are discussed at length in following chapters. Suffice it to say here that antiquity of lineage is a very important attribute of aristocratic standing, perhaps the most important, but tempered with more recent power and wealth. Thus at the top are those families that not only are universally recognized as descendants of conquistadors and/or *encomenderos* but are fairly wealthy as well, while the wealthiest rank higher than those who can boast of nothing but a proven ancient lineage. But within the wider context of the *haute bourgeoisie* the aristocracy is perceived as a homogeneous group, as social and expressive relations with the plutocracy have unfolded during the terminal renewal (1940-1993).

As I have indicated, the Mexican aristocracy since its inception has been a fairly bounded group; despite enfranchisement in cities far apart from one another, this group always had a high degree of self-recognition, due mostly to extensive and long-standing matrimonial alliances and widespread genealogical ties spanning the country. The situation, however, has changed during the past two generations, particularly because of the significant degree of downward mobility experienced by the aristocracy and its concentration in Mexico City. At the same time, concentration in Mexico City has somewhat equalized the self-identification and boundaries of the group. Thus self-classification, recognition, and acceptance have increased in importance as mechanisms of maintaining the boundaries and consciousness of the group individually and collectively. This is an overt mechanism of maintaining group endogamy, which in traditional times (until 1910) was a natural aspect of the remaining seigneurial system. Today, in such a rapidly changing world, these subterfuges are almost meaningless, but the majority of aristocrats continue to discharge them in a vain effort to maintain the aristocratic worldview. Be this as it may, the ambiance of self-classification and recognition has endogenous and exogenous dimensions.

In Mexico City since the early 1950s the aristocracy has included individuals and families from at least twelve provincial cities. While the majority of these aristocrats had extensive networks of friendship and matrimonial alliances with aristocrats permanently enfranchised in the capital, this was not the case with those of other provincial cities. Some contacts and alliances of various kinds had always existed among aristocrats of provincial cities, but the situation was significantly different in Mexico City from 1940 onward. Throughout the entire migration period from 1920 to 1960 establishing credentials and being recognized as bona fide aristocrats were of primary importance, and in this context the following criteria have been the main mechanisms of self-recognition and acceptance.

First, in the absence of official titles of nobility, registers of *hidalguía* (gentry), and other written mechanisms establishing aristocratic affiliation, name recognition was the first attribute of identification. By themselves, of course, patronymics did not establish aristocratic standing, but they were the first step toward this end. Family name in conjunction with physical type (namely, features that betrayed total European ancestry or the least non-European mixture) set the stage for further aristocratic claims. It should be noted that in many cases, particularly concerning the most distinguished and well-known families enfranchised in Mexico City and two or three provincial cities, family names are so well identified and so much in the aristocratic consciousness that name recognition alone established aristocratic affiliation.

Second came establishing city of origin and urban and regional connections, which meant basically determining social relations to locally well-known aristocratic families. This exercise was important to the extent that it helped to position aristocratic families of long standing and those of more recent origin, that is, local plutocrats who had achieved aristocratic status within a generation or so.

Third, perhaps the most salient attribute of aristocratic recognition was establishing the name of the hacienda or haciendas formerly owned by a family. This subterfuge was not so much a question of determining whether a family was aristocratic or not but rather of establishing antiquity of aristocratic lineage. Even though in the case of most landed estates throughout colonial and early republican times there was a fairly low degree of continuity, the great landed estates since the middle of the eighteenth century had been in the hands of distinguished aristocratic families in several provinces of the country.

Fourth, establishing genealogical connections between aristocratic families from the capital and those in the provinces and among the latter was the last and strongest attribute that created recognition and aristocratic standing. Quite frequently, genealogical and matrimonial ties had been dormant for generations, sometimes for more than a century; but upon being recognized they immediately established social bonds and inclusion in the network of the aristocratic family doing the recognizing. In the final analysis, established genealogical and matrimonial ties, no matter how old, were the main attributes that determined the position and social networks that migrant aristocratic families acquired upon settling in Mexico City.

Taken together, the foregoing mechanisms of recognition and attributes conferring aristocratic standing became an integral part of the realignment of the aristocracy in Mexico City from the end of the armed phase of the Mexican Revolution until the new plutocracy began to assert itself forcefully. The activation of these mechanisms, individually or in conjunction, resulted in the configuration of the Mexican aristocracy in Mexico City in the fashion described in this book.

Exogenously, the aristocracy since the early 1950s presents quite another panorama, as viewed by the plutocracy, the political class, and the upper-middle class proximate to it. Each one of these classes regards the aristocracy differently from the standpoint of its own interests, prejudices, and aspirations. In one respect, however, all of these classes regard the aristocracy monolithically, a gestalt that does not account for the ranking and fragmentation that the aristocracy has undergone since its concentration in Mexico City. Again, the exception is the dozen or so oldest or most distinguished aristocratic family groups that are distinctly known to most people in the upper echelons of the stratification system. In this context, name recognition is a very important factor, and family name serves as the initial and rallying consideration in aristocratic identification by plutocratic, political, and upper-middle class sectors. Thus family names such as Rincón Gallardo, Romero de Terreros, Cervantes, Cortina, de Ovando, Icaza, Pérez de Salazar, Sánchez Navarro, Villar Villamil, Martínez del Río, and another score or two are well known among the foregoing sectors of the stratification system. When they are mentioned in a variety of contexts and situations, they connote aristocratic affiliation and to some extent collectively denote the aristocracy as a class. Until about the early 1970s name recognition of the aristocracy extended to a wider spectrum of Mexican society, including the more educated classes; but such recognition is fading fast.

More significantly, the superordinate sectors mentioned above and the educated in general (realistically no more than 2 percent of the population of Mexico City) are historically aware of the aristocracy, perhaps vaguely, but accurately as far as regarding the social class described above as the former ruling class of the country, the former *hacendado* class with diversified economic interests. Particularly among the educated (some of them upper-middle class, but mostly solid middle class) aristocrats are remembered as the exploiters of the past but also in the contemporary context as the *sociedad* (society), mistakenly as "the Porfirian aristocracy," and resentfully as "those decadent people that caused Mexico so much damage" or "those who believe they are a divine caste but who no longer count for much." These and other derogatory references to the aristocracy today are another expression of the fact that Mexico's middle classes discriminate only on the basis of power and wealth.

Centering on the plutocracy (as the upper-middle class is socially close to both the aristocracy and plutocracy), what are the mechanisms of aristocratic recognition and the ambiance of interaction of these two superordinate sectors? In every context of the last superordinate (aristocratic) renewal throughout most of the twentieth century, answers to these questions have been framed in structural and expressive terms. Since the new plutocracy of Mexico began to emerge in the late 1920s, it has been in contact with the aristocracy, increasingly in a position of economic superordination but socially under the guidance of the aristocracy, until it began to assert its independence and create its own social life in the early 1970s. Thus former hacienda ownership, the country-city axis, and lineage and genealogy are for plutocrats as well part of the aristocratic allure and means by which to identify and relate to aristocrats. In other words, self-classification, recognition and acceptance, and the gate-keeping activities that go with them are the same endogenously and exogenously.

Returning to specific demographic considerations, let us consider a few preliminary facts about fragmentation of the aristocracy. The aristocracy today is no longer a fairly united and organic social group as it had been until the late 1950s. Since then it has become fragmented into perhaps a dozen identifiable segments composed of six to ten family groups. These segments today exhibit the degree of organic unity that the aristocracy as a whole exhibited more than a generation ago. Fragmentation has been the result of occupational differentiation, physical distance within Mexico City, and original (before settling in the capital) kinship and genealogical relationships. Fragmentation, however, has not diminished the self-image of the aristocracy as a social class and its position in the stratification system of the city.

Demographic Configuration of the Plutocracy Today

The Mexican plutocracy is not an easy social class to demarcate and analyze; it does not have the unitary configuration and organic worldview of the aristocracy. Yet throughout the seventy years since the end of the armed phase of the Mexican Revolution, the plutocracy has carved a distinct and powerful niche in the superordinate stratification of the country. Given the effects of diffusion, and the fact that for the past two generations the economic world system has transcended national boundaries, the new plutocracy of Mexico today is not in any way significantly different, socially and economically, from those of the United States, Europe, and other countries of the world.

It should be realized that there is very little continuity from Porfirian times to the present, because the Mexican Revolution not only terminated the traditional landed system of the country but also significantly transformed the old banking, industrial, and trading establishment. On the one hand, many numbers of the aristocratic *hacendado* class were also business leaders engaged in various economic enterprises. These activities, to be sure, were much less disturbed than the obliteration of the landed system; and members of the aristocracy who had a more diversified economy were able to survive economic disaster fairly well. On the other hand, the Porfirian plutocratic establishment, which included some aristocrats but mostly upwardly mobile plutocrats at that time, did not survive well, despite the fact that its wealth was primarily in banking and industry. As possessors of the most visible sources of wealth, Porfirian plutocrats suffered from the rapacity of the Revolution; and when the armed revolt subsided, most of their economic enterprises were in a bad state of affairs in the capital as well as in provincial cities. Thus the plutocracy with which the aristocracy has been in interaction during the past two and a half generations is almost exclusively of postrevolutionary origin.

The decade of the 1920s represents the gestation period of the new plutocracy, during which a new breed of business leader–entrepreneurs (covering every aspect of banking, industry, manufacturing, and trade) began to create the modern economic infrastructure of Mexico. Until the Calles regime, the economic infrastructure and practically all other infrastructures of the country were still in a state of turmoil, and one cannot really speak of a plutocracy exercising ruling functions independently of the political class. Rather, one must regard this decade as ushering in a new economic outlook and a new kind of business leader–entrepreneurs that launched Mexico on the road to modernity. While throughout this and two subsequent decades there were many foreign interests operating in Mexico, they were never part of the national plutocracy. But from this point onward it began to grow by the inclusion of foreign business leader–entrepreneurs, who did become members of the new plutocracy.

Beginning in the early 1930s, the incipient plutocracy began to grow during a period of uninterrupted prosperity, amassing increasingly larger fortunes until World War II. During this era the new plutocracy became a force to contend with, and from this point onward it acquired the first attributes of a ruling class. To some extent this was because in the middle of the 1930s politicians—some of them of bona fide revolutionary extraction—began turning into plutocrats after a stint in high office. Primarily, however, there was a new outburst of entrepreneurial activity that created large modern business concerns employing thousands of people. The great state-owned enterprises (railroads, oil, the postal system, and a few others) were, of course, still the industrial backbone of the nation; but the private sector of the economy—increasingly controlled by surging plutocratic magnates—continued to create new sources of work and wealth, which for the first time since Porfirian times gave this nascent social class a ruling function. During this period an unspoken understanding of mutual economic goals, procedures, and the general modus operandi began to shape the relationship between the plutocracy and the political class. As its ruling power increased, the budding plutocracy became aware of itself as a fairly distinct segment of the superordinate system. This awareness entailed typical ruling functions such as influencing national economic policy, a voice in the government's formulation of labor policy, and establishing guidelines regulating its relationship to the political class. The ruling party and past high officials kept a tight rein in running the country and promoting "revolutionary" actions that on the surface made Mexico a socialist state. In reality, despite the massive land reform and a number of other apparently socialist measures, the country was a tightly centralized, semidemocratic system with a mixed economy. This period, finally, triggered the expressive awareness of the plutocracy—that is, probably the majority of plutocrats became socially aware and sought ties with the aristocracy.

From roughly 1946 to the early 1970s the plutocracy reached maturity as a ruling class and began to differentiate. These processes of differentiation operated along the power-and-wealth axis and between the socially upwardly mobile and those essentially impervious to the lure of aristocratization. There is a correlation between these two variables: the least wealthy and most wealthy plutocrats have shown the lowest inclination to social upward mobility (that is, to acquire aristocratic expressive trappings), while those most upwardly mobile have been plutocrats in the middle range of wealth and power. As I have indicated, the Mexican plutocracy as a whole cannot easily be circumscribed as a social class, but its upwardly mobile sector, with which this book is exclusively concerned, can be configured in a meaningful fashion.

More significant is the degree of wealth controlled by the plutocracy in its banking, manufacturing, and commercial enterprises. Throughout this stage of development, plutocratic magnates had quite a diversified economy; but most wealth was generated in banking and manufacturing, ranging from heavy interests in major banks to a wide range of large manufacturing enterprises. In this wide spectrum, 30 to 40 million dollars was probably the minimum wealth needed in order to qualify for the status of plutocratic magnate. Fortunes of 50 to 100 million dollars were common, and a considerable number of plutocratic magnates had fortunes surpassing 200 million dollars, while a handful of fortunes were larger than 500 million. The total number of plutocratic magnates enfranchised in Mexico City in the foregoing categories probably surpassed 500, with perhaps another 600 in provincial cities in the category of 30–40 million dollars. This provincial category has little or no bearing on the present study, while perhaps 300 Mexico City plutocrats are upwardly mobile and have been in acculturative interaction with various aristocratic segments for at least a generation. Finally, during this developmental stage the Mexican plutocracy was increased by a considerable number of capitalists of foreign extraction, mostly Europeans, Near Easterners, and a few North Americans. With few exceptions, Near Eastern and North American plutocrats have not joined the ranks of the socially upwardly mobile, while European plutocrats have done so almost without exception. Most of the European upwardly mobile plutocrats were Spanish, Italian, and French and almost invariably settled in Mexico City. In several ways they became among the most upwardly mobile plutocrats, which may be because the French and Italians in particular had a better class position to begin with. Indeed, several of them were aristocrats (some of them titled aristocrats) and in such cases very quickly became aristocratic plutocrats with extensive social networks in the Mexican aristocracy. To summarize, by the early 1970s a ruling class of plutocrats had come into existence, which by virtue of their wealth and power — including plutocrats of political extraction — exercised significant influence in the affairs of the nation.

After the early 1970s the new plutocracy can no longer be so termed; for during this short generation it has consolidated its position as a ruling class, particularly in recent years, due to changes in "revolutionary" rhetoric, privatization of the economy, and the more outright participation of political plutocrats in the economic affairs of the nation. In other words, the earlier distinction between economic (business leaders) and political plutocrats is disappearing, if not almost gone. One can no longer speak of perhaps most plutocrats as *nouveaux riches*, as they have been rich and powerful for nearly two generations. Expressively, plutocrats have learned from the local aristocracy — and within the context of the wider international world of business — as much as they need to erase or successfully hide undesirable or unbecoming behavior and manners of the "new rich." Uppity aristocrats would not necessarily consider most of the more socially conscious plutocrats to be members of their group. In most respects, however, there is widening recognition, even admiration, of the plutocrats on the part of aristocrats, for behaving, acting, and on the whole discharging a lifestyle that is not essentially different from the aristocratic ideal. Or, as one aristocratic informant accurately puts it, "Many of our millionaires, great entrepreneurs, who not so long ago were coarse and uneducated people without any 'social' behavior, have become very refined. They now behave very decently and properly [code words for aristocratic behavior]; it is admirable how they have learned many of our customs and are worthy of our friendship and recognition." In absolute terms, the wealth of the plutocracy has increased, particularly in the case of the largest fortunes in the country. According to *Forbes* magazine (June 1994), there are more billionaires in Mexico than in any other Latin American country: twenty-four in all. This gives Mexico the dubious honor of being the fourth country in the world in terms of private fortunes, after the United States, Germany, and Japan. According to this account, the richest man in Mexico is worth 6.6 billion dollars. Five individuals or families have fortunes ranging from 2.5 to 5.5 billion, while the remaining eighteen fortunes range from 1.1 to 2.4 billion. It should be noted that these enormous fortunes (for a still industrializing country such as Mexico) are directly or indirectly the product of the intense privatization that has been taking place during the past decade, a process centered mostly in Mexico City. A similar concentration of wealth has been taking place throughout the country, albeit less spectacularly. There are many more plutocratic magnates today than in the early 1970s, and in several of the bigger cities of the country there has also been a great growth of private wealth. The richest family in Mexico, according to *Forbes* magazine, is of provincial extraction. As far as I am aware, it has not gone through a process of "aristocratization" derived from the national scene; rather, whatever social and expressive changes it has undergone are due to involvement in the wider international context of business.

I have mentioned the class position of the foreign plutocracy, and a few remarks on the domestic plutocracy are in order. The information on this matter is sketchy, but its general outline can be established. First, the rags-to-riches syndrome probably accounts for a third of all plutocrats today, that is, individuals of modest origins (probably in the range of lower-middle class) with little or no formal education and almost invariably of provincial provenance. I am not aware that any present-day plutocrats in the highest range of wealth came from this background. Most of these plutocrats occupy the lowest wealth niche, with fortunes in the range of 50 to 75 million dollars. This group includes domestic and foreign plutocrats: the former mostly from cities that became large manufacturing and trading centers after the 1930s (most notably Guadalajara, Monterrey, Puebla, Ciudad Juárez, and a few others); the latter most often from Spain and the Near East (mostly Lebanese and Palestinian Christians). A few of these are among the medium-to-richest plutocrats, but only recently (during the past decade or so) have they become socially and economically visible.

The second group consists of individuals of middle-class origins with a university education, including the law, engineering, and finance. This category includes most plutocrats and the great majority of politicians-turned-plutocrats. The former almost always gravitated to the capital, for the National Autonomous University of Mexico has always been a magnet that attracts students from all over the country. Some plutocrats in this category had no education at all, but they are a distinct exception, while some went abroad to further their education. As a group this is the best formally educated plutocratic group, the most professional from the financing, manufacturing, and overall business viewpoint. The majority of the medium-to-richest plutocrats, almost invariably with fortunes of more than 300 million dollars, fall into this category. Among the most socially conscious, they have been the backbone of the plutocracy, constituting for nearly two generations the acculturative expressive counterpart of the aristocracy. This category accounts for nearly half of the entire plutocracy and is almost exclusively enfranchised in Mexico City.

The third group includes individuals with the best class position at the beginning of their plutocratic careers, many of them upper-middle class. A considerable number of plutocrats in this group had ties to the aristocracy before the onset of their plutocratic careers, and many of them migrated to Mexico City from provincial cities at the time of the aristocratic exodus. This group is also the best educated in terms of Culture (with a capital C), and from the beginning it has been the most socially and expressively active of the entire plutocracy. Families in this category are the most acculturated, have had the longest-standing relationship with the aristocracy, and now constitute the leadership of the new superordinate "aristocratic" class that is almost *ad portas*. From the viewpoint of class formation, it constitutes the group to emulate, and its most outstanding members must indeed be considered the leaders that have done the most, and most creatively, to blend power and wealth with the values and orientation of social and expressive achievement and aspirations.

Fourth, and in a category by themselves, are foreign plutocrats, most of whom have been characterized above as having the best original class position. They quickly became a significant aspect of ongoing plutocratic developments, and part of the aristocracy, by virtue of having already incorporated an expressive array virtually identical to that of the local model. Indeed, a significant degree of expressive acculturation undergone by the Mexican plutocracy originated in these foreign elements, independently of the local aristocracy. In terms of wealth, this elite group again falls into the middle range of local standards: economically they are not among the most influential plutocrats, a factor that is counterbalanced by their expressive and social prominence.

Let us briefly put in perspective the main segments of the plutocracy in terms of expressive acculturation and degree of upward mobility. There is, of course, a significant degree of idiosyncratic variation, but the entire range of Mexico's plutocracy may be categorized as follows. First are individuals who are opposed or indifferent to expressive acculturation—that is, socially not engaged in upward mobility in terms of either the aristocratic model or other models presented to them in the context of their economic and entrepreneurial milieux. While enjoying the power and wealth that come with plutocratic status, they do not engage in any of the expressive activities so much a part of superordinate stratification: public and private presentation and display, participation in the cultural life of the city, socialization in aristocratic-plutocratic circles, intermarriage with aristocrats, philanthropy, sponsoring artistic events, and so on. These plutocrats are regarded by aristocrats and upwardly mobile plutocrats alike not only as *nouveaux riches* (entailing the worst social connotations of the term) but as individuals inimical to the interests of the plutocracy as a social class. This is a difficult group to categorize. According to standard sociological analysis, individuals in this category—given their power and wealth—are upper-class members of the superordinate stratum; according to the structural-expressive definition of class adopted in this book, however, they are not. Indeed, this segment of the plutocracy falls somewhere on the fringes of the superordinate system: structurally part of it but expressively not even upper-middle class. Expressively this plutocratic group, constituting perhaps slightly more than one-third of the plutocracy, is part of the political class, of politicians-turned-plutocrats, and of an assortment of groups in the middle classes. Its members are tied to many circles in the life of the capital, but they keep a low profile and are the least visible sector of the plutocracy. The group includes mostly individuals in the low range of wealth and with the lowest original class position. This sector of the plutocracy is the newest, as most of its members have achieved plutocratic status within the past twenty-five years or so.

Second, perhaps another third of the plutocracy's membership is composed of individuals who are both upwardly mobile and seeking social recognition. Although this group is older than the foregoing category, the initiation of its members' plutocratic careers does not extend beyond the mid-1940s, while the majority acquired plutocratic standing no earlier than 1960. This group of plutocrats came somewhat late into the game of upward mobility; and, probably until the early 1970s, many exhibited a degree of reticence about acquiring the trappings of the at that time established aristocratic-plutocratic ambiance. Since then, however, plutocrats in this category have engaged in the game of upward mobility and have now established solid networks with various segments of the aristocracy and the most traditional plutocracy. Most plutocratic families in this category have not yet acquired the full expressive array that would put them in the mainstream of plutocratic achievement. They have played the game well, and there are probably no expressive domains that they have not tried in achieving parity with the traditional plutocratic sector. Some of them have established matrimonial alliances with aristocratic families; and in several ways the members of this sector are closest to the aristocracy, in the sense that they have not yet experienced the syndrome of having arrived and beginning to innovate expressively. In terms of original class position, plutocrats in this category range from solid middle class to upper-middle class, while in terms of wealth they are today at all levels between medium and large fortunes. This category includes most politicians-turned-plutocrats, who have found it easier during the past fifteen years to shed their pseudo-revolutionary stance.

Third, the members of the last sector of the plutocracy, constituting slightly less than one-third, are and have been the most upwardly mobile since the beginning of Mexico's last renewal of elites. This group of plutocrats includes those who initiated their upwardly mobile career in the late 1920s and early 1930s, individuals with the best original class position, and the richest and most influential members of the class. They represent the structural and expressive core of the Mexican plutocracy, its social leaders, and the most innovative sector of the new superordinate class of the country. Plutocrats in this category today come primarily from upper-middle-class backgrounds, including some Porfirian plutocrats. In terms of wealth this group includes members of the three categories discussed above, but most of them are in the upper reaches of wealth. The worldview and expressive array of this group of plutocrats are the closest to those of aristocrats and in terms of manners and behavior in most social domains almost indistinguishable from them. Finally, foreign plutocrats fall somewhere between the second and third categories: most Spaniards and Near Easterners in the former, and most French and Italians in the latter.

To summarize, the plutocracy described above constitutes essentially the ruling class of Mexico, mostly centered in the capital but with provincial representatives in the majority of the most important industrial and commercial cities of the country. It is difficult to estimate today the total strength of this countrywide plutocracy, but my guess is that it is no larger than 2,000 families. Of these, about two-thirds are enfranchised in Mexico City—that is, their varied enterprises may be located in many places throughout the country, but they reside permanently in the capital and their social life is exclusively centered there. Discounting the non–upwardly mobile sector of the plutocracy enfranchised in Mexico City, there are roughly 850 plutocratic families with which the aristocracy is, and has been for two generations, in a relationship of structural and expressive acculturation. This sector of the Mexican plutocracy (basically the second and third expressive categories discussed above) represents the model to be emulated by the rich and powerful and the epitome of the *ad portas* superordinate class of the country.

CHAPTER 2

THE RELATIONSHIP
OF CLASS AND ETHNICITY
Somatic and Racial Considerations

Mexico is a complex nation state where phenotypic categories and characteristics blend with cultural categories and definitions in capricious, contextual, occasionally contradictory, and always baroque individual and collective types. Racial and physical categories that originally (in the sixteenth and seventeenth centuries) had clear and precise denotations have throughout the centuries acquired cultural denotations, with an array of connotations that only time, place, and context can make specific—terms such as *blanco* (white), *europeo* (European), *indio* (Indian), *negro* (black), *mestizo* (various combinations of white and Indian), *mulato* (various combinations of white and black; a rarely used term), *criollo* (originally a Spaniard born in Mexico but now a hopelessly contextual and imprecise term), and many extensions, variations, and corruptions of these basic terms. This intricate, convoluted, and occasionally jocose mosaic obtains from the lowest to the highest ranks of the country's stratification system and is often interdigitated with ethnic and cultural denotations.

Racial Composition of the Aristocracy and Its Ideational and Physical Underpinnings

Let us examine the contexts of aristocratic racial admixture and its consequences by briefly outlining how they have evolved since the Spanish Conquest.

From the Conquest onward, miscegenation was the law of the land. Spaniards procreated first with Indians and from the middle of the sixteenth century with black people. Marriage among the basic stocks was rare during the first half of the sixteenth century; but it increased from then on, so that by the middle of the seventeenth century New Spain had become a pluriethnic society. After the middle of the sixteenth century, black slaves arrived in considerable numbers; they were settled mainly along the Gulf coast, particularly in the state of Veracruz, and in several regions of the Pacific coast, especially in the states of Guerrero and Colima. Although there were some black slaves throughout the viceroyalty until the beginning of the nineteenth century, by the late eighteenth century they had been largely absorbed into the Indian-mestizo population and had ceased to be a distinct ethnic group. By the first quarter of the seventeenth century several terms that had originally denoted specific racial categories had already acquired cultural attributes and connotations. This is most distinctly the case with the two most common terms of the colonial system: Indian and mestizo.

For perhaps the first fifty years after the Conquest, the term "Indian" referred almost exclusively to the overwhelming majority of the colonial population (that is, those living in Indian congregations but occasionally intimately associated with the Spanish cities and towns of the viceroyalty). In other words, "Indian" denoted a purely racial category. The term then began to change rather rapidly as Indians settled permanently in mining camps, towns, and Spanish cities—that is, it began to acquire cultural characteristics. Three generations later, by the middle of the seventeenth century, the term essentially denoted a cultural category: Indians were those who practiced an Indian culture—the many acculturative-syncretic entities that had emerged throughout the confrontation and accommodation of Spanish culture and regional variants of pre-Hispanic Indian culture. The definition of an Indian since this early period has been not racial but essentially cultural, and it is not an exaggeration to say that this has remained a constant aspect of Mexican society until the present.

The term "mestizo" is intrinsically complementary to the term "Indian"; mestizos are part of a single sociocultural continuum. Originally, and probably for no more than two generations (until perhaps 1570 or so), the term "mestizo" denoted exclusively the racial category of the progeny of a Spaniard and an Indian. By the end of the sixteenth century it already included various admixtures of Indian and Spanish, as more and more Indians settled in urban areas. By the end of the seventeenth century the term "mestizo" had probably acquired the entire range of meanings and social and cultural denotations that it has had from the nineteenth century onward: a mixture of Indian and European; various degrees of admixture of Indian and European; phenotypic Indians who have culturally acquired mestizo status; at the local level, non-Indians (with many derivations and regional variations); and several other racial, cultural, and racial-cultural denotations at the local, provincial, and national levels. Throughout most of the sixteenth century the process of mestizoization entailed mostly Spanish and Creole fathers and Indian mothers; but by the end of the century it had taken a more fluid form, entailing various degrees of European and Indian combinations. By the middle of the seventeenth century, perhaps a generation later, the process of mestizoization had acquired the diversification that was characteristic of Mexico by the middle of the nineteenth century, representing the normal, fluid, and kaleidoscopic mosaic of ethnic phenotypes that has characterized the nation until the present.

Until past the middle of the nineteenth century the term "white," as a racial category, denoted almost exclusively individuals of Spanish blood; only since that time have other Europeans and Near Easterners settled in Mexico in significant numbers, a process that steadily increased until the late 1940s. As a racial category the term "white" does not have the same denotation as, say, in the United States and other colonial situations in the recent past. Rather, along the entire spectrum of the Mexican stratification system from Indians to aristocratic milieux, specific terms denoting nationalities (Spaniards, Lebanese, foreigners, Europeans, gringos, and so on) or physical and cultural characteristics (*güeros* [light-skinned people], *catrines* [city slickers], *criollos güeros* [blondish creoles], and so on) are employed instead to refer to whites. The term *blanco* (white), however, is occasionally used in Indian communities and regions where there is a clear Indian-mestizo dichotomy that is sufficiently ambiguous to include light mestizo phenotypes. In urban environments the ethno-somatic situation is configured by a gradation of mestizo phenotypes, on the one hand, and white Europeans, on the other, with a no-man's-land of light mestizos who (in the popular perception of color and somatic categories) are regarded as white Europeans. Occasionally this last category is denoted by the term *criollo* (Creole), primarily to indicate an essentially Spanish ancestry. Urban environments, and increasingly rural environments, may be characterized as a mosaic which does not denote the varied ways in which whites are perceived and how whites perceive themselves. The interdigitation of cultural, ethnic, and somatic traits and perceptions and manipulations in the pluriethnic society of Mexico are not well understood, but certain known themes bear directly on the subject at hand.

First, as individuals move from the bottom to the top of the stratification system, cultural characteristics and perceptions tend to recede and phenotypic inputs increase in the categorization of individuals and groups. For example, at the local level Indian or even mestizo cultural inputs predominate over phenotypic inputs, given the fundamentally uniform somatic configuration of most rural environments. At the opposite extreme, there is much less somatic manipulation: individuals (but seldom groups) are categorized essentially in terms of phenotypic characteristics, although whites and *criollos* are perceived and may regard themselves through the screen of putative cultural characteristics.

Second, the manipulation of cultural and phenotypic characteristics and perceptions is an inseparable aspect of the process of upward social and ethnic mobility that has characterized Mexico for centuries. Upward mobility of any kind has been fluid but always underlined by somatic characteristics as an advantage in the social categorization of phenotypes: Europeans have greatly predominated in most aspects of the social and cultural life of the country, and only since the 1910 Revolution has the situation significantly changed. To put it descriptively, the overwhelming majority of the lower classes are phenotypically Indian, while the great majority of the upper classes are phenotypically European. Not even the 1910 Revolution was able to redress this fundamental fact of Mexican society: the social, ruling, and political classes of the country are still primarily constituted by European phenotypes and light mestizos. This strongly diagnostic characteristic has been changing during the past two generations, however, and Indian phenotypes are appearing with increasing frequency among the political, economic, and even social elites of the country. But the most socially prominent, the richest, and the most powerful sectors are still dominated by individuals exhibiting distinctly or predominantly European phenotypes.

Third, even though Mexico is overwhelmingly a racially Indian country, culturally it is essentially a European, Western country. The syncretism and acculturation that have been going on for more than four centuries have affected mostly religion, several domains of material culture, and certain aspects of social and personal interaction: in the wider world beyond regional Indian and mestizo milieux and in the cultural baggage that migrants from rural areas bring to the cities. To put it differently, Mexico has retained many traits, complexes, and institutions of its colonial past, some of them inimical to a more equitable, less European-biased society. I particularly have in mind standards of beauty and physical appearance, which are essentially European. This is easily confirmed by looking at the predominance of male and female European phenotypes that populate television and other graphic forms of advertising. In the context of categorizing ethnicity, and in the range of phenotype variations, European standards of beauty and ideals of physical appearance play an important role. On the one hand, they provide guidelines on how to improve, heighten, and even change one's physical appearance in order to bring it closer to the idealized phenotype; and, on the other hand, they provide a model of somatic and phenotypic perception in passing from a subordinate to a superordinate social class or ethnic category. For example, individuals, primarily males, may marry European-looking women in order to enhance their progeny's phenotypic status; people may favor social interaction with European phenotypes and subtly influence children to do the same; in cases of the often significant phenotypic variation found within families, parents may favor the more European-looking children to the detriment of the more Indian-looking children.

The aristocracy must now be placed in historical perspective with respect to the reconstruction above in order to analyze it endogenously and exogenously. Let us first settle the terminological question. As in the case of the original categories of Indian and mestizo, there is some confusion concerning the term *criollo* (Spaniard born in Mexico or in any part of the New World) as contrasted with *peninsular* (Spaniard born in Spain). Throughout colonial times these two categories constituted the superordinate stratum of New Spain, and the richest and most powerful individuals among them constituted the aristocracy. For at least a generation after the Conquest, until 1550 or so, the European presence in New Spain included exclusively *peninsulares:* original conquistadors, royal officials of a variety of sorts, and later arrivals, including merchants, artisans, and holders of royal grants. By about 1575 the category of Creole had come into existence, entailing not only a difference in place of birth but a range of cultural characteristics that defined it and distinguished it from the category of *peninsular.* The distinction and cultural configuration of Creoles and *peninsulares* remained more or less constant throughout colonial times: stereotypes enshrining cultural and behavioral differences, generally negative. The term *peninsular,* as defined above, remained unchanged until Independence, while the term "Creole" came to denote more than the issue of Spanish parents.

Much has been written about the differences and antagonisms between Creoles and *peninsulares* for more than two and a half centuries. In my view, this stance has been exaggerated. Even though *peninsulares* always monopolized the highest political offices of New Spain and constituted its political class (a deliberate policy of the Spanish Crown to keep the colony under tight royal control and to avoid undue seigneurial highhandedness on the part of the Creole *encomenderos* and *hacendados*), the ruling and social class of the colony since the second half of the sixteenth century had always been centered on the Creole aristocracy. Moreover, since the great majority of *peninsulares* came to settle, their children or grandchildren became Creoles. Indeed, one can conceptualize the category of *peninsular* as a transitory status on the way to becoming Creole. Although there is no reliable information, it is doubtful that more than 20 percent of Spaniards who came to New Spain returned to the mother country; sooner or later *peninsulares* became Creoles, including many of the highest royal officials of viceregal and royal-justice rank. Thus, for more than two centuries, the *peninsular* class was always small but sufficiently rich and powerful to have constituted a fertile and attractive source of matrimonial and economic alliances for the Creole class, particularly the aristocracy.

For about one hundred years after the category of Creole came into existence (roughly until 1670), it essentially retained its original, nuclear denotation: the children of parents of pure Spanish descent. There are exceptions, of course, which are duly noted in the following discussion. From that period until the end of colonial times, the term "Creole" came to include a variety of phenotypes that did not correspond to pure Spanish parentage. At the onset of the nineteenth century, two decades before Independence, the population of New Spain was about 6.5 million: roughly 1 million were classified as Creoles, 2 million as mestizos, and 3.5 million as Indians, with a sprinkling of no more than 16,000 *peninsulares* (von Humboldt 1966:218). The Creole population presents problems in that perhaps a third of it was not Creole in the original, genotypic definition of the term. Rather, at least 300,000 Creoles were light mestizo phenotypes who were culturally defined in that superordinate category, just as Indian phenotypes were classified as mestizos upon acquiring non-Indian culture and/or by settling in cities and towns away from Indian communities. In the traditional fashion described above, passing from one ethnic category to another entailed the manipulations that Indians engaged in when seeking mestizo categorization: acquiring cultural characteristics of the superordinate group and emphasizing phenotypic traits of that group.

This fluidity is corroborated by the failure of the policy of the Crown during the middle of the eighteenth century to classify all possible combinations and recombinations of the basic racial stocks (Indian, black, and Spaniard) into a repressive system of *castas* (castes). Throughout the remainder of colonial times and during republican times until the Mexican Revolution of 1910, the term "Creole" came to denote Spanish phenotypes as well as light mestizos and perhaps other cultural-phenotypic denotations at the local and regional levels. In any case, if we assume that there were roughly 700,000 Creoles and *peninsulares* at the end of colonial times, the phenotypically European population of Mexico in 1821 (more than 10 percent of the total) was proportionally greater in relation to the total population of the country than at any period until the present, which is roughly 7 million in a population of more than 90 million (XI Censo General de Población de los Estados Unidos Mexicanos; Fernando Cervantes, personal communication, 1987). The fluidity of the ethnic and stratification systems diminished from Independence onward, and the Indian population, the passing population, and the various admixtures of mestizo populations became more endogenous and self-contained. The situation did not change much after the Mexican Revolution of 1910; only recently, during the past two generations, has the system regained its colonial fluidity. This is a startling demographic fact that requires detailed investigation.[1]

The Mexican aristocracy, of course, is racially part of the evolutionary process described above, but with a few distinct characteristics. The aristocracy originated with the sixteenth-century conquistadors who became *encomenderos*, founders of towns and cities, and subsequent recipients of royal grants. Throughout that century this budding ruling class remained largely endogamous, intermarrying occasionally with other prominent Creoles and *peninsulares* arriving in the colony. Indeed, New Spain's social and ruling class throughout colonial times was a Creole aristocracy that renewed itself twice by the incorporation of the richest and most powerful new people of the Creole-*peninsular* sector of the population. The first departure from this virtually endogamous pattern came early in the development of the aristocracy: the intermarriage of conquistadors and later of *encomenderos* with prominent Indian women of the *tlatoani* (kingly) and *tecuhtli* (lordly) classes. The Spanish Crown recognized the status and the landed wealth of these ranks of the Indian aristocracy; and the main incentive for conquistadors and *encomenderos* to marry noble Indian women was access to more land than could be sought from the Crown. We do not know how common intermarriage was, but it occurred; and I have been able to identify more than ten cases. The reverse situation—the marriage of noble Indian men with Spanish women—

was very uncommon, except for some of Motehcuzoma's descendants, one of whom was later awarded the title of count and had settled in Spain by the second half of the century (Dorantes de Carranza 1970:98). Indeed, several aristocratic informants readily acknowledge being descendants of prominent Indian rulers and lords and are proud of this heritage.

This early admixture was a thing of the past by the onset of the seventeenth century, and the aristocracy settled into a rather strictly endogamous pattern for a century and a half: aristocrats married their own kind or upwardly mobile plutocrats, always of Creole or *peninsular* extraction. Apparently, aristocratic resistance to marrying outsiders not of strictly Spanish descent was significantly reduced during the second half of the eighteenth century, and light mestizo phenotypes in significant numbers contracted matrimonial alliances with aristocrats. This can be explained in terms of the fluidity in the social and economic domains that characterized the last decades of colonial domination after the unsuccessful and rather disastrous experiment of the *casta* system. Class barriers hardened after Independence, however, and the aristocracy once more became highly endogamous and has remained so until the present. There are exceptions, of course, but today it is rare to find mestizo or marginal phenotypes in the few thousand surviving members of the aristocracy. In summary, the aristocracy is basically of Spanish stock, to some extent more recently modified by the infusion of other European stocks, mainly French, Italian, and English.

Endogenous Configuration: The Dynamics of Phenotypical Reality and Ideal Self-Image

With some exceptions, the aristocracy today is phenotypically European. My observations of some 1,500 men, women, and children indicate that they range from a few nordic-like types to standard Mediterranean. I am aware that these are rather imprecise categories and that it is a risky business to mix somatic characteristics and cultural traits and behavior. I shall be careful in reaching conclusions and keeping within the boundaries of what is actual and what is normative or expected.

First of all, it should be noted that the Mexican aristocracy, as defined in this book, is a small group, almost a village in the midst of a great metropolis. Uniformity prevails: in language, culture, and behavior as well as in phenotypical appearance. There are differences and divergences, of course, but these are expected, considering the pluriethnic society of which the aristocracy is a part. This is particularly the case in the realm of the somatic composition of the aristocracy, where differences and divergences are interpreted through the cultural prism. One last caveat: what the aristocracy conceives itself to be and several of the consequences that follow from it are not exclusive, for the aristocracy shares several of these somatic conceptions with other segments of European extraction in the upper echelons of the country's stratification system. Thus, in analyzing the aristocracy, I am also concerned with junctures of groups proximate to it.

Let us first present the somatic facts. The Mexican aristocracy today is primarily of Spanish stock, although during the past five generations it has received infusions from several European nationalities. Although these infusions are noticeable in many families, they have been of only medium significance. Non-European, Indian genetic inputs are also evident in a few families. In my observation of perhaps one-fourth of the aristocracy's membership (more than 150 informants and their families, at many weddings and other social affairs), individual males and females exhibiting non-European phenotypic traits are rare. I would say that such individuals constitute less than 2 percent of the entire aristocratic population, that is, roughly 100 individuals (I have arrived at this figure based on interviews of informants and their families, totaling about 1,000 men, women, and children). This percentage includes males and females in all age groups, and they are found mainly in certain entire families for more than a generation and in recessive phenotypes in otherwise standard European phenotypic families. This statement needs explanation.

In the case of recessive phenotypes, I observed seven individuals (four males and three females) whose parents, siblings, and progeny were standard European types, while they themselves exhibited Indian phenotypic traits. They range from light mestizo to unmistakable features associated with the "typical Mexican" phenotype. The most distinctive phenotypic traits in my observations (readily pointed out by aristocratic informants, who are sensitive to any deviation from standard phenotypic perceptions in their own group) are the following: brown skin, dull black hair, very round face, slight epicanthic fold, rather flat nose, and a few other not so specific traits. This set of traits may be characterized as that *je ne sais quoi* that aristocrats (and indeed most white people in Mexico) perceive and verbalize about a phenotype that deviates from what they conceive as being of "pure" European stock. In the perception of recessive phenotypes, the implication is that in a particular family there were non-European ancestors two or more generations ago.

In fact, in three of the above cases older informants were able to pinpoint the male, female, or both in a matrimonial alliance so many generations ago that had been responsible for the recessive phenotype. In the case of an entire family exhibiting non-European phenotypic traits, the situation is the same as described above with respect to individual somatic characteristics. The difference, however, is that it is well known among most aristocrats why the entire family deviates phenotypically from the standard: in the case of bona fide aristocrats in the immediately ascending generation, a male and/or female married a mestizo phenotype; in the case of a plutocratic family of mestizo extraction, an ancestor achieved aristocratic standing through marriage.

Aristocrats are well aware of these families; they are not discriminated against socially, but they are certainly regarded as deviant and are talked about in uncomplimentary fashion. In the particular case of a very aristocratic family, I was told in no uncertain terms that many of its members were mestizo phenotypes and had been so for three generations. In fact, I counted thirty-seven references in my field notes, by as many informants, indicating that members of this family have been phenotypically different since the grand-parental generation. Indeed, there is a high degree of preoccupation among aristocrats about phenotypes, or as several informants euphemistically put it, "por tener buena facha" (to have a good appearance; that is, to look European).

A few remarks about the non-Spanish European component of aristocratic somatology are in order. For at least five generations, roughly since the French Intervention, aristocrats have contracted matrimonial alliances with males and females of German, French, English, and Italian extraction and in a few instances with North Americans of Anglo-Saxon extraction. This European component is relatively minor, but it is readily detected in some groups of the aristocracy. My educated guess is that it accounts at the most for 8 percent of the aristocratic population. In other words, the entire range of non-Spanish phenotypes is about 10 percent, including the 2 percent of mestizo phenotypes. Most of the matrimonial alliances with individuals of European extraction were contracted more than two generations ago, either in Mexico or abroad. They include males and females from prominent plutocratic or upper-class families, including several titled individuals. It should not be assumed that the relative incidence of blond, light-eye phenotypes among aristocrats is due mainly to these inputs, for there was a significant incidence of these traits before the middle of the nineteenth century, to judge by the hundreds of portraits in aristocratic households. In a nutshell, the Mexican aristocracy, with the exceptions noted above, exhibits a range of phenotypes that is typically European and that the Mexican lower-middle and lower classes would distinctly categorize as *gente güera* (light-skinned people), to denote a group different from the entire spectrum of mestizo and Indian phenotypes.

Within the nordic and mestizo extremes noted above, the aristocracy is a fairly homogeneous group, exhibiting the whole range of phenotypic variation of Spain: the light complexion of the north; the medium-light complexion of the center; and the darker, more Mediterranean complexion of the south. Statistically, the medium-light complexion predominates, but with significant clusters of fair and Mediterranean types at both extremes, with the former predominating. The incidence of blond and auburn hair is perhaps as high as 25 percent, while the hair color of the majority ranges from light to dark brown, with a very small percentage of black hair. The incidence of light eyes (blue, gray) may be as high as 30 percent, with a sprinkling of green eyes, and the majority ranging from hazel-brown to dark brown. About 10 percent of men and women may be described as tall (more than five foot ten to six foot two for males, and five foot five to five foot nine for females), but the great majority are significantly shorter, averaging perhaps from five foot five to five foot nine for males and five foot one to five foot four for females. Both males and females are generally slenderly built; and, although there are a few fat or overweight people, the overwhelming majority of aristocrats are thin types and keep themselves fairly fit. This last trait is, of course, a cultural characteristic, very much a part not only of the aristocracy but of the upper-middle class to the top of the stratification system. Things are changing, however, and they have been doing so for a generation. As more and more aristocrats marry plutocrats of foreign extraction, the children of the present generation are becoming taller and fairer. Be this as it may, the above description of the somatic configuration of the aristocracy is incomplete but sufficient to analyze the aristocrats' expressive attitudes and physical conceptions of themselves.

The great majority of the aristocrats have very definite and standardized ideas about what the phenotypic configuration of the group "should be." Lurking below the surface—not always cogently verbalized by the average aristocrat but eloquently expressed by old, educated informants—is the notion that the Mexican aristocracy, as an integral part of the Spanish aristocracy, is of visigothic extraction ("somos de descendencia goda," as several informants stated in no uncertain terms). This assertion is a residual notion of the concept of the last conquerors, and it colors a significant part of the behavior of the aristocracy. Thus many aristocrats' ideal conception of themselves is as blond

Teutonic types, although—being realists—they hasten to add that such types have been altered by mixtures with other peoples, particularly early marriages with the Indian aristocracy and later alliances with mestizo phenotypes. As nebulous as this conception is, it does nonetheless configure the phenotypic ideals of the aristocracy; and, more to the point, it plays an important role in the configuration of its expressive culture. Closer to reality is the almost universal perception of adults that the ideal that underlies their phenotypic constitution is the blondish, light-eyed type of northern Spain. What they have in mind, of course, is the Celtic phenotype that is still quite common in northwestern Spain. Given the acknowledged admixture with the Indian population after the Conquest, the 25 percent of blondish types lends some credence to the aristocracy's claim; but, more significantly, it colors the ideal standards of beauty universally held by its members.

For females these standards include white, alabaster skin; medium blonde or auburn hair, straight or slightly curled; light eyes, preferably blue or greenish blue; medium height and thin body conformation; large, expressive eyes, with long lashes; fine, well-proportioned features; a small mouth and nose; and above all elegance and gracefulness in every movement, from walking and sitting to gesticulating and resting. (The last standard, of course, is culturally expressive but as much a standard of beauty as the other somatic characteristics, at least until a generation ago; young aristocratic males and females, like youngsters from other classes of society, are in revolt against the standards of the past.)

For males the standards of physical beauty may be specified as follows: white to bronzed skin; light to dark brown hair, preferably lightly curled; big eyes of any shade from light blue to light brown; tall but not too tall; full bearded but not hirsute; broad shouldered, well muscled, but lean and well proportioned; elegant of movement but measured and grave of mien. (Not specified but implied is the standard that men do not have to be handsome; rather, as in the case of women, it is more important to be elegant and graceful in every aspect of physical behavior.)

Given the phenotypic and cultural uniformity of the aristocracy, these standards of physical beauty are realized to a rather high degree. It is not necessarily the case that the majority of aristocrats are beautiful or handsome, for the combination of these standards is no more likely to occur than idealized standards are in any other population. Culturally, however, it is a well-known fact that good class position enhances whatever physical attributes people have, and from this standpoint the Mexican aristocracy is a physically attractive group of people, by their own standards as well as those of other European peoples.

Let us focus on the ideology and *imago mundi* underlying race and ethnicity within the endogenous boundaries of the aristocracy and the consequences that follow from them. There is a great preoccupation with race, particularly with the somatic characteristics exhibited by members of the aristocracy. In several ways this preoccupation is shared with all groups of European extraction and with that segment of Mexican society vaguely defined as *criollos*. In a pluriethnic society, in which race is important but not entirely determinant in drawing the boundaries between class and ethnicity, this preoccupation is understandable. Indeed, individuals in the more upwardly mobile sectors of the population—particularly at the top of the stratification system—are never entirely certain about their racial extraction, even in cases where phenotypes are clear-cut or fit their cultural definitions and perceptions.

This ambivalence, and to some degree uncertainty, is an important ingredient in the aristocracy's self-perception and its perception of other classes and social groups. It colors the most salient aspects of the social life of the group, from friendship and marriage to entertainment patterns and interpersonal behavior. Phenotypic characteristics are one of the key variables that configure the most central domains in the expressive life of the aristocracy. How does this concern with somatology affect endogenous relations?

There is no overt discrimination against individuals and families that do not phenotypically conform to accepted European standards, as specified above. By discrimination I mean reservations concerning intermarriage, invitations to social and religious affairs, and personal interaction. There may be some residual feelings of exclusion for purposes of matrimonial alliances, particularly when these phenotypically deviant individuals or families are on the fringes of the aristocracy (that is, when aristocratic status was achieved during the last renewal). But no such hesitation applies to the three families in this category that are among the most prominent aristocrats. If there is no discernible, ostensible discrimination, however, it most certainly takes place at the subliminal verbal level.

The most common statements about these individuals indicate not only a patronizing ambivalence but also a sense of personal commiseration: "People say that they mated with Indians; the mixture with Indians, blacks, and mestizos sometimes persists after many generations." "I don't know how, but in this family a mestizo type shows up once in a while." "Once in a while there is a 'salto atrás' [literally, backward jump, a reference to one of the categories of the eighteenth-century system of *castas* but also a rather accurate gloss for what I have called a recessive phenotype], and in that family there have been several." "Almost all members of that family have some Indian features, and I know the poor ones resent it." "Francisco X has always been the object of talk because he is darkish and has coarse features." "Pedro X is in every respect a very distinguished person, but his very mestizo face makes him look as if he did not belong to our group." "Since I was a little girl [this informant was eighty-three years old in 1985], I remember that aristocrats have had the illusion that we are all of pure European blood, but the truth is that when one least expects it the Indian blood shows up."

These statements give a fair idea of the attitudes of most aristocrats toward those who do not conform to phenotypic standards; but they also indicate that most aristocrats are realists and know that some Indian blood does flow in their veins. This reality is confronted by aristocrats when they look at portraits of ancestors from the later seventeenth century to the first half of the nineteenth century, for many families have ancestors that in varying degrees looked phenotypically mestizo. Moreover, the history of racial admixture in several families is well known to most aristocrats going back to the middle of the nineteenth century. Some of these atypical phenotypes occur in old aristocratic families, while most occur in aristocratic families of the last renewal, that is, not more than three generations ago.

This ambivalence about race has another dimension that is seldom verbalized but nonetheless still present among older aristocrats with intellectual inclinations. I refer to an almost atavistic pride in knowing that, irrespective of the aristocratic ideal of being of pure European descent, Indian ancestry is part of their racial composition. Pride in acknowledging a mestizo component has two sides: one intellectual and to some extent synthetic and one aristocratic, more in line with the traditional *imago mundi*. Intellectual pride in acknowledging a mestizo component rests on the realization of the great cultural achievements of Mesoamerican Indians as one of the pristine civilizations of the world, and it is shared with all educated Mexicans of the middle classes. This pride is not shared by the aristocratic majority; it is an illusion and for many a conceit of an aristocratic minority, but it does play a role in the tolerance and fairly complete acceptance of those aristocrats who do not conform to the standard European phenotype.

Aristocratic pride fits in well with the ideology of the group, but it is of limited incidence. Almost every aristocratic family that can trace its lineage to the sixteenth century boasts of having had a most noble Indian ancestor, most often of *tlatoani* rank. It is difficult to say how reliable these claims are, but my guess is that the majority are true and can be documented. I am well acquainted with nine such cases, the best known of which is the marriage of Luisa (Tecuilotzin was her Nahuatl name) Xicohtencatl, daughter of the main lord of Tlaxcala, to Jorge de Alvarado, brother of Pedro de Alvarado, second in command to Hernán Cortéz, conqueror of Mexico (Gibson 1952:199). A contemporary descendant of this marriage takes unbounded pride in being atypically related to such an illustrious Indian family. He put it well when he told me that "nobility has nothing to do with race; Xicohtencatl was as noble as the noblest of Spaniards, and I am as proud of him as of any of my European ancestors." This informant perhaps exaggerates, but similar claims from other informants leave no doubt that contemporary aristocrats are very proud of being descendants of the ancient Indian rulers of the country. Several other informants claimed to be descended from important *caciques* (probably Indians of the *tecuhtli* class, the second rank of the pre-Hispanic nobility) in the sixteenth and seventeenth century, but such claims are not made for descent from important Indian nobles after the end of the seventeenth century. Whether real or imagined, these claims undoubtedly indicate that the Mexican aristocracy today is aware of this early noble Indian ancestry (Ortega y Pérez Gallardo 1908:118–147). In summary, pride in having Indian blood (albeit this is to some extent an illusion and always in the distant past) has served to palliate overt discrimination toward fellow aristocrats who do not conform to European phenotypic standards.

Exogenous Considerations: The Dynamics of Interaction with the Plutocracy and Upper-Middle Class

It is important to place in perspective the racial components involved in the interaction between the aristocracy and other segments of Mexican society. This is particularly so with the plutocracy and upper-middle class, but the analysis here is extended to other social classes and groups directly or indirectly related to the aristocracy. The dynamics of interaction of class and ethnicity, as modified by phenotypic perceptions, are best illustrated in dyadic-group relationships. The following analysis proceeds sequentially with reference to the aristocracy, from the top to the bottom of the stratification system. Moreover, this analysis and the following section illustrate how class ideology, ethnic self-classification, and somatic perceptions are manipulated.

The plutocracy does not present the phenotypic uniformity of the aristocracy. As discussed above, however, the higher the class, the more European phenotypes are likely to constitute its membership. Basically, not only the plutocracy but local provincial plutocracies and the upper-middle classes throughout the country are overwhelmingly constituted by white and light mestizo phenotypes. Thus the proximate classes with which the aristocracy regularly interacts are somatically much less different from the aristocracy than all other classes in the stratification system, which are regarded as mestizos and Indians. As a corollary, aristocrats, plutocrats, and the upper-middle class conceive of themselves as ethnically and somatically different from the rest of the population, notwithstanding observable exceptions. Another way of putting this fundamental juncture of the stratification system is that these superordinate sectors of society are perceived by the masses of the Mexican population as ethnically and somatically white.

The aristocracy interacts with the plutocracy mostly on a footing of equality as far as ethnicity is concerned and in terms of somatic perceptions. The exceptions (that is, phenotypically non-European types) are accepted by aristocrats in the same fashion that they accept exceptions endogenously. Conversely, most plutocrats—while sharing the same self-image and conception of social interaction with aristocrats *vis-à-vis* all other classes—have no reservations about accepting or seeking aristocratic rapprochement, since the aristocracy is perceived as being of thoroughly European origin. In other words, whatever is being socially or economically maximized in aristocratic-plutocratic interaction, non-European phenotypical characteristics are minimized. This is well exemplified by one of my most perceptive informants: "There lived in our hacienda a very sly Indian who used to say that as people acquire city ways and make money they become whitened, and I would add that those around them also whiten them. This is the reason why the few in our class who exhibit mestizo physical traits are not discriminated against and are the same as the blondest of aristocrats."

This is another important juncture that characterizes the entire spectrum of the stratification system, with slight variations. As people ascend the social scale from Indian to *haute bourgeois*, the entailed principle remains the same: the more European an individual looks at the top—and, concomitantly, the less Indian an individual looks in the middle and lower rungs of society— the more it helps to succeed and achieve social, economic, and perhaps even political goals. This basic phenotypical principle has multiple variations that enhance, impede, or smooth the grooves of social mobility and govern many domains of social interaction. While one could say that Mexican society is as racist as U.S. society, the cultural manipulation of phenotypes makes the former more humane and less destructive than the latter.

Returning to aristocratic-plutocratic interaction, in the case of phenotypical deviations that may affect a few aristocrats and some plutocrats, money and power on the one hand and social position on the other tend to "whiten" those in interaction in the above-described fashion. Nonetheless, racial considerations color the context and ideology of interaction, to the extent that aristocrats and plutocrats share the same exclusive "European" image of themselves *vis-à-vis* all other social classes and groups. That bond facilitates social relations and has been a significant input in the formation of the *haute bourgeoisie*. This example illustrates that class and ethnicity in Mexico are almost invariably underlain by phenotypical manipulation of racial considerations, which increases in intensity in direct proportion to phenotypical variation, that is, endogenously and exogenously along the stratificational system.

The category of the upper-middle class includes a variety of groups that again share a rather high phenotypic denominator: the majority of people self-identified as being of European extraction (in Mexico City and in all large urban centers of the country), being of foreign extraction, or belonging to that rather nebulous category *criollos*, light mestizo phenotypes. It should be clear that I am not using the label "upper-middle class" in the standard fashion of U.S. sociology. For the purposes of this book, the upper-middle class is defined as a combination of structural, mostly economic, attributes and a large expressive component but significantly modified by ethnic-phenotypical components. Thus the class system of Mexico and of most Latin American countries entails social, physical, and expressive factors that may not be that different in, say, the United States, when the standard sociological approach to stratification is modified by nonstructural criteria such as the interplay of sociopsychological and physical-expressive factors and the influence of propinquity and group self-definition.

The relationship of the aristocracy to the upper-middle class may be characterized as social clientship, reciprocal but with a certain degree of condescension; upper-middle-class individuals and families, without overt signs of subservience, accept the relationship in a socially subordinate role. The more desirable aristocratic/upper-middle-class relationships are framed by the phenotypical condition that the upper-middle-class individuals be of European extraction. Since these dyadic relationships are unconstrained, it is almost invariably the case that upper-middle-class individuals and families related to the aristocracy are white and bound by the same racial attitudes of aristocrats toward mestizo and Indian populations.

The upper-middle class has been a significant complement to the Mexican aristocracy for generations. Since the middle of the nineteenth century, the upper-middle class has defined the effective outer boundaries of the aristocracy and provided a support group with significant implications: as a source of personnel for the discharge of social events in the life and religious cycles and not infrequently as a source of matrimonial alliances in more recent times. The upper-middle class is defined as the rung of the Mexican stratification system most expressively similar to the aristocracy, without the power and wealth of the plutocracy. So conceived, the upper-middle class constitutes the necessary complement to the dwindling fortune of the aristocracy in the contemporary setting, given the small number of aristocrats. Upper-middle class personnel constitute a highly upwardly mobile group, assiduously cultivating aristocratic ties and not infrequently vying for matrimonial alliances. This is particularly the case with foreign personnel and "familias propias" with long-standing ties to aristocratic families. Indeed, if endogamous marriages are not possible, traditional aristocrats would rather have their offspring marry into these families than into plutocratic families exhibiting non-European phenotypic traits and expressively far apart from aristocratic standards. For less traditional aristocrats, however, power and wealth count more, and phenotypical and expressive considerations are not as important.

The foregoing description indicates that at the top of the stratification system class and race exhibit a high degree of correlation: the great majority of the aristocracy, plutocracy, and upper-middle class are populations exhibiting European phenotypes, which serves to catalyze their interrelationship and configure a rather uniform vision of all other populations of various mestizo and Indian mixtures. The exceptions to this standardized conglomerate of European phenotypes are "whitened" as a function of power, wealth, and subtle cultural attributes that emulate social superiors. Thus the attitudes of the aristocracy, plutocracy, and upper-middle class as a white population toward the overwhelming majority of the Mexican ethnic-stratification system are uniform: we may have different social positions, but we are of the same racial stock, which makes us different from the rest of the population.

This somatic worldview dominates class and ethnic relations as one goes down the stratification scale. Exceptions are always accommodated by the principle of upgrading or downgrading people's class and ethnic position according to how European or mestizo-Indian they look. The manipulation of somatic traits increases in the middle and lower rungs of the social system as people play the endless game of upward mobility. As the middle and lower classes do not discriminate except in terms of power and wealth, the aristocracy, plutocracy, and upper-middle class are viewed by them as an undifferentiated complex of the white population of the country. It should be realized that the situation is more complicated, given that among the middle classes of the country there are several million phenotypically white people. I have not studied this situation systematically to attempt significant generalizations. But what I know of these people of essentially European descent, *qua* individuals, is that they share pretty much the same attitudes and have the same vision as the superordinate classes of the country. This is particularly the case in provincial cities that—with the exception that they may not have local aristocratic and/or plutocratic nuclei—are similar to Mexico City in terms of stratification.

In conclusion, the strong consciousness of kind exhibited by all phenotypically white populations throughout the country *vis-à-vis* all other populations amounts to a type of racism that is maintained in check by subterfuges, the most salient of which is the cultural manipulation of phenotypes in the contexts of upward mobility and the individual pursuit of economic and social aims.

Mutual Perceptions and Self-Image of the Superordinate and Subordinate Classes

With a modicum of individual variation, the superordinate classes (from here on, the aristocracy, plutocracy, and upper-middle class unless otherwise indicated) exhibit significant differences in categorizing the vast mosaic of mestizo and Indian phenotypes. Aristocrats, being the most isolated from the population at large, tend to be the least discriminating (except perhaps in distinguishing light mestizo phenotypes from what they regard as a homogenized population of mestizos and Indians) and are also the least sensitive, beyond their own milieux of social interaction, to accepting the cultural manipulation of somatic traits.

This is accurately exemplified by a 76-year-old aristocratic informant in 1985:

I remember when I was a child of fifteen that we interacted with many people of all social classes in a more intimate fashion and at several levels: professionally, from superior to inferior, in popular celebrations, on many occasions when different social classes and groups kept their distance, and in a variety of situations when everybody kept their place, respected each other, and where the old Mexican proverb 'juntos pero no revueltos,' we may gather together but we are not the same, applied very well.

Despite revolutionary transformations that radically changed the ruling functions of the aristocracy, this informant clearly describes the still dominant social position of his class in the mid-1920s. He goes on to describe the respect, even homage, that the middle and lower classes still accorded aristocrats, their wide networks of interaction among all social classes, and how their dominant position enabled them to interact with personnel of all stations in a relaxed and confident manner. This state of affairs came to an end by the late 1950s, and now the great majority of aristocrats have withdrawn, drastically reduced their once large networks, and developed an aversion to their Mexican roots. This is primarily expressed in their intolerance to everything mestizo and Indian and tendency to lump together all nonwhite populations irrespective of class and ethnicity. In this ambiance of rejection of what they once dominated and controlled, members of the aristocracy have exacerbated racial and cultural intolerance and engaged in what some of its more enlightened members regard as unbecoming behavior that contravenes their still strong sense of *noblesse oblige*.

Generically lumping together the middle and lower classes, regardless of phenotypical differentiation, many aristocrats employ unbecoming labels such as *la indiada* (that mob of Indians) and *la naquiza* (literally, that herd of *nacos*, a corruption of Totonaco, the name of an Indian group on the Gulf Coast). This deprecating attitude, by the way, is shared by the other two superordinate classes (including their small mestizo phenotype membership) and also quite common among the white population everywhere in the country. Here again the cultural nuances that have traditionally accompanied phenotypical categorization are downplayed. For example, many aristocrats refer to themselves as Creoles in the original denotation of the term and do not accept the term as denoting a light mestizo phenotype population. In other words, many middle-class people commonly use the term *criollo* to refer to themselves when they fit this phenotypic category.

It should be noted that it is in this ambiance that the greatest cultural manipulation of phenotypical characteristics takes place, that is, among the middle rungs of the stratification system. Aristocrats make fun of these manipulations and regard them as an uppity activity on the part of these light mestizo phenotypes, unaware that they do the same when one of their own occasionally does not conform to white phenotypic standards. Thus aristocrats regard the great majority of the Mexican population as a phenotypically Indian mass, which is not basically incorrect since the genetic pool of the country is overwhelmingly Indian.

On the other side of the coin, the middle classes as a whole are not aware of the aristocracy as a distinct social category. Only the educated among the middle classes retain a modicum of name and status recognition of the aristocracy, almost invariably colored by strong negative connotations, as noted above. These sentiments are generally less accentuated by the significant membership of European phenotypes in the middle classes, including most people of recent foreign extraction. These populations are more aware of upper-class categorization and almost invariably can discriminate according to traditional criteria beyond power and wealth, particularly in provincial cities, where the aristocratic presence was a fact until about fifty years ago. But for the overwhelming majority of the middle-classes the aristocracy does not exist as an identifiable category.

Except at the local (municipal and provincial city) level, where there is a lingering memory of the traditional ruling class of the country, the aristocracy is an unknown entity to the working classes. For aristocrats, however, the working classes embody the most pejorative aspects of the *naquiza* and elicit the most blatantly prejudicial attitudes. By contrast, there is a certain idealization of Indians, which is the only instance of many aristocrats' recognizing the cultural aspects that enter into the definition of an ethnic group (that is, Indians enfranchised in local communities defined as practicing a distinct subculture). Indians in their communities are perceived as pristine, uncontaminated by the outside world, almost as children that need protection. This version of the "noble savage" is voiced by the best-educated and older generation of aristocrats. They patronizingly regard Indians as well behaved, courteous, friendly, devout, loyal, respectful of others, faithful to their traditions, and living in a stable and satisfying environment. The downside of this idealization emphasizes the painful transition of Indians to the culture and society of the nation as they are corrupted by their incorporation into the *naquiza*, which illustrates some of the worst aspects of Mexican culture. This is a vision of Indians shared by other sectors of Mexican society, particularly educated *criollos*, foreigners, and many upper-middle-class people.

Of all the superordinate rungs of the stratification system, aristocrats are undoubtedly the most knowledgeable about Indian culture and society, since until three generations ago they were intimately tied to the land. Plutocrats and upper-middle-class people are on the whole appallingly ignorant of Indian culture and society, and pretty much the same can be said about the middle classes of cities throughout the country. It is almost as though there were a concerted effort to ignore this ethnic stratum of the population.

Many aristocrats, by contrast, do know about Indian society and subliminally identify with several aspects of its culture. More objectively, many informants—while recognizing the exploitative conditions of the hacienda system—remember the loyalty of their Indian peons during the revolutionary years and how many *hacendados* were protected during the dangerous armed phase of the Revolution.

Very much in the limelight in terms of recognition by the population at large, the plutocracy is nonetheless the most remote socially from most classes of society. In traditional Western society going back to the early Middle Ages, aristocrats maintained a close proximity to the various rungs of society, and their social and economic ties extended all the way down to the people they dominated. But in modern times—particularly after the middle of the eighteenth century, in the change from agrarian to industrial society—the distance between the emerging superordinate class (the industrial *haute bourgeois* magnate class) and the working and middle classes became progressively wider, as the center of gravity of production moved from country to city. Thus in Western society the plutocracy today is much more removed from the people than the aristocracy was from the commonality before the end of the *ancien régime*. This is also true in contemporary Mexico, of course, where the plutocracy is more aloof and remote from the rest of society than the aristocracy ever was before the 1910 Revolution.

Plutocratic informants betray a rank ignorance about the Mexican social system that does not affect production, distribution, and consumption. Almost to a person, several dozen plutocratic informants were not able to verbalize a coherent picture of their social class *vis-à-vis* the stratification system as a whole, specify whatever bonds tied them to the social system beyond the boundaries of upwardly mobile aspirations, or describe another segment of Mexican society in concrete or relative terms. They had a clear view of themselves as the mainstay of the country's economic system, as the creators of a private sector that operated more efficiently than the government, and as the architects of moving Mexico into the developed world.

The upper-middle class, both in the capital and in provincial cities, is comparatively very small by the standards of industrial countries but many times larger than the combined strength of plutocrats and aristocrats. The reader should remember that this class is not primarily defined in economic terms but rather as a combination of attributes that include lineage and tradition as well as economic position. Thus in any of the large cities of the country there are many individuals and families who may be classified as upper-middle-class by the standards of U.S. sociology, but only a fraction belong to this class in terms of the combined structural-expressive criteria defined above. To be sure, the people classified as upper-middle-class in this book are economically affluent by Mexican standards (with disposable incomes ranging from 50,000 to 100,000 dollars per year), but they can also boast several generations of lineage and tradition—that is, they have been *gentes propias* since at least the turn of the century.

This syndrome also applies to the middle and lower rungs of society and certainly influences the passage from Indian to mestizo status: the expressive criteria are different, the economic conditions are less stringent, but the principle remains the same. In fact, the transformation from Indian to mestizo is as pregnant with expressive attributes and attitudes as the aristocratization of the plutocracy and the *embourgeoisement* of the aristocracy, and I have closely observed the same phenomenon among populations ranging from the lower to the middle rungs of society in several milieux of the Central Highlands.

The upper-middle classes of the country are the best educated, as in all countries of European extraction. In this book's definition of this class, it stands at the threshold between the tiny superordinate stratum and the rest of society, a characteristic trait of Western stratification that no revolution since the eighteenth century has been able to change. In this sense the upper-middle class is the homologous equivalent of the gentry in modern times and the various forms of the knightly class from Roman times to the early sixteenth century. Much larger than the social, ruling, and political superordinate classes, the upper-middle class of Mexico constitutes a buffer zone between the distinctive superordinate and subordinate major segments of society.

With variations and different combinations of structural and expressive attributes, the upper-middle class, as redefined here, constitutes a combination of fulcrum and catalyzer of social and economic action. In Roman society the *equites* (knights) constituted the economic mainstay during the late republic and early empire. In feudal times the knights were the military elite and constituted the basic unit of the landed system. In modern times, at least until the late eighteenth century, the gentry–*haute bourgeoisie* embodied the main elements in the transformation process from estate to class. And since the onset of the nineteenth century the *haute bourgeoisie* has been the pivotal class in the economic and social configuration of the "democratic" state. Since the 1910 Revolution this class has begun to catch up with its counterparts in most countries of Western tradition. Today the upper-middle class is evolving toward a significant position of intellectual and perhaps even political saliency buttressed by its traditional interest in education, the arts, and a consciousness that has characterized the many local provincial intellectual elites since the onset of liberalism during the first half of the nineteenth century.

Interclass and Interethnic Relations and the Reinterpretation of Cultural and Racial Perceptions

Finally, I would like to offer a few generalizations about the overall mechanisms of interclass and interethnic relations as colored or reinterpreted by phenotypic perceptions. My aim is to place the stratification system in dynamic perspective as individuals, families, and groups move from the bottom to the top.

First, in Mexico's pluriethnic society there is no well-defined correlation between class and ethnicity, given the social and racial fluidity of the stratification system in the twentieth century, particularly during the past two generations. Ethnic categorization is generally a function of the social mobility that individuals and families experience as they rise from Indian to mestizo status and from the lowest to the middle rungs of society. At the top of the system ethnic categorization is even less significant, as the population in these superordinate rungs is much more homogeneous and consists mainly of European and light mestizo phenotypes. In this scheme of things, there are fundamentally four operational categories that may be termed ethnic: (1) whites (of European and Near Eastern extraction); (2) light mestizos (*criollos*, a rather imprecise category including several somatic shades); (3) mestizos (also an imprecise category including many somatic variations); and (4) Indians (irrespective of linguistic group, except perhaps at the local level). These are the basic categories that are racially manipulated within the context of specific classes and in the ambiance of upward mobility. Coterminously, these are also the primary ethnic categories that are perceived as constituting the main sectors of society. In this respect there is an overall correlation between ethnicity and the main blocs of the stratification system: whites and *criollos* as constituting mainly the superordinate stratum; mestizos as constituting the overwhelming majority of the population; and, rather ambivalently, Indians, viewed both as a racial-ethnic category (in their communities and regions) and as a cultural component (present in the lower rungs of society) in transitory terms.

Second, phenotypic considerations play a differential role in the categorization of people and the perceptions that these categorizations engender. The general operational principles have been discussed above, but how do they work in the three main blocs of ethnic classes of Mexican society? At the superordinate level, phenotypical factors are most important in the definition of class and in the perception of class membership of aristocrats, plutocrats, and the upper-middle class. Put it in reverse: since this sector of society is comparatively very small and overwhelmingly white, any deviation from putative phenotypic standards is noticed and manipulated accordingly. Functionally, then, the manipulation of phenotypes has the sole purpose of sanctioning class membership and psychologically generating acceptance. While there are differences among aristocrats, plutocrats, and the upper-middle class, the white common denominator tends to equalize matters in their internal phenotypic perceptions while presenting a uniform external set of attitudes toward those racially different from them.

At the middle, predominantly mestizo level, phenotypic factors are not significant in determining and defining class membership, since gradations of mestizoization are difficult to categorize. But phenotypic traits are greatly manipulated in upward social mobility and in maximizing specific economic and social ends that require being perceived as whiter or of a better class position. This is particularly the case in the upper rungs of the middle mestizo sector, where the highest degree of phenotypic manipulation takes place. Thus, given the perceived phenotypic uniformity, ethnicity is not a significant variable in mobility and the maximization of social and economic goals. The cultural manipulation of somatic traits and behaviors associated with them acquires its maximal expression: extension of the term *criollo* to include Indian phenotypes; "usurpation" of somatic manipulations from the upper rungs of society; the enhancement of European phenotypic traits in action and behavior; matrimonial alliances with lighter phenotypes to enhance white features; and so on. In this kaleidoscopic ambiance the mestizo middle classes manipulate and transpose cultural and physical traits in the pursuit of personal and group-induced social and economic ends. I do not mean to imply that these are universal patterns of behavior and action; but the higher the socioeconomic station of individuals and families in this enormous sector of the social system, the more conscious they become of the advantages of culturally manipulating phenotypes, given certain goals.

The third bloc in the Mexican stratification system is more complex than the definition given above. It is composed of the following rungs: the urban workforce, most of them one generation removed from rural environments, of both mestizo and Indian extraction; mestizo peasant populations; and Indians enfranchised in Indian communities. A significant percentage of these are Indian transitional populations, that is, in the process of shedding Indian culture and acquiring the ways of the national, mestizo culture. Phenotypically, these populations are very similar; as I have indicated, it would be difficult to discriminate significantly among them. Ethnically, however, the situation is most important as Indians become culturally mestizo in communal, regional, and urban environments. This process entails both the acquisition and incorporation of many mestizo traits spanning the entire cultural spectrum and the abandonment of many Indian customs and institutions. Ethnicity, then, is the most significant variable at this level and is entirely defined in cultural terms. In other words, in the process of upward mobility or the maximization of specific social and economic goals, neither Indians nor mestizos engage in the manipulation of phenotypic traits. There is no need for these subterfuges, because access to social and economic resources among these populations does not involve in any way "improving" one's phenotypic appearance. Nonetheless, individuals still engage in the manipulation of phenotypical traits as an expressive activity and in order to enhance the standards of beauty and demeanor that the national culture imposes upon them.

Finally, the perceptions of themselves and of others in each of the three main blocs of classes are highly significant in conceptualizing the stratification system of Mexico. They provide a kind of road map of the system as it emerged from the seigneurial situation of the nineteenth century and how it is changing toward a twenty-first-century, modern industrial class system. That is a topic beyond the scope of this book.

CHAPTER 3

THE REALIZATION OF EXPRESSION IN THE ETHNOGRAPHIC CONTEXT

I have deliberately postponed discussion of the methodological considerations underlying this book. It is more appropriate to undertake this task based on some of the main domains of expressive realization, as presented in the foregoing chapters. That procedure should be more meaningful to the reader than discussing methodological matters in abstract form. This departure from traditionalism has been dictated by the fact that there are no models for presenting an expressive ethnography, particularly one that extrapolates to other social classes.

Some Methodological Considerations for Ethnographic Description and Expressive Analysis

·

Basic Assumptions and Their Interrelationship

Substantively, this monograph is primarily an ethnography of the Mexican aristocracy during its period of rapid decline, roughly from the late 1940s to the present, but grounded on the four decades after the Revolution of 1910. From the analytical viewpoint, this study is concerned with the entire superordinate class of Mexico, based on a structural and expressive description of the aristocracy.

The structural dynamics of class formation and mobility are well understood and are analyzed at length in *The Wages of Conquest.* Not so the expressive components of this equation, which have been discussed (Warner 1960: Baltzell 1966) but never well understood. Here the problem is centered on the exclusive and inclusive expressive array of the aristocracy and—extrapolating from it—on those of the *haute bourgeoisie* and to a degree other sectors of Mexican society. I have established that the exclusive array of a social class is perhaps never more than 20 percent of its entire array. The present book puts this approximation on a firm foundation and, more saliently, analyzes the distribution of domains within the array that the class shares with other classes of Mexican society. At the heart of this analysis of expressive culture is the distinction between the exclusive and inclusive array as a conceptual *sine qua non* for understanding class formation and mobility.

The exclusive array of the aristocracy, as embodied in a specific number of domains encapsulating its ideology and worldview, defines this social class *vis-à-vis* all other classes of Mexican society. From the behavioral standpoint, the realization of the exclusive array constitutes the distinctive configuration of the aristocracy, as perceived by other classes. The perceived behavior, social image, and representation of the aristocracy encompass roughly one-fifth of its expressive culture, while it shares the remainder of the expressive array in varying degrees with other classes of Mexican society, from Indians to plutocrats. This proportion, however, has not remained constant and has been significantly reduced since the Revolution of 1910. The exclusive array of the aristocracy constitutes the universe of domains sought by plutocrats. On the other side of the equation, expressive domains of the plutocracy are also being incorporated by aristocrats, while the political class and the ranking sector of the upper-middle class have remained basically unaffected. Thus the process of expressive acculturation that is shaping the *haute bourgeoisie* is centered on the exclusive array of the aristocracy-plutocracy, as the defining ideology and *imago mundi* of the emerging superordinate class.

The inclusive array is just as significant to conceptualize, but for different reasons. First, it constitutes a general index of the involvement of the aristocracy in the expressive manifestation of manifold cultural, stratificational, and ethnic sectors of Mexican society. It places this social class within the global expressive involvement that must be determined in order to gauge the intensity and extension of individual domains.

Second, establishing the configuration of the inclusive array of the aristocracy is a good indicator of the changes that this social class has undergone since its demise as the ruling class of the country. This task provides an index of the *embourgeoisement* of the aristocracy and the extent to which the plutocracy has been aristocratized. At the same time, the analysis of specific inclusive domains pinpoints the junctures at which the incorporation of elements is most extensive and the extent to which these junctures are molding the process of expressive acculturation.

Third, comparing how specific inclusive domains are realized in different ethnic and stratification milieux is at the core of conceptualizing expressive culture *vis-à-vis* the social structure. I demonstrate that the principles of expressive realization—and the configuration of the expressive array in terms of domains and subdomains—are the same across social classes. Differences in expressive configuration of classes and groups are due to ethnicity, demographic constitution, size, and economic affluence. The global expressive array of the aristocracy, for example, has shrunk during the past generation, and that of the plutocracy has expanded, due mostly to economic affluence.

Interplay of the Standard and Expressive Ethnographies

This section presents the general *modus operandi* that has guided the organization of the book, based on the proposition that it is best to analyze the expressive array after a standard ethnography has been generated. The implementation of this strategy, however, varies from one cultural domain to another.

Presentation by chapters follows the standard ethnographic format, except that the configuration of content is adapted to the exigencies of the expressive description and analysis. The standard ethnography emphasizes the ideational order of the aristocracy centered on stratification and class consciousness, kinship and organization of the household, ritualism and religion, exhibition and display, manners and mores, and concern with the past.

Substantively, the standard ethnography of the aristocracy constitutes the bulk of the description, while enough ethnographic information on the plutocracy, upper-middle class, and other sectors of the stratification system is presented to place the expressive domains of these various interacting sectors in perspective—that is, establishing common elements, significant departures, and convergences.

Expressive Analysis of the Encompassing Domains of Race, Class, and Ethnicity

·

General Guidelines and *Modus Operandi*

In this section I analyze the expressive dimensions generated by the encompassing domains of race, class, and ethnicity. The aim is twofold. First, to establish the parameters generating expressive domains and subdomains that are realized in most ethnographic contexts. The exercise exemplifies the configuration of the exclusive and inclusive array of the aristocracy, of the other sectors of the superordinate class, and to a degree of what the entire Mexican stratification system shares inclusively. Second, the following description establishes the form that structures the expressive analysis in all subsequent chapters.

On the surface it would appear that domains such as race, class, and ethnicity (relatively straightforward and not too affected by underlying "what-ought-to-be" constructs) would not entail any significant expressive components—quite the contrary. As the description in chapters 1 and 2 indicates, these domains are pregnant with expressive attributes and entailments.

Physical type, presentation of the self, and in general the way one moves and bears oneself are the hallmarks of aristocratic self-definition and identification by others. Phenotypically, individuals cannot fundamentally alter their physical presence, but one can certainly present oneself socially and culturally so as to enhance certain traits and diminish or divert attention from others. In this general ambiance, the manipulation of phenotypical traits acquires expressive significance and colors many domains.

The expressive analysis proceeds along two different axes. The first involves the inherent attributes that the dimensions of class, race, and ethnicity have in themselves—that is, what I call natural expression. The second entails the consequences of these attributes in the domains of upward and downward mobility—that is, conflictual expression, intimately tied to changes in the configuration of a class or group of people. With respect to inherent attributes, the expressive dimensions of race and class (but not ethnicity, which does not play a significant role in superordinate stratification) of the aristocracy are the focal points of analysis. Whereas race is a fairly unifying entity, class becomes the more restricted domain in which expressive behavior takes place. With respect to the consequences of these attributes, the analysis is centered on mobility, as the aristocracy is in its terminal stage as a functioning social class. What will survive is name recognition, and above all a large number of domains that have shaped the expressive array of the new superordinate class that is in the process of formation.

Since there is no precedent for the description and analysis of the expressive array and its constituent domains, the best way to proceed is to isolate domains and subdomains after describing the main ethnographic categories. The criteria for determining the structural or essentially expressive composition of ethnographic domains and subdomains are tentative, but I have been able to formulate some practical guidelines that generate sufficient reliability. First, few ethnographic domains have no expressive components, and this is especially the case with social stratification and mobility. The main expressive domains of the central focus of this book are lineage and heredity as the hallmark of aristocratic affiliation; manners and mores that perpetuate aristocratic membership; behavior and actions that distinguish them from other superordinate classes; factors that enhance or impede mobility; and a special concern with exhibition and display. Broken down into many subdomains, these five major domains constitute the core of the expressive array of the aristocracy. Second, as a corollary of the foregoing point, the main conceptual task here is to establish the expressive coloration, or degree of expressive constitution, of all the domains and subdomains of the array along the entire ethnographic spectrum. Third, while a primary task is the identification and delimitation of domains and subdomains, their full expressive meaning is achieved only when they are relationally positioned within the entire array.

In a situation of rapid transformation, such as the one that the Mexican aristocracy has been undergoing during the past generation, it is difficult to ascertain the operational configuration of expressive domains. This is due mainly to the transference of so much of the aristocratic *imago mundi* to the rising *haute bourgeoisie*, which blurs the exclusive and inclusive boundaries of behavior. Thus expressive domains that were exclusively aristocratic until the onset of the Revolution have been incorporated by most plutocrats and are now perceived to be the common property of the entire *haute bourgeoisie*.

Exclusive Expression: Surviving Domains and the Mechanics of Plutocratic Transference

The exclusive expressive domains of the aristocracy concerning race are centered mainly on lineage and heredity and presentation of the self. Lineage and heredity constitute the necessary structural conditions that condition the manipulation (distortions, exaggerations, and reinterpretations) of the aristocratic tradition, thereby generating expressive domains in several related environments: a strong concern with genealogy; establishing the excellence of apical ancestors; exalting the consequences of the Spanish Conquest; magnifying the role of prominent ancestors socially and historically; buttressing aristocratic claims with pictorial representations and historical accounts; remembering titles of nobility and other dignities (*mayorazgos* [entails] and membership in military orders) that the family had in the past; and in general magnifying and elaborating on past aristocratic achievement (family coats of arms, wearing rings with the arms of titles of nobility that the family once had, etc.).

Racial or more precisely phenotypic considerations generate an associated complex of expressive domains: enhancing European features; manipulating physical appearance; cultivating elegance of movement and mien; improving physical features by dress and the culture of the body; fostering standards of physical conduct in the young; clearly specifying standards of beauty; and in general emphasizing what aristocrats consider their own phenotypical characteristics *vis-à-vis* all other classes or groups in society.

The main subdomains of lineage and heredity, as specified above, are best analyzed in the context of kinship, stratification, and mobility. Therefore, only the following categories define the expressive culture of race: the aristocratic claim to social superordination based on birth; the assertion that the Mexican aristocracy had its inception in the conquistadors, who were of Gothic descent; the standards of definition, recognition, and acceptance of group membership as an endogenous process; presentation of the self designed to enhance aristocratic standing and class membership; standards of beauty, elegance, and poise emphasized to secure recognition and mobility into aristocratic circles; and manipulation of place, circumstances, and quality of birth and heredity to advance specific aristocratic goals. The first three are nontransferable domains that will come to an end when the aristocracy ceases to be a functioning social class. The other three are "transitional," that is, they have been in the process of being adopted by the *haute bourgeoisie* for more than a generation.

First, from the classical Greeks onward, aristocracy has been not "the rule of the best" but "the rule of the best born," and a large superstructure of expression has been built around this notion. Thus much of the expressive life of the Western aristocracy has been constructed around this central core: aristocracy is in the blood; it is bequeathed by one's ancestors and passed on to one's descendants. As the power and wealth of the aristocracy diminished, this belief lost efficacy, and claims to superordination became exclusively expressive; what remains of the aristocracy during the past two or three generations is an expressive model to emulate. Based on claims of lineage and heredity, a large complex of expressive domains has been generated, which may functionally be explained as mechanisms of adaptation and survival that have by now been largely spent.

Second, although the great majority of Mexican aristocrats are sufficiently realistic not to claim descent from conquistadors, they conceive of the Spanish Conquest as a sort of origin myth of their class—a legendary construct that validates their claim to superordination with the subliminal function of generating consciousness of kind. The myth of the last conquerors, in a distorted fashion, of being of Gothic descent, is the core of the racial consciousness of the aristocracy and the origin of much expressive behavior. This is the cornerstone of the aristocratic *imago mundi*, which is seldom verbalized and remains mostly unconscious but is clearly manifested in specific behavior. What are the subdomains of race, class, and ethnicity in which this expressive behavior is realized?

One subdomain involves creating the illusion that aristocratic standing is still something one is born with. Specifically, this stance translates into glorifying the past. Thus most aristocrats enshrine the household, are obsessed with heirlooms that remind them of what they once were, and are unable to divest themselves of valuable art, furniture, and other domestic accoutrements even if this results in diminishing genteel standards of living.

Storytelling and genealogical concerns are expressive activities that validate standing and assuage the loss of aristocratic power and prestige. While *petites histoires* concerning family affairs, haciendas, and ancestral households are written by only a few male and female aristocrats, genealogical concerns occupy the attention of many. Although they may not engage in systematic study of individual ancestors or entire families, they can verbalize long lines of lineal, collateral, and affinal kin. This expressive activity, however, has little acceptance among the young. For adults, retreating into the past worked well as long as aristocrats were effective social leaders and participants in the expressive process of acculturation of the plutocracy, that is, until roughly twenty-five years ago.

Third, the game of self-recognition, important until a generation ago, is another domain that is almost gone but is still part of the expressive array of the traditional core (perhaps less than 30 percent of all aristocratic families). Self-recognition and acceptance—involving knowledge of former hacienda ownership, genealogical connections, marriage alliances, and place of origin—were important when the aristocracy was concentrated in Mexico City but are no longer so. The residual function of self-recognition and acceptance is well exemplified by an 80-year-old informant: "Remembering who we were, what we had, and the preeminent place we occupied in Mexico helps us to ease the pain of pondering what we lost and how unimportant we are today."

Fourth, presentation of the self as an instrument of enhancing aristocratic standing and class membership is a major expressive domain that, in equivalent forms of manifestation, is found in all social classes; and much of what I say here is shared by aristocrats, plutocrats, and the upper-middle class. This domain of expression is basically underlined by the notion that the perception of somatic traits can be manipulated in order to magnify the worldview of any social class or group. As stated above, this expressive ambiance is accurately verbalized by a perceptive informant: "the higher people aspire socially, the whiter they become." This syndrome has two aspects: the explicit behavior and actions of the upwardly mobile that tend to enhance European phenotypic traits and the implicit recognition accorded to them by those in superordinate social position because of their power, wealth, or other desirable characteristic.

Fifth, the game of cultivating and enhancing traditionally accepted standards of beauty, elegance, and poise spawns a rather large and diversified complex of expressive domains and subdomains. Here again, the interplay of physical and cultural elements constitutes an expressive whole at the core of superordinate mobility and class acceptance. While beauty is defined largely phenotypically, elegance and poise are essentially culturally defined; and in different degrees all three can be manipulated for specific effects. Since aristocrats, plutocrats, and the upper-middle class are phenotypically basically European and share much of the ideology of racial superiority, essentially the same somatically derived forms of expression underline much of this complex of expressive behavior.

Sixth, the game of establishing social identity in terms of where one was born, one's antecedents, and the quality of one's ancestors is also a generalized model of expressive activity. For example, since the demise of the *ancien régime* the upper-middle class has constituted the main support group of the declining aristocracy, and this was very much accentuated in Mexico after Independence. Considering that the aristocracy was always a minuscule segment of the country's population, the upper-middle class marked the social outer boundaries within which the social, ritual, and public life of the aristocracy was discharged. Throughout generations, this kind of social contract created bonds of clientship binding aristocratic and upper-middle-class families, given the large number of expressive domains that prolonged social contact had generated. Some of these families acquired aristocratic recognition, although the majority remained in that rather ambiguous status of clientship. But all these recognized or client middle-class families came to internalize the manipulation of lineage and heredity very much as aristocrats have always done. This takes place by creating pedigrees, sometimes distorting genealogies, and in general by slightly mythologizing an ancestor or exaggerating the achievements of another that would be difficult to disprove. More recently — and with power and wealth behind them — plutocrats are doing the same, particularly by creating and mythologizing a past to pass on to their children that they know cannot be acquired through the process of expressive acculturation with the aristocracy: they are, in other words, creating the lineage and hereditary trappings of a future "aristocracy."

Inclusive Expression: Aristocratic Inputs, Plutocratic Extensions, and the Mexican Stratification System

Three expressive domains (the fourth, fifth, and sixth) that until three generations ago had been exclusively aristocratic are now the property of the entire superordinte class or *haute bourgeosie*. I interpret this as an index of the aristocracy's success as an expressive acculturative agent. In this section I discuss the overall ethnographic contexts and stratification guidelines that spawn the expressive domains engendered by race, class, and ethnicity.

The first and perhaps the most encompassing principle of stratification that generates expressive behavior in specific ethnographic domains is encapsulated by the well-known Mexican saying "juntos pero no revueltos" (literally, "together but not scrambled," meaning roughly: we may gather together, but we are not the same). This is a diagnostic guideline to action that applies from top to bottom of the Mexican stratification system but is more stringently efficacious in the higher rungs. This system is at the same time quite closed and quite open. In other words, while upward class mobility is not nearly as fluid as, say, in U.S. society, social interaction among the classes is significantly more fluid. From a slightly different perspective, the fluidity of social interaction in Mexican society stems from the fact that class barriers are much more difficult to breach than in U.S. society: in Mexico the security and distinctness of class membership permit social interaction without loss of class status; in the United States the impermanence and blurred boundaries of classes do not allow such free social interaction, and barriers are behaviorally set up to ward off loss of status.

The superordinate classes of Mexico — particularly the aristocracy — have traditionally interacted with personnel of the middle and lower ranks of society in the social milieu of the "juntos pero no revueltos" syndrome. This takes place in many contexts and ambiances involving direct social in-

teraction. These interactions occur mainly in several kinds of nonrecipro-
cal clientship relationships involving peoples ranging from middle-class to
working-class and servants: becoming ritual sponsors (*padrinos*) of individuals and groups; honoring requests to participate in celebrations of merchants
in the city and former "retainers" in the country; participating in social celebrations of families related by economic or working ties; and so on. All these
occasions involve rather intimate interaction between superordinate and subordinate personnel in which they all know that they have gathered together
but social barriers remain very much in place. Aristocrats are particularly
adept at this kind of interaction, almost invariably in a relaxed and pleasant
ambiance, in which superordinate patronizing is consciously suppressed and
subordinate uppityness seldom occurs.

Fluidity of behavioral interaction is a characteristic of rigid class systems,
in which people are always well aware of status position, as class membership
is more ascribed than achieved. By contrast, in loosely stratified systems there
is frequently more segregation among the classes, which quite often generates
a significant degree of customary endogeny. This is particularly the case in the
upper and upper-middle rungs of society. Fluidity of class membership and
mobility, in short, create a situation of either perceived endogeny or inability
to interact with people below one's class. By contrast, rigid systems develop
interactional subterfuges of the "juntos pero no revueltos" variety that permit a more relaxed ambiance of social interaction between the superordinate
and subordinate sectors of society.

This general guideline to social action entails entirely inclusive domains of
expression that span several sectors of Mexican society. Indeed, one could say
that the flexibility of the stratification system, by allowing fluid social interaction among the classes, spawns the largest and most important expressive
field conditioned by more circumscribed domains and subdomains centered
on the economic, social, religious, and even political life of the nation. They
can be specified as follows.

1. One domain includes, first, the ambiance of downward behavior and
action—that is, the motivation and consequences for those who are superordinately placed to engage in patronizing social interaction. This context involves a significant measure of utilitarianism, of course, but the achievement
of this goal is always expressively couched. Second is the ambiance of upward
behavior and action—that is, the reasons and effects for those who are subordinately placed to engage in subservient social interaction. This context also
involves utilitarian aspects but less than the foregoing context, for upward

interaction (mobility) is always more expressive. The third element includes the manifold contexts and occasions when individuals and groups of different social classes come into unstructured public interaction, which makes the Mexican stratification system appear more fluid than it is.

2. Another ambiance in conditioning expressive domains and subdomains is the manipulation of phenotypic traits and cultural reinterpretation of them, a juncture that is accurately denoted by the folk wisdom of the saying "la gente se emblanquece a medida que hacen dinero" (people become whitened to the extent that they acquire wealth). This is a rich, expression-generating context that encompasses a great deal of behavioral interaction in a wide spectrum of Mexican society, because the standards of beauty and phenotypical desirability at all levels are European. From Indians to aristocrats, Mexicans view people through the prism of European phenotypical ensembles and act to maximize specific ends in view: social advancement, economic advantages, and even political and religious goals. How is this expression-generating context realized in the various strata of Mexican society?

First, there are two aspects to this question: individual and collective self-perception and how individuals and classes are exogenously perceived. The aristocracy perceives itself as phenotypically European; and, other things being equal, individual aristocrats extend social recognition to others in terms of somatic appearance—namely, to plutocrats and members of the upper-middle class that are regarded as akin to them. From this viewpoint, then, the superordinately placed are "socially" regarded as phenotypically European. In this context, expressive manipulation takes place, and the somatic characteristics of individuals that deviate from the phenotypical standards of aristocrats tend to be minimized—that is, they are "whitened" and made more appealing. This is the generalized syndrome that applies to the three sectors of the superordinate class considered here. The political class does not fit this socio-phenotypical characterization: although its perceived composition ranges from Indian to European, it is stereotyped as an essentially mestizo sector beyond the *tolerable* phenotypical manipulation of "white" aristocrats, plutocrats, and the upper-middle class. The superordinate class as a whole, however, is perceived by the overwhelming majority of the subordinately placed as the "whitest" sector of society by virtue of the power and wealth it denotes. According to the ideology of race and ethnicity, this position in society generally commands more honor and respect than are accorded to the common citizen. It should be noted, though, that this still subservient attitude of the ordinary citizen is rapidly changing.

Second, in the middle strata of society (the putatively middle and lower-middle classes) the same situation obtains but with significantly more fluidity. In this vast spectrum, it is not so much the striving for social recognition that leads people to manipulate somatic appearance (namely, to enhance European phenotypic traits or "whiten" individuals for social gain); rather, they make conscious decisions and take specific actions to bring individuals and groups (families, kin, and networks of friends) closer to the European standards of beauty and appearance that Mexican society imposes. The self-perception/being perceived contrast also obtains—but with a greater emphasis on being perceived by others as a means to an end, not necessarily for social advancement, more for specific economic gain, and always constrained by the ideological standards of European somatology. The ostensible model that to a significant extent guides the behavior and action of individuals and groups in this middle stratum is omnipresent and manifested in many "cultural" and communication environments: advertising, television, cinema, and even the graphic arts. In this general ambiance of an exogenous, imperialist ideology of color, somatic characteristics, and standards of beauty, middle-class individuals and groups engage in multiple expressive manifestations.

Briefly, the manipulation of phenotypes to enhance the connotation of European traits or to increase other peoples' perception of individuals and groups as more European may henceforth be encapsulated as "the cultural whitening syndrome."[1] What is the manifestation of this syndrome in the middle strata of Mexican society, and what are its consequences? Primarily, the syndrome serves as an ideological guide to action that fosters the maximization of European traits or, conversely, makes less noticeable the presence of Indian-mestizo traits. Thus the generated expressive behavior is centered on personal physical presentation and the conscious desire to demonstrate European ancestry.

The syndrome is realized at all levels of the middle strata but is probably more pronounced among individuals and groups of the solid middle class, where it acquires an element of upward mobility—namely, the desire to be enhanced socially after a level of economic affluence has been achieved. Secondarily, and with the most generalized incidence in the upper rungs of the middle strata of society, it includes practices aimed at "improving" one's phenotypical appearance or being perceived as more European, either immediately or for the benefit of one's progeny. This is expressively achieved by association with individuals who are closer to the ideal standards of physical appearance, which frequently entails preferential behavior and undue respect to them, even when they may be poorer or have less power. This, of course, is a characteristic of those who are upwardly mobile, while the majority of individuals in the middle of the stratification pyramid pay only symbolic lip service to the constraints of ideological standards of physical appearance and comportment.

Third, at the bottom strata of Mexican society (the rural and urban poor and the transitional and traditional Indian population) the cultural whitening syndrome is also significantly realized. The vast majority of Mexicans composing these strata are self-perceived and perceived by the rest of society as phenotypically undifferentiated, as there is often no or only slight somatic discrimination between Indians and mestizos. Distinctions are essentially cultural, even when at the local or regional levels people use terminology that may denote racial characteristics (such as "white," *güero*, and several other racially loaded terms used by Indians to refer to non-Indians, and terms such as *indígenas*, *inditos*, and other equally racially loaded terms used by mestizos to refer to Indians). In most rural areas of the country where large numbers of Indians are to be found, given that phenotypical differences between Indians and mestizos are generally either nonexistent or difficult to pinpoint (by individuals and groups culturally defined as Indians or mestizos), does somatic discrimination (distinction) take place? The answer is yes, but it is blurred by cultural considerations.

Similarly, much the same obtains in urban environments, with the significant difference that the syndrome at this level is exhibited mostly by mestizos vying for specific economic aims or involved in upward social aspirations. Whether they are Indians and rural mestizos or both of these categories in urban environments (or culturally and locationally in transition), the ideology of the cultural whitening syndrome compels the bottom, most numerous sectors of the stratification system to engage in the physical and symbolic manipulation of phenotypic traits. This manipulation may be self-directed (in unconsciously behaving in certain ways so as to bridge the somatic gap between phenotypic perception and ideologic imperatives) or other-directed (in consciously acting or making decisions that will affect the way in which individuals and groups are perceived by those in one way or another above their station).

To summarize, the ideology of the cultural whitening syndrome is a powerful generator of expressive realization at all levels of Mexican society. It cuts across race, class, and ethnicity and configures many expressive domains in the social, economic, political, and even religious life of the manifold rungs of the stratification system.

3. Not directly related to race and somatology but very much a part of class and ethnicity is the high sense of exclusivity and restricted consciousness of kind that characterizes Mexican society. These characteristics translate into guides to action that have very important implications for understanding class formation and mobility as well as transition from one ethnic group to another. Together with the foregoing principles, this syndrome constitutes a triad that explains much of the dynamics of stratification and the new realignment of classes that has taken place since the Revolution of 1910. The combined effect of these three principles or guides to action demonstrates how much the stratification system of the nation has changed, while retaining some traditional characteristics: the system has become significantly more open and fluid, but persistent constraining factors render it somewhat different from the systems of Western industrial nations with a longer democratic tradition.

First, exclusivity and consciousness of kind among the aristocracy and developing plutocracy may be regarded as gate-keeping mechanisms: among the former, as a last stand before impending disappearance as a functional group; among the latter, as an index of increasing power and wealth. Let me explain. In 1957 a book entitled *Registro de los trescientos y algunos más* on the socially prominent of Mexico City was published. It included more than 300 families of prominent aristocrats and plutocrats at that time. Many of the most prominent aristocratic families refused to be included in the book, which contained pictures of married couples, debutantes, and assorted familial information. When I asked one of my most insightful and knowledgeable informants (in his early fifties when the book appeared) to characterize the book, he answered, "Ni son todos los que están, ni están todos los que son" (Not all those who are included count, and not all those who count are included). I am unable to convey in English the beauty and epigrammatic quality of this informant's answer, which must be explained anyway.

My informant objects to the book as a collection of social sketches that include many rich and not so rich plutocrats, some of whose social standing he does not concede to be better than middle class, who were powerful enough to have their names included in the register. He himself refused to be included and was taken aback at the willingness of several prominent aristocrats who acceded to being included in the register. My informant did not object, however, to having his family reported in the social sections of the capital dailies, on the grounds that it was a traditional manner of letting the outside world know of an event that had taken place *en famille* involving interaction among persons of equal rank. In no uncertain terms he emphasized that aris-

The Mexican Aristocracy

tocratic consciousness necessarily entailed exclusivity of social interaction, particularly when it was projected to the wider society. He also maintained that "true" aristocrats had gone underground, assiduously avoiding the public display that had been so much a part of the aristocratic image when they were still the dominant social class. In other words, he implied that exclusivity was natural when the aristocracy was dominant because allowing outsiders to admire them enhanced the aristocratic image; but when aristocrats were no longer rich and powerful, exclusivity had to be maintained by avoiding exposure in every possible way.

In the plutocratic sector, exclusivity and consciousness of kind take significantly different forms, which are essentially those of a class still in the process of formation. While plutocratic consciousness of kind is not nearly as strong as in the aristocracy, exclusivity certainly is—and it centers on power and wealth. This is the protective coloration that is probably found in all modern stratification systems: a strong sense of enclosure exhibited by the rich and powerful from outsiders seeking economic, political, or other benefits. Thus Mexican plutocrats are characteristically exclusive in avoiding contact with ordinary folk not related to their business or the socially subordinately placed. As they have grown socially secure, their exclusivity has grown proportionally, thereby becoming much like that of the aristocracy. The aristocracy's exclusivity stems from a sense of entitlement that cannot be fulfilled economically, reinforced by ancient claims of superordination that can no longer be verbalized (except in the secluded ambiance of the household). In contrast, the exclusivity of the plutocrats is pragmatic and is mainly the expression of the power and wealth they command, which demand to be exercised unconstrained by unnecessary ties.

The expressive-structural juncture described above is starkly manifested in the words of a plutocratic informant:

> The so-called Mexican aristocracy is an anachronism. Undoubtedly there was an aristocracy when the great *hacendados* were the owners of the land and the economic force of the country. But now aristocrats do not count for much, and still less their pedigrees and pretensions of being descendants of conquistadors. Now what counts is money and power, and those who know how to acquire them are structuring the new ruling class of Mexico. Like King Boabdil [the last Moorish king of Granada, who was reproached by his mother upon the fall of the city to Ferdinand and Isabella in 1492], they do well to weep like women for what they did not know how to defend like men.

These are the harsh words of a well-educated but tough plutocrat, who knows that the way of the future is his and not that of arcane and ineffective aristocratic claims. Ironically, however, he has assiduously cultivated aristocratic mores and manners and is married to an aristocratic woman. This example attests both to the pragmatism of most plutocrats and to the effectiveness of aristocratic expression. Indeed, it also exemplifies the mechanics of the aristocratic-plutocratic interaction that has shaped the realignment of the superordinate class of Mexico for more than two generations.

Second, when I say that the stratification system in particular and Mexican society in general are characterized by exclusivity and a group-endogenous consciousness of kind, I essentially mean to convey the fragmentation of a pluriethnic country composed not only of many ethnicities but of disparate social groups that have not entirely coalesced into a distinct nationality. The Revolution of 1910 was, of course, a crucial step forward; but Mexican society still exhibits colonial traits that have conspired against its maturation as a national state. In no domain of culture is this fragmentation more apparent than in the process of nation building. Indeed, the concept of citizenship in Mexico is weak, and it does not transcend the community or at best the region.

Fundamentally, most people in Mexico, in different degrees and from top to bottom in the stratification system, recognize and are constrained (have rights and obligations) by the following categories: kin, ritual kin, friends, and neighbors. Beyond the realm of action and behavior of these categories, there are no effective social categories that regulate and control the social life of Mexicans. This, of course, is another way of saying that the category of citizen and the institution of citizenship are weak, and some segments of the population lack them altogether. In the ambiance of kinship, *compadrazgo* (ritual kinship), friendship, and neighborhood, the social life of the people at all levels of social integration is generally smooth, redounds in well-structured groups and networks, and seldom entails irreconcilable situations. But in the ambiance of citizenship, in the context of the wider world, the situation changes rather dramatically: disorganization abounds, there is little respect for laws and regulations, and consideration for the rights of others is minimal and usually enforced by immediate retribution. Perhaps an example may clarify what this means in the lowest rungs of the stratification system, as a base to outline what transpires as we ascend the social scale.

In Indian and the majority of traditional rural mestizo communities, kinship, *compadrazgo*, friendship, and neighborhood are the fundamental institutions that configure the social life of the people. These institutions are sufficient to structure an orderly, smooth-functioning society in which the rights of others are respected, there is collective responsibility, and duties and obligations are adequately discharged. One can thus speak of a highly developed sense of "citizenship" that is determined by both the small and circumscribed nature of the local group and the "sacralized" nature of social relations. When communities become secularized by the process of rapid growth, in time being transformed and becoming part of the national world, this "sacralized form of citizenship" begins to decline. Moreover, when individuals leave the community and settle permanently in the city, they bring with them the same social categories that efficiently organize the traditional village. In other words, integration into the national framework, collectively and individually, entails the continuation of kinship, *compadrazgo*, friendship, and neighborhood as the only recognized categories that structure orderly social life. I interpret this as a form of exclusivity that generates a consciousness of kind within the groups that these institutions condition, which tends to exclude most behavioral responsibility beyond their confines. Evidently, these categories are insufficient to structure orderly social life in the global context of the nation. Thus the citizenship that is necessary for the proper functioning of a nation is never developed, and disorganization becomes the norm. Everything beyond the sphere of influence of these institutions does not seem to have the same importance, leading to disregard for the institutions, rules, and obligations that bind the body politic of the nation.

In the middle rungs of the stratification system, exclusivity and consciousness of kind have basically the same functional constitution described above, except that they are differentially manifested. Sacralized folk citizenship does not obtain in the same efficacious communal fashion, as kinship declines and *compadrazgo* acquires a significant vertical, patron-client component. What survives of the folk ambiance is the continuous reliance on these two institutions, but in a reduced form and with a greater emphasis on friendship and neighborhood. The net result, however, is essentially no different than what obtains in the transition from folk to national life. Middle- and lower-middle-class culture is centered on the ambiance of the aforementioned institutions. Consciousness of a clear notion of citizenship is still weak and does not structure behavior and social relations in the impersonal domains of the nation. Another way of putting this is that the great majority of Mexicans have a keen sense of personal duty and responsibility but a weak sense of impersonal, abstract sense of right and obligation toward fellow citizens. Education is making a difference, however, and citizenship is increasingly asserting itself.

The three sectors of the superordinate class, despite being the most educated segment of the population (with the exception of rather small intellectual groups of the middle classes), have not developed an adequate consciousness of citizenship and are not basically different in this respect from the middle and bottom sectors of the stratification system. The aristocracy, plutocracy, and upper-middle class are the most self-contained rungs of society, and each in its own sphere of interaction is as isolated from the rest of society as Indian or mestizo folk communities are.

In summary, race, class, and ethnicity are generators of a vast complex of expressive domains in themselves; but at the same time they condition many other domains in the total expressive array across the stratificational spectrum. Directly and indirectly, race, class, and ethnicity account for most of the exclusive expression of the aristocracy; but it is important to know how they function throughout the stratification system in order to elucidate the range of the inclusive array of the aristocracy and of the other sectors of the superordinate class of Mexico.

CHAPTER 4

THE ORGANIZATION OF
URBAN LIVING

Settlement, Residence, and the Household

Since the foundation of the Spanish city on the ruins of Tenochtitlan, Mexico City has been the political, economic, social, and religious capital of the vice-royalty of New Spain and afterward of independent Mexico. A significant percentage of the aristocracy was always concentrated in Mexico City. At no time since 1530 did Mexico City harbor less than 30 percent of the national aristocracy, and at times it was as high as 50 percent. With the exodus from the provinces to the capital beginning after the 1910 Revolution, practically all of the aristocracy became enfranchised in Mexico City.

Prerevolutionary Residential Patterns and
Changes from 1910 to 1990

In the civic center of Mexico City today (roughly a square of some 100 city blocks surrounding the *zócalo*, the city's central plaza) hundreds of sixteenth-, seventeenth-, eighteenth-, and nineteenth-century buildings have survived rather intact the tremendous growth of Mexico City in the twentieth century, particularly after 1950. A good many of these buildings are former residences of aristocrats, most of them built between the middle of the seventeenth century and Independence (1821). Several of these establishments may be termed palaces, while the majority are best described as large mansions. At least a dozen are excellent examples of colonial architecture. The residence of the marquesses of San Mateo de Valparaiso (1786)—better known as El Palacio de Iturbide, because for a short time it became the residence of Agustín de Iturbide, first emperor of Mexico (1822–1823)—is a very elegant late Mexican baroque building exhibiting distinctly Italianate influences, now owned by the Banco Nacional de México. The residence of the counts of Santiago de Calimaya (completed in 1762 but with many late-seventeenth-century elements) is a massive and seigneurial establishment attesting to the wealth and social prominence of the Gómez de Cervantes family during the last century of colonial times. It is now the Museo de la Ciudad de México. The residence of the counts of Valle de Orizaba (1745), better known as the Casa de los Azulejos, is an exquisite majolica-tile-covered building unique in Mexico, now owned by a well-known chain of restaurants in the city. There are at least thirty other colonial mansions in the civic center of the city that can be identified as the residences of prominent aristocrats by the end of colonial times (Tovar y de Teresa 1990:76–87).

By 1910 many aristocratic families still resided in mansions within ten city blocks of the *zócalo*, the majority of which were large establishments. Occasionally occupying half a city block, these are still imposing two- or three-story buildings, with dozens of high-ceiling rooms clustered about two or three consecutive patios and coats of arms displayed on elaborate facades. The size and excellence of aristocratic residences reached their peak in the eighteenth century, as attested by the three described above and many others, both in Mexico City and in provincial cities such as Puebla, Guadalajara, Guanajuato, Quéretaro, Oaxaca, and a few others. Throughout the nineteenth century these mansions were continuously inhabited by their aristocratic owners; but during the second half of the century, because of modernizing tendencies and a desire to escape from the hustle and bustle of the central city, began the exodus toward the growing suburbs that has been going on until the present.

This seigneurial pattern of residence, intimately associated with the heart of the city, began to change during the last two decades of the nineteenth century, due mainly to European influences after the French Intervention. By the end of the Porfiriato the majority of aristocrats were residing in several exclusive neighborhoods (*colonias*) established in the periphery of the city, some of which until two generations ago concentrated a large number of aristocratic households. The Colonia Roma was the most noteworthy example until it was overrun by the enormous growth of Mexico City. The process accelerated in the following decades. By 1955, when most provincial aristocratic families had settled in the capital, few aristocrats still occupied ancestral residences in the central city; and by 1970 none remained. Thus two distinct periods of urban residence are identifiable outside the central city since the beginning of the

Porfiriato: the building of modern residences in the newly established *colonias* between roughly 1880 and 1920 and the exodus of provincial aristocrats to Mexico City from 1935 to 1960, which required new housing in several of the city's upscale neighborhoods (Olavarría 1945:67–108).

The first period introduced a new style of architecture, based on French and other architectural features, which came to be known as the *casa porfiriana*. This more functional house, which accommodated the modernizing trends of the time, replaced the old colonial residence. With architectural changes came a new concept of household decoration and display that was largely of European origin. The *casa porfiriana* demanded not only a new conception of interior decoration but an extensive array of modern furniture, ceramics, carpets, and a rather large roster of accessories such as curtains, tapestries, silver ornaments, silverware, china, and assorted bric-a-brac, mostly of French, English, and Italian origin. The traditional decoration of the ample and high-ceiling mansions, developed mostly during the last fifty years of colonial rule, was rather simple, sparse but characteristically dignified. The aristocratic mansion created an ambiance of almost Japanese calmness and elegance, which came to contrast with the more elaborate modern aristocratic household by the end of the Porfiriato.

Many of the European styles and manufacturers of furniture, porcelain, china, and other items of decoration in vogue at the time made their appearance in the Mexican aristocratic household. They blended well with some traditional appointments, particularly paintings, majolica, and silver ornaments. The Porfirian household was significantly smaller but surrounded by gardens that the compactness of the central city had never allowed. It also had modern conveniences lacking in the traditional mansion, including functional kitchens and, by the turn of the century, bathrooms — one of the innovations that diffused from the United States during this period. It should be noted that traditional mansions in the central city, which had continued to be inhabited by aristocrats until the late 1940s, also underwent important modifications in decoration, in the rearrangement of rooms, and in the addition of modern conveniences. By the onset of the Mexican Revolution, the aristocratic household had been transformed; perhaps more than in any other utilitarian and expressive domain, this social class had internalized the modernizing trends of the time. Combining European innovations with traditional patterns of decoration and display, the aristocratic household made the transition from a traditional to a modern world with dignity and elegance without appreciable loss of time-honored value (Alvarez 1990:40–73).

The second period is related to both the tremendous growth of the city and the migration of provincial aristocrats to the capital. Between 1910 and 1930 most aristocratic households were still located in the central city and adjacent *colonias*, within a radius of at most three miles from the *zócalo*—Roma, Santa María la Ribera, Condesa, Cuauhtémoc—and along the Paseo de la Reforma, the main avenue of the city. No new household architecture made its appearance until about 1930 or so, with the resurgence of a neocolonial style that combined colonial elements with modern architectural features of French and Italian origin. The result is a kitschy, nondescript combination of traditional and modern elements that until the early 1950s became the rage among some aristocrats but mainly among the rich and powerful. The appearance of this architectural style coincides with the establishment of several new upscale, fashionable *colonias* increasingly distant from the central city: Lomas de Chapultepec and Polanco. From then on there is nothing characteristic of the aristocratic household, as new elaborate mansions spanned many styles but were entirely associated with the rich and powerful plutocracy, including the political class (Buelna 1940:75–101).

The final episode in the residential distribution of the aristocracy in Mexico City is the great influx of provincial aristocrats who—gradually since the end of the armed phase of the Revolution (1919) but massively after 1935—migrated to the capital. The great majority of these families did not have a residence in Mexico City; but by the late 1950s most of them had bought or built houses in the *colonias* established during the first period and in *colonias* in the best sections of the city that had come into existence as the megalopolis expanded and engulfed many independent towns and villages. Some aristocratic families had owned residences in these towns since the nineteenth century; a number of them were country retreats until after World War II, which made these locations appealing to provincial aristocrats in the process of resettling in the capital. These newest fashionable residential areas were located in the southern part of the city: Coyoacán, San Angel, Pedregal, San Jerónimo, and a few other enclaves. Mexico City has continued to grow, but few elite residential areas have been established in the last twenty-five years. Thus by the mid-1970s aristocratic households were located in all the *colonias* or sections of the city mentioned above.

The great majority of households in these elite locations are, of course, residences of plutocrats, politicians, members of the upper-middle-class, and the most affluent sectors of the city's population. Unlike the distinct architectural style that characterized the aristocratic household until about 1930 (the old colonial mansion and the *casa porfiriana*), the architecture of the past sixty years—mostly a reflection of the newly rich and powerful—has not developed a distinctive style. Rather, the new mansions span a wide spectrum of styles, ranging from occasionally gaudy renditions of provincial and modern French architecture to nondescript modern architecture of several provenances. One common element of the mansions of the rich and powerful of late is the high walls or elaborate and massive iron fences that surround them, a reflection of a strong desire for privacy. During the past two generations, coinciding with the maturation of the new ruling class of the country, this feature of the mansion has been exaggerated for reasons of security and protection. Quite often, for example, the mansions of plutocrats and politicians from the outside look more like redoubts than private residences (Vargas Martínez 1971:109–198).

The general pattern of aristocratic settlement in Mexico City today is dispersed, and residences are found in most affluent *colonias*. There is a certain clustering of households, however, in the most fashionably traditional (since 1920) sections of the city such as Lomas de Chapultepec and its environs and within a radius of two miles of Chapultepec Park. Every elite section of the city includes a mix of the rich and affluent, and the houses vary greatly in style, size, and construction. None of the houses of aristocrats today can compare to the frequently palatial houses of many plutocrats and politicians, which, as a manifestation of power and wealth but not in architectural excellence, are the equivalent of the former colonial mansions and palaces of the aristocracy. Indeed, the houses of most aristocrats are modest compared to those of plutocratic magnates; they are mostly indistinguishable from the houses of the affluent upper-middle class. In addition, a considerable number of the least affluent aristocrats live in apartments, which further diminishes their social status as perceived by the *haute bourgeoisie*.

The dispersion of aristocratic families in the city has an aspect that has diminished the social cohesion and visibility of the group. Until about 1945 the aristocracy could still be regarded as a fairly localized group, because most families lived within a radius of two miles (roughly centered on the Colonia Roma). This factor facilitated social interaction in the houses of the most affluent aristocrats and in a few clubs and hotels. These were centers that hosted the brilliant social life that aristocrats could still afford, as the rising plutocracy was not yet sufficiently rich and certainly had not become sophisticated enough to challenge the aristocracy socially. The arrival of provincial aristocrats coincided with the trend toward residing in the fashionable sections that triggered the expansion throughout the city after World War II, particularly among young families. Dispersion throughout the megalopolis initiated the splintering of the aristocracy into several functional segments determined by distance within the city and residential location prior to the provincial exodus to the city, beginning massively in the mid-1930s.

In summary, isolation from kin and friends has augmented aristocratic loss of recognition and social prominence. The old sense of community fostered by relative propinquity is gone, and large numbers of aristocrats gather together only at weddings, still large and elaborate affairs that may bring together thirty or forty name groups, including as many as a thousand adults and children.

The Household as the Last Bastion of Aristocratic Exclusivity and Self-Identity

In terms of settlement and residential exclusiveness in Mexico City, then, there is nothing distinctive that sets the aristocracy apart from other superordinate classes of society today. Nothing in the residences of aristocrats, be they houses or apartments, denotes the social status that they still residually have. The external appearance of residences is not an indicator of social prominence or a perceived symbol of status recognition, as their mansions were until two generations ago and as the mansions of the plutocracy are now. The decorations and what residences contain are another matter altogether, and therein lies the last distinctive material complex of the aristocracy.

The Household as a Shrine to the Ancestors

The Mexican aristocratic household may be aptly characterized as a "shrine to the ancestors." It is the last material symbol that distinguishes aristocrats from plutocrats and other members of the superordinate class. More importantly, the household is the identifying core, the fulcrum of aristocratic consciousness, and the last bastion of exclusivity. Looked at from this standpoint, the household is the last redoubt, where aristocrats can be themselves and be reminded of the social power and status they once had. The aristocratic house or apartment itself—the receptacle of the shrine, if you will—is largely irrelevant: most aristocratic abodes in the city, with a few notable exceptions, are little more than comfortable and unostentatious when compared to the mansions of the rich and powerful. Only the content, arrangement, and display of the aristocratic abode are relevant in understanding it as a material symbol assuaging the loss of power and status.

In this section I first describe the traditional household as it was structured two generations ago and then point out how the situation has changed for most middle-aged and young aristocratic families. First of all, there was a clear division of space within the household: the "public" domain of exhibition and display and the private sphere of domestic living. This is the domestic division of space in the colonial mansion that was in effect until the Mexican Revolution and more or less survived until the last mansions were sold or confiscated by the government.[1] The symbolic, social, and ceremonial implications of this division of space were never as stringent as those of the aristocratic household of Meiji-restoration Japan (Sugiyama Lebra 1993:155–164), but it nonetheless configures a significant portion of the Mexican aristocratic household. Moreover, it is only the public domain of exhibition and display that constitutes a shrine to the ancestors, for there is nothing saliently different about the private sphere of domestic living as compared, say, with that of the plutocratic household.

The public domain in the aristocratic household is exclusively confined to the living room, dinning room, library, one or two family rooms (drawing rooms), and adjoining areas (hall, entrance hall, stairwell). As late as 1950 the well-appointed household included all these rooms arranged in various patterns designed for maximum display. The more elaborate households included two living rooms and dining rooms, usually of large proportions and occasionally interconnected to accommodate large gatherings. The general conception of the houses built by aristocrats after they vacated their colonial mansions and *casas porfirianas* (from 1940 onward) was to preserve some of the seigneurial features of these residences with more modest economic means. Most aristocratic residences today are conservative, with only two or three houses in the modern architectural style for which Mexico is deservedly renowned. The number of aristocratic households today that may still be regarded as elaborate but more modest versions of former mansions is no more than 20 percent. These households represent the ideal to which all aristocrats aspire, were they to become rich again.

Before describing the public configuration of the household in this section I catalogue its contents and provenances in order to assess their significance as symbols and as objects of decorative and artistic value. Throughout three centuries of effective domination (roughly from 1580 to 1910) the Mexican aristocracy accumulated a great deal of art, furniture, fine crafts, and household accessories (including china, flat silver, silver ornaments, ceramics, rugs, books, and so on). Some of these objects were handed down through generations, and it is fairly common to have a history of the most prized objects going back to the seventeenth century. Every aristocratic family today has a few objects that are categorized as heirlooms, while some grandparental-generation families may have many of them waiting to be inherited by their married sons and daughters. In fact, it is a standard practice upon marriage to provide couples with heirlooms, which become the centerpieces of their new homes. The most prized heirlooms are portraits of ancestors, landscapes of old haciendas, religious paintings, and furniture such as armoires, *secré-taires*, and chests of seventeenth- and eighteenth-century origin. More recent heirlooms of nineteenth-century origin abound, which include the same cate-gories but do not have the same symbolic and affective value.

The household has many more appointments than heirlooms in these cate-gories; they date mostly from the last period of great wealth enjoyed by the aristocracy, that is, from the French Intervention onward, when aristocrats came under the influence of French, Italian, and English styles of household decoration and display. This is most notable in living room and dining room furniture, porcelain, landscape painting, and tapestries, but it also includes miscellaneous bric-a-brac. These artistic and decorative appointments were imported directly from Europe; and furniture in particular is of the high-est quality, including pieces by the most famous manufacturers of the time, such as Chippendale, Chabot, and Miranelli. Heirlooms, in contrast, are al-most exclusively of Spanish origin but mostly made in Mexico. From the early seventeenth century onward, cities such as Puebla, Morelia, and Guanajuato have been deservedly famous for the fine manufacture of ceramics (majolica), inlaid (marquetry) furniture, lacquer work, and other fine crafts of house-hold decoration. Most importantly, portraiture, landscape, and other forms of painting have always flourished in Mexico, and some able artists since the middle of the seventeenth century have painted members of the aristocracy.

A third category for household decoration and display includes objects ac-quired after the aristocracy ceased to be the ruling class of the country in 1910. Due to the religious conflicts that characterized Mexico from the middle of the nineteenth century to the late 1920s a great deal of religious art (statu-ary, paintings, and religious furniture) became available in the open market. Also, the modernizing trends triggered by the Mexican Revolution, which af-fected mostly the rising middle classes and the new rich and powerful, de-valued the excellent traditional crafts of the country (wood-paneled screens, chest of drawers, armoires, ceramics, and assorted bric-a-brac) in favor of mostly French- and Italian-made or copied household appointments, quite often with little or no decorative or artistic value. (This is the most blatant, unusual case of cultural devaluation and lack of appreciation for tradition that I know of in my forty-five years of ethnographic and historical research in the country.) As a consequence, roughly between the late 1920s and the late 1960s, antique stores, flea markets, and private homes became the source of a large array of art and crafts at ridiculously low prices.

As the most "cultured" social segment of society during this period, aristocrats were the most avid collectors of these objects, sharing honors with small groups of intellectuals who valued tradition and were not blinded by the dubious benefits of modernizing trends. The acquisition of pre-Hispanic art (statuary and pottery) can also be explained by this syndrome. Appreciation for these artifacts was so low that museum-quality pieces were readily available in large quantities, spanning all Mesoamerican traditions, from Olmec to Mexica. Many aristocratic households contain good collections of pre-Hispanic art, but plutocratic households even more so. Plutocratic magnates have been avid collectors since about 1960 and now have the best private collections in the country. This is one of the few expressive activities that plutocrats initiated independently of the aristocratic model. This general devaluation of the country's artistic tradition is now over, and in the short period of a generation a significant segment of the population has learned to value pre-Hispanic and colonial cultural production. Prices have skyrocketed as a consequence, and there is no longer much to be had in the open market.

The traditional aristocratic household circa 1950–1960 had a very large array of appointments that occasionally included all the categories and styles described above. There is, of course, a significant degree of variation in terms of quantity, provenance, and the way in which objects and groups of objects are symbolically regarded by the family. But there is also a common core of meaning and guidelines that structure the decoration and display of aristocratic households.

First and foremost, the distinction between heirlooms and all other appointments is most important in the configuration of the household as a residence and as a shrine to the ancestors. The distinction must be placed in ideological perspective. From the utilitarian viewpoint, the aristocratic household is designed to enhance the elegance and taste of exhibition and display. The standards of elegance and taste are, of course, self-centered and self-generated, but they do have cross-cultural validity, as they adhere closely to the standards of all Western aristocracies. To put it differently, variants of the Western aristocracy have indisputably been the local arbiters of superordinate elegance and taste until today. This is a subjective matter, difficult to conceptualize. To a certain degree it is more appropriate to leave it unspecified, except to the extent that it entails important social symbols and constitutes the discriminating element of the aristocracy as a class: that *je ne sais quoi* that distinguishes the aristocratic household (and by extension a large roster of behavior) from all other households. The validation of this standard of elegance and taste rests on the fact that the aristocracy has always been the beacon of appropriate behavior in matters pertaining to decoration, display, and social manners for the superordinate upwardly mobile, even long after it lost its power and wealth. Thus the household is the fundamental symbol of aristocratic identity in a vanishing world, a symbol validated in feedback fashion by how deeply its realization has influenced the configuration of the household of the rich and powerful. This is the ideological foundation in which the aristocratic household is embedded as an abode and as a shrine to the ancestors.

The original meaning of "heirloom" was entailed household and personal property inherited by the firstborn. After the eighteenth century the term evolved. Today it denotes any kind of fine property that has been passed through generations and has symbolic value as an index of social status. Among Mexican aristocrats, heirlooms are household and art objects that have been in the family for at least five generations; most of them extend to the eighteenth century, and a significant number to the seventeenth and sixteenth centuries. Aristocrats seldom regard objects with provenance from the second half of the nineteenth century as heirlooms, as the object's antiquity is supposed to denote the owner's antiquity of lineage. Heirlooms are the centerpieces in the decoration of the household, about which all other appointments are arranged. They invariably occupy the most prominent position in the arrangement of the public domain of the household, particularly the living room and entrance hall. They constitute a mnemonic reminder of the aristocratic status of the family: the older and more numerous the heirlooms, the more illustrious the status.

I arrived at the notion of heirlooms and envisioned the notion of the household as a shrine after analyzing the results of a questionnaire administered to an opportune sample of twenty-five aristocratic families. Husband and wife were asked to rank their twenty most valued household possessions. There was remarkable agreement concerning the kinds of possessions that respondents ranked as the top five: portraits of ancestors (including churchmen, nuns, and important personages of colonial and early republican times); paintings of old haciendas (including landscapes of landed estates and assorted buildings that had been the property of the family); furniture known to have been in the family for many generations (primarily armoires, *secrétaires*, chests, and tables); religious art (mostly paintings, statuary, and ornaments associated with the haciendas and ancestral towns or cities they controlled); and special collections of ceramics, books, and silver assembled by some prominent ancestor. In follow-up interviews, it became evident that individual items of these top-ranked categories were held in much greater esteem than the rest of the vast array of household appointments; they evoked an image of the past that was of fundamental importance for the aristocratic family. Heirlooms center on the ancestors (what they looked like, where and how they lived, and what they accomplished) and are the symbolic and affective links to the past that sustain aristocrats' pride and self-identification in a world that increasingly considers them irrelevant. In summary, the household has evolved from being a center of aristocratic display where the ruling class of the country (until the Mexican Revolution) demonstrated its power and wealth to being a private sanctuary that helps to assuage the loss of former status and a refuge from what most aristocrats consider a hostile world.

Decoration and Arrangement of the Household Public Domain

The household viewed as a shrine to the ancestors is configured as follows. The household's public domain constitutes the chapel-receptacle: the physical structure of the shrine. The decoration and utilization of spaces may be in a variety of styles—classic, baroque, neoclassic (modern)—depending on the number, quality, and nature of the appointments. In other words, the receptacle may be arranged in many variants of a basic theme: the display of heirlooms for maximal symbolic effect. In this scheme of things, the heirlooms represent the icons and images of veneration, including furniture or paintings but most strikingly and literally portraits of ancestors. While cultural conventions of arrangement are observed (that is, the disposition of utilitarian furniture such as tables, chairs, sofas, lamps, breakfronts, and so on), the primary intent is to display the most prized heirlooms (of the five categories specified above) in a manner that enhances the prominence, accomplishments, and antiquity of lineage of the family. The pragmatic social aim of the shrine's structure is to demonstrate the aristocratic standing of members of the household, which has two distinct aspects. Endogenously, the shrine is a place affording protection, as the outside world is invariably regarded as inhospitable to the stubborn claim of aristocrats that they are still the best in society. This is the ideological cornerstone that supports the notion of the household as a shrine to the ancestors; they are quite literally patron saints, protectors of the family and providers of safety and comfort no longer afforded by an outside world which is regarded as beyond a tolerable measure of control. Exogenously, the shrine is a validating symbol of aristocratic standing, a demonstration to outsiders that however low the family may have sunk in the scale of power and wealth, its former exaltedness demands recognition and respect.

It is equally important that the household as shrine to the ancestors must be decorated with as much elegance and grace as aristocratic standards can muster. These standards are analyzed in the expressive section, including the intricate nuances they specifically entail. At this point, a few remarks may help to place matters in perspective.

First, there are no explicit guidelines as to the number of appointments that may be displayed in the household public domain or their manifold combinations. Thus the baroque household may involve variegated combinations of paintings, furniture, china, and accessories (draperies, carpets, leatherbound books, and all sorts of bric-a-brac) of different provenances that, to a high degree, validate the characterization of this style as the abhorrence of empty spaces. Without giving the impression of excess, baroque households are veritable old-fashioned museums of fine art and crafts.

The classic household, in contrast, is a sober combination of appointments, the accent being on the strategic display of choice heirlooms, to a significant extent enhancing the symbolic presence of portraits of ancestors and particular pieces of furniture intimately associated with the history of the family. The highest expression of this style, for example, is the display of a piece of furniture next to a portrait of an ancestor in which the piece is also depicted. I have recorded seven cases of this form of expressive display, the most notable being a lady of the highest rank (both a countess and marchioness) at the turn of the eighteenth century resting her hand on a *secrétaire* of late-seventeenth-century origin. These are exceptions; but they illustrate the drive and creativity of aristocratic families in configuring households as outstanding shrines to the ancestors, particularly when for a variety of reasons not much has survived in the inventory of heirlooms and fine art and crafts. Implicit in the display of the classical household is the expressive imperative that had more appointments survived, the family would have opted for the baroque style of display.

Finally, the modern (or neoclassic as I call it) style of the household as a shrine is the least elaborate, has the fewest heirlooms, and includes more contemporary appointments than the other two. This means essentially that, for one reason or another, the household did not manage to hold onto whatever appointments had been in the family until about 1910. From the viewpoint of elegance and taste, however, the modern household is not inferior to the richer and more elaborate baroque and classical households, and every detail of decoration and display is used to advantage to compensate for the lack of traditional appointments. The few heirlooms are perhaps more strikingly and prominently displayed amid the modern furniture and art than in the other two types of households. While the household may look more modest and relatively subdued, the importance of the ancestors is no less emphasized than in the baroque and classical households.

Second, great care is taken to integrate the blending of occasionally very different categories and varieties of appointments that the household displays. For example, the living room or library may include appointments as different as pre-Hispanic antiquities and nineteenth-century French porcelain but displayed in such a way that there is no apparent dissonance, as harmony is generated by the placement and combination of items in relation to other appointments in the room such as tables, chests, and breakfronts. In the same fashion, furniture ranging in origin from seventeenth-century Spanish and Mexican *secrétaires* to eighteenth- and nineteenth-century French and Italian armoires blends effortlessly in the same room. From this standpoint, the public spaces of the aristocratic household are basically baroque ensembles, as there is a strong tendency, whenever possible, to display the greatest density of appointments. This tendency goes back to the first half of the eighteenth century, when the baroque style in church and civil architecture achieved its highest degree of excellence and permanently marked many aspects of Mexico's cultural life.

Another basic principle of decoration and display is the meticulous concern with colors, shades, and the blending of tones in the arrangement of accessories and their environment. This applies not only to curtains, drapes, rugs, and upholstery but to the lampshades and materials that adorn tables and other pieces of furniture. Although the guidelines for decoration and display are not explicitly stated, the accent is on a pattern that emphasizes an assumed ideal of elegance that will be pleasing to the ancestors, as the family continues the traditions of those to whom the shrine is dedicated. The analogy that comes to mind is that of a visual mantra, deviation from which will displease the ancestors and cause them to look unfavorably upon the family. This implicitly magical belief is well expressed by one of my most perceptive informants: "The portraits of our ancestors, and the furniture and the art objects they bequeathed us, attest to the high status [old ancestry] of our family, but they also mean that the care with which we continue to remember them, without in the least deviating from the norms that have always been required in the decoration of our household, guarantees that they will continue to look favorably upon us, as if they were still among us." This (and similar statements by informants over seventy years of age) leaves little doubt that the household is indeed a shrine to the ancestors.

Closely associated with these guidelines for household decoration and display is an inherent tendency to avoid the kitschy, tacky (*cursi*), and ostentatious presentation of the *nouveau riche* household, generally associated with the richest, most powerful, and often socially non–upwardly mobile sector of the plutocracy. Aristocratic families are loath to resemble the *nouveau riche* in any way, implicitly assuming that this is undignified for the ancestors and detracts from their symbolic role of "protectors," as the *lares* and *penates* of the family.

In essence, I am addressing the incidence of the three types of households described above and how and to what extent the household has changed over roughly fifty years. Probably the majority of aristocratic households as late as 1950 were done in the baroque style, with a high percentage of classical households and a small number of modern households. During the provincial migration to Mexico City, aristocratic families whose heads were more than sixty years old had enough appointments for their children to set up either baroque or classical households upon marriage; only those most affected by the land reform and other economic consequences of the Revolution had no option but to set up sparser modern households.

By 1980, however, the situation had changed greatly for two reasons. Although no heirlooms were ever sold even during the worse years of economic dislocation between 1920 and 1940, many household appointments were ultimately sold in order to survive, thereby diminishing the total stock of paintings, fine furniture, silver, ceramics, and so on owned by most household heads in their early old age. But the number of independent households has increased since 1960, and the total cache of heirlooms and manifold appointments of ancestral (1920–1950) aristocratic households has been reduced by outfitting the households of newly married couples ranging in age from twenty-five to forty. It has always been a standard aristocratic practice that upon marriage couples are provided with heirlooms from both sides of the family, which invariably become the centerpieces of the household's public domain. Thus the bulk of the decoration of the households of most couples younger than forty in 1990 (and many older than that) has been done with newly acquired appointments. As a consequence of this division of heirlooms and fine appointments, most aristocratic households today are decorated in the modern style. With a few notable exceptions, the change has affected almost exclusively couples younger than fifty-five or so. But there are many baroque and classical households of couples in their early old age and late middle age, as in cases when the husband, wife, or both did not have any siblings and inherited everything when the parents died.

Finally, I reiterate that, however modest average aristocratic households may be, there is always that *je ne sais quoi* that distinguishes them from the households of plutocrats and other rich and powerful families. Several of that 20 percent of remaining baroque and classical households are veritable treasure troves of art and crafts. This is particularly the case with outstanding pieces of colonial furniture, majolica, and religious art. Indeed, many of the colonial pieces shown at an exhibition of the Metropolitan Museum of New York City in 1990 entitled "Thirty Centuries of Mexican Splendor" came from aristocratic households. For example, a seventeenth-century ivory-covered *secrétaire* of Mexican origin came from the household of one of my chief informants and was insured for $900,000. The best majolica pottery and several religious and secular paintings in the exhibition were lent by aristocratic households. These facts give an idea of the wealth still to be found in many aristocratic households, several of which may be appraised as containing more than 15 million dollars' worth of art and crafts. This does not mean, however, that these families are rich, for whatever they own may literally be regarded as entailed, not to be sold but to pass on to their descendants. This fundamental belief has been eroding, however, and aristocrats of the younger generation (essentially those about to be or recently married) are seriously questioning this overwhelming concern with the past as inimical to their continuing to be part of the superordinate class.

Country Retreats and the Material and Social Implications of the Rural-Urban Axis

For thousands of years the rich and powerful have had country retreats. By Greco-Roman times aristocratic living invariably entailed a country place, sometimes elaborate villas, to escape the constrained palatial existence in the city during most of the year. Thus a fairly structured rural-urban pattern of living came into existence in the aristocracy of Western society, a pattern that has remained constant until the present in all variants of this social class, including the powerful plutocracies that came into being after the demise of the *ancien régime*.[2]

Beginning in modern times, but with a much higher degree of incidence after the demise of the *ancien régime*, this dual pattern of residence has been thoroughly adopted by the *haute bourgeoisie* and in the twentieth century by members of the more affluent social classes who can afford a country place.

From Hacienda to Country Retreat

Until 1910 the hacienda was the country retreat for the majority of aristocratic families. By then there were a few aristocratic families which no longer owned landed estates because their economy had become entirely urban based, although there were always the haciendas of consanguineal or affinal kin where extended periods could be spent away from the city. Until 1910, then, the city-country axis was basically a seasonal phenomenon: two or three times a year the family would spend weeks and occasionally months in the hacienda, especially during the summer and for shorter periods during Christmas, Holy Week, and All Souls'–All Saints' Day. This was a rather standardized pattern, more or less regulated by the hacienda's distance from the city and the types of agrarian enterprises associated with it. Thus the city-country axis was an annual phenomenon and had a strong utilitarian component: respite from urban living was regulated by the annual cycle.

The configuration of the city-country axis began to change during the last two decades of the Porfiriato. Aristocratic life became more urban—that is, less time was spent in the hacienda during the summer—and almost all the aristocratic families that had resided most of the year in their landed estates reversed the pattern and became urbanites. By the onset of the 1910 Revolution, the aristocracy had significantly diminished rural living, which became a permanent pattern that was never reversed: first due to the great destruction of haciendas until 1920 and then with the end of *latifundia* after the 1934 land reform. Since then those who managed to hold onto manorial hacienda residences not too far from the city have refurbished them, and they may now be regarded as country retreats that are visited periodically. Most hacienda manors were so badly damaged that they could not be repaired and lie in ruins. Some manors, mostly far away from the capital, managed to escape destruction during the Revolution, have been repaired and improved, and still perform the same residential function of prerevolutionary times. Most of them, however, have been bought by plutocrats or expropriated by politicians; and many have become veritable showcases of opulent country living, combining the charm of colonial architecture with every luxury of modern life. There are probably no more than two or three of these stately homes still in the hands of original aristocratic owners.

The urban-country axis during the past forty years may be characterized (to coin a Spanglish neologism) as *weekendismo*. By this I mean a country place that aristocratic families (and now many affluent families of the superordinate ranks of society) can repair to on a weekly or biweekly basis to cope with congested city living. This characterization, however, should be expanded to include the country retreat for more prolonged periods of residence for the main ritual events in the annual cycle (Christmas, Holy Week, and All Saints'–All Souls' Day), a continuation of the prerevolutionary pattern. With the exception of a few hacienda manors, as noted above, the average aristocratic country retreat today is generally comfortable, sometimes architecturally interesting (such as modified structures of nineteenth- and occasionally eighteenth-century origin), but not lavish by comparison to the plutocracy's country mansions. The great majority of country retreats are located within a radius of 80 to 100 miles from Mexico City, that is, within two to three hours' drive.

The most common variations of this pattern are the following. First, parts of a few old hacienda mansions have been refurbished, and they are the most attractive and elaborate country retreats owned by aristocrats. But most of the hacienda mansions that survived the revolution (in reasonably good condition) within a radius of 200 miles of Mexico City are no longer owned by aristocrats. Second, many country retreats are located in the lands of former haciendas that owners were allowed by law to retain after the land reform of 1934. These small estates, usually no more than 200 hectares, generally involve some profitable agrarian operation, and the house may be a refurbished old structure or new structures built during the past twenty to forty years. Occasionally these can be attractive retreats, in that materials of old hacienda mansions were used for their construction. Third, and least common, are "urban" country retreats: country homes owned by aristocratic families in small communities in the Valley of Mexico before the megalopolis entirely engulfed them. In sections of Mexico City such as Coyoacán and San Angel there are a few Porfirian and other structures of early-nineteenth- and late-eighteenth-century origin, with ample gardens and other country-like amenities. Before the Revolution they were indeed country retreats, located within two to three hours' ride by horse and carriage. These are the earliest of such country homes that today have become either permanent residences or Sunday retreats for aristocratic families whose main residence is in a more centrally located part of the city.

Perhaps as many as 60 percent of all aristocratic families own a place in the country in one of the above categories or one acquired more recently and usually not related to their own former haciendas or old structures of Porfirian origin. Some aristocrats, however, have managed to buy and refurbish small hacienda manors that were rendered basically uninhabitable by the Revolution and subsequent land reform, including some ancillary structures such as ranch houses, mills, and *batanes* (fulling-mills). All these structures have been transformed into attractive country homes, but most of them are located quite distant from Mexico City. Closer to the city, country places are new structures that have been designed by architects or the owners themselves in a variety of styles, including Swiss chalets, neocolonial structures, and modern houses blending well with the natural environment. These country homes are built on farmland bought for agricultural exploitation, ranging from 50 to 100 hectares, but more commonly on small parcels of land ranging from three to ten hectares. The poorer families invariably have access to country places of kin and friends, so that it can be said that the entire aristocratic group in one way or another participates in the urban-country axis.

With the exception of the entirely refurbished old haciendas, significant parts of them, and structures built in the second half of the nineteenth century, the average aristocratic country retreat is a moderately small establishment, architecturally tasteful but not an outstanding structure. It is outfitted with all the modern conveniences, comfortable but not luxurious, and generally has easy access to the city. Many of them have swimming pools, tennis courts, park-like grounds, and extensive gardens. The more affluent aristocrats keep sizable stables, while a considerable number have three or four horses. The house itself is designed to accommodate the nuclear family and at least three or four guests, while the more elaborate establishments could accommodate at least twenty people at any one time. Accommodations are generally spacious and well appointed and on the whole have the same division of spaces of the city residence, although not as formal. The country residence is designed for relaxation, but a good deal of effort is spent in making it elegant and appropriate for ceremonial occasions.

The Social and Psychological Ambiance of the Country Retreat

The furnishings and decorations of the country retreat exhibit a conscious effort to replicate as much as possible the bygone hacienda manor. This is done by using furnishings and appointments that were salvaged or survived the dismantling of manors or by acquiring them at auctions and from antique stores. Fine crafts are a very important part of the decoration, and many items that would not fit well in the city residence find an appropriate place in the country residence. The same concern with elegance, balanced decoration, and display underlying the city residence is also found in the country residence. If the public spaces of the city residence have been conceived as a shrine to the ancestors, those of the country residence may be regarded as a votive symbol of the hacienda, as the validation of aristocratic status of bygone times. There is, of course, a mixture of traditional (pre-1910) and more contemporary furniture, crafts, pictures, and manifold decorative items. The following appointments are among those most commonly found in country places: local artisan furniture or furniture that belonged to hacienda manors but is not elegant enough to be displayed in the city residence (such as armoires, tables, chairs, breakfronts, mirrors, chests, screens, and chests of drawers); religious furniture, sometimes of rather large proportions, generally from hacienda churches and chapels (such as retables, benches, chairs, and ornamental trunks); religious art (such as paintings or wooden sculptures of saints, *ex-votos* [votive oils on tin or copper], and many manifestations of the Virgin Mary and Christ, including crucifixes); and assorted art (such as the less distinguished portraits of ancestors, landscapes, and depictions of old structures associated with the haciendas). In addition, of course, there is the array of modern utilitarian furniture and accoutrements that makes the country residence cozy and comfortable.

This is a description of the country residence of the most affluent aristocratic families, which probably includes roughly 30 percent of those who own a country retreat. The average country place, however, is a more modest abode that aims at what I have described above. There are always items of furniture, paintings, and religious or secular art that remind the family of ties to the hacienda, making this abode another mechanism to assuage the loss of status and wealth. From this standpoint, the country retreat represents not only a respite from the hustle and bustle of the city but a second line of psychological defense. This is the view of the middle-aged and older generations, whereas for the young the country retreat is little more than a place to have fun of a different sort than in the city.

Psychologically, the country home comes closest to recreating the hacienda, after three generations still a powerful symbol of status in the consciousness of most aristocrats. This vanishing syndrome is significantly enhanced when the country home is located in former hacienda lands or is part of the manor itself. From this standpoint, the country residence is an extension of the city residence. Both constitute a social-psychological-physical environment where aristocrats can be themselves, celebrate themselves, gather strength, and thereby be sustained by remembering the past, and conduct their most exclusive ritual and ceremonial gatherings. Just as in the city residence, aristocrats engage in several social behaviors that contain subterfuges that subliminally redound in elements meant to assuage their loss of status and the recognition that they are little more than a phantom social class.

The country residence as an extension of the city residence, *weekendismo*, and the annual cycle of activities are part of the same visiting pattern that regulates the social and religious calendar of the aristocratic family. The weekly or biweekly visits to the country serve both a utilitarian aim (the same for all those families fortunate enough to have a place to escape the constraints of the city) and a ritual aim (the celebration of birthdays, *santos* [name days], and sometimes social-ceremonial events such as christenings and first communions). The extended periods of residence in the country house are almost invariably related to the main events of the annual cycle. Not all families trek to the country, but probably the great majority of them spend one or two of these occasions there, particularly Holy Week. The periods of country residence for these events may be as long as two or three weeks, when guests are invited for a substantial part of the time. A few aristocratic families celebrate country weddings, most commonly among those who have managed to hold on to hacienda manors or parts of them, a practice that was common before the land reform. Finally, during the children's summer vacation, the country house is used for rather prolonged periods of residence, extending to several weeks, including children and adult guests.

In terms of social recognition and psychic capital, the country residences yield the highest dividends when located in regions of their former hacienda, as aristocratic families are usually well remembered by the most important people in the area. This is the case not only in the immediate regions where residences are located but in nearby towns and cities, where former *hacendados* are still remembered and remain even more in the consciousness of the middle and lower classes. Finally, the most affluent aristocratic families keep adequate stables of horses for pleasure and equitation. But the horse, as an important symbol of aristocratic status, is no longer a viable option for most families, and even the richest aristocrats cannot compare with the truly exceptional stables kept by plutocratic magnates.

Social and Material Adaptation to the City: Managing the Megalopolis with Restricted Economic Means

Until approximately the onset of the massive land reform of 1934–1940, and despite the ravages of the 1910 Revolution and the demise of the hacienda system, the Mexican aristocracy was the undisputed arbiter of social manners and behavior. In this role aristocrats constituted the model to be emulated by the rising plutocracy and all upwardly mobile people. These parameters for appropriate behavior, and the material base supporting them, ranged from dressing and fashions to entertaining and the organization of leisure. This domain of social interaction required an extensive network of business establishments that supplied the necessities for elite living. In this context aristocrats constituted a distinct and highly visible group, characterized by the way they dressed, the items they bought and where they bought them, the things they made fashionable, and the social image they projected. This ensemble of behavior and display, reported in the press and enhanced by word of mouth, constituted perhaps the main context in which the rising plutocracy began to acquire aristocratic manners, ultimately asserting itself as the most visible social segment in the capital.

Terminal Expressive Exclusivity of the Aristocratic Urban Environment: 1910–1960

During the Porfirian period Mexico City became fairly cosmopolitan, after the French Intervention reinvigorated and diversified the physical, business, and material landscape of the city. Many establishments made their appearance catering to the aristocracy and upper-middle class. The capital began to acquire the trappings of a European metropolis, ranging from tailor shops and women's fashion stores to tea rooms and restaurants. By the onset of the Revolution the center of the city and its immediate neighborhoods had become an elegantly disposed urban context. Harboring all the amenities of sophisticated living, Mexico City was the abode and playground of the small privileged classes of society.

Despite the loss of much wealth and the dislocation produced by the armed phase of the Revolution (1910–1920), social control of the city did not diminish; and aristocratic life and its plutocratic and upper-middle class extensions continued uninterrupted for another two decades. Although Mexican aristocrats did not derive much income from their landed estates after 1914, their urban property was left largely intact. The concentration of most aristocrats in the capital by about 1940 (and the fact that plutocratic fortunes were small until World War II) explains the aristocracy's continuing domination of the social scene for fifty years after the onset of the Revolution.

Social predominance meant primarily that the aristocracy, despite the catastrophic disintegration of the hacienda system, remained a discrete and distinct class for two generations. This is well attested by the attention that aristocrats received in the newspapers and magazines of the time and the recognition they elicited from the middle classes of the rapidly growing metropolis. In this ambiance, aristocrats set the standards of dressing, private entertainment, attendance at cultural events, public display, and in general most activities associated with leisure (elite sports, travel, games) of the city's superordinately placed. Because there was no other model, aristocrats were the undisputed arbiters of appropriate behavior, emulated by upwardly mobile plutocrats and vicarious fodder for the expectations of the middle classes.

Until the late 1940s the aristocracy was recognized as a distinct group by the middle classes in a city of approximately 4 million people. Recognition manifested itself in the way in which aristocrats behaved and displayed their public personae and most distinctly in their apparel and the places they frequented. Thus *la sociedad capitalina* (the city's society), as the aristocracy and those upwardly mobile people close to them were known, constituted a social group clearly discernible from the rest of the population. This distinctive perception of the aristocracy was enhanced by the low profile the political class presented in social affairs and by the inability of the plutocrats, despite the fact that in the 1950s they were sufficiently rich to create a distinct social milieu of their own. This was the last time that the Mexican aristocracy constituted the undisputed elite social class of the country. From then on, the aristocracy became an increasingly less distinct sector of a fragmented *haute bourgeoisie*, of which the new plutocracy had become the dominant sector. The new plutocracy has matured since then, and today it has become the ruling and social class of the country, largely enfranchised in the capital. How has this come about since 1950 or so?

Here we are exclusively concerned with the social ascendancy of the plutocracy and how it affected the expressive distinctness of the aristocracy and the aristocracy's loss of control over the urban landscape in which the social life of the capital takes place. This is a most important juncture for understanding the superordinate realignment of classes that has taken place during the past fifty years, and it has two aspects.

First, as long as the aristocracy was perceived as being on a par with the new rich and powerful, the aristocratic mystique evoked a significantly high degree of recognition among the middle classes, as the aristocracy's moderate wealth was sufficient to buy its members what they had made fashionable and therefore controlled socially. Another way of putting this is that interclass social recognition to a significant extent is posited on vicarious perceptions. From the mid-1960s or so this was no longer the case, as the new rich were perceived to have a much more opulent public life. Thus aristocrats no longer elicited as much recognition—having gone underground, so to speak—and vicarious perceptions shifted to the plutocracy. By about 1975 plutocratic magnates had monopolized the limelight; they were perceived as doing the most enviable things money could buy, making fashionable many things that aristocrats could no longer afford. The comings and goings of the rich and powerful became the steady diet of the city's dailies, and only occasionally did a prominent aristocratic wedding elicit enough interest to be publicly noted. Partly for economic reasons, but mostly because they did not want to be seen in the company of plutocrats they considered beneath them, the majority of aristocrats became an invisible group, eliciting recognition only from a very small segment of the best-educated social classes.

The second aspect is a corollary of the first. The distinctness of dress, personal presentation and display, and public behavior that the aristocracy previously had has been extended to the upwardly mobile plutocratic sector and, to some extent, to other wealthy sectors of society on the fringes of superordinate social status. Since the 1950s Mexico City has become an increasingly sophisticated metropolis that attracts many upper-class Europeans, further diluting the characteristic mark of the once distinct aristocracy in the capital. By as early as 1970 it would have been difficult to identify aristocrats by the most outward signs of behavior and action such as dress, the clubs they frequented, the shops and restaurants they patronized, and the cultural events they attended. These actions and activities have become the common property of manifold sectors of the capital's *haute bourgeoisie*.

Sociologically, this configuration of personnel (in Mexico City about 1 to 2 percent of the population) represents the extent to which the process of *embourgeoisement*-aristocratization has been expressively affecting Western superordinate stratification for a century and a half. The main difference between Mexico and Western European countries is that the superordinate sector of society is two to three times more numerous in Europe. In Rome, for example, the superordinate sector is about 6 percent of the population (Italo Signorini, personal communication, 1990), whereas in other capitals of Europe such as Paris and London it may be even higher. The reason for this difference must be attributed to Mexico's colonial past and its slowness in entering a mature industrial stage.

The Plutocratic, *Haute Bourgeois* Exclusive Environment of the City: 1960–1995

The past thirty-five years have witnessed the maturation of Mexico City's plutocracy, which after two generations of expressive acculturation and the acquisition of much wealth has become the dominant sector of the *haute bourgeoisie*. Adept students of aristocratic manners and behavior, the plutocrats now dominate the expressive public stage once monopolized by the aristocracy. The necessary condition of this developmental change is, of course, plutocratic wealth and the inability of significant numbers of aristocrats to generate new wealth after the Revolution; the sufficient condition is that the majority of plutocrats become socially upwardly mobile by learning from aristocratic models. The growth of the upper-middle class is a complementary aspect of the material transformation of the city as the expressive arena of the superordinately privileged. Indeed, without the moderate wealth and buying power of a sizable upper-middle class, it would have been impossible for the city to have established the elite commercial establishments to accommodate the expressive activities of the superordinately placed.

Discounting the city's long-standing museums, theaters, and cultural establishments and places of interest open to the general public, since the late 1950s Mexico City has witnessed the appearance of top-quality business and recreational establishments catering to that 1 to 2 percent constituting the city's elite population. Concentrated mainly in three or four sections of the city, they cater to a clientele that has unlimited or reasonable economic affluence to buy, attend, and patronize what they have to offer. But in the increasingly egalitarian ambiance of the city, these establishments, as in any great metropolis of Europe or the United States, are also occasionally frequented by affluent middle-class people. This is a universal phenomenon of modern industrial society everywhere, in which the old public exclusivity of the superordinately placed no longer obtains. Thus the Mexican *haute bourgeoisie* (henceforth denoting what remains of the aristocracy; the rich and powerful plutocracy, including many members of the political class; and the affluent upper-middle class, as defined above) does not in the public domain constitute an exclusive subdivision of society that can be distinctly circumscribed structurally and expressively, as the many variants of the Western aristocracy were until probably the turn of the twentieth century. But exclusivity and distinctiveness are still part of the new superordinate class of society in all modern industrial nations. In the context of Mexico City these attributes are manifested mostly in the privacy of the household, in clubs, and in activities that take place in public domains but are limited to those superordinately placed. Let us specify the nature and extent of these remaining exclusive domains before discussing the inclusive discharge of behavior that takes place publicly.

First, plutocrats (for different ideological reasons) have learned well from aristocrats to regard the household as a bastion of exclusivity, that is, confined to business associates and extended groups of kin and, most significantly, used for the purpose of building networks with upwardly mobile personnel and enhancing social standing. Not prone to allow anyone to take economic advantage of them, plutocratic families guard their privacy and foster exclusivity as much as aristocrats do. This is a task that takes significant effort, physically (as attested by the high walls and security systems almost invariably surrounding their mansions) and socially (by carefully screening and selecting individuals and families that are invited or admitted to their mansions), which enhances their aura of exaltedness as perceived by common folk. Upper-middle-class families, by contrast, exhibit no such concern with exclusivity and privacy, but they are selective about whom they admit into their midst, particularly concerning the maximization of upward mobility.

Second, in Spanish culture, unlike among the British upper classes, the culture of the club is rather poor; and, as an extension of the mother country, the Mexican upper classes exhibit the same lack of interest. Clubs have been part of the superordinate scene of Mexico City only since the second half of the nineteenth century, due to the modernizing influence of the French Intervention. By the onset of the 1910 Revolution there were probably half a dozen clubs with an exclusive aristocratic and plutocratic membership catering to some 2,000 families. There were no exclusively men's clubs in Mexico until after World War II; rather, these clubs were either family social clubs or clubs associated with horse racing and equitation. Between 1920 and 1940 the number of clubs increased by the introduction of U.S.-style country clubs and the establishment of equestrian clubs, including polo, which was introduced to Mexico in the 1890s. The number of country clubs (with an emphasis on the sports of golf, tennis, swimming) has increased since then; like their counterparts in the United States, they are somewhat significant social gathering places for the superordinately placed. Equitation clubs have proliferated, particularly after the decline of polo during the past thirty years. Throughout the most intensive period of aristocratic-plutocratic expressive acculturation (1940–1970), equestrian clubs were the most important gathering places for all three sectors of the superordinate class of the city, a trend that has continued until today.

The single most important club that for more than fifty years has served as a meeting place for aristocrats and plutocrats is the Jockey Club, the closest to the ideal of an exclusive, highly selective gathering place for people of acknowledged equal rank or aspiring rank in the English tradition. In the ambiance of this club many plutocrats learned the nuances and subtleties of aristocratic behavior. The Jockey Club is no longer the elite place that it was a generation ago, and few aristocrats and plutocratic magnates have kept up membership.

The closest to exclusive men's clubs are those that began to appear in the early 1950s and are now relatively common: banker clubs that extend membership to plutocratic magnates engaged a broad array of economic activities. These are common-interest clubs; they do not involve significant segments of the superordinate class in any particular activity, and they barely warrant the designation of social club. There are no other voluntary association groups that may be termed clubs, involving men or women engaged in the pursuit of specific activities. The poverty of free association groups in Mexico falling under the rubric of clubs, as they exist in most of northern Europe, may be explained by their traditional absence in southern Europe, where social display and intellectual interaction are mostly centered on the household (witness the French salon and the Spanish *tertulia*). The notion of the club was late in diffusing to Mexico and did so mostly in a connection with sports; it never acquired the social and psychological significance that it had in England or the United States, despite the proliferation of country clubs during the past fifty years.

Third, counteracting involvement in the culture of the club, there is a public domain in which plutocrats, aristocrats, and the some extent the upper-middle class are actively involved. More significantly, this domain (public to the extent that it entails the passive participation of the more-educated population of the city) brings together these three sectors into a kind of symbiotic relationship. This is the culture of display associated with some of the main banks, art galleries, and occasionally landmark buildings of the city. In particular, two banks (Banco Nacional de México and Banco de Comercio de México) and two or three privately endowed museums quite often sponsor exhibitions of art (painting, sculpture, pre-Hispanic art, and prints) and fine crafts (majolica pottery, colonial furniture, silver ornaments, religious artifacts, etc.). These exhibitions are open to the general public; but the items on display, the organization of the shows, and their inauguration are exclusively confined to plutocrats, aristocrats, and upper-middle-class personnel.

The symbiotic division of labor works as follows. Plutocrats are the organizers of exhibits as presidents or high officials of banks and as patrons of museums, some of which they were instrumental in establishing. But some plutocrats are art and craft collectors themselves and quite often mount exhibits of their own in these locales. Aristocrats, however, are the main providers of most of the colonial art, and their excellent collections of portraits, furniture, religious art, and majolica attract the most attention in these exhibits, as being closely associated with the social and cultural life of significant periods in the history of the country. The members of the upper-middle class (as I have noted in other contexts), by virtue of their ties to plutocrats and aristocrats, provide the numerical supporting role that enhances the significance of these exclusive gatherings within a rather public context. During the inauguration of these cultural events, the superordinate class of the city comes together, shines, and, in the eyes of the educated public, performs an important function that enhances its social recognition, regardless of whether the average attendant is able to discriminate among the social standings of the three sectors.

Since the demise of the *ancien régime*, commerce and trade—and more recently mass production—have greatly enhanced the democratization of society. The increasing availability and easy access to many of the necessities of urban and rural existence (dress, food, housing, medicine, transportation, entertainment, and so on) for a wide-ranging spectrum of the social system during the past 150 years have been a great equalizer. Indeed, many luxuries have become necessities; what was once in the exclusive orbit of the rich and affluent classes has become commonplace, and high fashions are now in the purview of the middle classes. The somewhat undifferentiated consumption of goods, services, and an extensive array of material objects (particularly associated with dress, sports, and entertainment) has made it extremely difficult today to sort people out and discretely categorize them. Except in the domain of potentates' extravagant consumption, the things people nowadays buy, use, wear, and employ are no longer good indicators of class position, as the rich and powerful and the middle classes share a rather high common denominator as consumers.

As a corollary of the general democratization of society as manifested in material goods and consumption, there are few exclusive places of business patronized by discrete clienteles. In Mexico City, New York, or London, as an example, people of the most diverse social and economic standings shop in the same stores and attend the same cultural events, the only constraints or restrictions being economic affluence and education. People from the queen of England to the moderately affluent commoner shop at London's Harrods; and one may find the richest or most powerful people in Mexico City shopping at Gucci side by side with average middle-class people. One cannot point to a single place of business and entertainment in Mexico City today that caters exclusively to the superordinately placed. The many stores that could be termed "exclusive" until probably the late 1940s are today patronized by anyone who has the money to buy whatever they sell. In a nutshell, as far as managing and negotiating what the city has to offer, money is the only significant factor.

The Material Establishments of the City Where Expression Is Most Intensely Realized

It is not my intention to offer a catalogue of the elite retail business world of the city but to analyze only diagnostic examples of class adaptation to city living. The most economic way to undertake this task is to categorize the establishments that—consistently and assiduously patronized by the city's superordinately placed—have the most expressive value for the goods and services they provide. Three caveats focus the analysis. First, in managing the city today there are basically no significant differences among the three components of the superordinate class. Second, what individuals may have learned or acquired abroad (in Europe or the United States) about satisfying their needs and expressive inclinations is internalized in the local context of the city, which until less than a generation ago was dominated by the tastes, proclivities, and drives for display of the aristocracy. A third caveat that must be kept in mind is that I am exclusively concerned with the socially upwardly mobile and not with the plutocratic rich and powerful who have elected to remain close to their usually original humble roots.

There are six types of establishments that have the most expressive value, centered on the following activities: clothing, food consumption, party giving, home entertaining, interior decoration and antique stores, and wedding celebrations and the churches where the religious ceremony takes place.

While clothing is one of the most important and extensive expressive domains, much of it is purchased abroad, as this is a much traveled class. There are, of course, many fine fashion shops, clothing stores, and accessory stores that are patronized for average consumption. Most of the well-known European and American fashion houses for women have stores in the city; but men's clothing is mostly custom made, and there are several tailor shops that cater to the usually well-dressed male.

Several elite food stores are patronized by the superordinately placed, including pastry shops, confectionery shops, delicatessens, liquor stores, and so on. These establishments cater not only to the everyday needs of plutocratic, aristocratic, and upper-middle class families but to special occasions such as birthdays, christening, first communions, cocktail parties, and other celebrations of a social and business nature. They are the sources satisfying the necessities of every aspect of the active home entertaining that goes on throughout the year. There are also three traditional catering services that can be hired to arrange and provide all the food and drink that is required for a celebration, from a wedding for 1,000 people to small cocktail party of a few dozen.

Interior decoration businesses and stores are a special case. While aristocrats may buy the finest materials (from curtains and carpets to all kinds of accessories) from these establishments for the decoration of the house's public domain, they would never deign to employ an interior decorator to appoint a new house or redecorate an old one. Indeed, many male and female aristocrats consider themselves experts in interior decoration, and some of them occasionally make it a business to decorate the houses of the new rich. Thus the employment of interior decorators is a business that caters almost exclusively to plutocrats and members of the upper-middle class. Antique stores, by contrast, are patronized by all three sectors, in addition to a small segment of the educated middle class. This is particularly the case with stores that specialize in colonial furniture, paintings, and a rather extensive array of items for household decoration and display. This is an expressive activity that has become widespread among the educated of all classes but especially among the superordinately placed.

Weddings, and the churches in which they take place, are an important expressive concern for all classes of society; and their importance increases upward in the social scale. Since colonial times aristocrats and plutocratic magnates have vied for the most architecturally distinguished churches in Mexico City, including the cathedral, to hold weddings. This has been a constant until the present; and in any given generation two or three churches in the city and its environs have become fashionable and highly sought out. Occasionally there is intense competition to secure these churches for the weddings of the scions of the city's privileged families, particularly in early fall and late spring, when most prominent weddings take place. Since World War II a few modern churches have become fashionable, but the lure of the old baroque churches still attracts the most competition for their use.

The wedding celebration ranks as the most important social event in the life cycle, and this frequently economically onerous occasion is again common to all classes of society. Indeed, comparatively speaking, the lower one goes in the social scale, the more onerous weddings become. Among the privileged of the city, aristocrats are the most affected economically, since the majority of them are not sufficiently wealthy to defray the exorbitant expense of a traditional wedding. Nonetheless, most aristocratic weddings are still large and expensive affairs, which take a significant toll on the finances of the average family. This is particularly the case when aristocratic women marry plutocratic men, a trend which has significantly increased during the past fifteen years. For this occasion aristocrats are loath to lose face and go to extremes to put on a good front. Plutocrats, in turn, "tiran la casa por la ventana" (throw the house out the window), as the saying goes, and often spend hundreds of thousands of dollars. These social events are the most elaborate gatherings in the social life of the city's privileged, sometimes including more than 1,500 guests, and they are duly reported in the press with great fanfare. Upper-middle-class families, many of them fairly rich, follow suit; but many which are not so affluent "empeñan hasta la camisa" (pawn even their shirts) to put on a brilliant wedding. Weddings for the privileged are more than tradition: they are nowadays, and have been for a generation, the most important social milieu, which brings together aristocrats, plutocrats, and the upper-middle class.

While many wedding celebrations still take place in the palatial country places of plutocrats and occasionally in the more modest country abodes of aristocrats, the majority take place in the best hotels, some of the finest restaurants with extended accommodations, or the three catering establishments mentioned above. Elite weddings involve a small industry: selection of locales, preparation and serving of food and liquor, flowers and decorations, music, and so on. In addition, there are the traditional events that precede the wedding celebration itself, which add significantly more expenses and the social involvements of hundreds of people: the banquet that accompanies the civil wedding, usually two or three showers, and assorted cocktail parties for social as well as business reasons. The wedding celebration is not only the most significant event in the life cycle but the most visible complex in the subcultural milieu of the superordinately placed that—discharged in mostly public accommodations—enhances the recognition of this group mostly by the middle classes of the city.

There is a second group of establishments with much expressive significance, associated with the following activities: attending sports, the theater, museums, art galleries, concerts and operas, and tea rooms as well as attending the inauguration of places of business, fashion shows, equestrian events, and charity affairs.

Significant differences exist among aristocrats, plutocrats, and upper-middle-class people in their engagement in sports; and age is a more important consideration than in the first group of activities. Polo, for example, used to be played by both plutocrats and aristocrats; but for economic reasons the latter have almost completely dropped out. Equitation, by contrast, continues to be practiced by both, as well as by considerable numbers of the upper-middle class. But, as I indicated above, these sports are played exclusively in private, restricted clubs. Golf, in contrast, is practiced by few aristocrats but is extremely popular among plutocrats and upper-middle-class people. Skiing, which involves travel to Europe or the United States, is mostly in the purview of plutocrats, but a considerable number of the most affluent aristocrats and upper-middle-class families also ski. The most popular sports practiced by all three sectors of the privileged are tennis, swimming, sailing and motor scooting, canoeing, and gymnastics. *Charrería* (Mexican style horseback riding) is a special case. This is a traditional sport that had been decaying since the last two decades of Porfirian times. Shortly after the Revolution it was revitalized by a group of prominent aristocrats, and the affair was widely reported in newspapers and magazines. They became highly visible in many circles of Mexico City, and the late 1940s was the last time a significant sector of the aristocracy was in the limelight and highly visible to the people at large. It goes without saying that (with the exceptions mentioned above) these sports are largely practiced in clubs and facilities open to everyone who can pay—there is no exclusivity involved.

All facilities involving music, the theater, the graphic arts, and the consumption of food and drink are potentially open to anyone who is sufficiently affluent, and again exclusivity is out of the question. Attendance at fashion shows and the inauguration of elite places of business, however, does have exclusive elements that preselect for power and wealth (plutocrats), residual prestige (aristocrats), and enough males and females sufficiently afflu-ent to serve as decoration (upper-middle-class personnel). The inauguration of places of business includes restaurants, boutiques, and specialty stores, which are sometimes owned by aristocrats but mostly by upper-middle-class business leaders. The inauguration is always accompanied by a cocktail party and occasionally by a dinner party, and it is advantageous for all concerned to have as many aristocrats and plutocrats as possible to lend distinction. At-tending fashion shows, by contrast, is an expressive occasion most actively centered on plutocrats, who are the owners of the department stores where they take place. Aristocrats and upper-middle-class personnel serve as the trimmings that give luster to this more business-like activity.

These affairs are reported in the daily press and constitute another venue of visibility for the privileged sector of the city. For aristocrats and pluto-crats, who generally wish to live as anonymously as possible, visibility is a mixed blessing; most members of the upper-middle class, however, welcome visibility and publicity as a significant aspect of their upwardly mobile so-cial aspiration, that is, the aura of superordination that accrues by being seen with the socially prominently and the rich and powerful. Attending charity and particularly equestrian events for aristocrats and plutocrats generates the highest degree of satisfaction in public presentation of the self, while for the upper-middle class such participation (that is, hobnobbing with aristocrats and plutocrats) is probably the most important expressive reward in the game of upward mobility.

There is a third group of establishments with medium expressive signifi-cance, associated with the following activities: nightclubbing, slumming, the culture of the body, body adornment, traveling, continuing education, and hunting and firearms. In all these activities there is a significant degree of variation, but all three superordinate groups exhibit a core of expressive real-ization that was originally at the center of the aristocratic array, which has now become part of the acculturative complex of the city's privileged.

Nightclubbing among urban aristocrats was a significant expressive ac-tivity until the late 1950s, when there were several quite exclusive, sedate establishments catering to the city's *haute bourgeoisie*, then in its most inten-sive stage of expressive acculturation. Now that both aristocrats and pluto-crats have basically gone underground, nightclubbing is primarily an upper-middle-class activity. Slumming, by contrast, is still somewhat part of the aristocratic worldview of the city: a kind of proprietary remembrance of the social control that aristocrats once so thoroughly exercised. (This is a good example of an expressive involvement that assuages the loss of a vanished way of life: behavior that can no longer be played out becomes a sort of game.) For example, after attending an important ball, nightclub, or early-morning social function, parties of several people would have a very late supper or very early breakfast in traditional cafes in the colonial section of the city. Until a generation ago it was almost *de rigueur* for early morning parties to end the evening with a tour of the Plaza Garibaldi, where the mariachi musicians of the city congregated. Particularly the Salon México (Aaron Copland's "El Salón México" was based on the music played there) was a magnet for aristocrats and a wide spectrum of the city's population. The night spot is now gone, and so is the ambiance in which the most diverse segments of the population interacted smoothly, according to the traditional Mexican dictum of "juntos pero no revueltos."

The culture of the body and body adornment entail several considerations that affect the behavior of the *haute bourgeoisie* as a whole and business establishments that cater to it. The realization of these domains is virtually identical for aristocrats, plutocrats, and the upper-middle class. Briefly stated, personal hygiene and the maintenance of the body according to certain standards of pulchritude are universal among the privileged. Aristocrats may have been the main carriers of these practices since early colonial times, but this cultural substratum is also present in several sectors of Mexican society. There is almost a fixation with personal cleanliness, affecting both men and women. People bathe daily, use a profusion of deodorants, and are always properly dressed. One often hears derogatory remarks about how dirty many Europeans are and how badly they smell. It is difficult to establish with certainty where this concern with cleanliness comes from, but it probably is rooted in pre-Hispanic culture, so much concerned with both ritual and physical cleanliness.

The culture of body adornment is highly developed, and women in particular are very conscious of their appearance, constantly striving to be up to date in the fashions of hairstyling, jewelry, and the use of the latest cosmetics. There are no exact standardized styles, but only the insistence that women look chic and properly groomed. Great emphasis is also placed on women's accessories (jewelry, shoes, handbags, scarves, gloves, and so on), and their styles, colors, and materials. For example, it is of prime importance for a woman to wear the right combination of shoes, handbag, and dress with the appropriately matching gloves and scarf. There is a great deal of focus on silk scarves, fine leather shoes and handbags, and so on. It is not pertinent at this point to detail all possible combinations, but women think that accessories are of paramount importance to the elegantly dressed woman that they always strive to be. Jewelry for women is another item of adornment that occupies a very special place in this domain of expression, ranging from heirlooms to contemporary items bought abroad or in a few well-known city stores. By contrast, although men are also concerned with projecting an image of elegance and are always properly attired, they are more conservative than women when it comes to personal adornment. For example, with the exception of rings, tie pins, and exceptionally fine watches, men do not wear jewelry.

Traveling abroad and in Mexico is an important aspect of the yearly cycle of the *haute bourgeoisie* and is closely associated with several elite travel agencies. Hunting abroad is almost exclusively associated with plutocrats. Big-game hunting trips are organized to different parts of the world, which may last for months and require much organization. On a more modest scale, hunting is still part of the aristocratic tradition, and many young and middle-aged men and occasionally women engage in hunting domestic birds (dove, quail, snipe, duck, geese) and game (deer, bear, armadillo) several times a year. Both aristocratic and plutocratic families may have excellent firearms collections, including shotguns, rifles, hunting rifles, and handguns. Several aristocratic families have superb hunting firearm collections of Belgium and British origin (Jeffries, Azcuant, Berno). As an important complement to hunting, there is a complex of dress and equipment, constituting an extensive array by itself. On a smaller scale, members of the upper-middle class also engage in hunting as an activity with significant expressive value.

Continuing education is almost exclusively an activity of women. Most young and early middle-age women (roughly thirty to forty-five) are college graduates, most commonly in psychology and art history, and some have professional degrees. After a woman has settled into married life and has borne the number of children she and her husband have planned (usually two or three), she often engages in some form of continuing education. Perhaps as many as 50 percent of all married women either take music and painting lessons from individual artists and academies or more formally enroll in specially designed programs in philosophy, art history, literature, music, and religion in the best private universities of Mexico City. Aristocratic, plutocratic, and upper-middle-class women generally are diligent in their studies but do not aim at securing higher degrees. Continuing education is basically an expressive activity that provides significant meaning to the inordinate amount of leisure time that elite women have.

Managing the megalopolis with restricted economic means is an apt characterization of the aristocracy when compared with the very rich plutocracy and the rich to affluent upper-middle class. In material and economic terms, the aristocracy is not a meaningful distinct category, and it has to be placed in the context of the other two sectors of the *haute bourgeoisie*. Here, as in many subsequent ethnographic-expressive contexts, the best way to make sense of this vanishing but still self-defining sector of the *haute bourgeoisie* is to analyze the aristocracy as a constituent part of a larger social category.

Expressive Analysis

·

Methodological and Analytical Notes

Defining expression is somewhat like defining time in Saint Augustine's philosophy: "'What, then, is time?' he asks. 'If no one asks me, I know; if I wish to explain to him who asks, I know not'" (Russell 1945:354). This has been my quandary since I became aware of the role of expression in the conceptualization of many aspects of culture: I know what it is, I ostensibly can identify it, but I cannot entirely define it and establish its operational relationship to the structure of manifold social phenomena. Before analyzing the data that have so far been presented, I discuss several issues here that were not entirely clear or were not addressed in my original statement on what the role of expression is in cultural analysis (Nutini 1988:377–397).

The basic vocabulary of expression was established by John Roberts and his collaborators (Roberts 1976; Roberts, Chiao, and Pandey 1975; Roberts and Chick 1979; Roberts and Natrass 1980; Roberts and Sutton-Smith 1962): domain, array, style, involvement, and so on. These categories are sufficient for an initial analysis of expression, and I have employed them in two of my studies (Nutini 1988, 1995). But the work of Roberts and his associates— fundamental as it was for bringing to the fore the role of expression in the description and explanation of social and cultural phenomena—is limiting, to the extent that they were almost exclusively concerned with very specific contexts (games, sports, and self-contained activities such as pantheons of gods, machine shops, combat flying, and so on). In an effort to pick up where W. Lloyd Warner (1942, 1957, 1959, 1961, 1963) and earlier students of expression (Allen 1935; Amory 1947; Ashburn 1944) left off, I widened the analysis of expression to include broad social domains that seemed to have a significant expressive component. First, I established that the defining characteristic of expressive culture is its noninstrumentality, that is, it represents an end in itself. This statement may be misinterpreted as saying that all culture is divided into instrumental and noninstrumental. This is decidedly not the case and needs clarification. Second, I identified basically three types of environments in which expression is realized (primarily expressive, at times expressive and at times instrumental, primarily instrumental). This categorization also needs clarification. Third, ostensively and intuitively I identified three types of expression, which I called natural or inherent, conflictual, and terminal. This typology is obviously incomplete, and there are other kinds that must be identified to advance the study of expressive culture. I aim to expand my original formulation by reexamining the relationship of expressive culture to the structural domains in which expression is realized.

A good starting point is to determine what expressive culture is and what it is not. Let us start with the latter. First, utilitarian-nonutilitarian distinctions are ontologically misleading, but such distinctions share clarifying value. The total ensemble of social action and cultural phenomena cannot be divided into patterns, activities, and domains that either have pragmatic value or represent ends in themselves. This is a false dichotomy. Epistemologically, though, it makes sense to distinguish between the utilitarian and nonutilitarian, because it forces one to determine the circumstances, contexts, and motivations that make behavior pragmatic or expressive. This is the crux of expressive analysis: to account for the motivation behind any behavior or action that cannot be accounted for by the effect of structural (ostensibly material) variables.

I am, of course, assuming that there are many kinds of behavior that cannot be understood or explained by structural or ideological variables alone. It goes without saying that if this premise is denied, then there is no such a thing as expression: what is called expressive behavior is caused by specific material conditions or the superstructures that these material conditions cause or provoke (ideology, values, worldview, and other cultural constructs). None of these constructs, for example, can entirely account for how one chooses a profession, why groups with the same economic and social configuration have different expressive styles, which strategies people employ in the acquisition of power and wealth, or (fundamentally related to this study) why in two and a half millennia of Western stratification—and possibly in all civilized traditions—the expressive culture of the aristocracy has been the magnet of superordinate upward mobility.

The most difficult task in the analysis of expression is to isolate what is pragmatic and what is an end in itself in understanding or explaining cultural patterns, activities, and domains. The reason for this is that expression is at once contextual and contextually defined and created. Thus expression may take place in any domain of culture, contextualized by time and space. It is equally true, however, that expressive behavior is generated by specific historical circumstances of an economic, social, political, and religious nature. In other words, contextualized expression is a universal phenomenon manifested in varying sectors of culture. In Western society the locus of contextualized expression is most naturally associated with sports, the arts, and some domains of religion and social organization, while in other societies it is possible to visualize quite different loci of realization. In this study, as a means of conceptualizing superordinate stratification and mobility, we are not so much concerned with universal, contextualized expression but with historically generated and contextually created expression.

Expression, as the concept is employed in this book, is an aspect of individual action but always within specific social milieux. Though expressive behavior has a psychological component, its collective realization makes it a cultural construct. As such, expression is a construct in the same class as ideology, belief systems (values), and worldview but a distinct species. Unlike ideology, expression does not entail any efficacy—that is, moral constraints, imperatives to action, and value directives. Unlike a belief system it does not generate any "thou shalts" or "thou shalt nots"; and unlike the *imago mundi* of a social group, expression does not set the guidelines and parameters for interpreting the world. Expression or expressive behavior comprises those aspects of culture that are not grounded on or able to be concretized by material constraints, demographic considerations, and adaptations to natural environments. Given these premises, expression may be defined as a necessary component of culture that conditions behavior regardless of cultural content but contextualized in a specific time and space. Specifying the conditions of time and space, then, becomes the cornerstone of expressive analysis. This operation permits us to establish the contextual realization of expression—that is, why a certain behavior or activity is at times utilitarian while at others nonutilitarian; and more importantly, it allows us to determine the consequences that follow from individual and collective action.

Finally, the expressive analysis of the following chapters has two explicit conceptual aims: to elaborate on conflictual and terminal expression in the context of aristocratic decline since the Mexican Revolution and to identify derivative types of expression in this social class throughout its inception, development, and decline. This extended exercise also aims to assess the relationship of expression to style, personality profile, individuality, and collective manifestation.

The Aristocratic Realization of Expression in the Declining and Changing Urban Context

Expressive realization is always posited on concrete social and economic historical conditions. For the Mexican aristocracy such conditions remained constant from its inception in the second half of the sixteenth century until the Revolution of 1910. Thus the expressive culture of the aristocracy today is a consequence of the enormous changes provoked by the Revolution. The expressive changes that have taken place during the past three generations are the result of the accommodations that aristocrats have had to make in order to survive as a social group, even though they realize that they are little more than a self-defined class exhibiting minimal recognition from other sectors of society. From this standpoint, the exclusive expressive life of the aristocracy has been confined to the household and kindred domains.

Before the Revolution of 1910 the aristocratic household was important but by no means the centerpiece of the expressive array of the aristocracy. Given the dominance that the aristocracy exercised in many aspects of Mexican society, this preeminent position was vested in the public persona that the class projected into the urban and rural contexts. Thus the overwhelming importance of the aristocratic household today may be regarded as a compensating mechanism for the great loss of public recognition that its members received from all sectors of society. The same is true of the country place as a continuing remainder of the hacienda as the landed source of aristocratic identification.

In fact, the retreat from an outward, public to an inward, private expressive emphasis is encapsulated by the symbol of the household as a shrine to the ancestors, which is marked by the changes from the central-city mansion to the *casa porfiriana* to the less elaborate modern household, from hacienda manor to country retreat, and including all modifications in the appointment and decoration of these abodes. Thus viewing the household as a shrine to the ancestors (and its symbolic extensions) is a more charitable way of saying that the household is really a shrine to "ego" (in the anthropological usage of the term). That is, the living aristocrats in the household (totally constrained by an *imago mundi* specifying that they are still the best born and as such deserve recognition from all sectors of society) are assuaged by these expressive involvements; or as John Roberts and Brian Sutton-Smith (1962:176) would put it, they engage in an expressive game designed to palliate conflict between the real world and what individuals think their position in the real world "should be."

From a psychological viewpoint, the household is a shrine to the self of aristocrats trying to maintain their sense of continuity with the past in a social environment that they perceive as hostile. The household as a shrine concretizes this struggle of an idealized self-image that needs to be sustained by attributes outside the psychological self for which the household serves well. It is a perfectly controlled mirroring environment. The household as a mirror of bygone greatness asserts aristocratic status identity much better than any psychological subterfuge that aristocrats may possibly engage in. The new social world of which they are part does not function as a mirror because the reflected image is that of a largely irrelevant relic individually and as a class. Consequently, the importance of the household as a shrine to the ancestors (a social representation complementary to its psychological interpretation as a shrine to ego) in the twentieth century increases in direct proportion to the decline of the aristocracy as a social class.

The household as a shrine to the ancestors is the best example of a historically contextualized construct that came into being as a result of specific economic and social changes in the global society in which the Mexican aristocracy is embedded. Also, the household as a shrine to the ancestors is individually and collectively a good example of the consequences that follow from the contextual realization of this expressive domain: a new expressive domain comes into existence (the household as a shrine to the ancestors), which in turn triggers new expressive behavior and action (the redefinition of the concept of the heirloom, the intensification of household decoration, the drive and creativity in generating new inventories of fine arts and crafts, the endogenous quest for self-assuagement, and the exogenous drive for social recognition through expressive display). Indeed, a case can be made that the most important expressive domains that aristocrats have engaged in since the Mexican Revolution entail similar social and symbolic consequences: palliating loss of status and wealth, generating continuity with the past as reaffirming status identity, and struggling for superordinate recognition in a world beyond their control. In the remainder of the analysis I emphasize the most salient domains of expression and the behavior that they engender.

The institution of the heirloom is crucial in understanding aristocratic mentality today. The heirloom is the single most diagnostic symbol of the downward transformation of the aristocracy in the twentieth century. It encapsulates the quiet despair of aristocratic families in coming to terms with the position to which they have been reduced during the past two generations. Prisoners of an ideology and worldview that constrains them from making the transition to a more *haute-bourgeois* existence, most aristocratic adults do not seem to generate enough creativity to effectively engage the "real" world in which they live, in order to achieve recognition according to the rules of the new superordinate game. Instead, whatever creativity and effort they manage to muster is directed to "unreal," traditional pursuits, of which heirlooms and the household are the focal points. This inwardly directed preoccupation distracts most aristocrats from becoming more acculturated to bourgeois ways and making their way in the world in plutocratic terms. Some liberal aristocrats realize that this is the only "rational" strategy to stay on top of the stratification scale: generate sufficient wealth to regain some of the recognition that was their birthright and pursue a life more in accordance with their former exalted status. This is the fundamental predicament that paralyzes most aristocrats, and the source of the expressive games they play: psychologically unable to make the transition to the real world of the present, they retreat to the glories of the past as a palliative for their inability to change.

The irony of this predicament is that most aristocrats, even the most recalcitrant conservatives, are well aware of what is involved in both remaining true to old aristocratic values and traditions and taking the acculturative plutocratic road. This is accurately voiced by a conservative aristocrat in the following terms:

> I have no illusions that the group [code word used by aristocrats to refer to themselves] will recapture our brilliant past, not even the position that we had in the late forties. We will soon disappear, and this is inevitable. The majority of families with whom I interact are faithful to their traditions; there is something very deep that prevents us from changing and acquiring a more congruent mentality with the style of things nowadays. On the other hand, there are many families that already behave almost like the new rich [deprecatory term occasionally used by aristocrats to refer to plutocrats] and imitate them in many things that are incompatible with the aristocratic way of being. My case is typical among the more conservative people. I have in my house things of much value, but it would never occur to me to sell them in order to capitalize a business enterprise, as I know several people from the group have done. When this mentality becomes generalized, our group will have come to an end.

This statement clearly expresses the inability of most aristocrats to change and adapt to new conditions (or, in Pareto's [1935:79] terms, to innovate creatively to stay at the top), the belated and not very creative willingness of considerable numbers of aristocrats to adapt, and the young being wholeheartedly coopted by the plutocracy. Moreover, the statement is a microcosm of the contemporary tendencies that characterize the terminal decline of the aristocracy, marked by social retrenchment and expressive retreat.

Let us examine several domains described above in order to determine expressive commitments that generate specific behaviors and actions or illuminate the individual nature of expression. First, overconcern with expression is a characteristic of Western aristocracies that increases in direct proportion to their loss of power and wealth. This process begins first with the onset of absolutism (ca. 1500) when their political power became increasingly vested in the Crown, and by the early eighteenth century they had ceased to be politically significant as an estate in society. This process resulted in much loss of wealth, as aristocrats, as a class, were never able to make the transition from landed to industrial and banking wealth. By the end of the nineteenth century, Western aristocracies were essentially expressive social entities in a world increasingly dominated by the plutocracy. In a nutshell, the loss of power and wealth is what increasingly propels aristocracies to emphasize expression, as a substitute for the exercise of economic and political power. This is the inevitable result of the predicament that when individuals and groups are too busy with the exercise of power and control there is less concern with expressive activities in order to perpetuate superordinate standing. The Mexican aristocracy, of course, is nothing more than a belated example of what the European aristocracies began to experience over a century earlier.

Take, for example, the fact that since the onset of class stratification roughly 200 years ago superordinate standards of elegance and taste in a large array of cultural domains have been aristocratic. There is no necessary or rational reason for this phenomenon, except that as the result of a long historical tradition these standards became the only model to be emulated by the upwardly mobile. As aristocrats lost power and control, they consciously cultivated traditional standards of behavior and action, thereby reinforcing the model as a surrogate for real exchange of material wealth. Cognitively, of course, it is beyond the scope of my competence as an anthropologist to ascertain why certain combinations of colors, mixtures of appointments, and arrangements of decorations in a household are elegant and tasteful.

Yet the cognitive aspects of the Mexican aristocratic household have explicit sociological meanings that can be handled fairly precisely and objectively. Take, for example, the combination of colors in the decoration of the household. This is a mixture of a perceptual code that probably applies to all classes of Western society and historically developed combinations peculiar to the aristocracy. The combinations of colors favored and most extensively used by, say, North Americans, Italians, and Spaniards differ greatly from the combinations of the Japanese. One would not expect to see mixtures of greens, reds, and grays in the fabrics of furniture and curtains of the aristocratic household, a pattern that is the norm and highly regarded in Japanese kimonos and screens but is offensive to Western taste in its own decorative settings. Complementarily, however, certain combinations of colors and shades are exclusive to the aristocratic household and the result of a long historical process (the Spanish tradition going back to the sixteenth century, some pre-Hispanic inputs, and more recently French and Italian influences). Thus the color combinations in the decoration of the aristocratic household today are the result of these two processes. Ultimately, of course, the validation of the color code is simply the expressive superordination enjoyed by the aristocracy for such a long time, which does not seem to have been challenged by the plutocracy or for that matter by any sector of Western society.

Second, slumming is a trivial expressive domain but highly diagnostic of conflictual expression as the result of drastic economic change. One of the most significant aspects of expression is individuality: individuals and groups striving for distinction and differentiation from others in order to achieve a higher place in the pecking order or to draw boundaries between me and you, us and them. Socially and psychologically, there is no difference between street gangs who wear certain apparel or hairdos as emblems distinguishing themselves from other gangs and Mexican aristocrats who conceive of the household as a shrine to the ancestors to assert their distinctness and social superiority over plutocrats. It is exactly in this context, but with an added component, that one can explain slumming among aristocrats until recently. Basically, as I indicated above, slumming survived as a symbolic activity of the social control of the city that aristocrats had for more than a generation after the Mexican Revolution. But the sufficient reason for the survival of this expressive array is the fact that plutocrats (for reasons of economic security) and members of the upper-middle class (for reasons of social insecurity) do not engage in slumming. As a kind of perverse volte-face (considering that they no longer have any social control over the city), aristocrats continued to slum in order to draw another differentiating boundary between them and the rest of the superordinate sector of society. Thus slumming is an expressive domain that enhances distinctiveness and exclusivity, another significant attribute of expression. This is one more example of the vagaries of the eternal pecking order that still characterizes superordinate stratification and is so well embodied in expressive behavior.

Third, of the three clusters of expressive domains discussed in the foregoing section, continuing education as a way for aristocratic women to spend leisure time is the clearest example of individual expressive behavior discharged in a well-bounded social context. Aristocratic women do not need and do not usually aim at a degree, and continuing education must be primarily regarded as nonutilitarian. It may be argued that this expressive activity has the aim of enhancing display (that is, projecting a more "cultured" image); this is true, of course, but it is a derived utilitarian activity beyond the original semantic field. More significant is the nature of the subjects that women most often take up, namely, history and psychology. History deals with the past and its greatness, which fits in well with an expressive orientation that was always there but has been so much enhanced since the beginning of aristocratic decline. And this is another significant attribute of the expressive culture of a well-bounded group or class: the strong tendency of the global array toward congruency, that is, that specific domains tend to become an expression of the same worldview, even during periods of change or transition. Psychology is concerned with the splendors of the mind, a noble but useless study, especially without a degree. Aimed at realizing some personal desire or aspiration, studying psychology becomes an end in itself, regardless of the fact that it may bring the added dividend of projecting a more knowledgeable image. The same can be said about the studies of philosophy, music appreciation, and art appreciation that aristocratic women also occasionally take up. Continuing education, then, is an expressive activity that fulfills an individual need but congruent with expressive adaptations that the aristocracy has had to undertake in order to maintain its identity in a changing stratification system.

Finally, I briefly return to the concept of expressive vicariousness, inasmuch as it affects the entire superordinate class and how it is perceived by other classes of Mexican society. The concept has two aspects: vicarious perception and vicarious attraction. These are complementary aspects; they bring together class mobility and class recognition and define the social pecking order. Expressive vicariousness is not a domain but a proclivity, which appears to be universal in Western society: the strong tendency of most people in a class or significant social grouping to aspire to a higher position in the pecking order. (This is a highly likely assumption—axiom, if you will—without which much of the work on stratification done during the past century would not entirely make sense. At least in superordinate stratification, upward mobility cannot be entirely explained without assuming expressive vicariousness.) The syndrome is a basically expressive construct because its primary motivation is almost invariably nonutilitarian, although it evidently leads to utilitarian consequences. In this scheme of things, expressive attraction is one of the main mechanisms of social mobility once most plutocrats have achieved a level of wealth, and the aristocratic way of life becomes the model to emulate. It is thus in the context of vicarious perceptions that vicarious attraction is realized. This conception of class and mobility, it seems to me, is more consonant with the manifold facts of stratification than the classification based solely on wealth and other so-called objective criteria.

CHAPTER 5

ᘐ

ECONOMY, MATERIAL CULTURE, AND POLITICAL PARTICIPATION

ᘐ

It is difficult to characterize the aristocracy as a distinct segment of the Mexican superordinate stratification system in terms of material culture and its economic base, except, of course, for the household and other core elements of the aristocracy (as analyzed in Chapter 4). Politically, however, the aristocracy is a distinct, if insignificant, social group; only during the past generation have considerable numbers of its members engaged in tangible action. In this chapter I contrast the organization of material culture, economic activities, and political involvement that characterize the three main sectors of the *haute bourgeoisie*, focusing on the aristocracy.

The Distinctive and Shared Material Culture of the Aristocracy

While power and wealth, or lack thereof, determine the position and expressive array of all classes in society, it is the configuration of material culture that most characteristically defines them. Thus it is common for two classes to have similar wealth and the same economic base and yet quite different expressive arrays. Even more commonly, classes with different degrees of wealth and economic bases may have similar expressive arrays. In both cases the difference or similarity is largely conditioned by the way in which wealth is used to generate particular ensembles of material culture. It should be emphasized that historical antecedents largely determine differences, while similarities are mostly the result of conditions of rapid change.

The Distinctive Traditional and Idiosyncratic Character
of the Aristocratic Material Array

Chapter 4 captures the fundamental elements of the "affective" material baggage of aristocrats as centered on the household, the city-country axis, and their overwhelming concern with justifying their belief that they are still the best in society. Nothing more needs to be said about these matters, except that they basically define the material distinctiveness of the aristocracy. Other aspects of the aristocracy's material life also contribute to its distinctiveness, however; and from an ethnographic standpoint, the aristocracy is worth describing in terms of Mexico's recent cultural history.

There are a number of ethnographic environments and practices that underlie several distinct complexes that perhaps three generations ago the aristocracy shared with various sectors of Mexican society—now disappearing from the urban environment across much of the stratification spectrum and in short supply in the material culture of the superordinately placed. The most salient of these are the preservation of traditional Mexican cuisine; a pervasive dichotomy between festive (ceremonial) and daily consumption of food; a consistent concern with ritualism and ceremonialism as part of the material celebration of sacred and secular festivities; a deeply ingrained sense of reciprocity and exchange; and a pronounced emphasis on protocol and etiquette. These complexes exemplify significant changes in material culture that Mexican society has experienced during the past seventy-five years. Let us analyze them in some detail.

First, the common conception of Mexican cuisine in the United States is a combination of a few folk dishes and recipes (mostly from central and northern Mexico, such as mole poblano, frijoles refritos, guacamole, fajitas, etc.) and traditional snacks (such as tacos, enchiladas, and tamales, which are now part of the English language but denote full-blown dishes, at least as they are listed in restaurants' menus). This is a poor conception of Mexican cuisine, which is highly diversified, includes several regional variants, and deserves the appellation of *haute cuisine*. Sadly, however, traditional Mexican cuisine greatly declined throughout the twentieth century, particularly since the 1940s. I attribute the decline mainly to labor-intensiveness of Mexican cuisine and the tremendous process of urbanization that the country has experienced since World War II. In urban environments, particularly in Mexico City, traditional cuisine has become standardized and simplified; ironically, its perception has become North Americanized. Undoubtedly a significant percentage of urban households spanning the middle and upper-middle stratification spectrum occasionally taste the delights of traditional Mexican *haute cuisine*. But the time-consuming effort of preparing traditional recipes and the uprooting effects of urbanization have nearly destroyed this culinary tradition.

In middle- and upper-middle-class households, the daily and festive cuisine has been "Europeanized." To be sure, the consumption of tortillas, beans prepared in different ways, and snacks (*antojitos*) and time-honored forms of cooking are still practiced, but the cuisine is no longer basically Mexican. Almost vestigially, to celebrate a special occasion a fine traditional recipe is prepared. In the public domain the situation is not much different. While there are still a few restaurants specializing in traditional regional cuisine, most restaurants in Mexico City (and in all large provincial cities) may be described as serving variants and combinations of continental cuisine (mostly French, Italian, and Spanish). It should be noted, however, that during the past decade there has been a renaissance of Mexican *haute cuisine*, and some of Mexico City's best and most expensive restaurants have revived a traditional cuisine that goes back to colonial times.[1]

Moreover, these restaurants are almost exclusively patronized by the superordinately placed and by foreign tourists. In summary, Mexican *haute cuisine* is almost a forgotten craft among the affluent sectors of Mexican society. As far as I am aware, the only exception to this generalization is among the majority of aristocratic households.

This is not to say that the majority of aristocratic households enjoy a steady diet of Mexican *haute cuisine*. Rather, this culinary craft is kept alive as a family tradition for festive and special occasions. Ideologically, *haute cuisine* is another way for aristocrats to underscore their individuality, Mexican traditionalism, and distinctiveness from the other sectors of the *haute bourgeoisie*. This is well exemplified by a 65-year-old female informant:

> Many ignorant and prejudiced people accuse us [aristocrats] of never having been entirely Mexican. But we are the depositories of many Mexican traditions that are on the verge of disappearing. Take, for example, traditional Mexican cuisine. There are no restaurants nowadays [1983] that serve it, and as far as I know, even less in private homes. However, there are still many of us who strive to maintain the tradition alive. Not daily, but on many occasions throughout the year, traditional dishes are prepared that the great majority of Mexicans are no longer acquainted with even by name.

Aristocratic women are proud of their culinary expertise and quite often are reluctant to make their recipes available to others. Many of them keep extensive *recetarios* (recipe lists), and several have contributed recipes to general books on Mexican cooking in Spanish and English. Although aristocratic women do not prepare the daily meals of the household, on the festive occasions when *haute cuisine* is served they do the basic preparations, mix ingredients, and supervise every stage of preparing a meal. Indeed, many of these women would qualify as professional chefs in terms of their culinary imagination and the complexity and extent of their recipes.

Recipes of the *haute cuisine* practiced in aristocratic circles have three provenances. First, traditional recipes (many of them going back to colonial times) are compiled in household-bound volumes or nineteenth-century publications. The symbolic value of these dishes is considerable; they are highly prized and are served in the celebration of the most important social occasions, often to impress guests with the excellence of the host's knowledge of this almost forgotten craft. Second are regional recipes, reflecting the location where members of the household had a hacienda or the provincial city associated with it. Recipes in this category, as the name indicates, are part of the regional cuisine of Mexico. They have been somewhat modified, improving the quality of ingredients and changing the presentation for more elegant consumption. This category of dishes is the most commonly served for the celebration of the events associated with the annual life and religious cycles. Third are originally created recipes, the labor of the most enterprising hostesses. These are usually created by combining traditional and regional recipes with elements of French and Italian cuisine; they involve changes in ingredients and condiments, variations in the form of cooking, and more functional forms of presentation. Dishes in this category are served on a variety of occasions requiring a more elaborate meal than the family's daily fare. Of the entire ensemble of aristocratic *haute cuisine*, these recipes come closest to what the family eats daily.[2]

There is a public aspect of *haute cuisine* that is part of the aristocratic environment—namely, the three catering services in Mexico City that are often employed by aristocrats and plutocrats. Two of them are run by aristocratic women and provide a wide range of services: preparing and serving food for breakfasts, luncheons, and dinners in private residences for special occasions; preparing and serving the food for weddings, balls, and cocktail parties at hotels and other public accommodations; and in general organizing manifold social events involving the consumption of food. With the exception of the restaurants mentioned above, these catering services are the main public expression of *haute cuisine* associated with the aristocratic milieu.

Second, the aristocratic lifestyle exhibits a traditional concern with categorically distinguishing between festive and daily consumption of food and drink and the quality and circumstances in which they take place. Admittedly, these five domains are not quantitatively important in the overall configuration of the aristocracy's material culture, but they are qualitatively and symbolically important to understanding the relationship between the aristocracy and the other sectors of the *haute bourgeoisie*. Be this as it may, most well-bounded social groups make a distinction between festive and everyday contexts in the consumption of food and drink as well as in many other domains in the celebrations of manifold events of the life and ceremonial cycles. Essentially, however, the extent and circumstances that determine this widespread phenomenon are differentially salient. In this respect, the aristocracy is quite different from the plutocracy and the upper-middle class, with which it shares so many germane expressive domains.

Another way of stating this difference is that aristocrats are expressively closer to Indians and rural mestizos than to the other sectors of the *haute bourgeoisie* in their pervasive insistence on qualitatively and symbolically separating the festive from the daily. This syndrome extends beyond the consumption of food and drink, as we shall presently discuss. Aristocrats have a monotonic preoccupation with what food and drink should be served for every festive occasion of their extensive social and ritual annual calendar. This preoccupation determines the dishes that are *de rigueur*, the wines and liquors that go with it, the tableware to serve them, and a considerable array of accessories (tablecloths, napkins, place-mats, serving implements, etc.) that accompany an elegant, well-appointed table. Some of these implements acquire almost the status of heirlooms (as defined in Chapter 4), many of them have been in the family for generations, and the entire ensemble constitutes an important expressive domain. Cocktail parties, birthday celebrations, and balls as well as the celebrations ranging from christenings and confirmations to betrothals and weddings involve precise combinations of these elements. Most households adhere faithfully to these standards and take pride in upholding a tradition that they consider so much a part of aristocratic behavior. It also takes a significant economic toll in many families which do not have the affluence to comply with the standards pertaining to the food, drink, and costly manner of serving them, even if they have the implements with which to do so. Although plutocrats and affluent upper-middle-class Mexicans exhibit some concern with separating the festive from the daily, they are not nearly as compulsive as aristocrats are.

Third, in ritualism and ceremonialism aristocrats are again more akin to Indians than to plutocrats and the upper-middle class. This, of course, is part of the Western aristocratic tradition, which in Mexico was reinforced by inputs of pre-Hispanic origin and the seigneurial ambiance that characterized the aristocratic ruling class from its inception in the sixteenth century. While the aristocracy was dominant, these expressive traits had a positive effect on its role as the social ruling class of the country: it fostered the public image of aristocrats and enhanced vicarious perceptions that made it easier for them to control the masses. This is no longer the case today, since the aristocracy is a moribund social class. In fact, these traits have significant detrimental implications for aristocrats by further sapping their economic resources.

The ritualism and ceremonialism that characterize aristocratic behavior have two manifestations: personal and celebratory. Personal ceremonialism is manifested in exaggerated punctiliousness, particularly among men, and in efforts at projecting *gravitas* that occasionally verge on the comic. This behavior does not entail material culture implications, but it does offend plutocrats and upper-middle class Mexicans who come into contact with aristocrats. It should be noted, however, that only a small minority (no more than 10 percent of those classified as traditional conservatives) have not been able to divest themselves of this behavior, which the majority consider not only no longer consonant with their diminished status in society but counterproductive to presenting an appealing profile in their interaction with the new rich and powerful.

Celebratory ritualism, by contrast, is still generalized and entails material consequences that affect families at all levels of aristocratic affluence. Any important aristocratic celebration is pregnant with ritualism of execution and display: from the place in which it occurs and the paraphernalia associated with it to the material means and the personnel required to execute it traditionally. Regardless of the sacred or secular nature of the event, the symbolic and the material are interwoven for maximal effect in the display that is the desired end of most aristocratic celebrations. Indeed, in this context there is no difference between the sacred and the secular, as ritualism is believed to be a necessary element enhancing the effectiveness and elegance of all celebrations. This belief is deeply embedded in a worldview that casts aristocrats as ritual specialists, which further specifies that they are diminished in status when they do not comply with the traditional ritual requirements that accompany manifold celebrations. This is a powerful reinforcer of traditionalism, particularly when most aristocrats have little more they can hang onto than a sense of superordinate status. In other words, aristocratic identity in decline hinges largely on a fragile ideological foundation, which during the past three generations has been enough to sustain them but is now nearing the end of its usefulness. The ritualism that accompanies the manifold complex of celebrations is economically expensive and is seriously sapping the status identity of aristocrats.

Every time an aristocratic family cannot afford a traditional wedding (with all its symbolic paraphernalia and ritualism), it is an unmistakable sign of downward mobility and loss of standing. Many aristocrats are aware of this and understand the corrosive effect of lack of economic means to implement the most cherished injunctions of their *imago mundi*. Many struggle to stick to the notion that upholding celebratory ritual standards perpetuates aristocratic status; some withdraw into a subterranean existence divorced from the constraints of tradition by not engaging in celebratory activities, which literally drives them to live in a world of dreams about the past. An increasing number of aristocrats, however, have given up upholding ritual standards as an illusion; they realize the futility of the traditional strategy and do not squander economic resources. This group understands that the best way to remain an aristocrat, or at least to stay at the top of the social hierarchy, is to generate wealth at the expense of the aristocratic tradition. This strategy entails the essence of *embourgeoisement*, and a significant number of aristocrats in this mold are by now structurally indistinguishable from plutocrats. Predictably, plutocrats and aspiring upper-middle-class plutocrats have, for nearly a generation, been engaged in ceremonializing and ritualizing their individual behavior and celebratory engagements. They have learned the lesson well. This juncture is another example of the process of expressive acculturation that underlies the terminal relationship of plutocrats and aristocrats: the aristocrats' lack of wealth fosters *embourgeoisement*, whereas the plutocrats' great wealth leads to aristocratization.

Fourth, the context of reciprocity and exchange that characterizes many aspects of aristocratic life is also a traditional behavioral trait that entails material implications with deep roots in Mexican folk culture. Since its inception, the Mexican aristocracy has always been a small, tightly knit group. After the Mexican Revolution and the aristocracy's concentration in Mexico City, its cohesiveness decreased. Nonetheless, aristocrats have largely retained traditional patterns of reciprocity and exchange that characterize the aristocracy as a folklike group.

Reciprocity in this context means essentially the *quid pro quo* that characterizes a large number of aristocratic interactions ranging from invitations to celebrations (weddings, baptisms, and many others), special events (exhibitions, musical evenings, literary reunions), vacationing (country places, old haciendas), and more pragmatic transactions such as a wide range of social and economic favors and support for special occasions (sponsoring cultural events, charities, inauguration of business, and so on). I am not suggesting that the aristocracy in Mexico City entails quasi-corporate social and economic functions. Rather, reciprocity obtains at the level of the kindred and nonresidential extended family groups. All of these interactions and transactions involve significant outlets of material resources that on the whole have a beneficial effect, given the low level of aristocratic affluence compared to the other sectors of the *haute bourgeoisie*. For example, there is no comparable reciprocity at work among plutocrats and the rich upper-middle class. There is no need for it, since they can finance any action or satisfy most desires without the help that is inherently afforded by reciprocity.

By "exchange" I mean primarily the giving of gifts for a large roster of occasions and events in the religious and life cycles. The main occasions and events are baptism, confirmation, first communion, and marriage; birthday, saint's day, Christmas, Epiphany, and All Saints'/All Souls' Day; silver-wedding and gold-wedding anniversaries; high school, university, and graduate school graduation; and religious ordinations for priests and nuns.

Fifth, protocol and etiquette are complexes that stand at the heart of the expressive culture of all Western aristocracies. Deeply ingrained preoccupations with precedence, insistence on exacting (traditionally sanctioned) behavior, and a sense that every occasion (secular or sacred) entails specific forms of address and comportment have been the hallmark of aristocratic life. In the case of the Mexican aristocracy, protocol and etiquette today are a pale reflection of what they were until the Mexican Revolution. Nonetheless, aristocrats still exhibit a significant proclivity for these traditional standards of behavior that for the outsider may seem not only out of place but stilted and pretentious. This is the almost unanimous opinion of plutocrats, who, despite their upward aspirations, have not been entirely acculturated to this aristocratic proclivity.

There are many occasions that demand traditional protocol and etiquette that aristocrats are loath to discard in favor of more modern, functionally less expensive ways. The invariable result is that much time and many material resources are wasted in activities and behaviors that outsiders may find inimical to the moderate affluence of most aristocrats. The inside view, however, reveals a positive psychological function: engaging in traditional protocol and etiquette (however simplified and formulaic they may be today) reinforces their self-image as a distinct segment of superordinate society. Aristocrats believe that they are the supreme masters of social manners, mores, and appropriate behavior and that discharging these standards not only compensates for their loss of status but also ensures that they will survive a little longer as a segment of superordinate stratification.

Protocol among aristocrats denotes the procedure, form, and precedence that accompany social interaction, particularly in the context of social gatherings and important invitations to events in the life and annual cycles. Whether at a wedding or a dinner party there are always specific traditional procedures that dictate which people are invited, where they are seated, and how they are served. The function of protocol, as the term is usually understood, is not to denote individual rank or status but to create an ambiance (illusion) that suggests to participants that events of such brilliance or distinction can be executed only by aristocrats. In this and many other contexts, the fundamental motivation of aristocrats is symbolically to affirm their distinctiveness *vis-à-vis* all other segments of society, an aristocratic conceit as old as Western civilization. This is a behavioral characteristic that underlies much of the expressive array of aristocrats, which in their decline has been highly detrimental to adapting to the economic realities of the twentieth century.

Etiquette, however, has partly to do with the implementation of protocol and partly with the discharge of personal expression. With respect to the former, etiquette constitutes the procedural means and forms that are embodied in protocol. For example, at a wedding banquet people are seated according to precedence, but the table is set according to certain rules of etiquette that permit creative elaborations that may enhance expressive quality. Or at more informal gatherings, such as high tea or a cocktail party, protocol is minimal; and the event is almost entirely underlined by etiquette: what kinds of tea and pastry are served, the china in which they are served, and the arrangement of edibles and implements on the table. Examples ranging across the entire spectrum of the social, religious, and economic life of aristocrats could be multiplied by the dozen. But they all entail the same results: emphasis on detail for the enhancement of expressive goals that may perhaps assuage the loss of status, but at the expense of deluding aristocrats into believing that they are still the best and inhibiting them from channeling energies toward more productive activities.

Personal etiquette is economically less costly and more idiosyncratic. It is realized mostly in the expressive domains of dressing, fashions, language, body language, traveling, and sports. These are the main domains that have traditionally defined the public image of aristocrats everywhere, but their overtness has also been the most fertile ground for plutocratic aristocratization. Initially, the greatest degree of expressive acculturation takes place in the public ambiance of these domains, which quickly leads to blurring the perceptive boundaries between aristocrats and plutocrats. In the Mexican case, socially upwardly mobile plutocrats are now virtually indistinguishable from aristocrats in the context of these expressive domains, particularly dressing and traveling. Indeed, they have become expressive innovators independently of aristocrats. As an example, take the specific case of morning and afternoon dressing for women. Aristocratic women are stylish dressers but on the conservative side. In this mold, they favor tailor- or ready-made suits and raw silk dresses, mostly imported from the United States and Europe. Most aristocratic women are impeccably dressed, always exhibiting the proper combination of colors, patterns, and accessories. But they are not necessarily fashionable, judged by international standards. The emphasis is on sobriety and quiet elegance, judged by traditional European standards.[3]

By contrast, most plutocratic women may be characterized as fashionable but not necessarily elegant (at least as they are perceived by aristocratic women). They often wear the creations of the best-known designers in France and Italy and are vicariously perceived by the upper-middle class as the epitome of fashionableness. The wardrobes of aristocratic women are relatively modest compared to those of plutocrats; the emphasis is on quality and classic pieces that can be worn from season to season. With vast wealth at their disposal, the wardrobes of plutocratic women are much larger, costlier, more diversified, and *dernier cri*. If we also consider the domains of traveling and sports, the same differential situation obtains. After they have learned from aristocrats the basic patterns of expressive behavior, the wealth of plutocrats permits them to innovate and diversify much more than aristocrats do: they can buy the best horses to play polo and to go riding; they can go on safaris to Africa and travel all over the world luxuriously.

The traditional distinctiveness that characterized aristocrats in dressing, traveling, and sports has been blurred. Only in the domains of language and body language have aristocrats retained a measure of distinctiveness; but plutocrats are fast learners, and—especially among the young—the differences have narrowed.

To summarize, much of the distinctive material culture of the aristocracy and some of its implications, as detailed above, center on a number of traditional themes and domains that have characterized most of the stratification spectrum of Mexican society. Despite great differences in economic affluence between aristocrats and Indians (and by extension rural mestizos and to some extent the urban poor), I have implied that they share several behavioral traits affecting their respective material culture. The dichotomy between festive and daily diet, a pervasive concern with ritualism and ceremonialism, and a deep sense of reciprocity and exchange affect the expressive material culture of aristocrats and Indians in the same way: they tax economic means, divert scarce resources from generating wealth, and inhibit the pursuit of more productive activities. Expressively, then, aristocrats in these domains are closer to Indians than to plutocrats. If one adds the preservation of traditional Mexican cuisine and the traditional concern with protocol and etiquette that characterized most classes (traits that have been waning for more than two generations), the aristocracy is one of the most traditional groups in Mexican society.

Shared and Diminished Material Culture of Aristocrats and Plutocratic Dominance

When aristocrats refer to plutocrats as *los nuevos ricos* (the new rich), the expression not only denotes snobbishness but connotes envy and resentment. Envy, because plutocrats are so much richer and can afford so many more things, which diminishes aristocrats' standing in society. Resentment, because aristocrats, faced with their inability to generate new wealth, subtly imply that plutocrats made their fortunes mostly dishonestly. Aristocrats and plutocrats share pretty much the same material culture; there is some expressive variation, of course, but the plutocrats have quantitatively, although not always qualitatively, more than the aristocrats. It would serve no purpose to detail the material cultural array of the Mexican *haute bourgeoisie* because, with probably minimal differences, it is the same as that of economic elites in Western industrial nations. Rather, I concentrate here on a few selected domains that are shared by aristocrats and plutocrats to demonstrate the economic dominance of the plutocracy and what this means expressively.

In terms of economic affluence aristocrats are a fairly homogeneous group. The majority are affluent, with relatively small percentages of rich and "poor" families. In terms of disposable incomes, the affluent majority (about 70 percent) range from $100,000 to $200,000 a year, with a mean average of about $130,000. At the top is a 10 percent minority of rich and "plutocratic" families with annual disposable incomes of more than $500,000. The "plutocratic" families in this category constitute about half, with disposable annual incomes surpassing $1,000,000. The "poor" families constitute about 20 percent, with disposable incomes ranging from $50,000 to $75,000 a year (most of them young married couples but including a significant number of middle-aged and old couples who never managed to better themselves economically, almost exclusively casualties of the exodus to Mexico City in the 1940s and 1950s).

These figures do not tell the entire story. First, even "poor" aristocratic families enjoy a standard of living better than that of well-established upper-middle-class families in the United States. If one adds the class recognition (which invariably results in various kinds of benefits such as social invitations, participation in cultural affairs, and outright economic gain) that these families accrue in the plutocratic and upper-middle-class circles in which they move, their standard of living is significantly enhanced. Second, disposable income does not necessarily correlate with net economic worth. Most aristocratic families have old houses (that have been in the family for generations), heirlooms, art, and other "symbolically" entailed property. As discussed in Chapter 4, these material possessions have an almost sacred status for aristocrats, and most of them would suffer economic deprivation before selling anything to improve their economic lot. Even among the aristocratic poor, there are a significant number of families worth millions in symbolically entailed property that would increase their disposable income several times, were they to sell part of it for some economic investment.[4]

Even if they are well off, the comparison with what they could afford to spend and squander when they were rich and powerful is the reality fueling aristocratic resentment of today's plutocratic wealth. Moreover, the inability to implement traditional standards of behavior and display is a great source of frustration to most aristocrats and the engine that propels them to engage in the game of replicating a pale reflection of the past. Thus the shared material culture of aristocrats and plutocrats with the most expressive value was originally the exclusive property of aristocrats, which today can be afforded mostly by plutocrats. Three examples are sufficient to put matters in perspective.

First, the plutocratic material complex of elite existence, ranging from residence and transportation to entertainment and presentation of the self, is more elaborate, expensive, and diversified than that of aristocrats. Aristocrats usually characterize the material objects of this complex and the behavior associated with it as ostentatious and *cursi* (tacky). This characterization may be true, but aristocrats forget that before the Mexican Revolution they were just as ostentatious as plutocrats and on a larger scale. To the trained observer, the differences between aristocrats and plutocrats in many domains of material culture are evident, but among the most acculturated and socially upwardly mobile plutocratic families differences become insignificant. Indeed, computing differences and similarities in the material culture is a good index of the degree of acculturation that these two groups have undergone. Be this as it may, there is generally a quantitative aspect that remains constant in measuring the *embourgeoisement* of aristocrats and the aristocratization of plutocrats. Putting aside considerations of quality (taste, ostentation, decoration), quantitative variables define the boundary between aristocrats and plutocrats. Thus plutocratic urban residences (including libraries, art collections, appliances, etc.), country residences (including stables and sport facilities), automobiles, wardrobes, and several other domains of superordinate living are more expensive, diversified, and on a larger scale. The same quantitative standard applies to forms of leisure and entertainment: the celebratory events of plutocrats are almost invariably more lavish and on a larger scale than those of aristocrats.

Second, with the possible exception of automobiles, high-fidelity music systems, and firearms, aristocrats are singularly uninterested in machines and manifold technological implements (computers, electronic equipment, photographic equipment, and machinery of the most diverse kind). Their interest in mechanical instruments is mostly confined to having well-appointed households with refrigerators, freezers, televisions, and other electrical equipment. Moreover, aristocrats place very little expressive value on any kind of mechanical or electronic implements; even automobiles and music sound systems have strictly utilitarian value. Predictably, firearms have much expressive value because they are associated with hunting, that quintessential aristocratic sport. Many aristocratic families have excellent collections of firearms, particularly hunting rifles and shotguns, which are prominently displayed in their country places.

Plutocrats, in contrast, place a great deal of emphasis on machines and electronic implements, and their lives are crammed with the latest and best technological innovations. The plutocratic household is usually equipped with the very best appliances and electronic gadgets that money can buy; plutocrats drive the most expensive cars, which until 1994 could only be imported at exorbitant prices; in general, they are perceived as being surrounded with the best technology available. This array of material implements is an important form of expression. It reflects most plutocrats' involvement with the world of business and manufacturing, which is invariably manifested in males and females, young and middle-aged.

Predictably, the fascination with machines and electronic gadgets and the execution of expressive activities associated with them are the consequences of wealth and how it was generated. (The reverse explains why aristocrats, with no history of practical technological involvement and not enough economic affluence, show so little interest in these expensive machine-related activities.) Among both male and females plutocrats, involvement with machine-related activities as an important domain of expression wanes as they grow older and, by age thirty-five or so, gives way to strong commitment to wealth-generating activities. More interestingly, as plutocratic families become increasingly acculturated to aristocratic ways, emphasis shifts to the finer material things of life: art collecting, craft collecting, decorating residences, and other activities such as hunting and breeding fine horses. By the time the head of a plutocratic family has amassed a fortune, almost invariably by age fifty-five or so, he is well into these activities.

Third, the final example deals with a domain that has always been central to aristocratic life, namely, the culture of the horse. Unlike the foregoing examples (which examine the circumstances of aristocratic disinterest and plutocratic dominance), the culture of the horse (now essentially reduced to polo and equitation, as traditional forms of Mexican horsemanship have essentially vanished at the top of the stratification system) has been monopolized by plutocrats. Aristocrats, to be sure, still practice equitation and may even play marginal polo; but the competitive sports are dominated by plutocrats. Aristocrats simply do not have the affluence to afford the exorbitant price of horses and the very expensive equipment and maintenance of facilities these sports demand. For example, the traditional excellence in equitation, once dominated by the army, is now a preserve of prominent plutocrats, who for two decades have successfully upheld Mexico's reputation in this sport. Polo, which was introduced by aristocrats before the turn of the century, never reached the level of excellence of equitation and does not have the same international standing. Until forty years ago, there were three aristocratic clubs; today they are controlled by plutocrats, in addition to seven other clubs. A few aristocrats play in these clubs by virtue of plutocratic connections, but none are prominent players.

For aristocrats to have lost such a central domain of expressive realization is both a painful individual experience and collective realization that social predominance can only be maintained with a certain level of wealth. This realization shakes aristocrats to the core of their social consciousness, to a greater degree than their inability to engage in other material cultural domains (more central to their present declining condition) that plutocrats can participate in with such easy display of elaboration and richness. For plutocrats, by contrast, the overshadowing of aristocrats at their own game is a triumph and the validation of achieved status. Adding to the culture of the horse, there are other elite sports such as big-game hunting, yachting, and motor boating that in the public domain of superordinate stratification confirm plutocrats as the social class of the country. The material culture of a class is the most determinant factor of vicarious perception (an inevitable component of superordinate recognition) and the most visible symbol of social success. From this standpoint, the aristocracy has ceased to exist as a distinct sector of the *haute bourgeoisie*.

The Aristocratic Economy: Traditional Sources and Modern Occupations and Professions

The main source of wealth for aristocrats everywhere has always been the land. In Mexico the size of landed estates from the middle of the nineteenth century until the Revolution reached tremendous proportions. The haciendas varied greatly according to size, the quality of the land, access to water, and the type of agrarian enterprises. The largest haciendas were in northern Mexico and in the lowlands of the Gulf coast, where most of the great plantations were located. In central Mexico (from Oaxaca to Zacatecas) the haciendas were smaller, generally more fragmented, but more valuable, given the better quality of the soil, accessibility to market towns, and irrigation. Property of 100,000 hectares within 150 miles from Mexico City or Guadalajara was generally more valuable than 1,000,000 hectares in Chihuahua or Coahuila. Indeed, there were moderately small haciendas, 5,000 to 15,000 hectares, in the states of Mexico, Puebla, and Morelos that were among the most valuable in the country because of irrigation, the intensity of cultivation, and an ample labor force (Nickel 1988).

Probably a third of aristocratic families had a mixed wealth-generating strategy: a combination of land exploitation and various economic activities ranging from banking and insurance to manufacturing and trade. Perhaps as many as one-fourth of the families did not derive their wealth from exploitation of the land, although most of them had small haciendas for pleasure and expressive reasons. These families were enfranchised mostly in Mexico City, and their wealth derived from banking, manufacturing, and insurance (Pérez de Salazar n.d.). This economic landscape changed with the onset of the Revolution—dramatically after the land reform of 1934–1940—and the majority of aristocratic families today have a diversified economic life as a sector of the country's haute bourgeoisie.

Agrarian Enterprises and Land Tenure

About 10 percent of aristocrats derive most of their income from cultivation of the land: staple crops (corn, wheat, potatoes, beans, lima beans, lentils, sorghum, etc.); commercial crops (sugarcane, coffee, grapes, etc.); horticulture (flowers, berries, fine vegetables such as asparagus and fennel); arboriculture (citruses, avocados, apples, peaches, pears, plums, etc.); agave for *pulque* production; and stock breeding (cattle, sheep, goats, pigs, horses). The land for these agrarian operations has two sources: parcels that aristocrats managed to retain in their haciendas after the 1934 land reform and land bought elsewhere, sometimes on a scale larger than the law until recently allowed. *Hacendados* could own land as allowed by law in addition to the *casco* (manor of a landed estate).

By 1950 about half of aristocratic *hacendados* had sold the land that the law allowed them to retain. They sold it either to peasants in nearby communities or to prosperous farmers. In areas closer to the capital the hacienda connection persisted longer; but by the late 1960s less than a fourth of former aristocratic *hacendados* derived income from the exploitation of their ancestral estates.

Aristocratic agrarian enterprises since the 1934 land reform may be described as medium-size farming and ranching operations. The typical aristocratic farm ranges from 300 to 600 hectares, although there are a moderate number of farms with more than 1,000 hectares under cultivation. Dry farming predominates, but there are many farms with a modicum of irrigation that range from 50 to 200 hectares. Stock breeding involves larger holdings; cattle ranches, for example, may reach 5,000 hectares in size. It should be noted that a hectare of irrigated land may yield ten times as much income as dry farming or ranching land. Thus the most affluent aristocratic farmers are those with the most irrigated land, which is invariably dedicated to arboriculture and horticulture.

All farming and ranching aristocratic families reside permanently in Mexico City, but they spend more time in the country than the great majority of families that do not cultivate the land as their main source of income. Their country retreats are more elaborate, particularly when they are hacienda *cascos*

The Mexican Aristocracy

or refurbished buildings of an ancestral estate; they are veritable secondary residences in which, at intervals, families reside for as much as three months of the year. In other words, farming and ranching families have the most balanced rural-urban orientation of all aristocrats: the closest replication of the traditional, prerevolutionary hacienda-urban pattern. But this is an easy extrapolation, to the extent that aristocratic commitment to the land is not what it was in prerevolutionary times, when the hacienda system reigned supreme. Rather, as one informant put it, "The people of my class are not good farmers and ranchers. The reason is evident: they have too many interests in the city which prevent them from being entirely centered on the land and exploiting it adequately. With a few exceptions, even those who make their living exclusively from agriculture do not work the land with the attention it needs. To say nothing of farmers like myself who cultivate land almost nostalgically, and what we realize economically is not much."

The last sentence of this quotation points to another form of aristocratic farming. By 1960 former aristocrats had sold most of the land that they were allowed to retain after the 1934 land reform; but many kept plots of 20 to 30 hectares, where the manor was located or a new country retreat was built. Also, many more who were unable to retain any land from their former estates frequently bought plots of land (10 to 20 hectares) where they built their country retreats. In both cases, some aristocrats on a small scale cultivate flowers (roses, gladioli, chrysanthemums, dahlias, carnations, etc.), fine fruits, fine vegetables, and other specialized crops. This type of cultivation earns aristocratic families considerable income, but it must rather be regarded as an expressive activity that keeps them tied to the land. Whether aristocrats make a living from agriculture or practice some agrarian activity for expressive reasons, the ideological pull of the land is still strong, even though commitment to efficient cultivation may not be extensively practiced.

The Professions, Higher Education, and Combined Economic Strategies

The tradition of aristocrats earning professional degrees and engaging in academic studies and research goes back to colonial times. In the nineteenth century there were several distinguished aristocratic jurists, historians, anthropologists, linguists, and naturalists who made important contributions to the country's scholarship. The law was always an important profession, and *hacendado* families invariably encouraged a son to become a lawyer to watch over their landed and other economic enterprises. Indeed, aristocrats literally monopolized the notarial profession. Notaries public (a law degree was a requirement) constituted a very important profession until the twentieth century, a situation that has changed little today. Some of the most prestigious *notarías* (notary public offices) in Mexico City are run by aristocrats. The medical profession was also attractive to aristocrats; many became physicians, more as philanthropy than as a means to earn a living. Some aristocrats obtained university degrees in architecture or fine arts and actively engaged in scientific research at the University of Mexico. This professional and intellectual bent stood aristocrats in good stead after the land reform and their concentration in Mexico City.

While there were always aristocratic doctors and lawyers, professionalization began in the 1920s; it greatly increased after the concentration of the aristocracy in Mexico City, and by the 1960s it had become generalized. Today probably 60 percent of all gainfully employed aristocrats earn their living mainly by practicing a profession. Most of them have private practices, but a significant minority work for larger concerns, including the federal and city governments. The main professions in order of numbers of practitioners are law, medicine, business administration, architecture, engineering (mostly civil and mechanical), accounting, and agronomy. There are a few historians, art historians, anthropologists, archaeologists, economists, psychologists, and literati, who teach at institutions of higher learning and do research in government institutes or (if they have other means of earning a living) work as independent scholars.

The most numerous professionals are lawyers and physicians. Among the former, there are a few well-known judges in the various levels of the judiciary system in Mexico City and several professors in the three most prestigious law schools in Mexico City. Most physicians have private practices or work for the Mexican equivalent of health maintenance organizations (HMOs), but some occupy medium to high positions in the federal and city health care system. In addition to being self-employed architects (owners of construction businesses or heading architectural firms) and engineers (owners of small to medium manufacturing concerns), aristocrats occupy medium- to high-level managerial positions in the city and federal government, particularly in the ministries of transportation, communication, and commerce. Almost all business administrators, accountants (including actuaries), and agronomists are self-employed.

Most aristocrats are educated in five of the most prestigious institutions of higher learning in Mexico: Universidad Nacional Autónoma de México, Instituto Tecnológico de Monterrey, Universidad Iberoamericana, Universidad

Anahuac, and Escuela Médico-Militar. In these institutions aristocrats obtain M.D., M.A., M.S., B.A., B.S., and occasionally Ph.D. degrees. Many go abroad for graduate education: until the late 1950s to Europe (France, Germany, and England), but since then mostly to prestigious universities in the United States. Postgraduate work in the United States is most commonly done in medicine, economics, engineering, and business administration; about half of those who study abroad obtain doctorates and almost invariably secure work in public administration.

Sixty years ago it would have been unthinkable for women to become lawyers or physicians; but the situation has changed rapidly since the late 1950s, and today there are many aristocratic women lawyers and physicians as well as architects, psychologists, historians, art historians, journalists, and publicists. The last two professions seldom attracted men; but since the beginning of women's professionalization they have become popular, and several aristocratic women have built successful careers in the media and advertising. Almost all women lawyers and physicians have private practices, whereas psychologists, historians, art historians, and architects either teach at several colleges and universities or do research in government institutes. There are also a few aristocratic women, with and without university degrees in education, who teach in private high schools and finishing schools attended mostly by *haute bourgeois* youngsters. A few women have obtained Ph.D. degrees (in anthropology and history), several have M.A.s (mostly in psychology), but almost all professionals have B.A.s. A few women have gone abroad for graduate work, but the great majority have been educated in the Mexican universities mentioned above.

With the exception of lawyers, physicians, and notaries public, the professions, academic disciplines, and research and teaching positions are not well remunerated. In order to generate a disposable annual income of $100,000 or more, the majority of aristocratic families must pursue mixed economic strategies. This means that more than half of professionals are forced to engage in money-making enterprises not necessarily related to their professions. Architects operate construction companies, engineers own small and medium-size factories, but aristocrats also frequently run businesses of various sorts unrelated to their profession, as detailed in the following section.

The professional involvement of aristocrats in government, banking, and manufacturing has been steadily increasing during the past thirty years. Significant numbers of lawyers, physicians, engineers, architects, and economists occupy middle-level and occasionally high-level executive positions in both the public and private sectors. Several are heads of departments, institutes, and research organizations in several ministries. During the last two administrations (1980–1992), two aristocrats became ministers of education and finance, the highest positions in government occupied by aristocrats since the Mexican Revolution. In the private sector they have been less successful, as there are no chief executive officers of the country's major corporations or presidents of the most important banks. A few, however, are chief executive officers of large insurance companies and investment firms, and many occupy medium and high executive positions in the country's largest banks and corporations located in Mexico City.

More visible are aristocratic scholars (mostly anthropologists, archaeologists, and historians), some of whom have achieved a significant degree of eminence. Since 1950 several aristocrats have been directors of the National Museum of Anthropology, the National Institute of Anthropology and History, the National Museum of Fine Arts, and the National Archives. There are several notable writers who add luster to the intellectual achievements of the aristocracy.

Finally, it is important to note the inherent social distance, fraught with potential friction, underlying the interaction of aristocrats with members of the middle classes (and to some extent with "nonacculturated" plutocrats) in the context of the professions and academic and bureaucratic environments. The best way to characterize this interaction is as a case of studious social avoidance on the part of aristocrats, another version of the "juntos pero no revueltos" syndrome. Indeed, it can be said that aristocrats in these environments lead a dual social life: they are condescendingly polite to their fellow workers and associates, but there is no interaction beyond the workplace. Considering that most middle-class personnel with whom aristocrats interact in the manifold contexts of employment are aware of the latter's standing, a tacit understanding of social distance develops, which is fostered by the vicarious perception that knowing middle-class people have of aristocrats. The situation is quite different in the workplace interaction of aristocrats and plutocrats. Aristocrats must bend significantly to plutocratic power and wealth, leading to social recognition.

Aristocratic Involvement in Banking, Business, and Manufacturing: The Plutocratic Component

A little-known aspect of the economic effect of the Mexican Revolution on the traditional landed aristocracy is that a number of haciendas were parceled out or sold as *pequeña propiedad* (any parcel of land of less than 100 hectares) in the interlude between 1919 and 1934, when—due to the exigencies of reorganizing the country—land reform proceeded at a very slow pace. Most *hacendados* expected that the early revolutionary fervor would peter out and therefore thought that if they held onto the land they would eventually consolidate their holdings. They were totally disappointed, for President Cárdenas redistributed most of the hacienda land of Mexico in six short years. But those who anticipated what was coming and sold out to well-off peasants and small farmers in the towns and villages near their estates were able to salvage part of their fortunes and invested elsewhere. In addition, by the time of the Revolution there were a significant number of aristocrats who owned moderate to large amounts of urban property in Mexico City and the provincial cities that they controlled before migrating to the capital. Since urban property was untouched by the changes brought about by the Revolution, these are two important sources of wealth of aristocratic families today. A third consideration bearing on aristocratic affluence today is that before the Revolution a considerable number of aristocrats engaged in manufacturing, trading, and other nonlanded business activities which were also not affected by the armed struggle. Thus these three factors account for most of the richest aristocratic families today.

Now most enterprises owned by aristocrats are small to medium in size: for example, factories employing 50 to 150 workers or white-collar concerns with 12 to 50 employees. Most of the factories are individually owned, but some are *sociedades anónimas* (corporations), usually entirely controlled by one person or family. Factories range from the manufacturing of textiles and plastics to small appliances and electronic parts. Moreover, businesses employing blue-collar workers include dairy-product factories, distilleries, automobile dealerships, and a few others. White-collar businesses include art galleries, antique stores, interior decoration stores, specialized boutiques, and other retailing businesses on a moderate to fairly large scale.

With the exemption of some lawyers and physicians, most other professionals, academics, and practitioners of academic disciplines working for government agencies do not generate enough income to make a comfortable living for the nuclear family, even when husband and wife have full-time positions—an increasingly common phenomenon. This large segment of aristocratic families almost invariably pursues a mixed strategy: a professional, academic, or government income combined with some business, manufacturing, and/or agrarian activity. This is the reason why about 70 percent of aristocratic families are able to earn an annual disposable income of $100,000 to $200,000.

Most of the 10 percent of rich aristocrats with disposable annual incomes of more than $500,000 are high-level executives in banking, investment, and insurance. No aristocrat is the owner or principal stockholder of a major bank or the largest insurance companies. The truly plutocratic aristocrats, with personal fortunes of more than 40 million dollars, are in the investment business. This category includes owners of brokerage houses, seats in the stock exchange, and diversified investment operations in real-estate and industrial development. There are about fifteen aristocrats in this category, and they command considerable influence in both aristocratic and plutocratic circles.

Political Participation and the Expansion of Ties with the Political Class

The political involvement of the Mexican aristocracy at the national level was always limited. Nonetheless, during the Porfiriato there were a few aristocrats in government and the diplomatic service. After the fall of Porfirio Díaz, aristocrats lost almost all political control at the provincial level, and in the capital they maintained a low profile until the end of the armed phase of the Revolution (1910–1919). It was not until the late 1930s that a few aristocrats were nominated to government posts, particularly in the diplomatic service and lower ministerial levels. For expressive reasons, the diplomatic service was attractive to aristocrats, but they were never drawn to participate in the distasteful (to them) process of seeking elective office.

At the national level, only a handful of aristocrats, as far as I am aware, have run for elective office since the Revolution. Thus aristocratic political involvement means essentially appointment to high- and medium-level ministerial office and the judiciary. Indeed, during the past fifty years, several aristocrats have served in the country's highest judiciary ranks, namely, on the Supreme Court and the various appellate courts. Beginning with the administration of President Gustavo Díaz Ordáz (1964–1970), increasing numbers of young aristocrats sought political appointments. Originally the main sources of recruitment were friendships established at the National Autonomous University of Mexico and ties contracted in the ambiance of country places by their parents. Since the late 1970s, however, many young aristocrats have obtained advanced degrees in public administration, economics, political science, and international relations in U.S. and occasionally European universities. Since the early 1980s the presence of male and female aristocrats in government has become a common phenomenon; and during the Carlos Salinas de Gortari administration (1988–1994), aristocrats secured government positions on their own merit.

At the end of the first year of the Miguel de la Madrid administration (1982), the General Directorate of the Presidency of the Republic published a directory of the fifteen to twenty most important positions in the twenty-four ministries of the federal government. It lists ministers, deputy ministers, heads and subheads of departments, heads of institutes, and other personnel. The directory (*Quién es quién en la administración pública de México*) includes more than four hundred officials in the federal government, a short résumé of each officeholder, and present position held. Three key informants identified eighteen aristocrats (more than 4 percent) of the total number of listed positions in the directory. The breakdown of positions was as follows: one cabinet minister (Foreign Relations); two undersecretaries (Programming and Budget; Urban Development and Ecology); six directors and deputy directors of national institutes; and nine assorted positions in six ministries, including parastate organizations.

The proportion of male and female aristocrats in government has increased significantly. In the estimation of a former cabinet minister, by the end of the Salinas de Gortari administration there were proportionally about twice as many aristocrats in government as in 1982. During the last three years of the De la Madrid administration and the first three of the Salinas de Gortari administration, three aristocrats had been cabinet ministers (Foreign Relations, Education, and Treasury). Two of the economists that negotiated the signing of the North American Free Trade Agreement (NAFTA) are aristocrats, and many others have been directors of government institutes and parastate organizations. Although we have no exact figures as to how many aristocrats today hold important government positions, in the opinion of several knowledgeable informants there are more than forty aristocrats in the upper echelons of the federal bureaucracy, which today has ballooned to more than eight hundred positions in twenty-seven ministries and five parastate organizations headed by officials of ministerial rank.

Although aristocrats have occupied positions of political influence for the past generation, they are not as a group part of Mexico's political class. Very few are PRI or PAN (Partido de Acción Nacional, the conservative opposition party) members or belong to any of the political cliques into which the PRI is fragmented. Rather, recruitment to the highest positions in the federal system depends on personal relationships with the president and prominent members of the ruling party, but based on specific expertise that potential candidates may have (especially technical knowledge in, say, economics, public administration, or international relations). Recruitment below the minister and the three closest officers (lieutenant minister, secretary general, and administrative officer) is done on the basis of merit. Under such circumstances, significant members of male and female aristocrats can compete well with the best-trained members of the political and intellectual establishment. This is most notably the case with economists, political scientists, public administrators, anthropologists, archaeologists, and art historians. Aristocrats have excelled in these professions and disciplines, and some of them are recognized leaders and well known in intellectual circles. As mentioned in the foregoing section, since the 1930s several aristocratic anthropologists and art historians have been among the nationally recognized authorities in these disciplines.

The Mexican appointing-to-office political system—and the patronage that accompanies it—is quite different from that of the United States. In the United States economic considerations (beyond required expertise, one would hope) play an important role in being appointed to high political office, particularly as ambassadors to important countries. In Mexico intellectual and artistic considerations play a far greater role. Quite often artists, writers, anthropologists, and other intellectuals are appointed to important posts. Both systems of political patronage (one done as a recompense for campaign contributions or economic favors; the other out of the probably misguided notion that intellectuals should be rewarded in this fashion) are inherently faulty: they detract from appointing the best-qualified individuals strictly on the basis of administrative, technical, or diplomatic merit. But I am not certain whether it is better to reward captains of industry or intellectuals with positions for which, in all likelihood, there are other personnel much better qualified.[5] The Mexican diplomatic service, however, has become more of a meritocracy during the past generation; comparatively speaking, there are fewer aristocrats in this branch of government today than there were two generations ago. This can be explained by the maturation and greater sophistication that the upper echelons of Mexican society have experienced since the 1950s.

Aristocrats in government have no power base as a group; nor can they be identified as belonging to any of the PRI factions or the opposition political parties that have acquired independent relevance during the past fifteen years. Whatever influence aristocrats in high office may have and exercise is strictly individual and is a function of the office they hold. Some aristocrats have had notable careers in some of the ministries, but probably more have been nominated to high office without the benefit of a distinct trajectory by excelling in intellectual or professional areas of expertise. Aristocrats who have achieved the rank of minister or have been nominated to positions near the top generally belong to the first category, while heads of departments and institutes belong to the second category. Interestingly, most aristocrats have qualms about the former, because they believe that they are part of the political establishment and did something unbecoming to achieve high office. No such reservations are expressed for the second category of political appointees, whom fellow aristocrats regard as having merited strictly on the basis of personal achievement. Again, it should be mentioned that this distrust, often bordering on visceral aversion, is shared by a broad spectrum of the privileged and middle classes of Mexican society.

Expressive Analysis

The analysis of material culture and the economy is an example of demonstrating several aspects of conflictual expression, whereas the discussion of aristocrats' political participation exemplifies terminal expression and expressive change. Moreover, this juncture is especially conducive to specifying the conditions of time and space in which some key aspects of the aristocratic expressive array have changed since the turn of the century. These ethnographic domains are propitious contexts for specifying how expression and style are related, assessing how individual and collective manifestations impinge upon upward and downward mobility, and determining how new forms of expression are being created, as a result of mobility.

First and foremost, the main characteristics of aristocratic material culture (*haute cuisine*, the categorical distinction between festive and daily food, the overemphasis on ritualism and ceremonialism, reciprocity and exchange, and protocol and etiquette) must be primarily regarded as expressive constraints that inhibit most aristocrats from coming to terms with their loss of power and wealth. Structurally, this quandary means that aristocrats, with few exceptions, have not managed to acculturate to plutocratic ways, thereby failing to adapt to the new social, economic, and political realities of the second half of the twentieth and early twenty-first century. This syndrome, according to Pareto (1935:456), is the result of a superordinate group's inability to innovate, leading inevitably to its downfall and extinction as a functioning entity. While a superordinate group still commands economic power (even in periods of decadence, when political power has escaped beyond its control), it is possible to be innovative and actively engaged in learning from proximate upwardly mobile groups (such as the plutocracy at various junctures since the Spanish Conquest in the development of the Mexican aristocracy).

The reason for this, of course, is that in the multiple transformations that the West has undergone for more than 2,000 years since classical times the estate system remained constant, with the aristocracy at the top. With the onset of the class system after the French and American Revolutions, and for a period of gestation since the establishment of absolutism, the aristocracy has been undergoing structural as well as expressive changes. During this period (roughly from 1500 to the present), the aristocracy gradually lost its power to innovate, particularly during the past 100 years. The expressive culture of the Western aristocracy, as a result, fashioned mostly ineffective innovative techniques that did not generate structural assets for survival in a world dominated by a rich and powerful plutocracy. This assessment applies equally to the Mexican aristocracy, as very few of its members have managed to acquire the necessary plutocratic wherewithal to continue at the top of the structural-expressive hierarchy.

The foregoing description of the five main cultural material domains of aristocratic expressive realization demonstrates how each has been detrimental to aristocratic structural survival. Their collective effect has been devastating, and it exemplifies the futility of placing an emphasis on specific forms of expression when the group or class does not have the material means conferred by power and wealth. To put it differently, expressive innovation (and undoubtedly aristocrats have been innovative since the 1910 Revolution, as shown above) per se does not necessarily entail positive structural consequences, unless innovation is aimed at generating wealth and power in any form. This, of course, is what Pareto means by saying that ruling classes come to an end when they cease to create. Take, for example, aristocratic *haute cuisine*. Aristocratic women have been quite innovative in improving on what was once a mildly salient domain before the Revolution, in the process preserving and improving on several aspects of traditional and regional Mexican cuisine. This innovation has probably engendered beneficial psychological results. But in no sense has it helped aristocrats to regain socioeconomic standing; nor has it been a means toward generating any kind of power and wealth. The same can be said of the other four material domains described above, inasmuch as they imply the squandering of precious assets in pursuits that aristocrats cannot afford or, more seriously, wasting millions of symbolically entailed property. In the name of bolstering a vanishing aristocratic identity, families do not use assets that could easily be liquidated for investment or capitalizing business enterprises. This quandary captures perfectly the conjunction of expressive commitment, structural conditioning, and the feedback effect that obtains between them.

Second, material culture also exemplifies the factors conditioning loss of status. The foregoing domains of aristocratic expression demonstrate the contextual nature of the phenomenon as well as how a domain is realized in different cultural and stratificational contexts. Let us take first the appropriation of an expressive domain by the plutocracy. What does this mean sociologically? The answer hinges on the saliency and visibility of the appropriated domain. One would not have expected that upwardly mobile members of the plutocracy would have acquired and improved on the *haute cuisine* or the ritualism and ceremonialism of aristocrats with whom they have been in contact for at least two generations. The reason is evident: these are expressive pursuits centered on the household, essentially devoid of a public component generating the visibility and vicarious recognition that upwardly mobile groups (the new rich) crave in the process of acquiring superordinate status. But plutocrats wholeheartedly acquired and made their own the culture of the horse and art collecting, which generates visibility and vicarious recognition.

The contextual nature of expression is borne out by ritualism and ceremonialism and the dichotomization of festive and daily food that aristocrats so distinctly share with Indians. The social, economic, and material context of aristocrats in Mexico City and Indian communities could not be more different; yet their expressive domains have essentially the same consequences. On the surface, they have the ostensible function of saving face, keeping up with the Joneses, and manifesting a natural desire for expressive realization (a universal aspect of expression that manifests itself in countless forms). Although the question of why, in these expressive realizations, aristocrats have much more in common with Indians than with plutocrats is not easily answered, I intuit that the most stringent, rigid domains of expressive realization are associated with the highest and lowest rungs of any stratification system. There is ethnographic and historical information which buttresses this assertion.[6]

Essentially the explanation I envisage is as follows. The source of the ritualism and ceremonialism of those at the top and the bottom of any stratification system is different, but their consequences are the same. In the case under consideration, for those at the bottom the source is magico-religious; and the pervading concern of Mexican Indians with events and occasions in the yearly cycle directed at effective propitiation of the supernatural (both Catholic and pagan) must be undertaken without deviating from exacting traditional formulae (embedded primarily in the cult of the saints, *compadrazgo*, and some aspects of kinship). For those at the top, the source is social and largely secular; and the rigor and monotonic concern of Mexican aristocrats in so much of their social life are focused on protocol and display, which are at the core of aristocratic identity. In order to be effective, the entailed rituals and ceremonies must also be undertaken with guidelines and the precision born out of centuries of tradition. In both cases, "effective" means essentially the same: for Indians, to make sure that supernatural forces will be propitious when they are entreated; for aristocrats, the secular aim of exogenously projecting a most advantageous image. Whether the emphasis on ritualism and ceremonialism carried to an exacting, undeviating extent is magico-religious or secular, its function remains the same: bringing about desired aims for the benefit of the individual and the group in accordance with clearly stated aspirations and ends in view.

This analysis is relative, of course, as the manifold segments of society between the bottom and the top do occasionally engage in similar kinds of ritualism and ceremonialism, but never in the manner described above. These are inner- and outer-directed activities that cast Indians and aristocrats as the ritual and ceremonial specialists of the Mexican stratification system. In both cases the fundamental structural consequences are the same: inhibiting a more "rational" adaptation to a changing world and fostering constraints that impede alternative strategies for preserving a dubious cultural identity that can more likely be preserved by the maxim "if you can't beat them, join them." This is the ironic predicament of preserving "Indian culture"; the more communities are involved with the outside world (essentially creating economic opportunities), the faster traditional culture will disappear. For aristocrats, in turn, the more they adopt the ways of the new superordinate class (essentially learning the economic creativity of plutocrats), the faster they will lose their expressive values and identity. In both cases, however, actors are not aware of these consequences.

Third, all five ethnographic domains discussed above define the material locus of the natural expression of Mexican aristocrats—namely, expressive patterns of long standing, which in one degree or another are shared by all Western aristocracies but modified by local (Mexican) constraints. These, together with those domains discussed in Chapter 4, further define the core of exclusive expression of the aristocracy as it has entered its terminal phase since 1910. And this juncture captures one of the most significant diachronic aspects of expression—that it accurately reflects the changes that a group or social class has undergone. For example, assessing how the material expressive array of the aristocracy (or any well-delimited social class) has changed between two proximate (two or three generations apart) or distant (centuries apart) baselines gives an accurate representation of the loss or acquisition of power and wealth of the aristocracy and its position in the global Mexican stratification system. To put it differently, independently of structural considerations, the expressive array of any significant social group is an accurate index of change and of differential upward and downward mobility. If there were no information, say, about the structural configuration of the aristocracy between 1910 and 1990 except its material expressive array, one could reconstruct how it evolved from a powerful class to a marginal, dying social class. It may be asked whether it is possible to know the expressive configuration of any group but not its structural configuration. Ethnographically this is likely (particularly concerning hunting and gathering and tribal societies), but not so likely among folk societies as parts of nation states and quite unlikely in recent times. It should be noted, however, that much of archaeology interprets the past, particularly in reconstructing the social life of a period, by extrapolating from remains that are basically expressive.

Fourth, political participation during the past generation is a belated involvement in a domain of public life that throughout the nineteenth century was constrained by a worldview and expressive array that effectively discouraged aristocrats from engaging in national politics. As a result, their only involvement was in local-level politics, which they deemed essential to safeguard their interests as a ruling class. This expressive change signals a drastic departure from traditionalism, the most diagnostic trait of terminal expression. Despite the conscious efforts of aristocrats in politics to dichotomize their public and private life, most of them sooner or later succumb to the inherent ambiance of *embourgeoisement* that politics entails. This is manifested by the overall erosion of aristocratic manners, frequent social interaction outside aristocratic circles, and increasing exogamous marriages. Unlike plutocratic *embourgeoisement*, which may foster the continuation of traditional expressive domains, political *embourgeoisement* does not take place. It should be emphasized that there is no discernible aristocratization of the political class, and the reason is clear: the original class position of politicians is lower than that of most plutocrats and, for some reason, politicians—before they become plutocrats—do not seem to have the urge that characterizes the expressive upward mobility that most plutocrats develop upon reaching a high level of wealth.

By contrast, the majority of plutocrats have engaged in a steady process of aristocratization (particularly in the most public domains as discussed above). The highest form of this process may be encapsulated by saying that the locus of material expression has shifted from machines and other utilitarian implements to art collecting and other so-called finer things in life. This aphorism captures the essence of plutocratic aristocratization and points toward the innovative expressive array that the new Mexican plutocracy is fashioning: based on old aristocratic patterns and domains, new forms of expression are coming into being. This process of aristocratic-plutocratic acculturation is the same as that which has been going on in Europe for more than a century. This apparently is not the case, however, with the powerful and immensely rich U.S. plutocracy during the past two generations. Until probably World War II, the U.S. plutocracy followed the European pattern; that is, it underwent a process of expressive acculturation similar to what I have described for the Mexican plutocracy. (This is clearly attested by the considerable number of U.S. plutocrats who married European aristocrats between the 1870s and 1940s, to say nothing of the great building boom of U.S. manors and mansions in the aristocratic European style, which television has enshrined as "American Castles.") The new U.S. magnates, however, are not playing this expressive game. The Bill Gateses and Sam Waltons seem to be going in a different direction. This suggests that the traditional expressive elements in Western society that accompanied upward mobility have come to an end and that a new expressive game is afoot.

Finally, two conclusions may be drawn from the expressive analysis of this chapter. First, expression is contextually determined when two classes engage in expressive acculturation. This is played out diachronically, as one social class replaces another as the ruling class of a country. The plutocracy, to put it differently, creates a new expressive array but to a large extent based on the traditional patterns of the aristocracy that it is replacing as the ruling class of Mexico. Second, more than any other cultural context, material culture and the economy are the most fertile grounds for upwardly mobile expressive innovation. More than any other major domain of culture (politics, religion, social organization), material culture and the economy embody the locus of expressive-structural realization as the most public, visible context where upward mobility is validated, and ultimately a new ruling class is established in the perception of the population at large. Thus in the following chapters (dealing with religion, kinship, and social segmentation) the expressive description and analysis are focused more on the aristocracy, for the plutocracy and other proximate groups have not been much affected by any discernible process of expressive acculturation.

CHAPTER 6

RELIGION

Ideology, Worship, and the

Ritual-Ceremonial Complex

It is well known that, as the largest and most widespread division of Christianity, Catholicism has many variants that usually but not always correlate with nation states. Thus Catholicism in France, Italy, and Spain exhibits quite distinct features; even within Italy there are significant differences between north and south, to say nothing of the differences between the somewhat "Protestantized" (in several pragmatic domains) Catholicism of the United States as contrasted with that of most European nations. The same, of course, obtains in Mexico. Mexican Catholicism is quite uniform throughout the country but exhibits a number of traits that depart significantly from the "standard" varieties practiced in Europe and the United States. The unorthodoxy of Mexican Catholicism increases from the top to the bottom of the social scale and is mainly the result of the process of religious syncretism and acculturation configured by the conversion of the Indians, which after more than four centuries has permanently affected all sectors of society. It should be noted, however, that aristocrats and Indian and rural mestizos share some elements that rather significantly distinguish them from the middle ranks of society.

The main unorthodox characteristics of Mexican Catholicism today are the retention of some medieval features of Spanish Catholicism that meshed well with several aspects of pre-Hispanic polytheism, rendering Mexican Catholicism more ritualistic, ceremonial, and pragmatic than Spanish Catholicism. In addition, Mexican Catholicism retained a magical component that surfaces in unexpected domains of the stratification spectrum. The Catholicism practiced by Mexican aristocrats is even more distinctly realized by socially entailed considerations. As in the Spanish system (the titled nobility and *hidalguía*) from which it derived, religion for aristocrats served as an ample domain for the realization of ostentation and display. To a significant extent this configuration of religion continued after Independence from Spain until the Revolution of 1910. The public aspects of this configuration gradually came to an end by the late 1950s.

General Characteristics of Mexican Catholicism

The Catholicism of all classes of Mexican society entails a rather high common denominator, but there are differences as one moves from the top to the bottom of the stratification system. The similarities are mostly ideological, that is, all Mexican Catholics (about 85 percent of the population) adhere in principle to the dogma of the church concerning doctrine, values, and teleology and the rituals and ceremonies that they entail. Although in the twentieth century there were attempts at secession from Rome by sizable sectors of the population, none of them were permanent; and Mexican Catholicism today remains dogmatically and administratively united. There are serious differences, however, in the praxis of Catholicism among the various sectors of society. These differences center primarily on the intensity and unorthodox discharge of ritualism and ceremonialism and the entailed consequences of doctrinal beliefs that greatly depart from Catholic dogma.

The unorthodoxy of rites and ceremonies is quite noticeable to the untrained eye as one observes the daily and festive practices of the various sectors of society. Transgressions of belief and dogma, however, can only be detected after careful observation and analysis of their entailments in the public manifestation of religiosity. For example, everything that we know about urban middle- and lower-class religiosity differs somewhat from Indian religiosity, with its elaborate ritual-ceremonial system centered on the cult of the saints, the *mayordomía* system, and several aspects of *compadrazgo*. Then there is the gradation of this substratum as it is found in rural mestizo communities and as it is brought to the city in the context of permanent migration, where in differential combinations it remains a permanent feature of the middle sectors of urban populations.

The greatest departures from Catholic orthodoxy are to be found in the realm of the fundamental doctrinal beliefs and injunctions that underlie Catholic dogma, which in themselves affect the discharge of the ritual and ceremonial life of the people in diverse ethnic and class contexts. These departures stem almost exclusively from three unorthodox domains which are the consequence of pre-Hispanic polytheistic components that—together with sixteenth-century Spanish Catholicism—shaped the syncretic nature of Mexican Catholicism.

The first aspect is the monolatrous component of Mexican Catholicism. (It should be noted that this is by no means confined to Mexico. In fact, it is found in many national or local varieties of Catholicism throughout the world: from Chinese Catholics in Hong Kong to the folk Catholicism of southern Italy, Sicily, and southern Spain [Nutini 1988:38–40].) Several anthropologists (see Linton and Linton 1950:13–21) maintain that most Christians throughout the centuries have been practicing monolatry (or polylatry) and not monotheism—that is, in behavior (psychologically) and in practice (ritually and ceremonially) no transcendental distinction emerges between God and the saints, including the many manifestations of the Virgin Mary. Whether or not the distinction between God and the saints is understood or explicitly made, the fact remains that in behavior and practice many sectors of Christendom are practicing monolatry, not monotheism. Indeed, at least in Catholicism, it may be difficult to be a theologically pure monotheist (witness the doctrine of the Holy Trinity).

This is certainly the case among Mesoamerican Indians today; and with various degrees of intensity it is present in all sectors of Mexican society. Most contemporary Mexicans have not internalized the theological distinction between God and the saints, even if they somewhat vaguely understand it; and in actual behavior and practice God is little more than a *primus inter pares*, a more powerful deity than the saints and the Virgin Mary. Because of the polytheistic inputs that came to reinforce the inherently monolatrous aspects of sixteenth-century Spanish Catholicism, Mexican Catholics never clearly distinguished between *latria* (the adoration of God as an omnipotent, omnipresent, and almighty entity) and *dulia* (honoring the saints as his exemplary servants and using them as intercessors). Even among educated Mexican Catholics, the confusion of *latria* and *dulia* is present in the cult of the saints as intercessors. Thus in Mexican Catholicism the manifestly monotheistic ideology of Christianity is behaviorally affected by the latent polytheistic ideology of pre-Hispanic survivals. The saints, including the Virgin Mary, are regarded not only as intermediaries between humans and the Christian God but also as supernaturals endowed with independent power and as dispensers of rewards and punishments in their own right.

The second aspect is the pragmatic nature of Mexican Catholicism and its surprisingly nonexistent or weak moral and ethical component. These two traits are entirely of pre-Hispanic origin: Mesoamerican polytheism (and probably all polytheistic systems) was and is almost exclusively concerned with propitiating the forces of nature rather than regulating human conduct. This inherited trait of Mexican Catholicism results in a greater departure from orthodoxy than monolatry does; and in the context of Indian and Mestizo folk religion it acquires pagan characteristics. Its most extreme form is manifested in traditional Indian communities.

The supernatural belief system of these communities has one general, predominant characteristic: to make the individual and the collective world of existence safe and secure by the proper propitiation of supernatural forces. The relationship between humans and the supernatural, then, is characterized by pragmatic and rather self-interested motives, for which the individual and the group expend a great deal of time and economic and social resources. All religious activities and behavior are individually and collectively aimed at propitiation of the supernatural in order to achieve certain finite goals. In fact, virtually the sole concern of Indian religion is rapport with the supernatural, whereas ethics, morality, and appropriate behavior are almost exclusively social concerns. This lack of moral and ethical components in Indian folk religion and the overwhelming emphasis on propitiation and pragmatic self-interest set this religious complex rather sharply apart from orthodox Catholicism, which is permeated with ethical values. The setting of standards for acceptable behavior is generally regulated almost exclusively by the social structure of the community. Failure to comply with ethics and morality carries social and economic punishments and sanctions but not supernatural sanctions.

This amoral configuration of religion may be characterized as a sacred covenant between the community (the social group) and God, the saints, and all supernatural forces. Humans and the supernatural are arranged in an established order in which each has rights and obligations; and so long as both comply with their respective parts, the world will run fairly smoothly. Humans expect from God, the saints, and other supernatural forces the necessary conditions for propitious existence. In return, supernaturals require respect, deference, a certain amount of love, and, above all, a firm commitment to try to please them.

This pragmatic and utilitarian conception of religiosity is not confined to Indian communities. It constitutes a substratum that in varying degrees affects the practice of Catholicism in all sectors of Mexican society: most pervasively in rural mestizo communities and the urban lower classes; less pervasively in the urban middle classes and superordinate class. Thus the gradation effect of utilitarian–non-normative religiosity decreases from the bottom to the top of the stratification scale.

There are two important facts to consider as folk Catholicism evolves toward urban manifestations. First, the collective aspects of the human-supernatural covenant gradually disappear; and by the time individuals and groups are permanently enfranchised in the city, the covenant becomes individually centered. Since there is no longer a strong sense of community, the *quid pro quo* obtains between the individual (and the individual's family and at most immediate kin) and the supernatural. Second, the complex of rites and ceremonies that in the folk context serves to communicate with and please the supernaturals naturally changes; but in the more secularized rural contexts and in the city, the complex does not necessarily diminish: new elements are introduced, and traditional elements are reinterpreted.

The third aspect is the magical component of Mexican Catholicism that transcends the boundaries of folk religion. This departure from orthodox Catholicism is more subtle than the first two aspects, and it is more difficult to establish how it is discharged. The magical complex includes elements of witchcraft, sorcery, and curing that again represent a confluence of Spanish and pre-Hispanic elements forged in the process of syncretism that crystallized by the beginning of the eighteenth century. In the folk context (from Indian-traditional to transitional-mestizo communities) witchcraft, sorcery, and curing are ideologically part of an undifferentiated complex that includes all Catholic supernatural. I have characterized this complex (Nutini 1988: 410–413) as an ideologically monistic system pluralistically discharged.

The efficacy of the monistic ideology and belief system of Mexican religiosity does not disappear in the transition from the folk to the urban-national context—far from it. It pervades the entire array of folk elements that survives the transition, which includes many elements of witchcraft, sorcery, and curing. Indeed, the religious ideology of the urban lower classes is not basically different from that of Indian and traditional rural mestizo communities, despite changes in structural realization that accompany the transformation. The religiosity of the urban lower classes includes a mixture of pagan, folk traditional, and orthodox Catholic elements that are practiced with apparently no contradiction. Individuals believe in witchcraft and occasionally consult sorcerers, engage in many unorthodox social practices (concubinage and abortion being the most common), and engage in orthodox Catholic practices (attending mass and occasionally taking communion) in basically the same fashion as the members of a folk community, namely, in the context of the same psychological ambiance and expecting to achieve similar results.

To summarize, the magical component of Mexican Catholicism practiced by the vast majority of the country's population (the folk Indian and rural mestizo population and the urban lower classes, probably 75 percent of Mexico's population) may be characterized as follows. The absence or weakness of moral injunctions and constraints, the pragmatic covenant that underlies the relationship of humans with the supernatural, and the efficacy of this magico-religious covenant in the discharge of several domains of the social structure fashion a religiosity that verges on paganism. The religiosity of the majority of Mexicans is, of course, basically Catholic in most outward appearances (the physical manifestations of the cult) and in theological principle, but it is vitiated by beliefs and practices that render it quite unorthodox and, at times, downright heretical. By labeling this configuration as endowed with a magical component, I mean fundamentally that there is a pronounced gulf between what the theology and belief system of Catholicism specifies and what the people actually practice.

Finally, a word about the Catholicism of the middle classes and more educated sectors, who probably constitute about 25 percent of the population of the country. The magical component of Catholicism in this environment is much less pronounced than what I describe above. First, the pagan component is more latent than manifest, but it is not exempt from occasionally explicit realization. The supernatural ensemble includes some non-Catholic elements; but middle-class and educated Mexicans are largely unaware of them, and religious praxis appears more orthodox than it really is. Second, with aristocratic religiosity as an exception, the extensive and diversified ritual and ceremonial folk complex no longer obtains, and religious praxis is discharged in a more or less unitary fashion but still on the basis of a surviving monistic ideology. Third, the magical element is mostly manifested in surviving beliefs in elements of witchcraft and sorcery and the willingness to consult traditional curers when medicine fails. Indeed, my information on educated upper-middle-class men and women in Mexico City exhibits a manifest ambivalence about the belief and practice of witchcraft and sorcery. This is exemplified by a female informant: "Yo no creo en las brujas. Pero de que las hay, las hay" (I don't believe in witches. But as for there being any, there are some). This aphorism characterizes much of the ambivalence that underlies the religiosity of the well-off and superordinate sectors of Mexican society.

This is also the ambiance that frames the Catholicism of Mexican aristocrats: highly ritualistic, ambivalent, and at times at odds with orthodoxy.

The Configuration of Ritualism and Ceremonialism

The ritual and ceremonial life of aristocrats (religious and secular) is very rich, a trait that they share with folk peoples. The annual cycle of all Mexicans is basically uniform, but aristocrats and folk peoples have woven about each event an extensive web of practices and meanings that sets them apart from the rest of society. The best way to express this difference is that for aristocrats and folk peoples religion has many more social implications than it does for the great majority of Mexicans. Thus, regardless of the fact that the manifold arrays of rites and ceremonies of aristocrats and folk peoples are differently configured and embedded in different socioeconomic milieux, the two systems share significantly the same ideological orientation and have similar socioreligious goals.

The main ritual-ceremonial events in the life and annual cycles celebrated by aristocrats are baptism, confirmation, first communion, presentation of a young girl in society, birthdays, marriage, silver wedding anniversary, golden wedding anniversary, death, wake, and burial; Christmas, Epiphany, Holy Week, Corpus Christi, and All Saints'–All Souls' Day; and occasionally the day of the patron saint of the bygone hacienda. These celebrations, of course, with varying degrees of distinctness, are practiced by most sectors of Mexican society, and there is nothing intrinsically different associated with aristocrats. Moreover, the object of this study is not to present a detailed ethnography but only to describe its expressive component and how it affects the life of the group in its terminal phase. Two examples, then, suffice to analyze the aristocratic ritual ceremonial system: the celebration of marriage and Epiphany— the first because it is one of the most ritually laden occasions in the life cycle, and the second because I have not seen it described and analyzed in the anthropological literature.

The Wedding: Religious and Social Implications

The events immediately leading to the marriage ceremony and its aftermath are unquestionably the single most important occasion in the life cycle. It is a fulcrum of expressive behavior replete with ritual and ceremonial activity of the most diverse nature. In prerevolutionary times weddings often took place on the hacienda, a practice that continued but gradually decreased until the late 1940s. Since hacienda and country retreat weddings are rare today, I confine myself here to city weddings.

In traditional European society going back to classical times, the wedding ceremonial complex sanctifying marriage has been the pivotal event in the social life of the community, from village to kingdom. This is especially the case with all variants of the Western aristocracy. One could say that even today, when most variants are arcane survivals of the past, the wedding complex is modeled after *confarreatio*, the patrician marriage of ancient Rome. The legal and long-lasting implications of *confarreatio* have long since ceased to exist in all variants of Western European society; but as a symbol and ideal they still frame the contemporary aristocratic wedding. Again, it should be noted that the organization of the aristocratic wedding is not significantly different from those of the upper-middle class and other elite sectors of European society; but its ritualism, social implications, and above all the concern with exacting ceremonial discharge are indeed different and require detailed examination. There are five domains that stand out as the basic component of the wedding complex.

First is drawing up the list of invited guests. Until the late 1950s weddings were enormous affairs, occasionally numbering more than a thousand guests. Since then weddings have been significantly scaled down; and since the mid-1980s aristocratic weddings seldom have included more than five hundred guests. Still, regardless of the number of guests, weddings are elaborate affairs that require much preparation and maneuvering, particularly when the families of the couple cannot invite all the guests that should traditionally be invited. Since the mid-1970s the parents of the bride and groom invariably have invited an equal number of plutocratic guests as well as upper-middle class couples that (as discussed in Chapter 3) constitute the outer circle of aristocratic social recognition. In the case of plutocratic guests, weddings are now the main avenue of reciprocating social interaction with business associates and assorted magnates who would not normally be invited to the household for more intimate affairs. From this standpoint, aristocrats regard weddings as basically in the public domain of their ritual-ceremonial life—that is, they are occasions when protocol (gate-keeping activities designed to protect their intimate social life) permits interaction with people who have not been accorded equal social status. The most conservative and traditional families still remain completely endogenous and refuse to invite people that do not, in their view, have aristocratic standing. These families do not constitute more than 10 percent of the entire group. Be this as it may, deciding who will be invited to the wedding initiates the ceremonial cycle.

Second is choosing the church where the religious ceremony will take place. Traditionally, aristocratic weddings took place either in the city's cathedral or in one of the main churches of the city, La Profesa. During the past forty years, however, things have changed significantly in that aristocrats, due mostly to the democratization of the church hierarchy which they once dominated, are no longer allowed special privileges. In a way this is a cosmetic change, for since the late 1960s smaller parochial churches throughout the city have accommodated the marriage needs of the superordinate class. Thus several of these churches (mostly late-seventeenth- and eighteenth-century baroque structures and a few modern, twentieth-century structures) have made a brisk business of catering to aristocrats, plutocrats, and upper-middle class families. In this sense there is no aristocratic exclusivity: today fashionable churches are contracted by all families of the superordinate class.

Churches have to be reserved months in advance not only because of demand, which may be fierce, but because weddings almost always take place on Saturday, either at noon or in the early evening. The decoration of the church for the wedding may be a major undertaking. This includes the decoration of the main altar and retable where the wedding will be performed, several side retables, benches and pews, and not infrequently the archway of the church's main entrance. The decoration includes several varieties of flowers (mostly gladioli, calla lilies, roses, carnations, and baby's breath), ferns, assorted foliage, and ribbons. A lavish church decoration effort can run into thousands of dollars; it may be done by gifted decorators from the family of the bride and groom or, more frequently, by professional florists. Some of the decorations that I have seen for weddings are veritable works of art in flower arrangement, indicative of a high expressive concern of aristocratic men and women.

Third is the choice of the locale for the wedding lunch or dinner and ensuing celebration. A small number of aristocratic families today have sufficiently large households to accommodate three hundred or more guests. The great majority of weddings, however, take place in special locales catering to the superordinate class or in seven or eight of the best hotels and largest restaurants in the city. Several of these establishments are owned by aristocrats, who know well how to cater to the requirements of aristocratic celebrations. Indeed two of these restaurants are old hacienda manors that have been engulfed by the growth of the city since the 1940s. They are excellent examples of eighteenth-century hacienda architecture, with elegant and spacious accommodations.

Food and drink are respectively of primary and medium expressive importance. Food requires a great deal of thought. Drink is a much smaller expense for aristocrats, compared to the extravagantly expensive lengths to which some plutocrats would go to put on what they consider a brilliant wedding (some weddings have been known to run into hundreds of thousands of dollars for liquor alone).[1] Thus, by what one might consider "international standards" of elites, the liquor served at aristocratic weddings and other celebrations is below average, as most aristocrats cannot afford $100 bottles of wine to serve to 200 or 300 guests. The food, however, is an altogether different matter. Indeed, subjective as this judgment might be, the best food that I have tasted in nearly forty years of work in Mexico has been at aristocratic weddings. There are essentially two types of menus served: traditional Mexican and basically French. In terms of delicacy and taste the Mexican menu is superior to the French. Intrinsically, the Mexican menu has more expressive meaning, regardless of whatever motivation aristocratic families may latently or manifestly have. It gives them the opportunity to try recipes that have been in the family for generations. When the wedding is catered, it is understood that the menu will be traditional Mexican, for this is their specialty. Most of these dishes have virtually disappeared from the repertoire of fine Mexican cuisine, except perhaps in a couple of restaurants (as discussed in Chapter 5).

Fourth is the civil wedding. Under the strict separation of church and state in Mexican law, priests, ministers, and rabbis are not empowered to marry; and religious and civil marriages are completely separate events. The civil marriage generally takes place one or two weeks before the religious ceremony, and this is standard practice among middle-class and superordinate-class people. What varies is where and how the civil ceremony takes place and how elaborate the event is. For folk people and the urban lower classes, civil marriage means a quick trip to city hall after securing a health certificate. For middle-class people it means the same; but the occasion may involve a small celebration, particularly in provincial cities, where it has become an indicator of upward mobility. For the superordinately placed, in contrast, civil marriage is a rather elaborate celebration, almost always accompanied by a dinner party. Plutocrats are the most ostentatious in celebrating civil marriage, but aristocrats are increasingly following in their footsteps.

All superordinately placed families are influential enough to have a justice of the peace come to the house to perform the civil ceremony, which is generally scheduled between 7 and 8 P.M. and is followed by an elaborate buffet dinner. Plutocratic civil marriage dinners may include 100 or more guests, whereas aristocratic ones are smaller and more intimate. This is a ceremonial occasion of considerable importance and has several sociological implications. First, unlike the configuration of personnel surrounding the traditional European wedding (upper-middle-class and up), the aristocratic wedding in Mexico is rather sparse; there is little emphasis on maids of honor and best men, and even *padrinos de casamiento* (wedding godparents) play a rather minimal role. Beyond primary relatives (the bride, the groom, and their parents), the only personnel of significance in the religious wedding are two pages of honor (*pajes de honor*; generally a boy and a girl, aged six to eight, closely related to the bride and/or groom) who help the bride with her train. For the civil wedding, by contrast, there is much emphasis on attending personnel, including the participation of the *padrinos de casamiento*, from four to eight *testigos* (witnesses, who sign the marriage certificate), and the *consuegros* (co-parents-in-law, that is, the parents of the bride and groom).

Second, the witnesses are mostly male and female relatives of the bride and groom; but occasionally close friends are chosen. The wedding godparents are almost invariably close relatives of the couple, as the purpose of *compadrazgo* among aristocrats (unlike among most other sectors of Mexican society) is to consolidate or reinforce relationships already existent rather than to expand networks of relationships. The co-parents-in-law are the central personnel in the civil wedding as the representatives of the wider network of kin. The wedding godparents, witnesses, and co-parents-in-law may be regarded as the body of peers that ritually instills in the bride and groom a consciousness of who they are and how they should behave in a socially hostile world. In subtle ways the couple is told that, even with limited economic means, there are ways to behave honorably as aristocrats. This is the main reason why the civil wedding includes mostly individuals of recognized aristocratic standing. Even in mixed marriages, the family of the aristocratic bride or groom manages to convey a consciousness of group expectations, regardless of the new milieu into which the nonaristocratic partner is to a large extent being incorporated. Almost invariably there are no conflicts of social interest. Before dinner is served, the bride and groom are admonished to be true to their roots, and this is the most overt formal occasion of reinforcing aristocratic values instilled in young men and women before marriage.

Third is the process of bequeathing the heirlooms to the bride and groom, traditionally the high point of the proceedings, which occurs when the co-parents-in-law announce the heirlooms that they are bequeathing to the bride and groom. During the past thirty years this practice has been largely abandoned, and only the most conservative families still practice it. This is a public statement of what the bride and groom already know. Their parents have privately told them, and the main function of this event is to impress upon the company the material-symbolic contribution made to the bride and groom as they begin a new life. Bequeathed heirlooms may vary significantly; but regardless of quality and quantity the symbolic meaning is the same: a final reminder of aristocratic standing. In summary, the civil wedding is sociologically more salient than the religious wedding, a ritual-ceremonial event redolent with admonitions and advice about the aristocratic way of life.

Fourth, and finally, are the three significant complements of the wedding cycle. First is the wedding dress and its preparation. Probably the majority of aristocratic brides have wedding dresses two to four generations old—that is, they were worn by grandmothers, great-grandmothers, or great-great-grandmothers. These are highly valued heirlooms, and brides take great pride in them. The basic form and style of the dress have been preserved; but in each generation some alteration had to be made, mostly in the configuration of the bodice, length and spread of the train, and elaboration of the headgear. To get an old dress ready for a wedding takes a significant amount of expressive innovation, and brides and mothers are justly proud of the finished product: combining the usually classic, streamlined style of an old dress with modern changes and/or additions. For the families of the couple, the high point of the wedding cycle is to see the bride and her dress being admired as she walks up the aisle of the church. Many brides have to wear new dresses that are purchased in one of two high-fashion stores in Mexico City; and if the parents are sufficiently affluent they may trek to New York or Paris to buy the dress. Even under such circumstances, something traditional is always added to the new outfit: a decoration in the train, a sash, a specially fine *azahar* (orange blossom), or anything that may qualify as a minor heirloom. There is an almost magical belief in the practice of wearing an old wedding dress or adding to a new dress something that has been in the family for a long time: that it will protect the couple by communicating the warmth that is attributed to heirlooms.

Second are the *despedidas de soltera* (showers) and *despedidas de soltero* (bachelor parties). Until the late 1940s showers and bachelor parties abounded. It was common for brides and grooms to have six or seven, extended over a period of three or four weeks before the wedding. Since then they have drastically diminished, and today it is rare for the bride and groom to have more than two. Showers are intimate affairs that take place in the homes of close friends and relatives; they are sedate gatherings, always accompanied by food and drink, and the guests are of the same cohort of the bride. The typical shower is a dinner party organized by one of the bride's best friends and attended by a carefully selected group of guests. Bachelor parties, by contrast, almost always take place in restaurants and night spots, are often risqué affairs, and are not as exclusive as showers. They are usually organized by friends of the groom and include a variety of guests, including friends, kin, and close fellow workers who may or may not be invited to the wedding. This is another way to reciprocate with personnel who have not been granted equal social status. Showers and bachelor parties may be rather large affairs, occasionally including more than fifty people. These aspects of the marriage complex, however, are much the same for plutocrats and upper-middle-class people and reflect a rather common denominator of the superordinate place in most of Western society.

Third is gift giving and reciprocity. These are deeply ingrained patterns of behavior among aristocrats and have traditionally been of great significance in the conduct of interpersonal relationships. This is especially the case with gift giving for marriage. It was probably the most important occasion in the life and yearly cycles of aristocrats when they went extravagantly out of their way to give valuable gifts. This was the traditional pattern until about forty years ago. Since then the quality and value (but not necessarily the quantity) of gift giving have been significantly scaled down. In traditional times the average gift ranged in the neighborhood of one thousand dollars. Silver was a popular gift, and couples frequently received enough items to last them for a lifetime (flat silverware, underdishes, bowls, candle holders, picture frames, ashtrays, candy bowls, etc.). With the price of silver having increased more than six times since the 1950s, few people can afford the munificent silver presents that were then the norm. I cannot go into the details of the very diversified gift complex; suffice it to say that it ranges from household goods and all kinds of utilitarian items to artworks and leisure items. The complex of gift giving is pretty much the same as that of plutocrats and the upper-middle class. Finally, marriage gifts help to cement and smooth the relationships binding aristocrats and plutocrats: among the most valuable gifts are those from plutocrats closely associated with the families of the bride and groom.

Epiphany: A Folk-Aristocratic Celebration

The second example of the ritual-ceremonial cycle of aristocrats is the celebration of Epiphany, variously known as Día de Reyes, Día de los Santos Reyes, and Día de los Reyes Magos. Epiphany in Mexican Catholicism marks the end of the Christmas cycle (December 16–January 6), one of the three most sacred and important in the annual cycles, the other two being Holy Week and All Saints'–All Souls' Day. It is celebrated by all classes of society and, beyond the folk context, by none more elaborately than among aristocrats. This is easily explained. Before 1910, when the landed aristocracy dominated the rural economic and social sectors of the country, Epiphany was a most important event in the annual cycle. It was one of those communal celebrations that for a brief period brought together all the personnel of the hacienda, from the owner to the lowliest peon. It was a day when presents were given to the peons and *acasillados* (indentured laborers) and other personnel. Everybody attended a mass, and owners and peons self-servingly interacted for a day, symbolically bridging the chasm that separated them. Several former *hacendados* fondly remember this act of paternalism, and former *acasillados* interviewed in the early 1960s regarded it as another high point in their former hacienda status. Today this vestige of aristocratic tradition is celebrated in a manner reminiscent of its folk roots.

The celebration of Epiphany in central Mexico was introduced by the Franciscan friars as part of their campaign of conversion and catechization of the Indian population. By the end of the seventeenth century Epiphany had been established as an important event in the yearly cycle; and it remained unchallenged until the onset of the twentieth century, when several aspects of the modern celebration of Christmas began to make a dent. This is especially the case with urban populations, where Christmas and Epiphany are celebrated with different emphases. But as far as gift giving is concerned, Epiphany is still more important, since the commercialization of Christmas — Santa Claus, and several other imports from the United States (the Christmas tree and sundry decorations) — has not diminished the traditional celebration among the great majority of the population (folk people and the urban lower classes). Only in most middle-class environments and among the superordinately placed is Christmas, U.S. style, more emphasized than Epiphany. Aristocrats celebrate both; but in their celebration of Epiphany, they along with folk people are the most traditional.

Epiphany today is a family celebration. Although it does include some religious aspects, here I first present its general configuration and meaning. It celebrates the first manifestation of the Christ child to the gentiles, personified by the Magi (Melchior, Caspar, and Balthasar). With minor variations, Western Epiphany has become standardized in terms of meaning, date, and peripheral activities. With the exception of Christians of the Eastern rite, this obtains worldwide. In Mexico Epiphany has many regional variations in belief and ritual.[2] It is not a *fiesta de guardar* (canonical holiday in the Catholic annual calendar) but customarily very important as marking the termination of the Christmas cycle. Parishioners are not required to go to mass; but significant ceremonial activity takes place at home, which for the great majority of Mexicans centers on the communal eating of a *rosca* (a round or oblong cake covered with sugar and candied fruit) and the exchange of gifts. *Roscas* come in many sizes and are decorated with various degrees of elaboration; bakers in the cities and rural areas make them to satisfy every budget and taste.

The central feature of the *rosca* is a small hidden figurine (*muñeco*, now made of plastic but traditionally made of wood). The hidden figurine symbolically represents the Child Jesus and the Holy Family's flight to Egypt to escape Herod's persecution, whereas the knife for cutting the cake symbolizes the danger to the Child Jesus. There is an intimate connection between Epiphany and Candlemas (February 2) and the blessing of the seeds and animals. Although there are significant variations on this theme, its central feature is that the person who gets the slice of *rosca* with the hidden figurine is supposed to host a party (lunch or dinner) for Candlemas. In the symbolic ideology of Mexican Catholicism, the significance of the connection between these two celebrations is that infants and children, specifically denoted by Epiphany, are strongly associated with fertility; and Candlemas, although ostensibly celebrating the purification of the Virgin Mary, is fundamentally a symbolic act of intensification (Nutini 1988:139–142). In the folk context the figurine of the *rosca* is blessed by a priest and kept with the image of the Child Jesus in the household Christmas crèche to be taken to church for the blessing of the seeds and animals on Candlemas. Among aristocrats the rite is simplified: the figurine of the *rosca* is placed in the crèche, where it remains for a few days until the crèche is dismantled.

The most affluent and conservative aristocratic households have chapel-like alcoves in one of the living rooms, with religious art on display and occasionally a small altar. This ensemble is used for religious occasions throughout the year such as christenings, first communions, and especially Epiphany, where the family and guests are assembled. In lieu of this formal facility, most aristocratic families simply gather in the living room decorated with some religious items to fit the particular event that is being celebrated (pictures and images of saints, special flower arrangements, lecterns, etc.) for partaking of the *rosca*. Then gifts are exchanged among parents and children and guests who may occasionally be invited. This is more symbolic than actual, for the main exchange of gifts has taken place on Christmas day. Then the company repairs to the dining groom for lunch or dinner, depending on the time of day when the ceremony takes place.

The symbolic importance of Epiphany is not gift exchange but rather the remembrance of things past—or, if you will, the proclivity of aristocrats toward vicarious re-creation of that which is gone and cannot be retrieved. Thus the eating of the *rosca* and the ensuing meal constitute another occasion to reflect upon the time when they were "true aristocrats and not the fantasy that still haunts us," as one informant puts it.

Ideological and Pragmatic Characteristics of Aristocratic Catholicism

In addition to its inherent and pragmatic ritualism, the religious ideology of aristocrats is characterized by social aspects that set it apart from the praxis of orthodox Mexican Catholicism. As detailed below, this is the most distinct aspect of aristocratic religiosity.

Catholicism as a Validation of Aristocratic Rank

The conquistadors of the sixteenth century vigorously asserted that by winning such vast domains for the Spanish Crown they were worthy of ennoblement in the best tradition of medieval Spain. They buttressed this claim by fictitiously casting themselves in the role of paladins of Catholicism in the process of conversion and catechization of the Indian masses. This is a role that *encomenderos*, early settlers, and their descendants composing the Creole aristocracy cultivated throughout colonial times. The role was reinforced by the middle of the seventeenth century with the transition from *encomienda* to hacienda as the basic institution of the Mexican ruling class until the Revolution of 1910.

The religious side of this equation may be regarded as a usurpation of the concept of "cristianos viejos," which throughout the later part of the Reconquest (1200-1492) denoted primarily stout defenders of the faith. This denotation, however, was appropriated by conquistadors and other superordinate personnel who constituted the budding Creole aristocracy. In this act of usurpation, aristocrats claimed validation of their social status, demanded special standing and privileges denied to the rank and file, and became the source of several domains of expression that were also mechanisms of religious and social control. First, aristocrats thought of themselves as a source of ritual and ceremonialism and became the undisputed leaders of many of the public religious events in the annual cycle. Second, aristocrats redefined the role of "defenders of the faith" by becoming the arbiters of religious etiquette and the watchdogs of morality. Third, aristocrats created chantries (*capellanías*), endowed religious institutions, and actively engaged in controlling the higher clergy by encouraging their own to pursue religious careers and to influence civil leaders to appoint them to positions of authority.

As long as the aristocracy remained the dominant class of the country it managed to influence and control many aspects of public religious life. Its control came to an end after the 1910 Revolution. But the sheer inertia of centuries of domination enabled aristocrats to prolong religious influence for another generation. After the late 1940s, however, nothing was left; and the public realization of their religious ideology had been transferred to the private domain of the household and extended environments.

Ideologies, particularly religious ones, have a significant power component: they are ideas that transmission has selected for benefiting those who espouse them. From this viewpoint, the religious ideology created in the sixteenth century had two aspects that benefited aristocrats. On the one hand, Catholicism was not only to be held up as the only true religion but also served as a mechanism of social control. By extension, it behooved the dominant aristocracy to assume the leadership, together with the clergy, in the campaign to instill Catholicism. On the other hand, and as a corollary, the notion that aristocrats were once the undisputed arbiters of Catholic ritualism and morality remains today a part of aristocratic religious ideology.

Validating rank through Catholic beliefs and practices made eminent sense as long as the aristocracy was the dominant class of Mexico. But what is the benefit for aristocrats after they lost all political power and most of their wealth? Or, if you will, what is the benefit for aristocrats today to believe that they are still the champions of Catholicism? Can an ideological construct entail other than material implications (such as validating rank and controlling people)? The answer to the last question is yes, whereas answers to the other two must be framed psychologically. From the first random information (1976) that I gathered on contemporary aristocratic religious ideology to structured elicitation (1990) from key informants, it was plain that there was no material benefit derived from the persistent belief of aristocrats that they are the paladins of Catholicism and its ritual and moral watchdogs. It was not until several years later that I realized that the benefit was psychological-expressive: then all the exaggerated claims of aristocratic informants, occasionally vehemently expressed, made sense. Succinctly, these ideological claims have the function (benefit) of palliating loss of power and wealth. This syndrome may be interpreted as a compensatory process by which aristocrats mediate between what they think they should be as a social class and what they know they are in the contemporary stratification system of Mexico. The need to confirm for themselves that they are still aristocrats, regardless of their lack of power and wealth, is so strong that aristocrats are driven to a nonreflexive state expressed when they verbalize, occasionally in a single extended sentence, what they are structurally ("we are an anachronism; we do not count for much any more") and what they conceive themselves to be ideologically ("but we are still socially the best and people should recognize it"). To the uninitiated this may sound strange, almost ludicrous, but it hides a significant expressive-psychological truth: people under stress (and Mexican aristocrats as a group are highly stressed) may be driven to almost any kind of self-protective measures to reduce pain and anxiety. In this case, religious ideology provides aristocrats with an excellent form of palliation.

Contravention of Customary Catholic Beliefs and Practices for Social Reasons

The ideological system of Catholicism has two components. First, and most encompassing, is a body of dogma that establishes the fundamental tenets of the faith: its ontology, theology, teleology, and configuration of the cult. With the exception of the configuration of the cult, this component of Catholicism was almost entirely established during the first five centuries of Christianity; and during the following 1,300 years it has rarely been changed or modified (for example, when the theological conception of the Virgin Mary was redefined in the fifteenth century and her worship was characterized by *hyperdulia*). The second component is a body of customary beliefs and practices sanctioned by tradition which has changed significantly in the history of Catholicism. The most salient customary changes, such as priestly celibacy and the general configuration of the annual cycle of celebrations, were established between the ninth and thirteenth centuries; but many others have taken place since then, the latest one of importance being the infallibility of the pope in the nineteenth century.

There is another dimension of the changing ideology of Catholicism that must be considered. Throughout the centuries Catholicism has had to accommodate to manifold local conditions as it spread throughout the world. As a concomitant aspect of this adaptability, Catholicism has been flexible in accepting deviations from dogma and customary beliefs and practices. For example, more than in all variants of Protestantism, the gulf between ideology and praxis in Catholicism is wide, which explains its diversification. In analyzing variants of Catholicism, it is important to keep separate the deviations from dogma and deviations from customary beliefs and practice; otherwise it is difficult to assess a particular variant with respect to putative orthodoxy (as theologically and teleologically defined). This is the standpoint that has implicitly underlined the characterization of the main variants of Mexican Catholicism and that explicitly frames the deviations of aristocratic Catholicism from putative orthodoxy.

Let us begin with deviations from customary beliefs and practices. It should be noted at the outset that in different forms and degrees aristocratic Catholicism shares deviations from orthodoxy with all other variants of Mexican Catholicism. I concentrate here on the most outstanding deviations: birth control, divorce, abortion, and loss of respect for the clergy.

Despite the insistence of the papacy, birth control among Catholics is practiced with impunity in countries worldwide, including those that are allegedly the most Catholic, such as Spain, Italy, and Mexico. As far as I am aware, the most conservative sector of Catholicism on this matter worldwide may be fundamentalist Catholics in the United States. In Mexico, even at the village level, priests seldom preach against birth control, and Jesuits in the cities often counsel people that birth control is a couple's personal decision.

In the case of Mexico's superordinate class, artificial birth control is generally practiced and is not a religious issue. Among aristocrats this attitude has been gaining acceptance since the late 1930s, and today is the rule among reproductively active couples. Traditional aristocratic nuclear families were generally large, occasionally including ten or more children; but as one 85-year-old informant put it, "it had nothing to do with religion but with our ignorance concerning family planning." Aristocrats in the intermediate and younger generations (ages sixty-five to twenty), however, openly state that artificial birth control is not part of the dogma.

In Mexico divorce was legalized in the late 1920s and involves a rather simple procedure. Regardless of the fact that Mexico is an overwhelmingly Catholic country, most of the people in most social classes take a liberal view of the practice. On the whole, divorce has become socially accepted: there are no serious social and religious implications, and it has been increasing in incidence for more than thirty years. To a significant extent this is the result of the rather low profile taken by the church. A divorced person cannot remarry in church, of course, and all the customary injunctions against the practice are formally in place. But most people usually do not pay much attention to such religious niceties, and in the lower rungs of society they are not even aware of them.

In the superordinate sector of society, the most liberal are plutocrats. Conversely, aristocrats are the most conservative, followed by the upper-middle class. Divorce among plutocrats is mainstream, and as far as I am aware its incidence is higher than the national average. The upper-middle class is mixed but closer to aristocratic conservatism. Aristocrats are still on the whole conservative, but things are changing rapidly at all generational levels.

Until the late 1940s divorce for aristocrats was nearly anathema. It meant social ostracism, overt discrimination in many domains, and avoidance of social and religious interaction. It was a real act of courage for a couple to divorce. But when marriage became intolerable, there was a way out to avoid the terrible consequences of divorce: separation without the possibility of ever marrying again. This action condemned the wife to a lifelong state of overt celibacy and appropriate aristocratic behavior, while the husband had a much easier time. He could take a mistress and with the necessary caution and propriety set up a *casa chica*.[3] There was no opprobrium for the husband engaging in this practice; but if the wife was caught in any romantic or sexual attachment, it was considered adultery. The Christian imperative that "what God joins together let no man put asunder" was universally believed, and those who dared contravene it had to suffer the consequences. In Catholicism, however, this sacred injunction has always been tempered by bureaucratic annulment of the marriage vows; those who had the money and thought they had a chance assiduously pursued it. The practice lent itself to many abuses as couples went to extremes, such as adducing technicalities that the marriage was not properly performed.

A generation later, by the mid-1970s, attitudes toward divorce had greatly changed. Divorce among aristocrats had become quite common, and ten years later it was about the same as the national average. Among the young and middle-aged (men and women in their twenties to early sixties) it was taken as a matter of course and as one of the consequences of modern life. Divorce was still a religious issue, and the most conservative still regarded it as totally against the law of the church. The majority no longer practiced the social ostracism that barred interaction with divorced people; only a small minority adhered to the old practices of having nothing to do with those who had dared to dissolve their marriage. Silent passivity and refusal to be in the company of divorced people characterized these strongly conservative aristocrats. Conservatism in this respect cut across the age grades from young to middle age to old age, as many informants older than eighty had bowed to the pressure of change. This is well exemplified by a 90-year-old dowager when I interviewed her in 1980 and asked her if she would receive at home divorced kin and nonkin: "If I did not receive them, almost no one would come to visit me. There are so many divorced people that one cannot any longer go against the trends of the time." This is a significant answer, which clearly implies that conviction had been waning at the expense of religious principle.

Finally, by 1995 the great majority of aristocrats had come to accept divorce as an unavoidable fact of modern life and at most times ignore its religious implications. Only a small ultraconservative majority cling to the traditional attitude toward divorced people and still regard them as having broken the law of God. But even these aristocrats grudgingly participate in social occasions where divorced people may be present. Annulment may occasionally be sought, but it is no longer an important component in the dissolution of marriage.

In no other context does aristocratic Catholicism exhibit greater flexibility in departure from orthodoxy than in the case of abortion. In other words, social considerations become more important than religious considerations when the honor and good name of the family are at stake. Almost at the outset of my research (1976), this aspect of aristocratic Catholicism was impressed upon me by a male informant in his early sixties. I quote him *in extenso* because what he said defined my subsequent investigation of several aspects of aristocratic religiosity:

> As I was telling you, one of the most characteristic aspects of religion among us [the aristocracy] is a ritual and ceremonial emphasis and not so much ethics and morality as a way of life. Perhaps an example may clarify what I want to say. If an aristocratic unmarried girl gets pregnant (and it happens much more often than people may dare think), I am certain that her parents would insist on an abortion and on covering up the affair by whatever means possible in order to avoid social scandal. This, in my estimation, is what the great majority of the families of our group [the aristocracy] would do. It seems to me that, simply put, social appearances take precedence over Catholic morality, which is against abortion. I am also sure that people [aristocrats] would invariably place social considerations above considerations of Catholic morality in order not to tarnish the name of the family. But I do not

know whether this type of behavior also obtains in the middle and better classes of Mexican society.

This is a very telling statement by a highly knowledgeable informant, which highlights three main points: the ritual and ceremonial bent of aristocratic religiosity, the social context of abortion and its incidence, and the liberal transgression of customary beliefs when considerations of a social nature are at stake. I have already dealt extensively with the first point, but the other two should be expanded to gain a thorough understanding of abortion and the social context in which it takes place.

During the fifteen years after the statement cited above, I had the occasion to test the informant's assertion concerning what parents would do if an unmarried daughter got pregnant. Needless to say, this was a most delicate situation, and it was impossible to broach the question of abortion to all 150 or so informants that I interviewed over the years. Only after I had interviewed informants two or three times, and I had established good rapport, did I dare ask "What would you do if an unmarried daughter got pregnant?" or variations of the question, depending on the circumstances and degree of *confianza* (trust) that I had established with the informant. I asked forty-nine informants (twenty-eight males and twenty-one females, in their late thirties to early sixties), and I received thirty-two direct answers. The other seventeen either refused to answer or evaded the question. Of the informants who answered (twenty-one males and eleven females), twenty-nine said that they would not hesitate to have the daughter abort, and three said that they would send the daughter away to give birth and then secretly put the baby up for adoption.[4]

Everything my original informant said about the social aspects of abortion was confirmed by subsequent interviewing, which continued until the summer of 1993. I could detect no changes in this fifteen-year period. Indeed, abortion for the reasons described above may have been a traditional practice of very long standing, perhaps an inherent aspect of the Spanish aristocracy going back to medieval times.[5] For the reasons stated, it was impossible to ascertain the actual incidence of abortion; but I intuit that my original informant was right in asserting that it takes place more often than people think. It is also fairly certain that resorting to such drastic action is the only type of abortion practiced by aristocrats. This was intimated by three middle-aged female informants (in 1992). They affirmed that in the great majority of cases, if a married woman became pregnant without wanting to be, she would most likely have the baby. They also stated that quite often an unmarried young woman who gets pregnant opts for abortion without consulting her parents; this is done in secret to avoid embarrassment and in order not to hurt her parents, knowing that they would undoubtedly agree with her decision. One of these outspoken informants, echoing what my original informant had said nearly fifteen years earlier, without mincing words asserted:

> What I want to say is that social considerations, and the stigma of an unmarried woman with children, weigh more than contravening the commands of the church. Everything is done very secretively, but I think the matter is the same: fathers, mothers, husbands, wives, and other responsible persons opt for abortion at the expense of the moral rule that prohibits it. It seems to me that to do the opposite condemns all those involved to all kinds of gossip, nasty talk, and suffering great pains. This is the way I think, and I believe the great majority of the group [aristocracy] thinks the same.

Under the above circumstances, how is abortion rationalized? It is not. Fundamentally, aristocrats simply sidestep the religious injunction, ignore it, and only occasionally offer the view that the Catholic position against abortion is not part of the dogma. All aristocrats who answered my question, and many others from whom I incidentally elicited information about abortion, said it did not occur for any other reason. At least ten informants asserted that there was no moral (Catholic) justification for the practice, contritely asserted that they could not control the weakness to place religious injunctions before social values, and left it at that.

Most interestingly, one highly educated and intellectually able middle-aged male informant offered the following explanation. He quite rightly asserted that the main concern of the church with abortion is not the destruction of the fetus (a physical entity) but of a soul. The soul of an infant, he went on to say, does not come into existence until after it comes out of the womb (until then it shares one with the mother); and therefore abortion does not involve the destruction of a soul.[6] It is doubtful that this opinion is shared by many aristocrats, even well-educated ones. Rather, fundamentally, aristocrats seem to have a profound sense of entitlement: as the paragons of Catholicism, they consider themselves entitled to interpret the customary beliefs of the faith as they please.

Since the onset of civilization in the Near East and in all pristine civilizations, the hand of power and the hand of religion have always made a common cause. King and high priest, ruler and seer, lawgiver and prophet, have been joined together as the enforcers of the higher ruling of a God or the gods. And so it has been in Western civilization since the beginnings of Christianity. The aristocracy (from king to humble knight) and the church (from pope to humble village priest) have invariably joined together in maintaining power over the masses and enforcing religious dogma. The effectiveness of this alliance has worked extremely well for most of the history of Western civilization and still has significant efficacy in the modern world. It is based on secular and religious powers' deferring to the ultimate authority of God.

This is an apt characterization of the relationship of secular power (the king) and religious power (the Catholic church) in Spain that was transplanted to the New World; and it explains the self-conception of aristocrats as defenders of the faith and as paragons of Catholicism. From the sixteenth century to the Mexican Revolution of 1910, the aristocracy and the church (with the exception of the regular orders until the end of the seventeenth century) enjoyed a very close relationship, religiously and socially. For more than 300 years many aristocrats became archbishops, bishops, and cathedral deans as well as well-known secular priests. At least until Independence, aristocrats had formal privileges; and from then on, until the Revolution of 1910, they had customary privileges usually not available to others, particularly in the provincial cities locally dominated by aristocratic *hacendados*. Chantries, rights of precedence in religious affairs, and the use of church facilities for many occasions in the life cycle were among the most common. This close relationship, and the privileges that went with it, gradually came to an end after the 1910 Revolution and by the late 1950s no longer existed. This may be explained by the general democratization of Mexican society that was triggered by the country's new leadership, emphasizing the native over the foreign, fostering the search for roots in the Indian past, and eliminating survivals from the colonial past.

As a result of these changes and the disappearance of any significant influence, aristocrats since the late 1950s have almost completely withdrawn from actively participating at all levels in church affairs. This is an aspect of the rejection of the new more democratic organization of the church that accords aristocrats no special status and with which they no longer have any affinity. Aristocrats rationalize this position by saying that the lower clergy has been vulgarized, that priests have become more concerned with social issues than with religion, and that their level of education has dismally fallen. Whatever the merits of these arguments, during the past forty years aristocrats have increasingly broken their traditional alliance with the hierarchy and the clergy essentially because they no longer cater to the needs of aristocrats or to their self-image. Aristocrats rarely participate in church-organized charities or in the occasional drives for church building and repairs and have almost entirely discontinued the practice of close relationships with individual parish priests or any priest attached to the household. Chantries have been abolished, and the intimate relationship that once bound the aristocratic family to the lower clergy is gone.

There are a few families that continue the practice of having a priest attached to the household to officiate at baptisms, first communions, and other ritual occasions throughout the year. Invariably, however, the priest is also an aristocrat or has been acculturated to aristocratic manners and mores. Be this as it may, as a result of the democratization of church affairs and their consequent irrelevancy to the new order, aristocrats have developed an aversion to the way in which Catholicism is managed and practiced today. In some respects this is a case of sour grapes; and the brunt of the antagonism is directed to the lower clergy, as outlined above. The traditional guidance that was sought from priests, the respect traditionally accorded to them, and the intimate ritual bond are no longer there.

The rejection of the clergy is a significant deviation from customary belief and practice that has had an effect on aristocratic religiosity. In other words, the change is part of a larger whole, and it has to do with the new form into which Mexican Catholicism has been molded during the past three generations. Basically, aristocrats bemoan that Catholicism has become more practical and has shed many traditions that were at the heart of their religiosity—namely, ritual and ceremonialism and concern with exacting display and execution. They lament the simplification of rites, the absence of dignity and pomp in ceremonies, and, in general, the lack of commensality that has afflicted Mexican Catholicism. To compensate, aristocrats emphasize the ritual and ceremonialism in secular life that they find lacking in religion. They longingly remember when traditional Catholicism conformed to their precepts and blame the transformation on a clergy that was unable to stem the tide of secularization. How could they do so, one informant asks, "when the priests' intellectual level has hit rock bottom, and even the Jesuits no longer know how to preach and confine themselves to children's clichés?"

Deviations from Catholic Dogma and Reconfiguration of the Cult

This section may be regarded as an exercise in how aristocratic Catholicism, including the religion of much of the superordinate class of Mexico, deviates from dogma. Deviations are subtle, mostly unnoticed by the casual observer, but they do configure a distinct variety of Catholicism. Conversely, there are also certain general tendencies that the many variants of Mexican Catholicism share, which, although well known, have not been properly placed in context.

I am not referring to deviation from dogma in traditional terms (that is, when such action had serious, occasionally fatal consequences) but to the consequences that follow from the church's inability to prevent or eradicate such deviations. Indeed, this is probably the main reason why Catholicism has engendered so many variants in the modern world. I have established that the several variants of Mexican Catholicism look more orthodox than they really are, and it is mostly at the ideological level that deviations are found and consequences can be determined. I concentrate here on five main aspects of aristocratic religiosity: the primacy of ritual and ceremonialism (the pragmatic component) over ethical and moral considerations; the monolatrization of Catholicism; the concept of the devil and teleology; its magical component; and the increasing philosophical transformation of Catholicism at the expense of orthodox beliefs.

What does it mean to characterize aristocratic Catholicism by the primacy of ritual and ceremonialism over ethical and moral considerations? What are the consequences of such a religious stand? And can this proclivity be regarded as a breach of dogma? The answer to the last question is yes, and the meaning and implications of this religious stand may be framed as follows.

First, the primacy of ritual and ceremonialism lends itself to breaking any precepts of the church more easily when dogma is emphasized. (This is the case, for example, in U.S. Catholicism, in which adhering to church dogma and custom is foremost, and religious praxis on the whole tends to be orthodox.) If this were not the case, one could hardly explain the facility with which aristocrats break injunctions against practices such as abortion for the sake of social appearance. This religious stand has always been part not only of the aristocratic tradition but of all superordinately placed sectors of Western society: a kind of entitlement stipulating that the few may be allowed to break the injunctions of the church—but not the common folk, for this lessens the hold of religion as an instrument of social control.

Second, emphasizing ritual and ceremonialism enhances the separation of belief and praxis, further eroding Catholicism as a moral blueprint for action; this ultimately renders religiosity either a formal system of behaviors or a kind of philosophy of life. Indeed, for traditional aristocrats the former has almost invariably been the rule, as religion serves the very important function of validating lineage and rank. By contrast, for most young aristocrats (males and females in their twenties no longer under the strong constraints of tradition and facing an increasingly impoverished existence unless they acculturate to plutocratic ways), religiosity has become mostly a philosophy of life: Catholicism provides precepts for a happy and ethical existence, and if one complies with them everything else is to some extent superfluous. To what extent these young people practice what they preach is difficult to say. What is certain, however, is that they are creating a mindset that seriously deviates from orthodox Catholicism as an integrated system of dogma, beliefs, and praxis.

Third, Catholicism emphasizes commensality through ritual and ceremonialism. This is a stance that, at least in the modern world, undermines principles of behavior and morality independent of dogma, thereby significantly disregarding social commensality (or, if you will, social responsibility beyond one's proximate group). Without immediate behavioral guidelines, and the injunctions of dogma fuzzily in the background, the practicing Catholic is left with ethical choices that can be easily manipulated for personal convenience. Thus defining religiosity in such restricted terms constitutes the overarching mechanism conditioning most dogmatic and customary deviations in modern Mexican Catholicism. Most Mexican Catholics are not aware of the decisions and actions that this conception of religiosity entails, but this is not true of aristocrats. Their sense of entitlement confronts them with the realization that they would not allow others what they allow themselves.

I have already stated the main parameters of monolatry in Mexican Catholicism, but it would not be amiss to expand the discussion in order to determine how it affects a specific variant of Catholicism. This involves two main aspects: the confusion of *latria* and *dulia* (and its psychological implications) and the proliferation of saintly devotions as an alternative to more central Catholic concerns.

First, well-educated aristocrats are aware of the distinction between *latria* and *dulia* and are able to verbalize what it means for the practice of Catholicism. Not so the great majority of aristocrats, particularly middle-aged and older women. In worshiping the saints and the many manifestations of the Virgin Mary, aristocrats on the whole endow them with power of their own to grant boons rather than serving simply as intercessors with God. For example, when a woman prays to Saint Jude (the patron saint of lost things) to help her find a valuable ring, her train of thought is not, "Please, Saint Jude, intercede on my behalf before the Almighty so that I can find my ring." Quite the contrary: she is actually endowing Saint Jude with power of his own and asks him to intercede directly. As I have indicated, this is another instance of the inherent difficulty of Catholics everywhere in practicing thorough monotheism, given the historical emphasis on saints and other sacred personages, which provides this branch of Christianity with an almost polytheistic (monolatrous or polylatrous) configuration. This aspect of Catholicism has been noted before, as it is found in probably all Catholic variants from putatively orthodox to marginal. What, then, is the purpose of bringing this point up in the present context? Primarily because it allows for the analysis of consequences in molding the religious praxis of a group. Let us place the problem in perspective within Mexican Catholicism.

Of all three sectors of the superordinate class, aristocrats are the most traditionally religious. They adhere to a Catholic praxis that is not altogether congruent with being part of the best-educated sector of the Mexican population, which includes a large segment of the middle classes. Catholicism among the educated is perfunctory, formal, and lacking in ritual-ceremonial activities. Aristocratic praxis, by contrast, is devotional and concerned with the cult of the saints. This is changing, but the majority of adult men and women can still be so characterized. It should be noted, however, that there is a rather marked difference between men and women, who are more devotional and prone to emphasize the "magical." This aspect of aristocratic religiosity is neatly encapsulated by a male informant: "We are not fanatics [the closest I can gloss *mochos* in English], but like all Mexicans we are indeed superstitious, especially women. We are inclined to see miracles everywhere, to see all kinds of supernatural things when there is a natural explanation, and in general to commend ourselves to the saints and all the Virgins and Christ in our religion more than we ought." Looked at from this perspective, aristocratic religiosity is closer to folk Catholicism (including that of the urban working classes) and in rather sharp contrast to the Catholicism practiced by roughly 25 percent of educated Mexicans, which is undoubtedly the most "orthodox," taking, say, mainstream Catholicism as practiced in Western Europe as the standard.

Aristocratic concerns with devotional activities (practically every female informant of the seventy interviewed was devotionally attached to a saint), participating in pilgrimages and processions, invoking supernatural intercession, or in general seeing the hand of the supernatural at work in extreme, and frequently not so extreme, situations are largely entailed by the mindset of monolatry. This is in sharp contrast to the Catholicism practiced by educated Mexicans and Western Europeans, as characterized above. Aristocratic

Catholicism, however, is rather rapidly evolving toward a more philosophical religiosity, in which neither ritual and ceremonialism nor devotional, folklike concerns play significant roles. As noted, this is the case with most aristocrats in their twenties and thirties.

But what caused traditional aristocrats, among all educated segments of Mexican society, to practice a ritual-ceremonial, devotional, and to some extent magically laden kind of Catholicism? Primarily, I think, the answer lies in aristocrats' close association with folk Indian and mestizo peoples in the context of the hacienda for hundreds of years. One informant explains it as follows: "It is possible that in the context of the haciendas, even after the Revolution and until a few years ago, all these occult things like necromancy, witchcraft, sorcery, and curing were practiced by peons, villagers, and Indians, but it is also possible that many of these things were believed and practiced by *hacendados* as well. Proximity to this country folk very probably had an effect, for as the saying goes, 'he who lies with infants wakes up wet.' " It is also a fact that folk nannies had a significant similar effect, for nannies today continue to have an influential and intimate effect in the early enculturation of children.

Thus the monolatrization of aristocratic Catholicism has fashioned an ambiance of belief and practice that most educated Mexicans have superseded. The education of that 25 percent of Mexicans (as specified above in terms of class composition) has eradicated most of the monolatrous aspects of the Catholicism that they shared with the folk and urban lower-class three generations ago. The reason is clear: they did not have the benefit of the two enculturative contexts that aristocrats have always had. As a result of monolatrization, in conclusion, the core of aristocratic Catholicism, beyond its pragmatic use for the validation of lineage and rank, departs significantly from the Catholicism practiced by the educated in all Western variants. Aristocratic Mexican religiosity is therefore perceived as discordant by educated observers, accurately encapsulated by an Italian nobleman of princely rank:

Mexican aristocrats practice a Catholicism that is more Indian than that of educated people, which the majority of them are. It is the type of Catholicism that I have observed in Sicily, where the common folk are still superstitious; they practice customs that have disappeared among educated people and have religious aspects bordering on the pagan. In more than thirty years of residence in Mexico, I have observed with interest the religious behavior of my Mexican friends; nothing like it may be observed in the Catholicism practiced by European aristocrats, upper-class people, and educated people in general, even here in Mexico.

On the whole, most practicing Christians are not well versed in, and occasionally are quite ignorant of, the dogma that regulates religious behavior. This is particularly the case with Catholicism, whose body of dogma is more extensive than that of all other variants of Christianity and has elements that go back to the onset of the faith. Beyond the basic dogma specified by the Nicene Creed, there is a vast domain of Catholic dogma about which most Catholics are vaguely aware and at times wholly ignorant. Indeed Catholic praxis throughout the centuries has been mostly based on customary behavior and what the faithful are told to do by priests. Except for theologians, most Catholics when they are asked cannot specify the reasoning behind their practice. At least this is my assessment of dogmatic awareness among folk, semi-educated, and well-educated populations in Latin America. In fact, there is little awareness of whether a deviation, when pointed out to them, stems from customary or dogmatic beliefs. In this ambiance of general lack of theological sophistication, all kinds of dogmatic deviations take place, covering a wide range of religious practices which synergetically make Mexican Catholicism quite unorthodox. What, then, are the consequences of dogmatic deviations concerning the devil, guilt, sin, and several teleological elements of Mexican Catholicism?

The concept of the devil in Catholicism has been changing for more than 200 years. Until about the beginning of the nineteenth century it would have been heretical to maintain that the devil did not exist, while today individuals may assert with relative impunity that the devil stands metaphorically for the epitome of evil, but belief in the devil is not essential for Catholic salvation. Theologically, the existence of the devil has always been an ambivalent tenet in Catholicism; it was never a dogma of the church, but for most of the church's history to doubt the devil's existence had heretical consequences as serious as contravening a belief of the Nicene Creed. In this niche the conception of the devil has had manifold interpretations with a wide range of consequences, depending on time and place.

Given the syncretic components of Mexican Catholicism, the devil has played a rather minimal role in religious praxis along the entire spectrum of the stratification system. At the folk level the devil is one of several personifications of evil and does not affect the discharge of ritual and ceremonialism in any clearly discernible way. Rather, the devil is the subject of legends, a sort of trickster and a harbinger of bad luck. In a more attenuated form, pretty much the same obtains in the religiosity of the rural and urban lower classes. In middle-class and educated environments the devil plays a more salient role as the objective personification of evil and as an entity; while the devil is no longer pictured with horns and trident, one must entertain the possibility that he is out there and may try to waylay you. But there is nothing in the entire spectrum of Mexican Catholicism that approaches the great concern with the devil exhibited in U.S. fundamentalism. Even American Catholics, I have noticed, have a more pronounced concern with the devil than Mexican Catholics.

Again aristocratic Catholics may be the most traditional of the educated classes; for them the devil is a shade more real. To elaborate: middle-aged and old aristocrats take a rather Manichean stance in which the devil acquires a greater presence; they conceive the devil as being evil incarnate, locked in combat with the good forces in humans. Indeed, the devil acquires a kind of religious negative existence not unlike that of a saint: one does not pray to or entreat him, but one is aware of him and takes appropriate measures to repel him. For the great majority of aristocrats younger than forty, in contrast, the devil is something personal, a sort of mental construction that manifests itself when one has done something bad or has a bad conscience. As such, the devil has ceased to be a Catholic supernatural in the traditional meaning of this term. This is a conception, by the way, that is shared by most educated Mexicans. All variants of Mexican Catholicism exhibit deviations from the customary-dogmatic conception of the devil, but the entailed implications are practically the same: this supernatural personage has essentially become a metaphor, does not shape any significant aspect of religiosity, and survives as a rather superfluous manifestation of peoples' desires for the concretization of evil and morally reprehensible behavior.

Mexicans of all classes have a weak sense of sin and guilt, which goes beyond the traditional lack of intensity of these religious elements in orthodox Catholicism as contrasted with Protestantism. The sacrament of confession and the emphasis on ritual and ceremonialism explain the difference between Catholicism and Protestantism. But what accounts for the difference between orthodox and Mexican Catholicism? Again, my answer is the influence of pre-Hispanic polytheism, which in the sixteenth century shaped the configuration of a syncretic Catholicism that has survived at all levels of society. The two most decisive aspects of pre-Hispanic polytheism that account for the weak sense of guilt and sin are its singular lack of moral and ethical components and, as a corollary, a conception of the afterlife that has nothing to do with reward or punishment. Synergetically these two polytheistic conceptions account not only for the weak sense of sin and guilt but for several teleological conceptions in modern Mexican Catholicism.

What does it mean to say that Mexican Catholics have a weak sense of guilt and sin? First, I wish to clarify what I mean by guilt. I am adhering to the semantic distinction that exists in English between "guilt"—meaning the feeling of deserved blame or the sentiment of having done something wrong—and "culpability"—meaning the realization of deserving blame or having been found to contravene a rule or injunction. There are, of course, other meanings to these glosses, but what I want to convey here is that "guilt" connotes what people feel after realizing that they deserve blame for having contravened or broken a culturally determined injunction, whereas "culpability" connotes only the realization of being responsible for neglect or having broken a rule or injunction but not a state of feeling that they have done something or left something undone—that is, irrespective of whether they deserve blame. (In Spanish the situation is even more complicated semantically: there is only the Latin root *culpa*, and *culpabilidad* means both "guilt" and "culpability"; *culpa* also means "blame." The advantage of English here is in having an Anglo-Saxon and a Latin gloss, while in Spanish only context discriminates between guilt and culpability.)

The modal personality of all people I have worked with in Mexican society (Indians and mestizos, the urban lower and middle class, and the superordinate class) is remarkably similar in several respects. While a feeling of guilt is seldom reported, individuals frequently express a sense of culpability, especially in the specific sense of having been found to break a rule or injunction. Guilt is short lived and can always be rationalized by self-consciously displacing blame—that is, by individuals arguing that in other related domains they behave impeccably and never do any wrong. For example, failure to attend mass on a given Sunday may produce a sense of guilt which is quickly diminished by assessing how often communion is taken. In fact, guilt seldom plays a significant role in shaping behavior, much less in seriously impeding any kind of social interaction. It may seem bold to say this; but as far as the manifestations and consequences of guilt are concerned, there are no differences throughout the entire spectrum from Indian to aristocrat in Mexican society. Moreover, whatever feelings of guilt and culpability this diverse population may exhibit are almost always stronger in the social than in the religious domain.

As a corollary, the concept of sin—the main generator of religious guilt in Christianity—is also weak in Mexican Catholicism. Original sin is preached from the pulpit, of course, but in such a perfunctory fashion and so rarely that it again does not have any meaningful or noticeable effect on religious practice. Priests and people in general do not have sin at the tip of their tongues, and there is nothing in the praxis of Mexican Catholicism that compares with the fire and brimstone of many variants of Protestantism. This absence is partly a characteristic of orthodox Catholicism but intensified by the peculiarities of Mexican Catholicism, as specified above. This view of sin and its place in religiosity is not particularly aristocratic; it is shared by other segments of society.

The teleology of Mexican Catholicism exhibits some significant departures from orthodoxy. The concepts of heaven, hell, purgatory, and the paths leading to them have undergone important changes during the past century in Catholicism everywhere. This is part of the general trend that may be characterized as emphasizing the here-and-now at the expense of the afterlife with respect to reward and punishment and the final destination of the dead. For the same reasons discussed above, Mexican Catholicism departs even further from what liberal theologians term "enlightened" Catholicism, as practiced mostly in Western Europe. Here again Mexican Catholicism exhibits uniformity, but there are differences at various levels of realization.

Among folk peoples the conception of hell as a place of eternal damnation was never accepted, and this attitude stems directly from the amoral configuration of pre-Hispanic polytheism. The most common expression of this stance among the people I have worked with (Indian and rural mestizo populations in Tlaxcala, Puebla, and Veracruz) is verbalized or implied as follows: "We are punished for our wrongdoings in this world, and there is no need for a place of punishment where we will ultimately end up"; and (more damaging to orthodox Christianity) people imply that they cannot understand a God so cruel as to condemn someone to eternal punishment even for the worst kinds of transgressions here on earth. Time and again I have heard these expressions from the most diverse informants in four decades of fieldwork. I have also heard similar expressions from adult aristocrats, but I do not know the extent to which they are generalized throughout the group.

The urban lower classes exhibit a slightly less divergent conception of hell, but it hardly plays a significant role as a deterrent to manifold kinds of behavior. Predictably, belief in hell and entailed religious consequences are most orthodox among converts to Protestant evangelism (Pentecostalists, Jehovah's Witnesses, Seventh Day Adventists, and several others), which has made great inroads in Mexico during the past fifty years. It is striking to compare these converts with lower-class Catholics: the converts at times sound like Christian fundamentalists in the United States, often verbalizing hell, damnation, and repentance, whereas among lower-class Catholics these precepts are seldom expressed and basically are not part of daily religious praxis. In fact, among converts this religious stance seems noticeably to enhance guilt and awareness of sin as manifested in their daily lives. For the middle and superordinate classes hell has a more tangible existence, but its ontological reality is nebulous. It does not seem to deter wrongdoing, and people do not refer to it in any systematic meaningful fashion. Hell is not necessarily denied; but its traditional physical location (in some infraworld) is no longer verbalized, and its allegorical representation no longer seriously evokes punishment for contravening moral and religious precepts.

In all Christian denominations heaven is the most confusing of all teleological concepts today. Its meaning and ontological configuration as well as the paths to reach it have changed greatly over the centuries. The rather drastic transformation (accommodation forced by the general naturalization of society would be a more accurate way of putting it) during recent times from a fire-and-brimstone, punitive mold to one of love and benevolence explains the decaying significance of hell and the emphasis on heaven and proliferation of interpretations. Indeed, the geography, demography, and sociology of heaven today, among both Catholics and Protestants everywhere, exhibit manifold variations, and most of them have become personal and idiosyncratic. This is the same in Mexican Catholicism at all societal levels.

From Indians to aristocrats, the configuration and teleological entailments of heaven are essentially the same. First, heaven is still overtly conceived as the ultimate destination of those who behave well according to Catholic morality. What is not specified (verbalized) are the kinds of behavior that pave the path to heaven, except to the extent that social rather than strictly religious precepts and ethics seem to be more determinant. In other words, failing to attend mass on Sundays or not taking communion at least once a year is less detrimental than failing to comply with one's obligations to kin and friends or being dishonest and a liar. Contravening a dogma of the church, behaving in any way "heretically," or disregarding behests of priests (whenever people are overtly aware of these serious transgressions, which does not happen often) does not fundamentally affect one's path to heaven. To put it differently, selectively complying with ritual and ceremonialism and social ethics are the main stepping stones toward heaven, whereas orthodox theological and teleological compliance does not play a significant role.

Second, the ontological configuration of heaven is to a large extent a personal, idiosyncratic construct that varies across the societal spectrum, determined mostly by class, ethnicity, and degree of education. There are significant overlaps, however, and one may find naive or sophisticated conceptions of heaven at all levels of the societal system regardless of education. They have a wide breadth of expression, ranging from the traditionally simple to the allegorically elaborate. It would be impossible to do justice to the expressive imagination that is exercised in placing, populating, and describing the social dynamics of heaven, but a few examples suffice to illustrate the range of expression. At one extreme, heaven is conceived as a static hierarchical tableau of the celestial court: a pyramid at the top of which are God the Father, God the Son, and God the Holy Ghost; below them is the Holy Family (the Virgin Mary, Saint Joseph, and Saint Anne), surrounded by the saints, as the principal courtiers; and at the bottom are the virtuous faithful in enraptured adoration. This is a static representation commonly expressed (not always coherently) by people in all classes of society. It is simply a conception of reward for good behavior and one of the most common medieval representations of heaven that has been reproduced countless times in Western art and in Mexican popular art, which may account for its prevalence. At the other extreme, heaven is little more than a vision of blissfulness with no particular location in time and space: an allegorical society of souls enjoying perfect happiness in the presence of God, in which behavior of any kind is never specified. This equally static vision of heaven has a number of variations and elaborations. Incidentally, Mexican Catholics are vaguely aware and seldom verbalize such teleological entities as Final Judgment and the Resurrection of the Dead, which is one more indication of their pragmatic disregard for established dogma.

Purgatory is the third Catholic destination of the dead. For all intents and purposes, purgatory—as a waystation to heaven—is gone from Mexican Catholicism. From Indians to aristocrats, very few informants could verbalize the conditions at death for going to hell, purgatory, and heaven (those who die in mortal sin go to hell; those who die in venial sin go to purgatory; and those who die in a state of grace [sinless] go to heaven). Moreover, only a few informants were able to verbalize the distinction between mortal and venial sin and the length of stay in purgatory, as specified in dogmatic teleology.

Several practices associated with purgatory have greatly diminished, except among folk people and the urban lower classes. For example, wearing a scapular guaranteed that the wearer would not die in mortal sin by inducing last-minute repentance. About three generations ago an alternative to the scapular came into vogue: wearing a medal with the Virgin of Carmel on one side and the Sacred Heart of Jesus on the other, pinned to a garment covering the chest. With diminishing incidence, this practice continues. One of the most common beliefs associated with the scapular and its surrogate is that an individual who dies on Saturday with one of them on goes straight to heaven; but a person who dies on any other day of the week goes to purgatory and stays there until the following Saturday and then goes to heaven.

To summarize, behaviorally the teleology of Mexican Catholicism has undergone rather drastic transformations. Dogmatic and customary components of the afterlife are no longer as significant in guiding daily religious life as they were two generations ago. This is a general characteristic of Mexican religiosity, and there is little in aristocratic belief and practice that is not shared with the rest of society. The global teleological complex outlined above has become latent, and it has little influence on the conduct of most people. Indeed, heaven, hell, and purgatory have become rather nebulous concepts, remaining relatively conscious only due to inertia.

Admittedly, aristocrats are comparatively as "superstitious" as other sectors of Mexican society. This self-evaluation was expressed by aristocratic informants on several occasions. By "superstitious behavior" I wish to denote a complex of magical practices spanning witchcraft, sorcery, curing, apparitions, and assorted supernatural phenomena that have their maximal expression among folk people and the urban lower classes. In varying degrees all sectors of society (except the most educated and enlightened individuals) exhibit this magical complex. Among aristocrats it manifests itself both in belief and in practice; again, the source is the former hacienda context and the continuing influence of nannies, who often come from the rural areas where former landed estates were located. Aristocratic involvement in this supernatural complex must be carefully qualified.

First, how pervasive is the belief in magic supernaturalism? It is difficult to say, but I would estimate that perhaps more than half of the adult population believes in some form of it. At least ten male and female informants affirmed that they believed in the supernatural power of certain individuals to affect the lives of others (read witches, sorcerers, and curers), in apparitions, and in several kinds of phenomena that could not be explained naturally. Shortly after the beginning of systematic data gathering (1979), one of these informants, a female, provided me with the following statement that guided subsequent investigation:

> The truth is that these beliefs are quite common among the known people [aristocrats], but many of them do not dare say that they believe in magic, in witches and sorcerers, and in other things that are considered superstitions. I have many female friends who believe in these things but do not affirm it openly. But in the intimacy of friendship and in small groups they do indeed admit it. Besides, I know that many of my friends, and at times their husbands, consult curers when things are going wrong [when scientific medicine is not working]. There are also many people who consult clairvoyants and have their fortune told all the time.

Second, under what circumstances do aristocrats engage in magic supernaturalism? This was a sensitive topic to broach. Many informants evaded my questions, but about forty male and female informants were sufficiently open to enable me to put together the following picture. Middle-aged and old women are the most likely to believe in some form of magic supernaturalism and consult practitioners or undertake some action with supernatural connotations. Men of all ages, however, are less susceptible to believing or engaging in magic supernaturalism; and I attribute this to the higher degree of formal education, particularly scientific training, that aristocratic males have traditionally had compared to females. Among males and females of the younger generations (below age forty), magic supernaturalism is much less prominent but still surprisingly strong among males and females between ages fifteen and twenty-five. I attribute this to the proximate influence of nannies and servants, which is eventually outgrown as the result of the parity in education that both sexes now achieve. These facts may be summarized as follows. The older generations, growing up in a much more traditional world (with a much less scientific educational background), will never outgrow their early exposure to magic supernaturalism. The younger generations, by contrast, deprived of the reinforcing traditional ambiance of their parents and grandparents, eventually outgrow their early indoctrination by age thirty or so.

The most common and pervasive context in which aristocratic magic supernaturalism is realized is in assigning supernatural explanations to unusual phenomena when there are natural explanations, as stated by the informant quoted above. This is an extension of the belief that Catholic supernaturals have power to influence the outcome of natural events, which pervades Mexican religiosity. There are not only magical practitioners that can influence the natural course of events, but also events and occurrences that are caused by magical powers beyond natural and religious control. In other words, an individual either believes or does not believe that there are events and occurrences that are inherently supernatural and acts accordingly. Aristocrats, and probably other seemingly educated sectors of Mexican society, believe that there are events that warrant supernatural explanations or situations that can be remedied by consulting individuals possessing supernatural powers. Thus magical beliefs and practices among aristocrats are compartmentalized and realized as elements of last resort but not categorically different from the beliefs and practices of folk peoples.

Third, the magical beliefs and practices of aristocrats (with the caveats of age, sex, and incidence stated above) include several manifestations of witchcraft and sorcery; curing and exorcism; apparitions and enchanted places; clairvoyance and predicting the future; the evil eye (*mal de ojo*), bad or evil air (*mal aire*), and *espanto* (fright); the qualities of hot (*caliente*) and cold (*frío*) inherent in foodstuffs and human psychological states; and assorted beliefs concerning *duendes* (fairies) and ghosts, amatory magic, control of people's will, miraculous cures, and miracles in general.

With different degrees of incidence and intensity, this magical complex is probably found in most social groups (classes) above folk peoples and the urban lower sectors of Mexico's population. Among the superordinate classes of society, I intuit that it is most pervasive among aristocrats, but I was unfortunately unable to record the nuances and complexities of its manifold realizations. Nonetheless, on the basis of the anecdotal data I was able to collect, the following generalizations are in order.

First, the magical complex is latent but always close to the surface of peoples' social awareness. It is seldom verbalized, but when enough *confianza* (trust, intimacy) was generated, informants would relatively openly verbalize the generalities of their magical involvements. With two exceptions (both females in their middle and late sixties), the fifty interviewed informants did not go into the details and circumstances of their beliefs and practices, though they invariably implied that magic supernaturalism is quite generalized among their adult peers.

Second, the most common active involvements (practices) are consulting curers both as a matter of course and more often when scientific medicine has failed; having their fortune told and attending seances; and minding the hot and cold distinction in the foods they eat; the most common passive involvements (beliefs) are the existence of ghosts and fairies; apparitions; miracles and miraculous cures; and the supernatural power of certain individuals to bend the will of others. With the exception of attending seances (which may occasionally involve groups of women), active magical involvement is done quietly, even to the extent of not telling family members and close friends, particularly when it involves consulting curers and other supernatural practitioners. Passive magical involvement—while not a matter of common expression—does occasionally come to the surface, primarily under unusual conditions or situations of stress.

Third, the existence of magic supernaturalism among aristocrats seems to be justified as an extension of Catholicism. Perhaps the religious rationalization of magical beliefs and practices is a better way of putting it, in that magic is regarded as a Manichean entailment of religion. Twelve years later (in 1991) I again interviewed the informant quoted above. She said:

> Not that I am an expert on magical and supernatural things, but I have read enough to realize that the Catholic church burned many women and men at the stake as witches and sorcerers, and three centuries ago the church could not have been wrong. I could not tell you why things are so different today, but I have no doubts that things could return to what they were 300 years ago. This is why I have never dismissed the possibility that there may be supernatural forces that men [and women] can manipulate for good or evil. I have discussed this with some of my intimate female friends, and this is why I know that the majority of our people over fifty-five or sixty continue to believe in these matters despite the fact that they do not talk about it.

This statement strengthens the incidence of my anecdotal information on magical supernaturalism among aristocrats.

Finally, a few remarks are in order about the transformation of aristocratic Catholicism that has been going on for more than two generations, which underlies both some customary and some dogmatic deviations. There is agreement among informants that since the 1930s religion has been changing steadily. Probably until the late 1940s aristocrats were "traditional." During the past fifty years or so, Catholicism has been significantly liberalized, and much of the public ritual and ceremonialism has been simplified. What has not changed is the social ritual and ceremonialism of aristocratic expression and way of life.

Fundamentally, we may characterize the transformation of Catholicism into a philosophy of life that will ultimately change religion into a more active and socially conscious activity. There is no longer the traditional devotion and dedication to attend mass, confess, and take communion; and much of what is done is *por el que dirán* (for appearances' sake) and not out of religious conviction. In effect, the ritual and ceremonial spirituality of Catholicism has been gutted, leaving an empty shell. The only domain that has retained the traditional characteristic of aristocratic Catholicism is its social aspects, which is tantamount to saying that public religious ritual and ceremonialism have been secularized.

The Realization of Worship and Organization of the Cult

To conclude the analysis, I describe the public practices of aristocrats and how they are related to the formal organization of Mexican Catholicism. This can be done briefly for two reasons. On the one hand, the foregoing sections detail much of the general ambiance in which actual praxis takes place, and the description simply serves to flesh out specific points. On the other hand, Mexican Catholicism is most orthodox in its formal organization, and there is not much that is different from what has been described as mainstream Catholicism elsewhere.

Liturgy, the Clergy, and the Local Congregation

The great majority of aristocrats are practicing Catholics, and most of them belong to a parish. In the old days aristocrats were tied to two congregations: the hacienda, which always had a large chapel and not infrequently a much larger structure, the equivalent of a small church; and the urban parish to which the family belonged in the capital or provincial cities, which they thoroughly dominated. The seigneurial ambiance of the hacienda congregation was under the guidance and control of the aristocratic family and its urban extensions. Quite often it included hundreds of parishioners (peons attached to the land, administrative personnel, and neighboring people), and it had either a permanent or a visiting priest from a nearby town. The religious annual cycle was exactingly observed, presided over by the *hacendado* family members or their representatives; for the ritual and ceremonialism that it entailed was very important, both as a validation of aristocratic rank and as an instrument of social control. In urban environments aristocratic families equally dominated the parishes to which they belonged, in addition to playing leading roles in the affairs of the cathedrals of Mexico City and the provincial cities where they resided. The oldest and most prominent aristocratic families quite often had side chapels in cathedrals and the biggest parish churches, where their members had the right to be buried. In summary, religion for aristocrats was one of the main arenas of public display and expressive realization, which congregations vicariously accepted as lending luster to their own religious life. After nearly two generations of decay this religious preponderance had come to an end by the 1950s; since then aristocrats have increasingly been distancing themselves from local congregations, to the extent that today they have practically nothing to do with the organization of the parish and the activities that it sponsors or provides.

This rather drastic transformation, as I have already stated, may be attributed to a conscious effort at all levels of the church to democratize. To reiterate, the main function of the parish for aristocrats today is as nothing more than a receptacle for discharging the formal obligations of Catholicism, as priests no longer play a significant role in their religiosity. The rejection of the lower clergy to a degree extends also to the upper clergy, and nothing remains of the intimate relationship that used to bond aristocrats and prelates.

The majority of aristocrats attend church, but in the conventional sense they are not devout Catholics. Most of them attend mass on Sunday and all canonical holidays, occasionally take communion, but seldom go to confession. Confession is a sacrament that is rapidly going out of style. Two generations ago aristocrats went to confession almost every time before they took communion. Now the majority of men and many women of all ages may confess once or twice a year or not at all. As one perceptive informant put it, "People go to confession late, badly, or never; this is due mainly to the fact that they have lost all notion of what this sacrament means." Most aristocrats no longer operationally distinguish between venial and cardinal sin, which is one of the causes of this phenomenon. In addition, the personalization of religious praxis has led many aristocrats to slight the notion of sin and its consequences even more than is the case with Mexican Catholicism as a whole.

Despite the recent restrictions of the church on private ministering and the elimination of privilege (roughly since the middle 1970s), aristocrats can always find willing priests, and occasionally a bishop, to perform rites and sacraments in the household. Thus most aristocratic baptisms, confirmations, first communions, and other events in the annual cycle take place in the privacy of the home. The only sacrament that always takes place in church is marriage, mainly because of the solemnity of the occasion and the large number of people involved.

To conclude, aristocratic Catholicism today is almost entirely private. The traditional public component of religiosity is essentially gone, and with it the last public domain of ostentation and display; the church wedding may be regarded as an exception, but this is an endogenous ceremonial occasion that satisfies the aristocratic self-image and not any desire to project a spurious exogenous image.

Devotional Activities and the Cult of the Saints

The private discharge of aristocratic religiosity is characterized by the propitiation and entreaty of the saints and devotional activities accompanying events in the religious and life cycles. Strictly speaking, this is at the heart of the Catholicism practiced by most aristocrats, and they regard this as the essence of their religiosity and spiritual well-being. Beyond sanctification of the sacraments and formal obligations of Catholicism, the religious life of aristocrats is inner directed and centered on the cult of the many manifestations of the saints.

Let us address the last characteristic shared by aristocrats and folk people: an abiding concern with and devotion to a large array of supernatural personages and activities placed largely outside the church's formal ritual and ceremonial context. Foremost are the devotional rituals and activities entailed by a large roster of male and female saints, Virgins, and Christs. While individual devotions may vary significantly, the global ensemble of sacred personages is surprisingly uniform among aristocrats. The most popular are the following: (1) Saint Michael the Archangel, Saint John the Baptist, Saint Jude, Saint Anthony of Padua, Saint Martin of Porres, Saint Joseph, Saint Francis of Assisi, Saint John the Evangelist, Saint James the Apostle, and Saints Peter and Paul; (2) Saint Anne, Saint Isabel, Saint Rose of Lima, Saint Catherine of Siena, Saint Cecilia, and Saint Theresa of the Child Jesus; (3) the Virgin of Guadalupe, the Virgin of Ocotlán, Our Lady of Carmel, the Immaculate Conception, Our Lady of Sorrows, the Virgin of Lourdes, Our Lady of Perpetual Succor, Our Lady of Candlemas, the Virgin of Zapopan, the Virgin of the Rosary, Our Lady of Remedies, the Virgin of the Defensa, Our Lady of Fátima, Our Lady of Solitude, the Virgin of the Assumption, Our Lady of Piety, and Our Lady of the Immaculate Heart; (4) the Sacred Heart of Jesus, Christ the King, the Divine Savior, the Divine Shroud, and the Ascension of Christ. Just as important as devotions are mixed or composite sacred personages: the Holy Trinity, the Sacred Family (the Child Jesus, Mary, and Joseph), and the Blessed Souls in Purgatory.

Of all the Catholic supernaturals listed above, the most numerous are manifestations of the Virgin Mary, including both European and exclusively Mexican manifestations. This is a reflection of the strong Marianism that pervades all classes of Mexican society. Also extremely venerated are the Blessed Souls of Purgatory, another feature of Mexican Catholicism that finds a strong expression among aristocratic women. Accounting for the popularity of this composite supernatural is the deeply ingrained belief, at all levels of society, that the souls in purgatory are the best intercessors on behalf of individuals who are about to die. The variations on this belief are multiple; among aristocrats, the most common is that the devotees of the Blessed Souls in Purgatory can always count on dying under circumstances not involving mortal sin. Thus Marianism and the cult of the Blessed Souls in Purgatory account for most of the devotional activities and inward religiosity of aristocratic women. The same is true of men, but to a significantly lesser degree.

Another significant factor in the foregoing list of supernatural devotions is the rather small number of manifestations of Jesus Christ as compared with the much larger numbers that I have compiled for folk and urban lower- and middle-class populations. In the folk context Marianism shares honors with an extremely diversified complex of local Mexican Christs, including several dozen manifestations. The local nature of these cults (and perhaps a less monolatrous operational concept of the deity) explains why the devotion of God the Son among aristocrats is confined to traditional, universal advocations such as the Sacred Heart of Jesus and Christ the King.

In more recent times the role of nannies has been important in instilling their own folk practices in their wards. Traditionally (roughly until the late 1940s) nannies came from the hacienda or the nearby region. This reinforced the devotions of middle-aged and old aristocrats in the context of the last days of the hacienda system, like the patron saint of the landed estate and its divisions and the many manifestations of the saints. Since about the 1950s nannies have come from many different regions not connected to haciendas owned by aristocrats. The devotional enculturation of aristocratic children by nannies reflects both their idiosyncratic bent and their regional origin. Beginning as early as age five, aristocratic children are told about the devotional advantages of entreating specific Catholic personages, and by their middle teens they are thoroughly indoctrinated not only in how to approach them but in a large body of lore surrounding the cult of the saints. This process of early devotional enculturation stays with most aristocrats until old age and constitutes a significant part of their inner religious life. During the past fifteen years, however, the role of nannies in this respect has greatly diminished because the traditional bond that tied them to the aristocratic family has been broken, and nannies have essentially become servants.

After the demise of the hacienda system and loss of control of the public religious life of the capital and provincial cities where they were enfranchised, the ritual and devotional life of aristocrats significantly diminished. Many religious practices that had been an integral part of these socioeconomic contexts have come to an end or have only marginally survived. This is the case with the following folk practices: *mayordomías* (stewardships) and *hermandades* (brotherhoods); pilgrimages and processions; visiting churches of the saints of one's devotion; rosaries, novenas, responsories; and celebration of special events in the religious annual cycle. All these activities and involvements demonstrate how much the traditional Mexican aristocracy shared religiously with folk peoples. It should not be amiss to record what has survived.

As a "folk community," the life of the hacienda was centered on the estate's church or large chapel, which was the hub of the religious life of the hacienda's personnel, from the *hacendado* family and manager of the estate, to the administrative personnel, to the lowliest *acasillado*. In this ambiance *mayordomías* invariably thrived in pretty much the same fashion as in the folk communities of the region from whence the peons came. The main *mayordomía* was typically that of the patron saint of the hacienda; but depending on its size and complexity, there were other *mayordomías*, usually of the most venerated regional saints. These traditional folk institutions were, of course, the religious property of the folk people who constituted the workforce of the hacienda. But the *hacendado* family was also an integral part of the rites, ceremonies, and manifold activities in the annual cycle of *mayordomías*; it lent luster to the religious life of the hacienda personnel, palliated their exploitation, and served as a mechanism of control for the *hacendado*. The *hacendado* family, under such circumstances, became quite knowledgeable about the practices that these institutions entailed. In the capital and provincial cities, in contrast, the equivalent roles played by aristocrats were confined to *hermandades* and sodalities associated with cathedrals and the main churches.

These involvements had come to an end by the late 1930s in the hacienda and the early 1950s in the capital and provincial cities. But for another twenty years or so aristocrats were still involved in some folk practices that were the norm in the traditional setting. Among the most common were pilgrimages, processions, and visiting churches of saints of one's devotion. Some of this traditional exposure survived migration to Mexico City, and to this day some of the most devoted aristocratic families may occasionally go on pilgrimages to the basilicas of some of the most venerated images, such as the Virgins of Guadalupe and Ocotlán. Processions did occasionally take place in the hacienda, particularly for the day of the patron saint and for Holy Week, and the *hacendado* family fully participated during these ritual occasions. The same was common in the context of the cathedrals and churches that aristocrats controlled in the cities. Little of this has survived today.

There is also a rather extensive array of traditional rituals and ceremonies that aristocrats have continued to practice but no longer in the mainstream of their religious life: rosaries, novenas, responsories, and wakes. For reasons discussed above, however marginal they are today among aristocrats, they have survived longer than in most middle- and upper-middle-class environments. In fact, in plutocratic circles and among the upper-middle-class elites they have almost totally disappeared, and they are regarded as rather quaint practices of the past. For example, rosaries are occasionally said by groups of aristocratic ladies after someone dies, for some occasions in the annual cycle, and individually as part of the propitiation and entreaty of the particular saints of one's devotion. This is almost exclusively a practice among women, and men seldom participate. Novenas are also disappearing; only the most traditional families still practice them as part of the annual cycle, such as Holy Week and All Saints'–All Souls' Day.

The traditional wake and responsories are no longer part of aristocratic religious praxis, and they are symptomatic of the great changes that Mexican religiosity has experienced during the past two generations. Saying good-bye to the dead has always been a very important aspect of religiosity in all classes of a society so much concerned with bloodshed and death. The wake and responsories were very important events in the life cycle, which in some milieux acquired almost grotesque proportions. Traditionally among aristocrats these two rites occupy a middle position between the almost pagan ambiance and activity surrounding death and burial among folk peoples and the perfunctory, sanitized ambiance of modern funeral homes (*pompas fúnebres*). Probably until the late 1940s the aristocratic wake took place at home. No later than twenty-four hours after a person's death, an elaborate catafalque was set up in the main room of the house, and visitation began immediately. There was plenty of food and drink, and kin made a special effort to prepare delicacies that would have delighted the deceased. Informants in their seventies (1980–1985) remembered the wake as a bizarre combination of sorrowful and happy elements. Over drink and food, kin and friends remembered the deceased, told jokes, and had a good time in one room, while in another the bereaved cried and sometimes grieved ostentatiously. This almost festive ambiance surrounding the wake is characteristic of Catholicism and is based on the notion that almost invariably people believe that the deceased are going to heaven, no matter how badly they behaved on earth, and this is a cause for rejoicing. Responsories were a part of the wake and were usually said at midnight before burial, but the most elaborate responsory took place at the graveside.

This traditional complex of the last event in the life cycle came to an end by the late 1950s, with an antecedent twenty-year period of steady erosion. As far as I am aware, no aristocratic wake has taken place in the household since 1985. The ritual and ceremonial elaboration described above is no longer present; gone are the responsories, the intense human interaction that accompanied the consumption of food and drink, and the intimate ambiance that undoubtedly helped the bereaved to endure the loss of a loved one. In the modernized and impersonal ambiance of the funeral home, none of this is possible; and while some welcome the change as an improvement on several of the almost pagan aspects of death and burial, most aristocrats feel that something positive has been lost by the demise of the traditional wake.

The devotional activities of the cult of the saints are the outward manifestation of private aristocratic religiosity—or, if you will, the way aristocrats relate socially and to some extent publicly to Catholic supernaturals. There is another aspect of private religiosity, however: the intensely personal manner in which individuals relate to the supernatural. These are the two main forms of relating to the supernatural, and with slight variations most aristocrats adhere to them. They represent respectively the mostly female and mostly male approaches to Catholic worship and entreaty. The former is more traditional and monolatrous, while the latter is more modern and orthodox. These two approaches are perceptively expressed by late-middle-aged male and female informants.

On the one hand, the predominant female perspective was expressed in the following way:

> Only God can do and undo in this world, and it is of him that we ask favors and it is He who grants the good things of life: health, prosperity, love, and everything positive. The saints [males and females] and Virgins in their various manifestations are conduits to reach God, and it is to them that we primarily pray and supplicate for intercession on our behalf. As far as I know, we rarely ask God directly, and it is thus that

among us [aristocrats] devotion to the cult of the saints is so important. We know that only God may grant boons, but unknowingly we attribute to the saints powers they do not have. Every person has saints and virgins of her devotion, many times forgetting God the Son and his manifestations, to the extent that *mandas* are almost never made to him. It is something very strange, and it seems that most of the people of our class respect God so much that supplication is invariably made through intermediaries, which is what the saints and Virgins are in our religion.

Mandas (promises made to God, Virgins, or saints in return for particular favors) are a widespread Mexican practice and still very much in vogue among aristocrats. This woman's statement falls somewhere in between the monolatrous context of folk peoples, in which the saints are virtually endowed with power of their own to grant boons, and the orthodox position that conceives of the saints strictly as intermediaries. This informant is ambivalent about the position of the saints, places God (supposedly God the Father) in a somewhat unorthodox, remote position (not characteristic of either folk or orthodox Catholicism), but does distinguish between *latria* and *dulia* (probably more distinctly than most aristocratic women). I intuit that this position is quite widespread in the religiosity of the superordinately placed and the middle classes.

On the other hand, the predominant male perspective is expressed as follows:

To tell you the truth, for me and all people of my class, the Holy Trinity is a mystery. I can more or less repeat what the dogma states, that is God the Father, God the Son, and God the Holy Spirit, but I do not know what the relationship among them is. I only know what the dogma says and I do not question it. I accept, obviously, that God the Son came to the world to save us, and it is to him that we refer as Our Lord Jesus Christ. It is to him that I pray and direct my devotion, whereas God the Father and God the Holy Spirit are far away and are recondite beings that I have never been able to visualize directly or intimately. When I am praying I have in mind the figure of Our Lord on the cross, that is, as in many of his representations in paintings here at home. It may be because I imagine that Our Lord may have looked like that, that I have his image so vividly in my mind. The image of God the Father is nebulous, and I can never visualize it clearly, whereas that of God the Holy Spirit many people visualize as a dove and a triangle, something that means nothing to me. On the other hand, many people of my class, especially women, instead address their supplications and prayers to a large array of Virgins and saints, a fact that I have always thought was something very Mexican and none too orthodox. What can I tell you? Everything is valid if you put your heart in the entreaty.

This informant's statement presents the more orthodox position in the mostly male-oriented, private religiosity of aristocrats. Some women, of course, do adhere to it; but there is no question that it is primarily a male attitude. It illustrates two significant facts. First, this is evidence of a religious stance that comes close to the ideal theological position of the church but retains a measure of unorthodoxy—namely, the relative slighting of God the Father and the significant unimportance of God the Holy Spirit. Second, and as a corollary of the first, the statement makes clear the inherent difficulty that Catholics have in giving equal weight to the members of the Holy Trinity, particularly in the context of individual, private religiosity.

Fundamentally, just as aristocrats have socially withdrawn and to a large extent gone underground, the same process has taken place in their religious life. Aristocratic religious praxis, which had a vast public, social context until 1910, had become mostly private by the late 1970s and (with the exception of some public ritualism, particularly associated with marriage) almost entirely centered in the household. Mass attendance has become perfunctory, and whatever is meaningful in the religiosity of aristocrats is a personal concern.

In conclusion, Catholicism (there are no avowed atheists or members of other religions among the informants, only three of whom admitted being freethinkers), particularly among the young and middle-aged, has been transformed into a kind of personal philosophy. Although based on Catholic principles and the commandments of the church, it no longer needs to be buttressed by traditional church-centered ritual and conventions of ceremonialism, which are seen as largely superfluous to being truly religious. Particularly the younger generation thinks that attending mass, taking communion, and going to confession are largely irrelevant if one leads a healthy, moral, and dedicated Christian life. The relationship to God has become something abstract, like the kind of rapport that one has with an absentee landlord. On the other side of the coin, Catholicism among aristocrats has lost its traditional commensality, and religiosity has become an individual matter in coping with the world. This characterization has become increasingly common among members of the proximate generation, and only the older, most conservative aristocrats remain true to what religion was two generations ago.

Expressive Analysis

Religion in most societies is one of the most expressively laden subdivisions of culture. This is certainly the case in the aristocratic culture of Western society. If we add the inherent ritual and ceremonial proclivity of the aristocratic way of life, the foregoing chapter is one long succession of expressive domains subsumed under a single array. Thus concentrating on the most salient domains suffices to exemplify the expressive principles in operation and the consequences they entail. This exercise reveals one of the most important aspects of expressive culture: its exclusive and inclusive components and their distribution in a culture or subculture.

Inherent aristocratic ritual and ceremonialism are the main factors that have fueled the transformation from the public to the private realization of religiosity, basically without a diminution of the overall expressive significance of this broad domain. Or, as I have implied above, expression has been privatized and secularized. The net result has been an expressive array that combines social domains with some domains determined by devotional activities. This process has entailed a significant degree of innovation, primarily for psychological and palliative purposes. This illustrates the power of expression as a springboard to action, even when conditions have drastically changed for aristocrats: from constituting the predominant social class of the country to being an almost invisible and economically insignificant sector of Mexico's superordinate class. I briefly describe here the most significant domains as the database for the analysis.

First, the history of Western civilization conclusively demonstrates that expression is at its creative best in periods of transition. This is the case, for example, in the transformation of European society from feudalism to seigneurialism in the twelfth–thirteenth century and the rise of courtly love; the process significantly changed the man-woman relationship in the superordinate class, but with subsequent implications for the whole of society. On a smaller scale and not as dramatic—but entailing the same principles and consequences—is the transformation of the expressive array of Mexican aristocrats when they ceased to be the dominant class of the country. When aristocrats could no longer afford (economically) to discharge much of their traditional expressive array or were prevented (religiously and socially) by the new organization of society from doing so, creativity was greatly enhanced. What happened most often was that elements that were strictly utilitarian acquired expressive meaning and significance in the new structural setting. Baptismal garments and wedding gowns, for example, were just components of these ritual occasions; they did not acquire outstanding expressive significance until at least two decades after aristocrats ceased to be the dominant class of the country. Much of the religious ritual and ceremonialism of aristocrats today has the same origin, as I have suggested, and has the capacity to serve psychologically as a compensatory mechanism for the loss of status. This compensatory ritual-ceremonial complex exemplifies the creative origins of expression in antecedent structural conditions. Moreover, this example illustrates the interplay of expressive and structural variables in the changes that most often accompany downward and upward social mobility.

Second, the elaborateness of the manifold aspects and ceremonies of the wedding celebration among aristocrats today is the structural equivalent of the classic Roman *confarreatio* but devoid of all legal and religious implications that it had until the rise of class stratification after the demise of the *ancien régime*. In other words, here we have the reverse of the foregoing situation: a structural domain or institution becomes essentially an expressive domain of realization as a concomitant aspect of societal changes—namely, the democratization of society, which in Mexico began more than a century later with the onset of the 1910 Revolution. Thus the extreme elaborations accompanying the marriage celebration are to a large extent structurally spurious; but expressively they continue to have great significance socially and psychologically. Among the most expressively salient of these elaborations are those through which aristocrats can compete with plutocrats: items for which money is not necessarily required and in which aristocrats have a traditional advantage over plutocrats (for example, cuisine, at which aristocrats excel, but not extravagant liquor, which plutocrats can afford; or the old wedding finery that only age and tradition can confer; and the several niceties of exhibition and display at which aristocrats are experts and of which they have always been the arbiters). This exemplifies yet another important attribute of expression— the persistence and "survival value" of specific domains and occasionally an entire array.

Third, the ritual celebration of Epiphany is a case example of conflict expression (Nutini 1988:394–395) that is the result of loss of status (or any other cultural loss) entailed by drastic, usually revolutionary, changes in the social structure. This is the kind of expression that Roberts and Sutton-Smith

(1962) developed in their "conflict-enculturation theory of model involvement," which postulates that among individuals and groups conflict is assuaged by engaging in a model (expressive style) that re-creates the present in terms of a usually idealized past. When they were the dominant class of the country, the traditional celebration of Epiphany for aristocrats was strictly a religious celebration with significant overtones of seigneurial control. In the contemporary setting Epiphany has been transformed into a social-psychological celebration that compensates for the great loss of status and control that aristocrats have suffered. I have already given several examples of this kind of expression, and in the present instance the only significant twist is that the contemporary expressive involvement takes place in the realm of religion and not in a social realm, which is rather unusual in cases of conflict expression.

Fourth, expression as an individual and collective phenomenon is a changing aspect of culture, constantly adapting to new structural situations and conditions but with most specific domains of any given array retaining a core of original content and meaning. The process of change and adaptation may go on for long periods, in many instances for centuries or even millennia. This is the case, for example, with many aristocratic expressive domains that had their inception at the beginnings of Western society and still retain social and psychological validity, not only in the dying aristocracy but in all sectors of superordinate stratification. The key terms of expression as a social phenomenon are "creativity" and "imagination," which, in my opinion, are at the heart of understanding and conceptualizing sociocultural change. In fact, it may not be farfetched to claim that the origin of most sociocultural change is underwritten by expressive considerations. Necessity (material, structural conditions) may be the mother of invention, but invention is triggered and initially guided by the need for expression (socio-psychological conditions). For more than three generations in Mexican religion (not only as practiced by aristocrats but by all sectors of society) the entire teleological array has been subjected to much expressive creativity in fashioning a new conception of hell, heaven, purgatory, the devil, and so on. More specifically, much of the new ritual and ceremonialism of aristocrats is another instance of expressive creative imagination that has transformed the structural realization of many religious and associated social domains.

Fifth, the validation of rank through religion has been a constant in Western aristocratic ideology and praxis since the early Middle Ages, at least since the First Crusade. In no other country of Europe, due mostly to the reconquest of the Iberian peninsula from the Moors, has this tradition flourished with greater force than in Spain. The ideology of the Spanish nobility (both *hidalgos* and titled nobles) as being the defenders of the faith and protecting the southern flank of Europe against the infidel played an extremely important role in shaping all religious, political, and military actions and involvements of Spain throughout its golden age of florescence and supremacy in Europe (roughly from the beginning of the reign of Ferdinand and Isabella in 1478 to 1650). This syndrome is most clearly seen in Spain, leading to the Counter-Reformation and the Conquest and colonization of the New World, the main motivation being respectively the returning of seceding Protestants to the fold and propagating Catholicism among the heathens of the New World. This is the ideology that underlay the Conquest and colonization of the New World. In New Spain it played a preponderant role in the formation of the Mexican aristocracy and served the ruling class of the colony and then of independent Mexico well for nearly 400 years.

The Mexican Aristocracy

CHAPTER 7

SOCIAL ORGANIZATION

The Configuration and Interrelationship of

Kinship Units and Institutions

General Characteristics of Aristocratic Kinship

Aristocratic kinship is basically bilateral but diverges from the standard Spanish system from which it stems: it is somewhat more patrilineally biased. This characteristic has nothing to do with any changes that the Spanish system underwent in Mexico; rather, it reflects differences between the standard Spanish system (that of the commonality while the estate system was in place and that of most Spaniards today) and the system of the aristocracy, which in Mexico has thrived from colonial times to the present. This difference, by the way, obtains in pretty much the same fashion in all Western European countries and can be traced to Republican Rome. Shortly after the reign of Emperor Justinian, the kinship system of the West had become essentially bilateral, whereas the aristocracy retained many traits of the patrilineal system of classical Rome.

This bilateral system may be characterized as follows. First, it does not entail distinct and well-bounded kinship units beyond the household; the system's patrilineal bias, however, configures a number of functional units in the organization of the group. Second, descent has important endogenous and exogenous social stratificational implications, but it does not entail determinant properties for kinship-unit formation. Third, residence in the context of Mexico City is dispersed, occasionally patrivicinal, and largely neolocal in the context of the household but has limited implication for kinship unit formation. Fourth, there are preferential forms of marriage, but again with stratificational rather wider kinship implications; thus group endogamy and some forms of kinship exogamy do not lead to the strict localization of significant units beyond the household. Fifth, complementary filiation, albeit in the context of cognation, is an important component in unit formation; affinity is the most salient feature that complements descent in fashioning operational kinship units. Sixth, kinship terminology is basically of the Eskimo type that is most commonly associated with the standard Spanish cognatic system; but it exhibits some features consonant with the system's patrilineal bias. Seventh, kinship behavior is undoubtedly the most patrilineally biased feature of aristocratic kinship and significantly configures it into a system that transcends the usual fluidity of cognatic systems. Let us discuss these features in detail and determine how they are interrelated.

There are three main kinship units with structural saliency: the nonresidential extended family, the kindred network, and the name group. None has strict residential and social unity, but they have significant functions in the lives of aristocrats at different levels of realization. Their configuration is determined by variegated elements of choice, localization, descent, and affinity, shaped in the context of Mexico City. While these three operational units do not exactly correspond to well-established units as they have been discussed by anthropologists for several culture areas (see Buchler and Selby 1968; Kessing 1975; Gellner 1987; Robichaux 1995), they denote sufficient kinship features which warrant application of the above labels. The following discussion may be interpreted as an exercise in redefining certain aspects of kinship in the urban context of a well-bounded, fairly endogamous and endogenous group. Let us begin with name group, which is undoubtedly the least common in kinship usage.

The Name Group as a Kinship and Stratificational Social Unit

·

Definition, Origins, and Strength

By "name group" I denote all those individuals, males and females, who bear the same patronymic. Those having the same patronymic consider themselves related, even though the relationship may be quite distant. The name a person bears (even young aristocrats usually remember patronymics up to the fourth ascending generation) is not only a kinship designation but an index of aristocratic standing. Although from a synchronic viewpoint there are patronymics and matronymics, strictly speaking, generationally aristocrats conceive of names as being handed down through males. Thus one's mother's, grandmother's, and great-grandmother's names are regarded as patronymics. At least ideologically, then, this is one of the most patent patrilineal biases of aristocratic kinship, which (as I discuss below) has significant structural implications.

It is impossible to determine exactly the number of patronymics, but there is strong agreement that there are between ninety and one hundred patronymics today that are universally regarded as aristocratic, with perhaps another twenty in a marginal position (that is, patronymics of families that have acquired aristocratic standing during the past three generations). There are roughly another fifty patronymics that informants remember but that have no representatives today. The twenty marginal patronymics represent individuals and their descendants who acquired aristocratic standing between the last two decades of the Porfirio Díaz dictatorship and World War II. The fifty extinct patronymics belonged to families that died out, or lost aristocratic standing, between independence from Spain (1821) and the end of the Porfiriato (1910) or to downwardly mobile families that for at least two generations have no longer been regarded as aristocratic. Formally, then, there are two types of name groups: those including all patronymics living at any given point in time and those including patronymics that are remembered by the aristocratic group but no longer have any individual representatives or patronymics of families that have opted out of the system. I would like to call the former the living name group (LNG) and the latter the genealogical name group (GNG).

Mexican aristocratic patronymics are not exclusive, as they are found in all classes of society. This situation, of course, is exactly the same in all Western aristocracies. Its origin can be traced to the late Middle Ages, when the increasing complexity of emerging national states required naming beyond occupation and place of origin. Commoners very often took the names of the lords to whom they were entrusted under the seigneurial system; thus, by as early as the beginning of the nineteenth century the most distinguished and ancient aristocratic names were in extensive use among all classes of society. From then on, the patronymic a person bore ceased to be an index of social standing.

Be this as it may, in Mexico the names people acquired after the Spanish Conquest have the following origins. Quite often the mendicant friars gave arbitrary patronymics to the Indians in their congregations, in addition to Christian personal names; the secular clergy later did the same in urban environments. Indians in the *encomienda* system often took the names of *encomenderos* when they made the transition to urban environments and mining camps. When they were baptized, Indian nobles were given Christian personal names and were endowed with patronymics; apparently they had the option of keeping their Indian names (and what they denoted in the original native setting became patronymics) or accepting a Spanish patronymic, frequently that of the Spaniard who customarily became the baptismal *padrino* (sponsor) for the occasion. Mestizos, in the original, racial denotation of the term, took the names of their Spanish fathers. After the hacienda system was instituted, by the middle of the seventeenth century, many of the peons took the name of the *hacendados*, a practice continued until the 1910 Mexican Revolution. I am certain that there were other ways by which people acquired names; but the net result is that by the twentieth century all Mexicans from Indians to aristocrats had the same patronymics and matronymics, and only context and economic circumstance determined the social standing of names. There are in Mexico today at least hundreds—perhaps thousands or tens of thousands— of people bearing most of the 120 or so aristocratic patronymics now in use. This, of course, is the same in all Western European countries.

Aristocratic patronymics have a wide variation in membership, ranging from 3 nuclear families and 15 or so members to 40 or 50 nuclear families and 250 to 300 members. The mean average membership, however, is about a dozen nuclear families and 55 or so members, including male and female adults and children. There are very few (about 7) patronymics with a membership of 15 to 25 clustered at one extreme, and even fewer (2 or 3) with memberships of 250 to 300 clustered at the other extreme, while the great majority cluster about the mean average. I cannot say with certainty the factors that affect the size of patronymics, but I do know that it has little to do with antiquity of lineage (that is, when the patronymic acquired aristocratic standing throughout any of the four renewals [Nutini 1995:218–220]) or social prominence and visibility today. Rather, it probably has to do with the kind of forced migration to Mexico City beginning after the Revolution of 1910; significant numbers of aristocrats stayed in their ancestral provincial cities, quickly became downwardly mobile, and fifty years later had dropped out of the aristocratic group. Downward mobility in general is another factor that has kept name groups small, which warrants separate discussion as a critical aspect of aristocratic dynamics.

Downward Mobility and Aristocratic Identity

The most common traditional reasons for downward aristocratic mobility have been primogeniture (*mayorazgo* in the Spanish nobiliary system), the effects of impartible inheritance, and, in general, the excessive economic requirements of maintaining aristocratic standing. Since the demise of the *ancien régime* and the spectacular rise of the *haute bourgeoisie*, idiosyncratic and psychological reasons have perhaps become more significant. This process is inherent in the process of *embourgeoisement* that all Western aristocracies have been experiencing for more than 200 years. This means essentially the economic influence that the *haute bourgeoisie* has exercised in transforming the aristocracy. Plutocrats have demonstrated to aristocrats that the only way to maintain superordinate status in the modern world is to divest themselves of cherished social and psychological patterns of behavior and acculturate to plutocratic ways. In the case of Mexican aristocrats, many have dropped out of their class in an effort to stay at the top of the stratification system; some in Mexico City after their concentration in the capital, more in the provincial cities where some stayed.

All fifty patronymics that informants still remember but of which there are no aristocratic representatives today are cases of downward mobility. For about thirty-five of the name groups denoted by these patronymics the cause was economic: they lost their wealth and were not able to recuperate. Most of these cases took place before 1910, when the aristocracy still socially dominated. Ironically, most of the richest families in Mexico at the time of Independence fall into this category, and by 1940 most of their descendants had lost aristocratic standing. The reason for this is that the bulk of their wealth was in mining and entrepreneurial activities, in which it became increasingly difficult to compete with the rising plutocracy after about 1850. By contrast, those whose wealth was more diversified, with most of it having been vested in the hacienda system, fared better. The other fifteen or so remembered patronymics without contemporary representatives were extinguished as a result of developments after the 1910 Revolution and the strong process of *embourgeoisement* that the aristocracy has been increasingly experiencing since then. With a few exceptions, the name groups denoted by these patronymics were of provincial extraction, and downward mobility took place in the ancestral cities that they controlled. In the isolation in which they remained after most other name groups migrated to Mexico City, they became part of the new plutocracies that quickly began to emerge locally after the demise of the Porfiriato. To understand the nature and source of downward mobility, however, these facts require careful assessment.

The foregoing reasons constitute the structural, necessary conditions for aristocratic downward mobility. But there is more to downward mobility, and the factors are mostly expressive. Or, if you will, they constitute the sufficient conditions that underlie the process of downward mobility: one may have been born in an aristocratic family, but to maintain aristocratic standing is contingent upon making decisions which are largely expressive in nature. Once all structural reasons for downward mobility are considered, it remains to be determined why, in a group of born aristocrats with the same position (that is, with more or less equal wealth and social standing in the group), individuals make different decisions: the great majority opt to uphold aristocratic standards no matter what the cost (otherwise the group would disintegrate), but some are not willing to pay the price (particularly under declining conditions) and opt out of the group. To put it quantitatively, since 1910 about 80 percent of born aristocrats remain so today, while the remaining 20 percent have become downwardly mobile. Wealth, of course, is a determinant variable in sustaining a viable aristocracy, and the lack of wealth ultimately results in its demise as a functional social group. Power and wealth per se, however, are not a necessary determinant of aristocratic standing individually, and collectively it may be a long time (as evidenced by the continuing viability of the European aristocracy since the demise of the *ancien régime*) before lack of them causes an aristocracy to come to an end as a functional group. Thus there are always sufficient expressive, idiosyncratic considerations entailing downward mobility, which probably accounts for most cases of aristocrats who drop out of their class of orientation. Downward aristocratic mobility due to expressive-idiosyncratic reasons has a tradition going back to classical times; but since the aristocracy began declining with the rise of class stratification, its incidence has greatly increased. This process, centering on the Mexican aristocracy since the demise of its *ancien régime* in 1910, requires clarification.

Acculturation to plutocratic behavior and praxis (*embourgeoisement* if you will) has been a threat to the aristocracy since the Western *haute bourgeoisie* became an economic power to reckon with. In the Mexican case, until 1910 the plutocracy played an acculturative role *vis-à-vis* the aristocracy; but plutocrats ultimately became aristocrats. After the Revolution, however, plutocrats were not only an acculturative factor but began to exert an economic and, to some extent, an expressive influence on aristocrats, given that their great wealth made it possible to fashion new expressive domains on their own. This reversal of expressive roles created an enticing ambiance for aristocrats to emulate now that their wealth had drastically diminished. This is basically the situation that obtained in the provincial cities just before most aristocrats migrated to Mexico City. Those who stayed behind made expressive choices to intermarry with local plutocrats and acquire their ways and by the mid-1980s had essentially lost aristocratic standing. This expressive choice, however, was to a significant extent determined by the isolation of provincial aristocrats from the bulk of their kind. In Mexico City, where practically the entire aristocratic group is enfranchised today, the same choice is occasionally made, suggesting that downward mobility is mostly expressively motivated. This is not to say that all aristocrats who marry plutocrats or acquire their wealth-generating ways become downwardly mobile. The situation is significantly more nuanced.

None of the richest aristocrats (those who either were able to salvage some of their prerevolutionary wealth or were well positioned to create new wealth afterward) have become downwardly mobile; on the contrary, they are among the most conservative aristocrats, but they must also be regarded as plutocrats by virtue of their wealth. They constitute no more than 5 percent of all aristocratic families belonging to seven name groups and are among the most prominent and visible members of the group. By contrast, it is among the poorest aristocrats (families that between forty and fifty years ago were barely making ends meet, had little money to engage in the minimum expressive activities behooving aristocratic standing, but were bona fide members of the group) that downward mobility has most often occurred. Downward mobility has basically taken two forms: incorporation into the plutocratic milieu or acquiring the status of *familias venidas a menos* (downwardly mobile families) leading an upper-middle-class existence. In the case of the former, the transition was made by marriage; and in the process more females than males lost aristocratic standing, ultimately resulting in entire families becoming downwardly mobile. It should be realized, of course, that this process is relative downward mobility, as it was only aristocratic standing that these individuals and families ultimately lost; gaining in economic standing, they remained solidly enfranchised in the superordinate class locally and nationally.[1] Individuals and families unable to cope with the onerous material requirements and social and psychological outlays that aristocratic standards demand simply give up and acquire middle-class behavior and rather consciously divest themselves of aristocratic manners, particularly ritual ostentation, flaunting personal and household display, and concern with glory of the aristocratic past. It does not take long for this new ambiance to set in; new social ties are contracted, and in less than a generation they are lost to the aristocratic group. This is not a new phenomenon, as interviews with descendants of six downwardly mobile families indicate that it has been going on since the middle of the nineteenth century; the Revolution of 1910 only increased its incidence.

What ambiance and mindset, we may ask, keep the great majority of individuals and families struggling to maintain aristocratic standing with such limited economic resources? The answer to these questions is at the heart of aristocratic identity—namely, the rock-bottom belief that being an aristocrat has nothing to do with power and wealth but is a matter of antiquity of lineage and how one acts and behaves (that is, expression). Being realists, most aristocrats are aware that power and wealth were the sources of their old ancestry and were what made it possible to fashion the refined manners of which they are so proud; yet they are unaware that this implies a contradiction, which to outsiders may seem like nothing more than a rationalization for their claim to exaltedness. As I have emphasized in several different contexts, the great majority of informants sincerely believe that being an aristocrat is in the blood and that those who opt out of the group had a defective upbringing that did not reinforce what they were born with. While an inadequate enculturating upbringing may have something to do with downward mobility, what sustains aristocrats' claim to exaltedness is the innate part of the belief that compels most of them to preserve the dream, being aware that they count for so little in the superordinate context of the country. These contradictory thoughts and feelings are seldom expressed, but they are always present in adult aristocrats and are probably the source of their social depression. Their behavior, however, bespeaks security and arrogance, which compound aristocratic depression. This mindset is rapidly waning among the younger generation of aristocrats everywhere; and when it disappears, the traditional concept of aristocracy will come to an end.

Meanwhile, most Mexican aristocrats (determinedly and hopelessly, as they are well aware) go about their business, behaving in the only way that tradition dictates. In the last analysis, and at the heart of this study, the last bastion of aristocratic claims to be the best in society is expressive realization. This is poignantly explained by a 75-year-old male informant:

> Little remains of what we once were and had. For people who know something about the history of Mexico, we are like a memory fading

with time, but somewhat irrationally we continue to consider ourselves on top of everybody. It is as if something irresistible compels us to continue to maintain tradition. Without any power, and with limited economic means, we take refuge in our personal lives, in the past, and in an array of behavior that is of interest to nobody but us. At the same time that we take pride in our folly, we instill it in our children, as our parents instilled it in us, and we forge ahead with our illusion. But there are few families that do not have close kin that have ceased to belong to our class because they did not have the strength of character and aristocratic conscience to maintain our traditions. It is not easy to be faithful to what we believe in, with the moderate means we have, and in a world in which we count for very little. Yet most of us obstinately cling to a past that no longer exists.

This quotation was elicited during an interview about liquidating this informant's assets (amounting to more than 10 million dollars in art, furniture, and a large array of heirlooms) and investing—thereby becoming a plutocrat—and is an excellent statement on the expressive constraints that keep most aristocrats from dropping out of the group. I also elicited the same intensity of feeling from many informants who have few assets to liquidate. Such is the strong consciousness of class that still maintains the aristocracy as a functional group.

Endogenous and Exogenous Implication of the Name Group

Although all those who bear the same patronymic consider themselves related in several degrees of consanguinity, the name group does not exhibit any significant degree of organic integration. This is particularly the case in the largest name groups, which may be divided into two or three branches whose members seldom gather together for any social or religious functions. Ideologically, however, those who bear the same patronymic have a high degree of consciousness of kind and are very much aware of the history of the name group (particularly the identity of the apical ancestor, when component families acquired aristocratic standing, the place of origin in Mexico and Spain, and its most illustrious past members). Needless to say, these concerns of the name group are most accentuated among those who can trace aristocratic standing to the sixteenth, seventeenth, and eighteenth centuries, who account for nearly 80 percent of all aristocrats. Even those name groups whose apical ancestors became aristocrats within the past 150 years exhibit the same attitude and are most likely to inflate the family tree and exaggerate historical facts.

The name group is the most amorphous of the operational units of aristocratic kinship; it is essentially a reference group with more stratificational than kinship features. From the viewpoint of kinship, name groups are the reference matrix for conceptualizing the formation of more functional units. More significantly, the patronymics that denote them are at the heart of understanding aristocratic identity, assessing antiquity of lineage, and determining the overall position of their bearers in the aristocratic group.

The gestalt that these classes have of aristocratic standing is focused on twenty-five or so patronymics (the most prominent being Rincón Gallardo, Cervantes, Romero de Terreros, Sánchez Navarro, Pérez de Salazar, Cortina, García Pimentel, de Ovando, Icaza, Villar Villamil, Martínez de Río, and Fernández del Valle) that were consistently verbalized by plutocratic and upper-middle-class informants.[2] Awareness of this reduced number of patronymics, then, is the extent to which the aristocracy is recognized by very limited sectors of Mexican society.

To summarize, the name group plays a salient role in the social life of aristocrats. Endogenously, it is the focal kinship unit with reference to which more functional kinship units are structured, and the patronymic that denotes it is the most prominent index of aristocratic rank. Exogenously, patronymics are the markers of aristocratic standing and denote how aristocrats are collectively perceived by the superordinately placed and educated Mexicans.

The Limited Cognatic, Exocentric Kindred as a Coalescing of Descent and Affinity

·

Emic Configuration of the Exocentric Kindred

Among Mexican aristocrats, the bilateral kindred (*parentela*) has a significant emic presence: it is verbalized by knowledgeable middle-aged and old male and female informants as a functional aspect of kinship. Thus I begin with a general account of what aristocrats themselves (as elicited from numerous informants) conceive the kindred to be and what that conception accomplishes organizationally and ideologically.

Unlike the name group, the aristocratic kindred is a bilateral (cognatic is a better denotation) kinship unit with considerable stability throughout at least one and as many as three generations. The individual is coterminously related to a group of families through male and female connections. It is not a fixed group, but its boundaries are fairly well delimited by variables and constraints. The kindred is a combination of egocentric (personal) and exocentric (nonpersonal, grouplike constitution) elements: on the one hand, entailing choices of associating with families patrilaterally or matrilaterally related to a married couple depending upon nonkinship factors; on the other, having some of the characteristics associated with a descent group, mainly a measure of stability through time together with a degree of circumscription. (The kindred thus considered is not a unit "in perpetuity" as Robin Fox [1967:163–173] puts it, but it does entail a combination of what Ward Goodenough [1964:76] has labeled the *ancestor-focus* and the *ego-focus*, namely, conceptualizing kinship systems from the viewpoint of the kin groups composing a society or from the viewpoint of the individual and personal kin.)

The kindred is a network of households configured by the bonds of patrilateral and matrilateral ties and affinal connections. Individuals initially belong to a kindred as members of their families or households of orientation. When individuals marry, the first step in network formation takes place. At the start of this process the bride and groom almost invariably set the direction of network growth by choosing to identify with either his or her already existing kindred, rather rapidly leading to the formation of strong social ties. In the majority of cases, due primarily to the patrilineal bias of aristocratic kinship but conditioned by other factors, couples affiliate with the network of the groom. This does not prevent brides, however, from actively seeking to incorporate into the budding network nuclear families from their kindreds of orientation. The dynamic of network formation is intensified by the action of the groom's and bride's parents and prominent members at the center of their existing kindreds to incorporate affines into the kindred in the process of formation. To put it differently, the initial step in the formation of a kindred group, or rather in the expansion of a limited existing kindred, is centered on newly married couples and the basic choices they make in siding with his or her kindred of orientation. This is a zero-sum game, in which it is always the case that in the initial steps of network formation one of the kindred loses and the other gains a household.

The process of growth, leading to stability, is not as mechanical as the foregoing description may suggest. Rather, the basic mechanism of formation is modified throughout its developmental cycle by exogenous (to kinship and residence) variables. The kindred network is not a perpetual entity, for its composition changes in structure and the character of its functions as households literally die out, families shift network affiliations, and individuals withdraw from active participation. In network growth, structural variables and personal factors come into play; but the result is most commonly realized as follows. The kindred is almost invariably anchored in or centers about ancestral households; this provides continuity to the network, which may remain basically stable for two or three generations. (This is conditioned by continuous or intermittent long-standing affinal relationships binding two or more name groups.) It must also be considered that younger households do become ancestral (that is, at the center of a kindred network), and in this context personal factors most significantly come into play in network growth. When the children of middle-age families marry, the shifting from centrality in the network sets in. As members of the third generation and those of the second approaching old age begin to die out, the center of gravity is further displaced; but for at least a generation the kindred as a whole and the households at the center remain stable. Permanence and change, then, characterize the developmental cycle of the kindred until a new cycle begins—namely, when new ancestral households come into being as the center of gravity of an emerging kindred.

Individual households which shift allegiance, or rather those which attach themselves more strongly to another kindred (slide is perhaps a more appropriate term), do so for personal and/or psychological reasons. This is a common phenomenon underlain by two factors. First, the aristocratic group is still mostly endogamous (although this is beginning to change rapidly, as more and more younger aristocrats are marrying exogamously); most people know each other well and have kinship ties of long standing, which facilitates the sliding of kindred affiliations. Second, there are genealogical ties going back to colonial times that bind bundles of families of various name groups, which also facilitate changing kindred affiliation without any significant detrimental consequences for all families concerned. Personal reasons may include friction between women and men and changes in attitude and interest on the part of a particular household and the majority of the kindred. While psychological reasons are more difficult to pinpoint, they revolve about feelings of not being appreciated enough or a greater sense of closeness to another kindred, particularly among women and occasionally children. But perhaps the most common structural reason for shifting kindred affiliation is economic: a particular household for self-serving reasons changes allegiance to another kindred whose families are more affluent or have greater access to material resources. No less important for changing allegiance to a proximate kindred is the perception that it may have a more desirable aristocratic standing.

From a processual viewpoint, the kindred undergoes a developmental cycle which may be described as follows. The greatest strength of the network takes place when the majority of the component families of the kindred have been married for at least five or six years and are related to two or three ancestral households. The network stays stable for about a generation or more until it begins to decline, when the children of most families begin to marry. The least strength of the kindred occurs when second-generation couples are about to be married, as they have not yet engaged in the process of network formation, to start the cycle all over again. There are variations, of course, depending mostly on economic factors and residential propinquity in the city.

Concerning the exocentric aspects of the kindred, it should be noted that the parameters that structure it are the eight name groups bearing the patronymics of the grandparents of husbands and wives. Thus when married couples slide or shift kindred affiliation they are associated with households related to them through parents and grandparents and affinal extensions. In the past this was occasionally extended to the great-grandparental generation; in the contemporary context, since 1900, this no longer takes place. The fact remains, however, that kindred affiliation is always within the familiar context of name groups to which husband and wife are closely related, that is, in the second and occasionally third degree of consanguinity and affinity. The kindred network, then, is more than a reference group; it is not an exacting and well-delimited unit, but it does entail a number of social, religious, and limited economic functions.

Except that it is expressed in anthropological terms, the preceding account is what knowledgeable, well-informed aristocrats conceive the cognatic kindred to be. As far as it goes, it corresponds to ethnographic reality to a remarkable degree. It leaves out, however, two important aspects: the detail of the exogenous and endogenous factors that configure the kindred and the functions that it involves. The remainder of this section complements this conscious perception of the kindred verbalized by informants.

There are two kinds of variables and factors that underlie the formation and organization of the cognatic kindred: structural and personal-idiosyncratic. Structural variables include the patrilineal bias of aristocratic kinship, the interdigitation of name groups, and the inherent rank of patronymics; settlement and spatial distribution in Mexico City; economic affluence and disposable wealth; and, more recently, exogamous marriage.

Personal-idiosyncratic factors include conflict of personality and friction among affines and consanguines; individual inclinations, style of living, and professional interests and commitments; and feelings of affinity and closeness engendered by early enculturation.

Interdigitation and Entailment of Structural Variables

The patrilineal bias of aristocratic kinship is perhaps the strongest factor in endowing the kindred network with exocentric, unitlike components. Informants are aware of this and know that it is connected to the role patronymics play in network formation, as indicated above. But how do these factors manifest themselves and what do they specifically accomplish? First, *ceteris paribus*, aristocrats are enculturated to gravitate and associate with members of their patrilines. From the moment of marriage, and their initiation in network formation, husbands consciously pursue this strategy and as much as they can try to steer wives from their own patrilines. In most cases wives resist, compromises are reached, and the network expands among the wives' patrilines as well. From the beginning of network formation, however, this patrilateral bias remains a strong factor in the configuration of the kindred. Second, in this context of a mild pulling of forces within the family the network grows, and exocentric elements exert the most influence in configuring the functional kindred. Another way of putting it is that the confluence of structural variables and personal-idiosyncratic factors has a positive or a negative effect in network formation and on the functioning of the kindred as an effective social unit. Third, patronymics, denotating name groups, also play an important role at this juncture, not only by buttressing patrilineal bias but more significantly by facilitating the positive confluence of divergent husband-wife preferences and proclivities. Specifically, above and beyond the pull of the patriline on both husbands and wives, the prestige and standing of patronymics have a significant effect in network formation. Based on ancient lineage, relative wealth, and distinction of their members in some area of endeavor, patronymics are functionally ranked within the aristocratic group. Often families gravitate toward the highest-ranked name groups to which husbands and wives are related, usually those denoted by their eight patronymics.

Traditional bonds of affinity that have united aristocratic families going back to the eighteenth and occasionally to the seventeenth century are another important factor. In such cases, affecting probably more than two-thirds of the aristocracy, the prestige sought by families in affiliating with the most prestigious name groups is largely neutralized, and personal-idiosyncratic factors become more important in network formation. By contrast, some 25 percent of families (those that achieved aristocratic status within the past 150 years) do not have such long-standing alliances; their patronymics are on the whole less prestigious, thereby making them more susceptible to seeking affiliation with those which are more prestigious.

The distribution of households within the confines of Mexico City during the past sixty years is another consideration in the configuration of the cognatic kindred. The network constituting the operational kindred is affected by the proximity of households, and it is always a factor in the choices that married couples make in network building. By itself residence is significant; but when coupled with other structural and/or personal-idiosyncratic factors, it becomes determinant.

Before migration of provincial aristocrats to the capital, beginning in the late 1920s and completed by the late 1950s, Mexico City was a fraction of the megalopolis that it is today. Moreover, the 60 percent or so of aristocratic families that had owned residences in Mexico City since the middle of the nineteenth century (including both the permanently enfranchised and provincial families who kept houses in the capital) were concentrated in the historical center of the city and two adjacent sections (*colonias*) in close proximity to one another. By the mid-1950s all this had radically changed. Provincial migrating families almost invariably settled in the upscale *colonias* that developed far apart, beginning in the early 1930s, and the great majority of families residing at the core of the city quickly followed suit (see Chapter 4). By the mid-1960s dispersion throughout the city meant that quite often closely related families were residing twenty or more miles apart.

Dispersion throughout the megalopolis has been the result of loss of wealth—that is, the inability of most aristocrats to maintain their former mansions in the colonial quarter of the city and nearby *colonias*, which has forced them to move to more modest abodes. The dislocation of provincial aristocrats also contributed to dispersion, not only by their own resettlement but by virtue of their sons and daughters marrying into old Mexico City families shortly after their arrival. In a nutshell, the demise of the original residential propinquity that traditionally characterized the aristocracy in Mexico City had a significant effect in the network structure of the kindred, which may be summarized as follows.

Patrilineal bias, the prestige of name groups, and attraction of the affluent as variables in kindred network formation and growth were realized best in the context of residential propinquity, when the overwhelming majority of aristocratic households were located in and near the historical center of the city. In the context of dispersion these variables continue to operate but are modified by personal-idiosyncratic factors which significantly alter the choices of husbands and wives in the process of activating ties to families in their parents' and grandparents' kindreds. A few examples illustrate this predicament.

First, when households are physically and socially isolated for any of the reasons given above along with circumstantial factors (that is, when everyday life is centered in locations in sections of the city far away from the majority of the kindred of orientation of husbands and wives), personal-idiosyncratic factors are most likely to be realized in the process of network formation. Families affiliate with the network of either husbands or wives irrespectively, based on considerations such as physical proximity to potential kindred households, closeness of interpersonal relations, common social and professional interests, and, in general, the bonds that are likely to counteract physical isolation in the city. The growth and stable configuration of the network upset the efficacy of structural variables. Of all the types of networks, the kindred network is the most fluid and optional. To a significant degree, however, the kindred maintains its integrity as a unit by virtue of the relational pull of patrilateral and/or matrilateral ancestral households which is exerted on dispersed households. Dispersion throughout the megalopolis means basically that the kindred network is somewhat reduced in terms of household composition and less efficient in functional discharge.

Second, in the majority of cases, most of the households of kindred networks exhibit a degree of residential unity within a *colonia* or adjacent sections of the city. In such cases, idiosyncratic-personal factors per se are less likely to influence the discharge of the other two structural variables. I am not implying that conflict among consanguineal and affinal kin, individual and professional interests, and early enculturation cease to have an effect on patrilineal bias and the inherent rank of patronymics or economic affluence and exogamous marriage but only that the effect of personal factors is not enough to upset the integrative effect of structural variables on kindred network formation. Thus household propinquity generates kindred unity and functional integrity, while dispersion has the opposite effect. In the few cases where all the households of a kindred are localized in a single *colonia*, the network approaches the constitution of a well-bounded social unit.

Since early colonial times (for several reasons but primarily because of the *mayorazgo*) the wealth and disposable income of aristocratic families have varied significantly. As discussed in Chapter 5, this is still the case today, even among closely related families. Thus all kinship groupings include a mix of affluent, rich, and comparatively poor families. In most name groups, for example, the majority are affluent, the rich may include one or two families, while the poor constitute a significant minority. This is an important variable in the formation and growth of the kindred, which is realized as follows. Poor couples in the initial stages of network formation, as well as families with a budding network, gravitate toward the rich and most prosperous families irrespective of the patrilineal bias, name group prestige, or dispersion in the city, thereby adding another factor to the often difficult process of making choices in kindred network affiliation.

What does it mean socially and economically for poor couples and families to chose kindred affiliation with rich and affluent families? Essentially, to be participant members of the social activities centered on the life and annual cycles and manifold social celebrations they cannot themselves afford and to enhance their image. This is seldom verbalized, but it is always in the minds of the more disadvantaged aristocrats as a factor in deciding to activate advantageous affiliations in kindred networks. Given the choice between affiliating with patrilateral households bearing distinguished patronymics but little disposable income and matrilateral households not so distinguished but rich, almost invariably couples at the onset of their networking careers would choose the latter. By the same token, it happens quite often that well-established families, based on considerations of affluence, shift lineally or collaterally in active kindred affiliation. Families doing the shifting do not expect any economic gain per se; the motivation is exclusively the possibility of behaving as aristocrats are supposed to behave, even at the cost of doing so vicariously.

With no power of any kind and limited affluence, economic considerations have steadily eroded antiquity of lineage as the main criterion of endogenous aristocratic ranking, and wealth has become increasingly important. This ideological change is manifested in both the intrinsic upgrading of rich aristocratic families of rather recent lineage (that is, families that achieved aristocratic standing within the past 150 years) and the attention they elicit from ranking aristocratic families. The implications of this change have altered the exogenous relations of aristocrats as well, particularly with plutocrats, entailing important consequences for the configuration of the kindred.

Aristocratic plutocratic marriage has always taken place; since the inception of the Mexican aristocracy more than four centuries ago, it has been one of the main avenues of superordinate upward mobility. This type of marriage has greatly increased during the past two generations, however, and is now quite common. Indeed, many aristocratic families today would have their sons and daughters marry rich plutocrats rather than impoverished scions of distinguished aristocratic parents. The initiative increasingly comes from young aristocrats themselves, as they are much more independent of their parents than they were a generation ago and make plutocratic acquaintances on their own in social, job-related, and manifold other contexts. This new phenomenon has seriously disrupted the configuration of the kindred—namely, the extent to which exogamous marriages affect the network due to the choices couples have to make and acceptance by the respective families and kindreds of husbands and wives. To a large extent the issue of acceptance underlies all other considerations and should be dealt with first.

Ideologically, as the situation stands today, plutocrats are more likely to accept aristocrats in building significant bonds among individuals, families, and groups. As invisible as they are to the population at large, within the superordinate sector of society aristocrats are regarded as being socially at the top, and there are many plutocrats who seek interaction with them. To this extent aristocratic standing still counts as an asset, which aristocrats use to maximize usually economic or utilitarian aims, while plutocrats use it to validate or secure social standing. Although aristocratic families may encourage or facilitate interaction with plutocrats, leading to matrimonial alliances, it does not necessarily follow that their kin may accept these exogenous relationships. By contrast, not only do plutocratic families welcome the alliance of their children with aristocrats, but their kin are more likely to accept them as affines and may actively encourage the establishment of social and occasionally economic ties with the family and kin of the aristocratic spouse.

The sex of the spouse makes an important difference in whatever ties and relationships come into being after an aristocratic exogamous marriage. An aristocratic husband generally manages thoroughly to incorporate his plutocratic wife into his family and kindred network, in the process becoming the agent in building limited but durable affinal ties between the couple's respective families and kin. An aristocratic wife, however, is seldom successful in incorporating her plutocratic husband and in functioning as the instrument of establishing ties between their respective families and kin. From the standpoint of kinship, then, both situations are asymmetrical and anomalous, but the latter more so than the former: aristocratic wives quite often become socially and interactively isolated from their families and kindred networks of orientation and frequently are in most respects ultimately incorporated into their husbands'.

The consequences of exogamous marriage for the formation and growth of the aristocratic kindred network are evident. In the case of male exogamy, the husband is only partially willing to affiliate with his wife's kindred, while—by not marrying endogamously—he is deprived of half of the options of network formation. In the case of female exogamy, the wife may be able to keep network affiliation with a few households of her kindred of orientation, but her household is basically lost to her potential aristocratic network. Thus, as a result of marrying exogamously, the kindred networks of male aristocrats are smaller than those of males marrying endogamously, whereas female exogamous marriages, with a few notable exceptions (when the plutocratic family into which the woman is marrying has had a long history of interaction with aristocrats), have an inimical effect on aristocratic kindred network formation and growth and basically represent a dead end. This statement, however, should be qualified.

On the one hand, most exogamous marriages are contracted by poor aristocratic males and females either on their own initiative or on that of their parents. The attraction is generally economic, but it is managed differently by males and females. Males invariably fare better than females, in that they are economically rewarded by access to well-remunerated jobs or business opportunities, while remaining actively part of their aristocratic milieu. Females, by contrast, gain access to the wealth of their plutocratic husbands, but at the expense of becoming significantly disconnected from their aristocratic background. In both cases, parents may be happy about the economic outcome of exogamous marriage, but it does not necessarily follow that they and their kin will actively engage in network formation with families of their children's spouses' networks.

On the other hand, matrimonial alliances are much less frequently established between the offspring of rich aristocrats and of plutocrats, primarily because the former are a small minority of the aristocratic group. These alliances, however, are more symmetrical than those of poor aristocrats who marry plutocrats for two reasons: most rich families that acquired aristocratic status after Independence (1821) are among the least conservative and consequently more open to exogenous overtures; the plutocratic families into which their offspring marry are generally well acculturated to aristocratic ways, not among the richest, but of solid upper-middle class extraction. Thus the similarity of factors on both sides of the equation leads to long-standing relationships in an ambiance of equality that is not present when exogamous marriages involve poor aristocrats. The consequence under these circumstances is a kindred network that has pretty much the same characteristics as the kindred network resulting from aristocratic endogamous marriage in which component households exhibit a degree of residential unity. Given the high status recognition among the superordinate class that aristocrats still command, the only exception to this generalization is that the kindred network, in terms of size, is skewed toward the aristocratic side of the equation.

Implications of Personal-Idiosyncratic Factors

I have already discussed some of the implications of the personal-idiosyncratic factors entering into kindred network formation and growth, as they interdigitate with structural variables. To complete the configuration of the kindred, in this section I briefly discuss the nature of the personal-idiosyncratic factors per se. This discussion should clarify the choices that individuals and families make in the process of actualizing or reinforcing ties within the kindred network.

Conflicts of personality and friction among affines and consanguines are perhaps the most salient factors. They most often begin before marriage but also quite commonly develop when couples are most actively engaged in network kindred formation, during the first five to ten years of married life. In the former case, they emerge from the proverbial antagonism between mother-in-law and daughter-in-law; differences of opinion regarding the wedding celebration and friction over the guests to be invited; conflict between the choice of spouse and parents' approval or disapproval; resentment on the part of bride and/or groom concerning the quantity and quality of heirlooms and inheritance provided by their parents; and several other factors. Invariably these early considerations have an important effect on a couple's process of kindred network formation by slighting, occasionally rejecting, or affiliating, sometimes entirely, with the bride's or groom's kin. Thus the end result of these choices is either a skewed kindred network or one that is composed primarily of families related to either the bride or the groom. In the latter case, conflicts of personality and friction usually develop early after marriage, affecting both affines and consanguines, and frequently result in the severing of budding affiliations with specific families on the side of the husband or wife. The most common reasons for this development are breaches of etiquette in failing to invite individuals and families to parties and celebrations in the annual and life cycles; among close kin, failure to choose particular individuals to be godparents for baptisms, confirmations, and weddings; and manifold occasions involving friction over children, social and economic favoritism on the part of parents and grandparents, and simply quarrels that get out of hand. These after-marriage factors have a significant effect in the growth of the kindred by skewing and/or limiting the network and not least by affecting its stability and functional discharge.

There is considerable variation in individual inclinations and aristocratic styles of living—that is, preferences for discharging one's social and personal obligations, patterns of entertainment, and, more basically, the professional interests and commitments that determine the degree of affluence and characterize the center of gravity of the family. Irrespective of patrilateral and matrilateral affiliation in kindreds of orientation, individual and families are affected by these factors. They entail manifold effects, for which, unfortunately, I do not have the data to give a more precise account.

Last but not least, the choices individuals must make concerning kindred affiliation are conditioned by early enculturation and the relationships established with consanguines and affines before marriage. First, the nature of aristocratic enculturation of children and young men and women influences the choices they will make as married adults. In other words, the views that conservative and liberal parents instill in the young about aristocratic behavior and tradition will have different effects in kindred network formation, and the growth of the network will reflect what was taught before marriage. Here again, there is a distinct tendency to choose affiliation with families that have an orientation similar to those of husbands and wives before marriage, irrespective of their original kindred. Second, every bride and groom enter into marriage with a set of well-established relationships with consanguineal and affinal individuals and families. The natural individual tendency here is to continue these relationships after marriage, which quite often conflicts with the wishes and proclivities of the spouse. While to some extent the patrilineal bias of aristocratic kinship favors affiliation with the husband's side of the equation, the wife usually strongly resists divesting herself of her own relationships; this may occasionally develop into a tug of war. This situation has been changing over the past generation, however, as younger couples usually make their choices based on compromise, disregarding some traditional aristocratic values.

Functions of the Cognatic Kindred Network

Although I have described the kindred as a network of consanguineal and affinal families, it does have functional attributes that warrant identifying it as a loosely articulated, significantly optional social unit. By this I mean primarily that the aristocratic kindred network may also be described as having some degree of institutionalization. The ensuing analysis makes this assertion explicit and complements the understanding of decisionmaking in the configuration of the kindred network.

The aristocratic kindred fulfills several functions of a social and religious nature, while it also exhibits some subsidiary economic and political functions. Specific functions are not the components of an encompassing safety system, but they serve as guidelines for both the activation of rights and obligations and the realization of cooperation and exchange. To put it differently, the institutionalization of functions in this case is not the organic, all-encompassing system that has so often been described by anthropologists for folk and tribal societies; rather it is a system of potential realizations that may be activated under conditions determined mostly by nonkinship factors.

The social functions of the kindred network are centered primarily on the occasions and events of the life and religious cycles. Members of the kindred are always invited to weddings, baptisms, confirmations, first communions, and, until quite recently, balls for presentation of girls in society. Invitation to these affairs is not automatic (read institutionalized), but it may constitute a breach of etiquette if an individual and/or family is not invited, which may become grounds for terminating active affiliation with that particular family. (If this is severally repeated by other families in the network, the slighted family may shift kindred affiliation altogether.) These occasions range in elaboration from a breakfast or brunch served for the occasion of a confirmation to the elaborate round of dinners, dancing, and showers of a traditional wedding celebration. Moreover, most aristocratic families lead an active entertainment social life including dinner parties, cocktail parties, and numerous social and cultural events such as birthday and anniversary celebrations, inauguration of art shows and business places, exhibitions of arts and crafts, and so on. All these occasions, directly and indirectly sponsored by aristocratic families, invariably involve the consumption of food and drink and occasionally are accompanied by music and entail rather elaborate displays. These various occasions generally include significant numbers of network kin, but unlike the celebrations of the life cycle, they are not *de rigueur*—that is, not being invited does not constitute a reason for considering oneself slighted.

In addition, there is a considerable amount of visiting throughout the year among the component families of the kindred network. This activity includes extemporaneous invitations to country places and old haciendas and more formal invitations for Christmas, Holy Week, and All Souls'–All Saints' Day.

It goes without saying that these invitations are often asymmetrical, for not all aristocrats have country retreats. Nonetheless, these gatherings constitute occasions when significant numbers of families in the kindred network get together, particularly when a wedding or an important anniversary takes place in a country retreat. In fact weddings in the country may constitute the only occasion when the great majority of the kindred network gathers together, since it also includes children, who are usually not invited to city weddings.

As discussed in Chapter 5, gift giving, exchange, and reciprocity are important aspects of the aristocratic worldview that obtain at all levels of realization. This is especially the case among individuals and families constituting the kindred network, where these activities, though largely spontaneous, acquire a measure of institutionalization and a high degree of realization. To reiterate, gift giving, exchange, and reciprocity are the social functions that characterize kindred as a stable, fairly circumscribed, and moderately continuous kinship unit.

The religious functions of the kindred network are slightly less salient than its social functions; but to a large extent they overlap with social functions, as they are largely centered on participation in the same events and occasions of the life and annual cycles. There are other religious events and occasions, however, that enlarge the functional discharge of the kindred as distinct from social networking: attending masses for the dead, sponsoring anniversary masses commemorating particularly prominent or beloved kin, participating in burial rites and ceremonies, attending wakes, and, occasionally, rosaries. Invariably large numbers of kin participate in these religious occasions, which quite often constitute a sort of rallying point. The presence of individuals and families makes them more likely to be invited to the more informal, always pleasurable social functions such as dinner and cocktail parties: grateful for their presence at these sad occasions, affected families regard them as a reminder that kin solidarity is most appreciated under painful conditions. From this standpoint, religious functions not only complement social function but in the conscience of the group are regarded as the highest form of kindred support and reliability. Considering that religion for aristocrats not only relates to the supernatural but constitutes a social force as well, these two aspects of the kindred network are essentially regarded as inseparable and functionally reinforce each other.

The subsidiary economic functions of the kindred network are related to the life and religious cycles. Unexpected economic help (*ayuda*) for several occasions in the life and religious cycles is fairly institutionalized: largely non-reciprocal but part of behavior patterns that characterize the kindred network as a whole. For example, some of the kindred families may help with cash or in kind to defray some of the expenses for a wedding, and the same obtains in the case of other occasions such as baptisms or important celebrations of a secular nature. The economic function of gift giving and exchange, which has already been discussed, demonstrates the rather close interrelationship of these three functions of the kindred network.

Finally, the kindred network has a few, more marginal, political functions; aristocrats play a minor role in public politics and generally do not run for elective office, so the term "political" should be understood to mean the politics of social life and support for a kindred member for some essentially public undertaking. For example, when a family sponsors an exhibition of arts and crafts in one of the main cultural venues of the city, or an individual aristocrat gives a lecture on some topic of public interest (music, art history, genealogy, and so on), large numbers of kindred members invariably attend. Just as significantly, the network can be counted on to facilitate the excelling of member families in a large array of social, entertaining, and intellectual affairs, some of which transcend the boundaries of the kindred. Thus the political functions of the kindred network are ultimately a mechanism for generating endogenous social power and bringing exogenous luster to the group among the superordinate class.

On balance, the overall functions of the network are sufficiently institutionalized to regard it as a cognatic kindred with a certain degree of unity and permanence through time. Like most aspects of aristocratic kinship, however, this overview of the kindred network is underlain by nonkinship factors, primarily a highly developed consciousness of kind and sense of tradition.

Household Composition and Strength of the Kindred Network

What is the overall configuration of the cognatic kindred in terms of constituting families and its overall numerical strength? Although in the foregoing account I have likened the kindred to a social unit by virtue of having a certain degree of organizational integrity and continuity, structurally the kindred is a network, as I have referred to it throughout. Thus, fundamentally, the kindred may be defined as a cognatic-related group of households (families and individuals) that may be potentially activated by the effect of nonkinship factors. In these terms, then, the cognatic kindred is a network; but for the manifold occasions in the life and annual cycle and other social events, it functions as a kinship unit. As a consequence, the individual and household strength of the kindred network must be assessed in terms of both its potential and actual operational discharge.

Potentially, the kindred comprises various categories of households, exocentrically related to one another, and drawn patrilaterally and matrilaterally. From the standpoint of "ego," denoting a married couple with unmarried children, the network includes all those households related to the husband and wife by (1) parental and (2) grandparental links: (1) Fa, FaBr, FaSi; FaBrSo, FaBrDa, FaSiSo, FaSiDa, and their unmarried children; Mo, MoBr, MoSi; MoBrSo, MoBrDa, MoSiSo, MoSiDa, and their unmarried children; (2) FaFa, FaFaBr, FaFaSi; FaFaBrSo, FaFaBrDa, FaFaSiSo, FaFaSiDa; FaFaBrSoSo, FaFaBrDaDa, FaFaBrSiSo, FaFaBrSiDa, and their unmarried children; MoMo, MoMoBr, MoMoSi, MoMoBrSo, MoMoBrDa, MoMoSiSo, MoMoSiDa; MoMoBrSoSo, MoMoBrDaDa, MoMoSiSoSo, MoMoSiDaDa, and their unmarried children.

Altogether, there are thirty-six patrilateral and matrilateral categories of households (fourteen at the parental and twenty-two at the grandparental generation) in the cognatic kindred network that can potentially be activated. Averaging roughly 2.5 nuclear families per category at the parental and grandparental generations,[3] the maximal potential strength of the kindred network is roughly 90 households. Considering that the aristocracy today is constituted by about 700 nuclear families, with perhaps another 300 nuclear families of marginal aristocrats and plutocrats by marriage, the household strength of the kindred indicates how much the aristocracy is integrated by kinship ties. Be this as it may, this maximal pool of households is the matrix out of which the operational, functional network is actualized by the effect of nonkinship variables and factors.

The operational kindred is much smaller, most often no more than half of its potential strength (that is, generally less than 45 households). There is variation, of course, but the seven networks that I concentrated on, which are representative of the group, range from two with about 30 households each to one with nearly 50 households.

As might be expected, the households most often intimately and continuously activated are those related to ego at the parental generation (1). Ideally, and to a large extent in practice, this category constitutes ego's most reliable set of households and, as discussed in the following section, the immediate matrix in which the nonresidential extended family is embedded. The set of households related to ego at the grandparental generation (2) is not necessarily slighted but represents, so to speak, ego's second line of defense. Another way of putting it is that—although both sets of households are subject to the effect of structural and personal-idiosyncratic nonkinship variables and factors in actualizing the kindred network—the grandparental-generation set is much more affected than the parental-generation set. For example, location and distance in the city and professional interests, to take a structural variable and a personal-idiosyncratic factor, are more likely to affect the activation of households in set (2) than in set (1). There are several combinations of nonkinship variables and factors that affect the actualization of potential households, and my data set in this domain warrants two generalizations: the closer the genealogical connection to ego, the more likely households are to be actualized; the more important the event, the more grandparental households (2) are likely to be actualized.

In conclusion, in this section I conceptualize the aristocratic cognatic kindred in an urban environment as entailing two complementary aspects: some of the institutionalized properties of a kinship unit and a network of households activated by nonkinship variables and factors. I have redefined the cognatic kindred as a fairly well bounded consanguineal-affinal kin group, which is functionally activated as a network of households. This, I believe, is a profitable way to look at kinship in an urban setting and a concept worth testing in other urban settings among other classes of society.

The Nonresidential Extended Family

·

Definition, Structural Elements, and Composition

The third unit of aristocratic kinship beyond the household is the nonresidential extended family. This unit has received significant attention in the kinship study of Mesoamerican Indian and mestizo communities. David Robichaux (1995:327) redefines the nonresidential extended family, which he calls "limited localized patrilineage," and correctly maintains that it is the fundamental kinship unit in traditional Mesoamerican communities. I originally identified the nonresidential extended family in my study of a Tlaxcalan municipio (Nutini 1968:149–152), which, with modifications, is used here to describe the social context in which aristocratic households in Mexico City are embedded.

In the present context, I employ the term "nonresidential extended family" as follows: "a group of consanguineally and affinal related households lineally and collaterally related, usually ranging from four to nine, comprising from two to four generations, and invariably residing in the same or adjacent sections of Mexico City." This is the smallest unit of aristocratic kinship beyond the individual household, which consequently exhibits the highest degree of social integration. Its membership ranges roughly from twenty to forty-five people, including adults and children. Fundamentally, the aristocratic and the folk nonresidential extended families are homologously and analogously the same, except that the former is not nearly as localized as the latter. The component households of the folk nonresidential extended family are invariably located within close proximity of one another, usually within a radius of 100 yards, while those of aristocrats in Mexico City are generally located within a radius of one or two miles. Given the size of community and megalopolis, the locality referent is not so different as to impede effective social interaction. It should be noted, however, that perhaps 5 percent of nonresidential extended families have a residential integrity that approximates that of its folk counterpart; most of its households are within two or three city blocks, and some are next to each other. This is usually the result of the massive resettlement of provincial aristocrats in Mexico City between the late 1930s and the early 1950s.

The nonresidential extended family is, so to speak, the hub of kinship interaction. From this standpoint, I find that kinship among aristocrats is more significant than among the other segments of the superordinate class and also more so than among most urbanites, except for those migrants to the city that have not entirely divested themselves of their original folk roots.[4] The aristocratic household is far from being the isolate that may seem to be the case among the elite sectors of society in any of the great cities of the world. Rather, it represents one of several levels of social interaction most intensely associated with the nonresidential extended family, which, despite a lack of residential proximity, approaches the discharge of this unit in folk environments.

As in the case of the formation, organization, and development of the cognatic kindred, the nonresidential extended family has four underlying, defining elements: a strong component of choice, determinative nonkinship factors, a potential and actual membership, and relative fluidity. Moreover, being directly embedded into the cognatic kindred, the nonresidential extended family is affected by the same variables and factors that structure the latter. Thus the description and analysis of this social unit here is brief.

The most common form of the nonresidential extended family is a group of households that has its inception when the children of a well-established nuclear family household marry and set up their own independent residence but retain strong ties to the family of orientation. Because of the patrilineal bias of aristocratic kinship, married daughters usually are drawn to their husbands' families of orientation. This is the original core of the nonresidential extended family, which generally extends over three generations, including married offspring. Processually, if in the next generation married grandsons retain strong ties with their grandparents, the household becomes ancestral or *troncal* (relating to *tronco*, the origin of a family) in the word of several informants. This standard form of the nonresidential extended family is occasionally modified by nonkinship considerations, the usual result being that newly married couples attach themselves to the wife's family of orientation, by overriding the patrilineal bias. These considerations are underlain by the entire array of variables and factors that configure the cognatic kindred, the most common of which are the greater affluence of the bride's family of orientation; distance and location in the city; conflict between father and son; and professional interests.

There are variations and extensions in the composition and development of the nonresidential extended family. First, it is quite common that strong ties with collateral households already exist when married sons and daughters separate from a budding ancestral household. These are usually households of brothers or patrilateral first cousins of the head of the ancestral household but may occasionally include the same matrilateral categories. In other words, the patrilineal bias is always significant in shaping these extensions but is modified by nonkinship factors that inevitably result in the incorporation of matrilaterally related (through consanguineal and affinal ties) households into the nonresidential extended family. Second, more distantly related households may be incorporated into the nonresidential extended family; these are either patrilateral or matrilateral, related to the head and wife of the ancestral household. These collateral extensions come into being by reasons ranging from serendipitous residential proximity and the pull of economic affluence to personal-idiosyncratic and professional factors.

There are, then, basically two types of nonresidential extended families, each with variations. On the one hand is the lineal or stem nonresidential extended family, with two variations: (1) those composed of exclusively patrilineal households (married grandfathers, sons, grandsons); and (2) those that occasionally include one or more bilineal households (married daughters). On the other hand is the joint or collateral nonresidential extended family, with three variations: (3) those composed of patrilineal households related to the head of the household (married brothers and male first cousins); (4) those that occasionally include one or more bilineal households (married sisters and female first cousins); and (5) those occasionally composed of more distant households patrilaterally or matrilaterally related to the head of the nonresidential family and his wife (male and female married cousins at the grandparental and parental generations).[5]

I do not mean to imply that these types of nonresidential extended families are realized exclusively — quite the contrary. While types (1) and (2) are often realized by themselves or in combination, most often nonresidential extended families are variegated combinations of (1) and (2), singly or jointly, and (3), (4), and (5). Beyond this generalization, there is little more to say about the incidence of the various forms of the nonresidential extended family. Two points, however, must be emphasized. First, the lineally related types, (1) and (2), as one might expect, are the most integrated and have the greater intensity of social interaction. This is due not only to the patrilineal ties that bind most households but also to the intensity of the affinal ties that result when married couples opt to attach themselves to the ongoing extended family of the wife. This is tantamount to saying that the patrilineal bias is not strong enough to upset the pull of the wife's household; the reasons for this are invariably personal-idiosyncratic. Second, by contrast, the collaterally related types, (3), (4), and (5), are more fluid and significantly more open to the options and choices entailed by the manifold complex of nonkinship variables and factors.

Similarities by far outnumber differences of the various type combinations of the nonresidential extended family. More significant, however, is the role of the ancestral household, particularly how it comes into being and ultimately comes to an end. It goes without saying that not all nuclear families become ancestral households upon the marriage of their male and female offspring. If this were the case, the nonresidential extended family would be a short-lived, one-generation unit, with more limited functions. Moreover, all collateral extensions would have to be considered potential nonresidential extended families in their own right. Rather, roughly only one out of seven nuclear families ultimately become ancestral when offspring marry and establish independent households. Thus the position of centrality at the hub of social interaction is achieved that is, determined by a combination of exocentric factors. In other words, ancestral households come into being as the result of similar but more personalized factors and variables discussed in the foregoing section. The patrilineal bias plays a preponderant role in that, *ceteris paribus*, individual households would most likely be part of a patriline rather than activate any other option. However, this consideration is invariably modified by nonkinship factors.

The saliency of the ancestral household is always present. It is the point of convergence of all types of social and religious activity and occasionally becomes the rallying point of any action involving all or most of the households of the nonresidential extended family. The main reasons for this position of the ancestral household are the qualities of social leadership of its head and his wife (usually in their late middle age or early old age, at their most influential), the respect the couple has achieved in aristocratic circles, occasionally the intellectual and/or professional standing of the head of the household, and, increasingly, the economic affluence of the family. For one or more of these reasons, certain households become exocentrically ancestral and are able to attract potential households—or, if you will, these are the considerations that generate the necessary pull for a household to remain ancestral. From the opposite viewpoint, however, there are personal considerations that shape the options of married couples to attach themselves to an ancestral household, such as a son upon marriage not getting along with his father or the death of the head of the household from which the son is separating. During the past generation economic affluence has become an increasingly important aspect of certain households' becoming ancestral.

Functions and Household Strength

Theoretically, the actual composition of the cognatic kindred network (with an average of forty-five households) constitutes the potential membership of the nonresidential extended family. Because of the emphasis on the grandparents-grandchildren focus that basically configures the nonresidential extended family and the greater importance of proximity, its potential membership is probably reduced to about half (that is, to no more than twenty-five households). This is the household pool out of which the actual, operational nonresidential extended family is constituted. Its membership ranges from four to eleven, although it rarely comprises more than nine households. In individual and household membership the nonresidential extended family is at its zenith when the children of first-generation couples are in their teens.

Lineally related households almost invariably are more numerous than collaterally related households, but the composition of the nonresidential extended family varies significantly over its usual span of two generations or so. In its early phase, households of young married couples lineally related predominate, whereas when it is about to come to an end (that is, with the expiration of the ongoing ancestral household) its composition includes a mixture of households of couples in middle age and approaching old age, in which collaterally related households predominate. Finally, in terms of cohesion, it is not always the case that closer, lineally related households are more predisposed and willing to cooperate socially and religiously than collaterally related households, given the quite frequent friction among siblings over inheritance and the lingering effects of the *mayorazgo*.

The functions of the nonresidential extended family are basically the same as those of the cognatic kindred network, the only significant difference being that the former's are more intensive and extensive than the latter's. Moreover, the nonresidential extended family has a stronger economic component than the cognatic kindred network. Nonetheless, the operational form of the nonresidential extended family is somewhat different, which is the result of closer kinship ties and closer residential proximity.

First, the patterns of social and religious interaction are more frequent and intimate. Members of the nonresidential extended family are the most common participants at cocktail parties, dinner parties, and all sorts of impromptu affairs that punctuate the yearly cycle. Second, visiting is more frequent, extemporaneous, and informal; hardly a week goes by without members of a particular household interacting with one or more households for a specific reason or no reason at all. Third, there is a good deal of mutual economic help, which seldom obtains within the wider network of the cognatic kindred. Widows, quite commonly in dire straits, are helped in kind and cash; occasionally, loans are secured among members of the nonresidential extended family; and the more affluent households can often be a source of help in securing better economic opportunities. Fourth, the men and women of the nonresidential extended family can be counted on to help in kind, cash, and/or services for organizing the celebration of the main events in the life and yearly cycles. Fifth, although any member of the cognatic kindred network is an appropriate choice, almost invariably ritual kin are chosen within the nonresidential extended family, particularly for baptism and marriage.

To conclude, the aristocratic nonresidential extended family is a structural distillation of the cognatic kindred network, as no exact meaningful boundary separates them. The nonresidential extended family may be considered an activated network of households entailing the closest and strongest kinship beyond the household. Although it is not as localized as the folk extended family, it fulfills the same functions and could probably be defined as a limited localized patrilineage in Robichaux's (1995) terms. I did not do so because of the element of choice that the aristocratic nonresidential extended family has as contrasted with the more institutional character of the folk nonresidential extended family. In all other respects, they are structurally the same.

The Nuclear Family Household

As I have indicated, at the turn of the twentieth century the percentage of extended family households was high. By the time of the ethnographic present of this study (1990–1995) the extended family household had virtually disappeared as a permanent or long-lasting residential arrangement; and the twenty or so households that I have identified are temporary, generally not lasting more than two years. These extended household arrangements are usually the result of the inability of young married couples to set up independent households right after marriage. This temporary, most often patrilocal, residential arrangement allows couples to get on their feet economically and to separate as soon as possible. There are also a few truncated extended families; they come into existence when widows or widowers attach themselves until they die to the households of married sons or daughters to whom they are particularly close. Thus the nuclear family is the only significant social component of the household today. I have described the physical component of the household in sufficient detail to embed its social component (see Chapters 1, 4, and 6). This section is concerned exclusively with the latter.

Constitution and Numerical Strength

The number of children per nuclear family among aristocrats until the Mexican Revolution was very high; it was not uncommon for married couples to have ten offspring or more; the average family had five or six, as evidenced by twenty-five complete genealogies of name groups and published accounts (see Ortega y Pérez Gallardo 1908). Since then the numerical strength of the nuclear family has steadily declined. By the mid to late 1930s it was still common for married couples to have four or five children. After the end of the massive migration of provincial aristocrats to Mexico City, procreation declined even further, and couples seldom had more than four children. More than a generation later, at the time of the ethnographic present of this study, most aristocratic couples have two children; a considerable number may have three, but it is a rarity for couples who have been married since 1975 to have more than three.

There is a pronounced discrepancy between the ideal strength of the nuclear family and the actual number of children that the overwhelming majority of aristocratic couples have. The ideal of a large progeny is still present today; but in practice the great majority of aristocrats carefully plan their nuclear families, as they are well aware of the economic disadvantages and disastrous demographic consequences of reckless procreation in the modern industrial world. On the one hand, dealing with dwindling affluence and the economic exigencies of educating offspring while maintaining their standard of living has become second nature to the overwhelming majority of male and female aristocrats, thereby resulting in careful family planning. On the other hand, there is the wider to a large extent intellectual preoccupation with overpopulation in Mexico and the world at large. Overpopulation, for example, is viewed as perhaps the main scourge of the country, which, together with corruption, has been the main agent in keeping Mexico from achieving the status of a modern industrial nation.

Thus aristocrats regard overpopulation as taxing the economic resources of the nation but more seriously as causing the shrinking of physical space (such as cutting down forests that should be preserved as natural resources), disfiguring the land (such as clearing mountain slopes for unproductive agriculture), causing rural crowdedness, and contributing to urban congestion by the frantic growth of towns and cities. In short, overpopulation is considered an evil that enlightened people should work to redress personally and induce others to do the same.

In Chapter 6 I have discussed the religious and social attitudes of aristocrats toward artificial birth control. Suffice it to say here that it is almost universally practiced by reproductively active couples, its most common forms being the pill and intrauterine devices. More significant are the planning and intervals of conception. Until the mid-1970s the first childbirth generally took place between one and two years after marriage. Since then this initial period has frequently been extended, sometimes to three or four years. The most common reason given by couples for this practice is, in the words of a wife in her early thirties, "to take a breather without the worries of baby caring, and to get to know each other better before getting into the conjugal marriage track." The second and third childbirths are usually spaced every two years and may occasionally be extended for another year's interval. The reproductive career of most women married since the late 1980s is generally over between nine and twelve years after marriage. There are variations, of course, based on all kinds of imponderables (such as late marriage, difficulty of conception, and so on), but this birth planning has become quite standardized among young aristocratic couples.

Another fairly constant aspect is the age of marriage, which, with some exceptions, usually takes place at twenty-five to thirty for men and twenty to twenty-five for women. It should be mentioned, however, that until quite recently among the more conservative families marriage—especially for daughters—was considerably and sometimes greatly postponed. The exclusive reason for this delay was the parents' expectations for a suitable prospect, given the still high degree of control exercised over offspring of marriageable age. Conservative parents expected their children to marry partners of equal aristocratic standing; when there were no available prospects, marriage was postponed until parents died or offspring managed to break the shackles of tradition. It was not unusual for women to be married for the first time past the age of forty, whereas men generally were able to break the parental bond sooner. This practice is much attenuated today; but while it was in full force, until more than a generation ago, the waiting for Prince [Princess] Charming syndrome caused much unhappiness among young people. During the past fifteen years arranged marriages have pretty much come to an end; and today the decisions of when, how, and whom to marry have become largely those of the bride and groom.[6]

Authority, Social Control, and the Changing Perspective

The nuclear family is the hub of aristocratic life. Although tied to larger kinship aggregates, as detailed above, it has its own independent existence as a social, economic, and religious unit. With the decaying incidence of the extended family since the turn of the century and its virtual demise today as a long-lasting unit, a new practice quickly developed: a nuclear family is established when the groom is in the position to support his bride and offspring to come. Nonetheless, in the majority of cases the bride and groom are economically dependent on their nuclear families of orientation for four or five years after marriage. Occasionally the prospects of newly established nuclear families are strengthened by the contribution of working brides with a university degree or a small business of their own. The general intent on the part of the bride's and groom's parents is to provide the budding nuclear family with a sound economic basis. Thus (as I have indicated in several places) parents, particularly those of the groom, provide the couple with significant economic help, beyond whatever heirlooms they may confer at marriage. This help is usually provided in cash, furniture, artwork, silverware, and not infrequently a plot of land to build a house or a house ready to be occupied.

Until a generation ago (roughly the late 1960s) the nuclear family was a very close and integrated unit. Despite the traditional aristocratic *pater familias* image, husband and wife had an even hand in running the household, exercising authority, and maintaining control over their children. Decisions concerning economic, social, and religious actions and activities affecting the family were made in common. There was, however, a division of labor. The husband, as the main provider, was mostly responsible for economic decisions and the allocation of resources; he was the authority image but most of the time, at least with the children, behaved as the proverbial consenting uncle. The wife ran the household on a daily basis, had control of its economy, and was in charge of the servants; she was directly involved in supervising and disciplining the children and had the most contact with them. These roles were sufficiently fluid so that there was a significant amount of overlapping. Serious disagreements were rare; and at the parental level the household, in the great majority of cases, was a smoothly run operation. From an early age, children fully participated in the social life of the family—that is, in the patterns of visiting, exchange, and manifold interactions concerning the life and annual cycles. Indeed, from the time the infants began to walk, they were fully integrated into the life of the family and the social and religious relations with other kin and nonkin families in the aristocratic group. Parents exercised a high degree of control over their children, carefully screening whom they could interact with and when they could invite them home and above all making sure that, in the widespread code expression, they were GCU (*gente como uno*, people like us). Children, and young people until marriage, were strongly enculturated to interact endogenously; and effective pressures and constraints were always effective in controlling those who rebelled. Even the exogenous relations that were tolerated, some of which led to exogamous marriages with plutocrats, were conducted according to aristocratic rules and patterns of behavior.

Things had greatly changed by the time of the ethnographic present of this study, and they are now in significant disarray. This applies mostly to the children's generation (particularly those who were born since the early 1980s), for in the parental generation the relationship between husband and wife remains relatively the same; they have retained the same expectations of their children and still try to enculturate them to their own largely traditional ways, but they are aware that they are fighting a losing battle in achieving these goals. Significant numbers of parents, however, are more receptive to their children's choice to contract exogamous marriages with rich plutocrats (a process that has gained momentum since it started two generations ago), a strategy that insidiously saps their overt expectations. The result is that even preteen children today have the kind of freedom and choice that would have been unheard of twenty years ago; but teenagers and young people approaching marriage have gotten out of control, at least as their parents assess the problem. This is true compared to what the situation was a generation ago but not so compared to the behavior of teenagers and young people of the superordinate classes of society in Europe and the United States, among whom parental control has become extremely difficult to enforce. In fact, the revolt of young Mexican aristocrats is mild, and in most sectors of Western society today it would be taken as a matter of course.

This newly found independence is overtly expressed in many domains of behavior and action. In dress, for example, young people have given up probity and quiet elegance (at least as demanded by Western aristocrats) and adopted the ragged, unencumbered attire of the young everywhere, which makes it difficult to classify individuals by the clothes they wear. Parents hope that their children are experiencing a passing fad and that after marriage they will return to traditionalism. It is too early to tell, but my observation of young men and women from ages eighteen to twenty-five during the past ten years lends some support to this expectation. The force of early enculturation is still an effective agent in upsetting the force of fashion and peer pressure as young people settle down.

Chaperoning was given up more than a generation ago, and today teenagers can go about with little direct supervision. While the more conservative parents may still be able to exert a measure of restraint on their children's comings and goings, most families have simply given up and allow them a wide latitude in dating, frequenting public venues of entertainment, and staying out quite late at night. Boys and girls start dating at thirteen or fourteen but generally do not form steady relationships until three or four years later. Serious relationships leading to marriage are rather short lived, seldom lasting more than two years. Today "entente" best characterizes the state of affairs in the aristocratic nuclear family. Parents significantly temporize with their offspring, rarely confronting them directly, while trying to retain control in order to continue the process of aristocratic enculturation. Teenagers and young people, in turn, do not unduly antagonize their parents, do comply with the basic tenets of aristocratic behavior (except in dressing and leading a fairly independent life), and in the process lead a kind of dual existence.

Teenagers and young people before marriage are still full participants in the affairs of their families of orientation. Despite their newfound independence expressed in manifold domains mostly outside the household (fashion, dressing, music, dancing, entertainment, liberty of movement, choice of friends, and so on), they have not abandoned aristocratic behavior; in all social and religious events in which the family participates they comport themselves as they have been taught. The disadvantage of this dual kind of behavior is that it breeds tension for both parents and young people and more seriously creates an ambiance of downward social behavior that saps traditional aristocratic integrity.

Despite these deviant features, the nuclear family continues to fare relatively well but is inexorably undergoing a process of *embourgeoisement* that is symptomatic of the entire aristocratic way of life. Young people question the futility of upholding the aristocratic tradition but still conform to it as a card in the game of making an advantageous exogamous marriage. Parents have been encouraging this strategy for the past decade; but the young harbor serious doubts, essentially taking the position that the attraction for plutocrats who marry them is not their behavior but their name. This assessment of the young is undoubtedly more accurate than their elders' view; but either essentially creates a threat to aristocratic manners and tradition. The revolt and drive for independence of the young are to some extent temporary, significantly offset by early enculturation once young people settle into married life, thereby giving the older generations the hope that all is not lost.

The Allocation of Resources: Social and Religious Functions

In spite of the changes that the nuclear family has undergone, it remains largely a socially and religiously integrated unit, in which economic resources are an important element in welding together parents and offspring as long as they reside together and to a significant extent after the latter establish their own families, as I have indicated above.

Offspring are economically entirely dependent on their parents until they get a job and acquire a measure of independence. For young women, this is rarely the case even after they graduate from college or obtain a postgraduate degree; they remain, as the Mexican expression goes, *hijas de familia* (family wards) until they marry. This has been changing, and more and more young women secure gainful employment before or after graduation. Parenthetically, young women in this category tend to avoid marriage for four or five years longer than is the norm. Young men, in contrast, quite often get jobs sometimes even before graduation, either in an area pertaining to their future profession or in some family enterprise or through connections to the pluto-cratic establishment. This is a sort of on-the-job-training for preparation be-fore marriage. Until offspring begin to earn, however, all expenses they incur (pocket money, clothing, entertainment, education, and so on) are paid out of their parents' income.

Rich parents indulge their offspring nearly as much as the proverbial pluto-cratic new rich, which many aristocratic parents view as another manifesta-tion of *embourgeoisement*. The great majority of parents, however, are just well off and have to manage their incomes and economic resources carefully in catering to their children's needs while maintaining a proper aristocratic stan-dard of living. Thus the heaviest demands on the family income are allocations for the education of offspring (this also includes activities such as music, art, and equitation lessons and other expensive extracurricular activities), keeping the family in adequate aristocratic style, and the manifold commitments to events in annual and yearly cycles (including the onerous discharge of wed-ding celebrations and occasionally expensive social commitments).

Offspring are passive recipients of these benefits and do not participate in the economic decisions, which are entirely in the hands of parents. Husband and wife function well as a team in allocating resources and making decisions. While the husband is most often the only earner, income allocation and dis-posal is always done jointly. Indeed, the wife may have a greater voice than the husband in the actual planning and execution of the manifold social and religious activities of the nuclear family.

The nuclear family household is the pivotal unit in the social life of aristo-crats; it is the locus of realization of all events in the annual and life cycles as well as the source of all secular celebrations involving adults and children. All social activity that aristocrats engage in has its source in the nuclear family, from the relatively simple task of giving a cocktail or dinner party to the elaborate staging of a wedding celebration. The institutionalized aspects of the nonresidential extended family and the cognatic kindred network are not so much automatic as activated by members of the nuclear family and their closest kin. For most social and cultural events throughout the year the nuclear family can fend for itself; but there are always unforeseen events (such as an untimely death or an impromptu affair involving many guests) that require the cooperation of close kin, who can be activated on the spur of the mo-ment. For the most important events of the life cycle (when personnel and resources are most needed), members of the nuclear family, including young people and their immediate kin, fan out throughout the nonresidential extended family and cognatic kindred network in order to generate resources. These, in a nutshell, are the most significant social functions of the nuclear family.

Finally, the nuclear family is also the convergence point of religious celebrations from baptism to marriage and all events of the religious cycle in between—they are basically family events, tightly integrating parents and offspring. The routine practice of religion is also a function of the nuclear family: going to mass, attending funerals, participating in christenings, and similar activities are undertaken in common. During the past decade, however, teenagers and the young—as part of their revolt—have become more independent of their parents in religious devotions, have developed their own ways of expressing themselves religiously (for example, joining religious study groups and doing charity work), and are now reticent about participating in their elders' traditional religious practices (for example, attending wakes and funerals).

Despite its exclusive functions and self-reliance, the nuclear family is by no means an isolate. On the contrary, it is well integrated into the wider networks of the nonresidential family and cognatic kindred. From the name group to the nuclear family household, the function of kinship is important in structuring the social and religious life of aristocrats.

Inheritance and the Lingering Effects of the *Mayorazgo*

Due to the *mayorazgo* and the patrilineal bias, aristocratic society has historically had a kind of semipartible inheritance system. By this I mean that the firstborn male inherited the bulk of the family estate, while subsequent male and female offspring shared what was left, with the former almost invariably being favored over the latter. Dowry was the most often used mechanism for providing daughters with an inheritance; this was usually economically onerous, and parents quite often enticed daughters to join religious orders, which required a smaller dowry. That was the general state of affairs until the end of colonial times. Since then inheritance has become increasingly more equitably partible; but until the end of Porfirian times many aristocratic families still adhered to the *mayorazgo*. It is only in the past three generations that this relic of the past has formally ceased to exist, but not without some persistent effects. During the past seventy years sons and daughters have inherited fairly equitably, but sons are still somewhat favored over daughters. Let us examine the nature and kind of economic assets that are inherited (both during the lifetime and after the death of parents) and the general procedures of inheriting.

The small minority of plutocratic aristocrats usually have substantial wealth in securities and investments in addition to real estate and other diversified assets. The great majority of aristocrats, however, have few investments and occasionally some real estate, consisting mostly of small urban properties, some agricultural land, and a retreat in the country. Inexplicably, families with medium wealth or tending to the poor end of the economic spectrum have the most extensive collections of art, crafts, furniture, heirlooms, and other valuable household property. As I have indicated, the value of these possessions may run into millions of dollars, which even young aristocrats would be reluctant to liquify for investment. Thus most parents now have few possessions to bequeath their offspring except for these nonliquid assets, which are invariably the main bones of contention among heirs. Regardless of the kinds of possessions that are at stake, inheritance practices among aristocrats are as follows.

Under Mexican law, the property of a person who dies intestate is equally divided among the heirs, regardless of sex or generation. This is rarely the case, as parents divide up the property before they die or leave detailed wills allocating possessions to their offspring. The most common practice, however, is that heirlooms and all property defined above as nonliquidatable are transferred to offspring at marriage and at other occasions in the life cycle. Moreover, when a parent dies, the other parent inherits the entire estate; as in the case of all industrialized nations, there are many more widows than widowers, so that the final execution of the will falls mostly into the hands of mothers. They distribute any remaining heirlooms and nonliquidatable property before they die, and what is left constitutes usually meager liquidatable assets.

Despite the trend toward equitably inheriting in the twentieth century, aristocratic males are often favored over females, who are supposed to be compensated by what their husbands bring to the marriage. This practice most often does not compensate wives, who—as part of the revolt against tradition—are insisting on equitable sibling inheritance across the board. This position is becoming the rule as the result of both the greater voice that women have in kinship affairs and the fact that husbands are not inheriting enough liquidatable and nonliquidatable assets. Thus practically all the squabbles and the friction they generate are experienced by siblings while one or both of their parents are still alive, beginning right after marriage with the allocation of some heirlooms, centered mostly on nonliquidatable possessions. Liquidatable possessions are the last to be distributed; this mostly comes after the death of the surviving parent and does not generate nearly as much friction and resentment.

The state of disarray of inheritance practices today is perhaps more the result of the lingering effects of the *mayorazgo* than of the patrilineal bias of aristocratic kinship. Favoring the firstborn male (the *mayorazgo*) tends to extend to brothers to the detriment of sisters; the basis of this largely unconscious stand is that, as the perpetuators of the patronymic, males should be provided with more ample means for the greater glory of the name. The younger generation, male and female, is conscious of the futility of such strategy and the friction that it generates. Nonetheless, the great majority of *mayorazgos* do not dispute their parents' wishes that favor them economically and confer more social distinction by giving them the most precious expressive possessions of the family. Thus the friction among siblings is compounded: complaints about the unfairness of the practice come not only from sisters but from brothers as well, who see no reason why the oldest should be favored. It should be noted, however, that this situation obtains in no more than a third of conservative families that still have enough heirlooms and precious art and furniture pregnant with aristocratic symbolism. This is particularly the case with family portraits of illustrious ancestors, not because they are the most valuable possessions but due to their expressive significance. If these items have not been given to the *mayorazgo* either at marriage or before the death of parents, wills include detailed clauses to that effect. On two occasions I personally witnessed the precise instructions given by an old patriarch on his deathbed to his wife concerning the portraits and heirlooms that were to be inherited by the *mayorazgo*. The consequences engendered by this archaic institution, which most aristocrats have given up as disruptive to their offspring, are fundamentally symbolic and expressive and exemplify the pain of divesting themselves of one more hopeless relic of the past.

Before concluding, a note on the *mayorazgo* and the incidence of the extended family is in order. When this institution was still an operational aspect of aristocratic kinship (roughly until the end of the Porfiriato), the incidence of the extended family was high: perhaps 25 percent of households harbored extended families. The explanation is simple. Because the firstborn inherited the bulk of his parents' estate, younger brothers, and occasionally sisters (depending on the economic prospective of their husbands), had no realistic option but to reside patrilocally after marriage. This was facilitated by the usually large mansions that most aristocratic families had in Mexico City and provincial capitals, which could easily accommodate several nuclear families. I have sufficient anecdotal evidence to support the assertion that until the end of the nineteenth century the extended family was an important household arrangement. Finally, another factor to consider is that residence in the hacienda invariably entailed extended family living, which in the contemporary context has continued as a temporary residential arrangement throughout the year: in country retreats and old hacienda mansions for the few aristocratic families that managed to keep them after the 1934–1940 land reform.

Marriage and Divorce

The organization of this book requires that the institutions of marriage and divorce, so critical and encompassing for understanding the transformations that the Mexican aristocracy has undergone since the Revolution of 1910, be described and analyzed in several social, demographic, and religious contexts. Chapter 1 discusses the changes and patterns of intermarriage between aristocrats and plutocrats. Chapter 2 puts the historical background of aristocratic marriage alliances going back to the sixteenth century in perspective, including alliances with Indian nobles. Chapter 5 examines the erosion of aristocratic manners and usages in the twentieth century due to exogamous marriage. Chapter 6 analyzes the social and religious implications of marriage and the wedding and places the incidence and consequence of divorce in social and religious perspective. Finally, throughout this chapter, marriage is analyzed in several contexts: preferential forms but with stratificational rather than kinship implications; downward social mobility due to exogamous marriage; the ambiance and form of marriage with plutocrats; and the disruptive effects of exogamy for the functioning of the kinship system.

There are no strict preferential forms of marriage or marriage prohibitions; existing preferences and prohibitions have stratificational rather than kinship implications. Until two generations ago first cousins were not allowed to marry. Today first-cousin marriage is not forbidden; it occasionally takes place, and those concerned do not even bother to inform ecclesiastical authorities. There is no exogamy beyond those related within the first degree of consanguinity.

As far as endogamy is concerned, again there are no clear rules regulating marriage based on locality or kinship unit membership. Despite the fact that marriage with plutocrats and members of the upper-middle class has been steadily increasing during the past two generations, the aristocracy still remains roughly 90 percent endogamous (1995). But exogamous marriages, particularly with plutocrats, are rapidly becoming common; and within a generation the aristocracy will most likely become an agamous group. This will signal the end of the aristocracy, as endogamy has been the main mechanism of maintaining it as a functional, fairly well structured group. Whatever survives will no longer be a distinct segment of the Mexican stratification system as described in this book.

Since the inception of the aristocracy in the sixteenth century, and after a short period of intermarriage with the Indian nobility, endogamy has had a dual function: preserving the social configuration of the group as a class and maintaining the racial purity of the group. When the aristocracy ceased to be the dominant class of the country after 1910, maintaining purity became the sole function of endogamy. As the economic affluence of aristocrats deteriorated, concern with phenotypic purity increased. Today what adult aristocrats resent most is that their sons and daughters have no compunction of marrying what they contemptuously call *nacos* (essentially individuals exhibiting various degrees of Indian phenotypic traits), as is increasingly the case. They no longer care whether their children marry the new rich or any nonaristocrats, as long as they are phenotypically European.

Most aristocrats today favor marriage of their children to foreigners of European extraction, regardless of wealth; this is an acceptable strategy, since most foreigners in Mexico are economically affluent and generally have upper-middle-class status. In summary, knowing that they are on the verge of disappearing, most adult aristocrats no longer worry about preserving the social integrity of the aristocracy as a functional group; but, fully aware of their racial prejudices, they are set on preserving the phenotypical integrity of their descendants. To judge by the marriages that have taken place between 1990 and 1995, most young aristocrats no longer share their parents' preferences and prejudices; beyond satisfying romantic expectations, the main consideration in choosing a spouse is economic affluence. This attitude greatly upsets adult aristocrats, but they accept it because they know there is very little they can do to counteract it.

The ideal form of marriage was traditionally among partners of equal social standing or, as several informants put it, *con iguales pergaminos* (of equally illustrious ancestry; this implies a degree of stratification within the aristocratic group, as discussed in Chapter 8). This ideal is no longer realized, except perhaps among ultraconservative families which have thoroughly managed to enculturate the young. As I have pointed out several times, however, most members of the younger generation have rebelled against what they regard as an antiquated and unrealistic way of thinking; marriage for them has become a personal matter that should not be clouded by aristocratic ideology, thereby opening a range of possibilities that older generations did not have. Marriage, the younger generation believes, should enhance personal fulfillment and not uphold ideals constraining social opportunities and economic security. If this new way of thinking can be realized traditionally, so much the better; but most young aristocrats would not hesitate to marry exogamously if their desires cannot be realized endogamously. Nonetheless, early enculturation has not been entirely forgotten, as they are not above consciously using aristocratic status in pursuing connubial aspirations.

Until World War II, the age of marriage was significantly younger than it is now; it was not uncommon for women to marry in their late teens and men not more than two or three years older. Since then the age of marriage has been increasing, and today it has risen by three to five years for men and women. There are exceptions, of course; but, other things being equal, men and women try to postpone marriage as much as possible. Two reasons for this phenomenon have been the pursuit of a university education for both men and women and entering into marriage with a substantial economic position. Age differences between bride and groom are seldom more than six or seven years, a significant change since the nineteenth century, when grooms were generally much older than brides.

Marrying consanguines or affines is very common, a practice that has not diminished, considering that the structure of endogamous marriage is breaking down. This, of course, simply exemplifies that the social circle in which young aristocratic men and women move is highly interrelated by bonds of kinship. Regardless of the changes that have taken place, adults still encourage the young to marry *parientes lejanos* (distant relatives) as a guarantee that unions are contracted with people of equal aristocratic standing.

Beyond the strong proclivity of marrying consanguines and affines, there are other factors that condition the initiation of marriage. First, propinquity played an important role before the aristocracy became concentrated in the capital by the late 1940s; most marriages then took place endogamously in the cities where aristocrats were enfranchised. With dispersed settlement in Mexico City, propinquity is redefined to include the contact that young people have at weddings, important social and intellectual affairs, and invitations to country houses and haciendas, which are the main environments for the young to meet.

Second, friendship involving both parents and the young themselves is an important aspect in the structural ambiance conducive to marriage. These friendships often lead to courtship and ultimately to marriage. The most salient contexts where friendships are shaped is through sisters; through the offices of parents, who may want to influence offspring to marry people of their choice; and through school ties.

Third, parents and grandparents are very much aware of pedigrees and family histories and in the marriage game are alert to the possibility of marrying children to partners of their own social standing. The parents of either a prospective bride or groom may search for an appropriate candidate; and when a target is decided upon, parents set about to make the situation propitious for the prospective groom and bride to meet. Often these stratagems pay off; just as many do not, but it is an accepted form of matchmaking. Frequently, by chance or design, both sets of parents manage to get the prospective couple together. In either case there is an air of conspiracy surrounding the machinations leading to marriage.

Fourth, friends or relatives early in life may engage in matchmaking. Quite frequently, when children are as young as ten, two mothers and perhaps their husbands may decide that their offspring should marry. When the time comes for the children to get to know each other, generally in the late teens or early twenties, parents do their best to encourage it. Probably as many as 15 percent of marriages in the aristocratic group are the result of this strategy. Arranged marriages in this and the foregoing sense have apparently been quite successful, for there is usually a commonality of interests that helps cement them into enduring nuclear families.

The great majority of aristocrats today are no longer rich, and many of them go through daunting economic straits trying to uphold traditional standards. Still, most of them would place aristocratic standing ahead of economic considerations in the marriage game. Although during the past two decades the ambiance has become more relaxed, preservation of endogenous traditions is almost an obsession with many of them. This aspect of the aristocratic worldview is the main source of rebellion by the young, and whenever possible they contract economically advantageous marriages, often against the wishes of their parents. As I have suggested above, parents are ambivalent about their children's marrying exogamously; as opposed as they may be, they accept the outcome as inevitable. This is the main reason for the increasing incidence of aristocratic-plutocratic marriage during the past generation. By now the situation has become generalized, and about the same proportion of young men and women marry plutocrats.

Traditionally, courtship (*noviazgo*) was fairly long, and the wedding seldom took place before the couple had been acquainted for two or three years. Courtship was rather controlled and took place mostly in the house of the prospective bride. Since in the great majority of cases marriages took place between partners whose families knew each other intimately or well, there was no formal presentation of prospective in-laws. When the relationship approached the point of leading to marriage, there was a formal reunion of in-laws in the house of the bride. Courtship from then on was marked by a great deal of interaction between the families of the bride and groom, including dinners, lunches, teas, and so on. In the case of endogamous marriages, this sequence of events has remained pretty much the same in the recent context of change.

Courtship involving exogamous marriages, particularly with plutocrats, however, has significantly changed. Nothing is usually done before the relationship develops into an impending wedding; frequently months go by during which the couple keeps the relationship very private, tests the situation, and prepares the respective families for announcing the intention to marry. The more difficult context to manage is always the aristocratic family, irrespective of sex, since the families of prospective plutocratic brides and grooms are invariably receptive to a socially upward alliance. Immediately after the intention to marry becomes public, both families take it as a *fait accompli*; and every effort is made to smooth the situation, which includes mutual invitations to formal dinners and creating a social ambiance in which the respective families may get to know each other. The final step is formally asking for the hand of the bride, which usually consists of an elaborate dinner party, particularly in plutocratic households.

Courtship is always an important period in the life cycle, for it conditions much of the future married life of the couple. It plays a determinant role in shaping their kinship relationships and whether they will become part of the exocentric kindred network of the bride or groom, as discussed above. This aspect of kinship network formation has remained fairly constant despite the changes that have taken place, and the only disruption has been the increasing incidence of exogamous marriages. In such cases, especially in aristocratic-plutocratic marriage, either the bride or groom (particularly the former) may occasionally be essentially lost to the aristocratic group by the virtual incorporation into his or her spouse's family.

The Mexican Aristocracy

Proof of virginity ceased to be part of the aristocratic tradition more than a century ago, and no living informant remembers it being practiced. Virginity for women, however, is the ideal among the parents of the present set of brides, although it is extremely doubtful that the majority are virgins at the time of marriage, given the rebellious mood of the young today. Most parents delude themselves that the old standard is still in place, which is a source of considerable amusement among the younger set.

The honeymoon, which follows immediately after the wedding, remains an important aspect of the marriage complex. Before 1960 the couple invariably went to Europe, even if less affluent families had to borrow the money. Nowadays many couples settle for more modest honeymoons in Mexico, the United States, and the Caribbean. In tune with the modernizing trends that characterize the rebellion of the young, during the past decade and a half many couples have foregone the honeymoon altogether and used the money for some practical purpose, such as investing in or improving their new household. None of this economizing takes place in the case of plutocratic marriages, which are characterized by great ostentation and the most expensive honeymoons, irrespective of whether the bride or groom is the plutocrat. As one aristocratic informant put it, plutocrats, in "trying to impress us, 'echan la casa por la ventana' " (go completely overboard).

Finally, the dowry was formally discontinued by the middle of the nineteenth century; even in colonial times it was not as prominent an institution as it was in Spain and other European countries. The bride brings to the formation of a new family heirlooms (pictures, furniture, silver, and so on) that are given to her by her parents at marriage or promised for the future, to which end the family of the groom contributes as much or more. Moreover, occasionally the bride and/or groom bring to the marriage a house or a site to build one, as some aristocrats still own a considerable amount of urban property. In the case of marriage to a plutocrat, the family of the bride or groom invariably provides the couple with a luxurious house or apartment.

In conclusion, in most respects marriage among aristocrats is not significantly different from marriage among the other sectors of the superordinate class, particularly given the process of *embourgeoisement* that the institution has been undergoing for two generations, as evidenced by the foregoing description. The difference in aristocratic marriage is exemplified by the fundamental idea of the *prestation totale* (Mauss 1923). A person to person interaction is never an isolated event but part of a total set of transactions dispersed through space and time. Thus marriage for aristocrats is not just an important event in the life cycle but at the heart of their institutional life, connected to other transactions in the kinship and stratificational system: it defines who they are as a group, serves as a mechanism of exogenous social identity, exemplifies the internal stratification of the group, and is a determinant factor in the formation of the nonresidential extended family and the exocentric kindred.

The religious context of divorce, some of its social consequences, and its transformation throughout the century are discussed in Chapter 6. Here I confine myself to the incidence of divorce, reasons for the practice, and its sociological implications, including some details not mentioned in Chapter 6.

The incidence of divorce among aristocrats today is slightly less than the national average, but it is growing rapidly and is likely to become much higher, which is the case with plutocrats and the upper-middle class. A few brave souls in the aristocratic group divorced before World War II, but this was a rarity. By the late 1960s divorce had become established as an option to terminate marriage; since then, according to the standards of the group, it has acquired alarming proportions: today perhaps as many as 20 percent of all marriages end in divorce within fifteen years.

Separation was the traditional way of *de facto* termination of a religious marriage. When annulment was not possible, separation was the next step. It should be noted that until about fifty years ago it was not difficult to engineer an annulment, generally posited on some technicality (that is, the ceremony or documentation of the marriage was not properly done). The Catholic church in Mexico granted annulment for three main reasons: insanity, impotence, and nonconsummation of the marriage. In the majority of cases, however, annulment meant simply that for social, psychological, or other reasons the couple could not endure an intolerable situation, which—by stretching the letter of canonical law—could be accommodated to the reasons for annulment allowed by the church.

The most common reasons for separation were sexual and psychological incompatibility, physical and psychological abuse of the wife, the husband's inability to support the family, and his constant infidelity. Old informants were unanimous in asserting that in separation the reasons for annulment allowed by the church were rarely invoked. The religious status and social condition of separated couples are amplified as follows.

Almost invariably separation was initiated by wives for the reasons stated above. Husbands rarely sought separation; and when they did, it was mostly due to sexual discontent or boredom. While the wife was condemned to demure behavior and lifelong celibacy, the husband enjoyed all the privileges of the Mexican double standard: he could engage in all kinds of sexual dalliances with impunity and occasionally set up a *casa chica* with a woman of lower social standing, generally of middle or upper-middle-class status. When a separated woman occasionally engaged in a liaison, it was done in secret; if she was discovered it amounted to adultery, entailing virtual social ostracism from the aristocratic group.

That was the state of affairs until the late 1940s, when the position of a separated woman began to improve. Although her peers did not condone her behavior, people in general were less eager to condemn her if she engaged in any romantic dalliance. The option of divorce rather quickly followed, as the majority of aristocrats realized the futility of separation if it was not enforced by traditional ostracism and strong social pressure. Thus separation as a way of terminating a marriage came to an end; and after the late 1960s, except among the most conservative, divorce became the only option. It is clear to most divorced informants that divorce developed from the notion of separation, as they would no longer put up with the hypocrisy that the situation entailed *vis-à-vis* the church.

As far as the church is concerned, nothing has changed. The consequences for the divorced couple are religiously drastic: they are *de facto* out of the church and cannot receive the sacraments or be ritual sponsors. In practice, however, most aristocrats do not pay much attention, and divorced men and women continue to go to church, take communion, and go about their religious devotions as if they were members of a congregation in good standing. This is helped by the fact that many parish priests do not subscribe to the official Catholic policy on divorce; and even if they go along with the church, they let people follow their own consciences.

Divorce among aristocrats today takes place almost exclusively among people who have been married for ten to fifteen years, that is, generally before age forty to forty-five. The same, in fact, was the case with separation. Divorce after fifty is considered an inadmissible indulgence and ridiculously out of place. Aristocrats share the notion of most educated Mexicans that if couples have lived together for twenty years, they can certainly make the necessary adjustments to stay together for the rest of their lives. The reasons for divorce remain the same as they were for separation. What has changed is that now couples may consult an analyst or marriage counselor when the relationship is in serious trouble. If this step does not work, they quickly proceed to divorce. Initially, the families and close kin of both husband and wife try to dissuade them from taking such a drastic step. But when they realize that continuation of the marriage is impossible, they try their best to facilitate the divorce as peacefully as possible and with the least notoriety. If the divorce gets nasty, as occasionally happens, specially designated kin intervene to ameliorate the proceedings. The main concern is no longer religious but social; in this respect there are the traditional qualms and reservations about the consequences of such a drastic step, which traditionally were real but today are no longer in effect, although aristocrats still fear them.

In most respects the configuration and consequences of divorce are essentially the same as in the United States; differences are due to some inherent structural features of the Mexican superordinate classes. The legal aspects of divorce are almost identical in Mexico and in the United States. The wife is awarded custody of the children, but the father has specific visiting privileges; only rarely is the father awarded custody, almost always because the mother relinquishes this customary right (usually for psychological reasons). Alimony does exist but quite often is not necessary, for most couples in the upper echelons of Mexican society marry under the law with *separación de bienes* (essentially a version of the prenuptial agreement in the United States) rather than having joint ownership of assets and possessions.

Traditional separation was usually bitter and disruptive and almost always led to severing social interaction among its immediate and extended actors. Divorce, in contrast, takes place with much less drastic consequences and in recent years in an ambiance of understanding and civility. Couples part amicably and frequently continue to see each other socially. Except among the ultraconservative, aristocrats no longer discriminate against divorced men and women in any social situation and keep to themselves whatever religious qualms they may still have. Thus during the past decade divorce has become part of the social structure of the aristocratic group.

Finally, a few comments on celibacy are relevant. Aristocratic bachelors and spinsters are extremely rare; even today—despite the liberating changes that have taken place—pressure to marry is put on those approaching thirty; a few men resist and hold on until age forty-five or so, while women who reach about forty most likely will remain spinsters. There are exceptions, of course, and two women informants recently married in their late fifties. In my sample of 150 informants there were no bachelors and one spinster past the age of sixty.

Compadrazgo (Padrinazgo)

Compadrazgo (ritual kinship) is one of the most important and widespread social institutions in Latin America and exhibits its most complex and diversified form in the Indian and rural mestizo communities of Mexico. With diminishing social and religious elaboration, *compadrazgo* is present in all sectors of Mexican society. Among the urban lower classes its significance and complexity occasionally approach the folk situation. Among the middle classes the incidence of types is probably reduced by half; its social and religious functions are considerably diminished, but it may acquire important economic and political dimensions. In the superordinate sector of society it is reduced to a minimum of expression but retains a core of religious and symbolic meaning.

It is among aristocrats that ritual kinship is the least important, whereas among plutocrats and the upper-middle-class one may speak of a viable *compadrazgo* complex not too different from that of the middle classes. In addition to sacramental types, plutocrats and upper-middle-class people contract at least three or four more types of *compadrazgo;* the ritual and ceremonialism are quite elaborate, and ritual kinship is used to maximize economic and political ends in an essentially asymmetrical and stratified fashion. Aristocratic *compadrazgo*, in contrast, is primarily endogenous, involves exclusively sacramental types, and has residually exogenous aspects.

Before analyzing *compadrazgo*, a brief discussion of ritual kinship terminology is necessary. It is confined to six terms and their plural forms: (1) *compadre* (co-father, male ritual kin); (2) *comadre* (co-mother, female ritual kin); (3) *compadres* (co-parents, ritual kin); (4) *padrino* (godfather, male ritual sponsor); (5) *madrina* (godmother; female ritual sponsor); (6) *padrinos* (godparents, ritual sponsors); (7) *ahijado* (godson); (8) *ahijada* (goddaughter); and (9) *ahijados* (godchildren). Unlike in the folk and lower-class urban contexts, there are no extensions of these terms to real kin of those related by *compadrazgo*. Moreover, ritual kinship terms may occasionally be used as terms of reference but almost never as terms of address. Terms denoting real kinship relationships are used instead. This is also the case in *compadrazgo* relationships contracted with friends, when godchildren refer to godparents as *tío* (uncle) and *tía* (aunt), and the godparents refer to the children by their given names.

Let us first place aristocratic *compadrazgo* in historical perspective. I should note that *compadrazgo* was always endogenous—that is, aristocrats would never ask individuals or couples that were not members of the group to be ritual sponsors. In the context of the hacienda, aristocrats were asked to be ritual sponsors for many occasions in the life and annual cycles; those asking them included personnel attached to the landed estate as well as assorted individuals in the region. Indeed, *hacendados* were a focal source of ritual kin; and *compa-*

drazgo under nearly feudal conditions may be regarded as a subterfuge, a sort of palliative, bridging the chasm between serfs and lords. (Parenthetically, this paternalistic extension of *compadrazgo* survives today in politicians' use of the institution to generate individual and collective support; for example, when they *apadrinan* [ritually sponsor] an entire graduating class in a rural or urban community.)

Moreover, ritual kinship among aristocrats was much more diversified than it is today and included traditional *compadrazgo* types of long standing, basically of two kinds. The first kind were types of *compadrazgo* dear to the folk personnel of the hacienda and surrounding region, such as bedding of the child Jesus in church, sponsorship of church paraphernalia, blessing of a saint or image, and blessing of the Holy Manger. These ritual sponsorships may also be regarded as a symbolic artifice employed by *hacendados* and their families to enhance their paternalistic image, thereby gaining people's respect and loyalty. The second kind were types that all segments of Mexican society traditionally engaged in, such as erection of a burial cross, blessing of a new building, setting the foundations of a new house, and relationships contracted on the occasion of a silver wedding anniversary.

With the demise of the hacienda system and the aristocracy as a dominant class after 1910, this extensive ritual kinship began to disintegrate; it was largely gone by the time of the land reform of President Cárdenas (1934–1940). Some aspects survived in the contexts of aristocrats' continued ownership of hacienda manors and ties to their city households: former servants and various personnel of the landed estate continued to regard erstwhile *hacendado* families as a source of ritual sponsorship. Nowadays this context of *compadrazgo* is not exclusively associated with aristocratic families; rather, it is very common among rich and prominent urban families. This is an aspect of Mexican patronage and clientship (what I have called elsewhere stratified-vertical-asymmetrical *compadrazgo*) in which the underprivileged seek to maximize economic and, to some extent, prestige opportunity by seeking ritual kinship ties with the superordinately placed. More significantly, the diversification of the traditional *compadrazgo* system in which aristocrats participated is gone, both as a realization of clientship and patronage and in the traditional types they engaged in endogenously. Also gone is the elaboration of accompanying rites and ceremonies, and the remaining types have been significantly simplified. With the demise of the hacienda system ritual kinship as patronage came to an end, whereas the disappearance of traditional *compadrazgo* types may be explained as an aristocratic reaction to middle- and upper-middle-class values that the aristocrats regard as *cursi*, which may be interpreted as a rationalization of the "us versus them" syndrome. This is a recurring theme (as I have indicated in several places) in the rearguard action that aristocrats have been fighting for group identity since their accelerated social decline began in the late 1940s.

Compadrazgo among aristocrats today is confined to the four sacramental types: baptism, confirmation, first communion, and marriage. This is strictly the case endogenously (that is, when aristocrats ask for ritual sponsorship), although exogenously they may accept being *padrinos* for all sacramental types as well as for nonsacramental types such as *graduación* (graduation from primary or secondary school), *parada de cruz* (erection of a cross for a variety of occasions), *bendición de casa* (blessing of a new house), and *primera piedra* (setting the foundations of a house). This is a residual aspect of formerly well-organized clientship or patronage that occasionally takes place with household personnel and in the region of former haciendas. It is not *compadrazgo*, and it should be referred to as ritual sponsorship. Many aristocrats take these sponsorships seriously; most probably adduce *noblesse oblige* as a reason for becoming *padrinos*, although the real purpose may be to assure themselves of the loyal service of people connected to them in various capacities.

Aristocratic *compadrazgo* is symmetrical and egalitarian, and it takes place primarily among members of the nonresidential extended family. More specifically, *compadres* are mostly chosen among relatives within the first and second degree of consanguinity but occasionally among friends. They are often siblings, parents, uncles and aunts, and occasionally grandparents and first or second cousins. The selection of ritual kinship sponsors is the responsibility of parents of the infant or child being baptized or confirmed; in the case of marriage, *padrinos* are chosen by the bride and groom in agreement with their respective parents; for first communion, prospective *ahijados* have a say in the selection. Another peculiarity, uncommon among folk and middle-class people, is that ritual sponsors do not necessarily have to be a married couple and quite often may belong to different generations. For example, the parents of an infant may choose as baptismal *padrinos* the husband's mother and the wife's brother or vice versa. There are many combinations that may include grandparents and friends. The reason for these strategies is to generate goodwill within the nonresidential extended family, to defuse a potentially disruptive situations, and to maximize some specific social end, particularly in the case of friends that parents may wish to bring close to the family.

This traditional configuration of *compadrazgo* form, selection, and overall ambiance is changing due to the rebellion of the young, along with greater contact and intermarriage with plutocrats. Increasingly, young parents are choosing *padrinos* among their endogenous and exogenous plutocratic friends, many of them with the explicit intent of network building or maximizing some economic or political aim. Aristocratic *compadrazgo*, in other words, is evolving from an environment that emphasizes reciprocity, exchange, and the absence of any type of intrinsic maximization to an environment emphasizing the maximization of economic, social, and other goals. Much the same can be said of the practice that began in the mid-1980s of plutocrats who ask aristocrats to become *compadres* for social reasons, and the latter accept for economic reasons.

Since most *compadrazgo* relationships are still contracted among primary and secondary relatives, the patterns of behavior, duties, and obligations are those of real kinship and not ritual kinship. However, this has to be qualified. Particularly in baptism and marriage, there is a special bond established between *padrinos* and *ahijados* which goes beyond the relationship entailed by real kinship. Godparents have an obligation to "dress" the infant at baptism, give a valuable present to the marriage couple, and give a substantial gift to first communion and confirmation children. In addition, *ahijados* must be especially respectful of *padrinos*, who must in turn be supportive of their godchildren, all of which goes beyond entailed real kinship relationships.

Compadrazgo contracted for reasons of friendship in the changing context is quite similar. The relationship that binds *compadres* and the behavior patterns that ensue are really those determined by the antecedent friendship that led to the sponsorship. When one considers that ritual kinship terms of address are never used and terms of reference only seldom, it becomes evident that ritual kinship is primarily a symbolic system that by itself entails few social, economic, religious, political, or any other functions that are not accounted for by kinship and friendship. Thus ritual kinship behavior is basically determined by the kinship behavior that obtains among *padrinos, ahijados,* and *compadres,* since *compadrazgo* contracted by reasons of friendship is not yet generalized. The social, economic, religious, and political functions of *compadrazgo* are those of kinship.

What is really significant in aristocratic *compadrazgo* are the rites and ceremonies of being baptized, confirmed, married, and taking first communion in themselves. After these central events of ritual kinship have been discharged, the relationship becomes *de facto* one more aspect of kinship—more intensified to be sure (for example, an *ahijado* and his *madrina* often become closer to one another than they were in the relationship of, say, nephew and aunt) but nonetheless subsumed under the behavior of kin in the household, nonresidential extended family, and exocentric kindred.[7] Thus ritual kinship among aristocrats is unlike folk *compadrazgo* in that the locus of importance of the institution is in its immediate ritual-ceremonial aspects and not in its permanent social aspects. *Compadrazgo*, in other words, is of the European variety, in which the dyad of primary importance is that between *padrinos* and *ahijados*, whereas the relationship among *compadres* is virtually nonexistent as far as any particular rites and obligations. In this light, ritual kinship is best characterized as *padrinazgo* (ritual sponsorship).

To round out the analysis, a brief description of the temporary and permanent aspects of the four types of *padrinazgo* is in order. First, the immediate, temporary obligations of baptismal *padrinos* to *ahijados* is to give them a special gift (usually a gold coin, an icon, or a silver cup), pay for the *bolo* (coins thrown at children by the *padrinos* right after the baptism; silver or gold coins handed individually to attendants, usually during the ensuing ceremonial meal), and present them with a small silver tray engraved with their names and the date of the baptism. Frequently *padrinos* pay for the lunch, dinner, or cocktail reception; but all other expenses are defrayed by parents. Infants are usually baptized one or two months after birth: either at ten or eleven in the morning or at six or seven in the evening, followed by a lunch, cocktail party, or dinner. The ceremony takes place either in church or at home; the rite is orthodox and usually officiated by a priest friend of the family. The permanent or long-lasting bonds and duties of baptismal *padrinos*, however, are determined by canonical custom; they include guiding *ahijados* to lead a moral life, supervising their religious practice, and assisting them if they become orphans. Conversely, *ahijados* are customarily required to revere *padrinos*, be attentive to their needs, visit them on their name day (*santo*), attend their funeral, and so on. How seriously these reciprocal duties and obligations are complied with depends on the age of *ahijados*; in most cases they begin to wane after adolescence and usually disappear after marriage.

Second, confirmation as a *padrinazgo* and rite of passage is less important than baptism. Until the mid-1940s confirmation was bestowed individually by a bishop, usually a friend of the family. Nowadays the great majority of confirmations are collective, and not infrequently groups of aristocratic boys and girls get together to be confirmed during the periodic ceremonies organized by dioceses. It is still possible to organize an exclusive confirmation for a group of aristocratic adolescents; but it is becoming increasingly difficult, given the recent democratization of the church. The celebration, duties and obligations, social ambiance, and ensuing patterns of behavior of confirmation *padrinazgo* are essentially the same as those of baptism; but they are less elaborate, and the participation of kin and friends is significantly lower.

Third, first communion *padrinazgo* is more important than that of confirmation (even though first communion is not exactly a sacrament of the church), because *ahijados* almost invariably have a voice in choosing *padrinos* and occasionally are allowed to make the choice on their own. The religious rite takes place in the late morning in the family parish church, and it usually involves several adolescents undergoing the rite together. After the mass is over, communicants and their invariably large entourages repair to their respective homes for a cocktail-lunch, a kind of brunch (*almuerzo*), consisting mostly of traditional Mexican delicacies (*antojitos*). The entire celebration is as elaborate and well attended as the occasion of baptism. The social salience of first communion is attested by the gifts that *padrinos* give to *ahijados*, which may be as valuable as those given at baptism, and by the ensuing patterns of behavior between them, which are in most cases longer lasting than those involved in baptism *padrinazgo*. To reiterate, the saliency of first communion *padrinazgo* rests on the choice of ritual sponsors, in which godchildren have a determinant voice; they choose godparents that are already reciprocally tied to them by strong bonds of affection.

Fourth, in marriage *padrinazgo* the temporary social implications are more important than those of baptism and first communion *padrinazgos*, but not the ensuing behavior patterns, which are virtually nonexistent. Two reasons account for this lack of permanent bonds: the manner in which marriage ritual sponsors are chosen and the fact that *padrinos* and *ahijados* are adults and not infrequently of the same age group. The *padrinazgo* relationship essentially survives as an aspect of the real kinship or friendship relationship between *padrinos* and *ahijados*, including all the ensuing patterns of behavior. *Padrinos* must give *ahijados* valuable presents such as cash or silver objects (for example, a large silver tray, a tea set, or perhaps something in the category of an heirloom) when they are primary relatives. But the structural significance of marriage *padrinazgo* resides in the selection of *padrinos*, which is done by the bride and groom in consultation with their respective parents. That is a delicate matter that must be handled with diplomacy and punctiliousness, so as not to offend members of the nonresidential extended families of the bride and groom; this also applies to the ubiquitous *testigos* (witnesses) attending the

civil wedding. As indicated above, the selection of marriage *padrinos* and witnesses is a structural aspect with important implications for kinship network
formation.

To conclude, let us summarize the most salient characteristics of aristocratic ritual kinship and place it in the wider context of Mexican *compadrazgo*.

1. Despite the changes that aristocratic ritual kinship has been undergoing
   for nearly two decades, it remains largely endogenous and contracted with
   close kin. This is in rather sharp contrast with the *compadrazgo* system of
   folk peoples and the urban poor (accounting for the majority of Mexicans),
   among whom ritual kin are mostly chosen among nonkin.
2. As a corollary of item 1, the main function of *padrinazgo* among aristocrats is to reinforce already existing kinship and friendship relationships
   or to generate propitious interaction among kin and friends. Among folk
   peoples and the urban poor, the opposite is the case: *compadrazgo* serves to
   expand relationships beyond kinship and create networks of mutual assis-
   tance and exchange. Thus one can speak of a *compadrazgo* system among
   the latter but not of a *padrinazgo* system among the former.
3. *Padrinazgo* among aristocrats is almost entirely subsumed under or determined by kinship, as evidenced by the ritual kinship terminology and behavior of godparents and godchildren. By contrast, *compadrazgo* among
   folk people and the urban poor has an extended terminological system and
   distinct patterns of behavior of its own.
4. Aristocratic *padrinazgo*'s most important components are the immediate
   religious rites and ceremonies of the occasions for which it is contracted.
   After these events, it becomes socially insignificant; independent of kinship, *padrinazgo* has no permanent aspects. The situation is rather drastically different among folk people and the urban poor. Though the initial
   temporary aspects of *compadrazgo* are also critical, what makes it a system is
   its permanent component, which in importance often rivals kinship as an
   institution in organizing many aspects of the social life of the community.
5. There are also a number of similarities underlying *padrinazgo* among aristocrats and *compadrazgo* among folk peoples and the urban poor. Two of
   them are the most salient. On the one hand, in both cases ritual kinship
   is basically a sacred institution (even an aristocrat cannot refuse to become a ritual sponsor), devoid of overtly social, economic, religious, or
   even political functions tending to maximize specific ends. In the changing spectrum from the folk to the urban context, however, *compadrazgo*

does acquire determinant secular aspects. On the other hand, ritual kinship in both situations is basically egalitarian, horizontal, and symmetrical in most of its endogenous contexts. This has to be qualified to the extent that aristocrats accept becoming ritual kinship sponsors for people not of their class, and occasionally even folk people use *compadrazgo* to maximize economic or political ends; in both cases the entailed relationships are stratified, vertical, and asymmetrical in most respects.

Expressive Analysis

With the exception of religion, kinship-social organization is the most expressively laden major domain of Western aristocratic culture. Whereas religious expression was realized when the estate system was in place, kinship and social expression are essentially realized in the context of decline that the aristocracy has been experiencing since the demise of the *ancien régime*. This is particularly true of the Mexican aristocracy since the 1910 Revolution, when the realization of public religious expression—so much a part of the aristocratic *imago mundi*—came to an end. In this ambiance of decline, kinship has become a much more important domain of expressive realization. Throughout this and the preceding chapter, I have implicitly discussed many of the most salient expressive domains realized in the context of kinship and social organization, and nothing more needs to be said about them. Several new domains of expression need to be reiterated, however, since they were created after the aristocracy ceased to be the dominant class of the country, the most significant of which are the following.

First, since its inception in the sixteenth century the *mayorazgo* has been an important mechanism of structural continuity; it was the source of much expressive realization centered on the person of the firstborn son but affecting entire extended families. The *mayorazgo* began to decline after independence and ultimately lost its legal status before the turn of the twentieth century. Today the *mayorazgo* as a customary institution and in a simplified form remains in place among perhaps one-third of aristocrats but continues to play a symbolic and expressive role. Married aristocrats of the younger generation regard it as an anachronism, as one 40-year-old informant put it, "a practice without rhyme or reason and in total disagreement with contemporary social mentality." Nonetheless, most adult aristocrats take great pride in the notion of the *mayorazgo*—namely, in the knowledge that in colonial times the family was prominent enough to endow one. Today it continues to be a source of expressive realization: letting people know that there was a *mayorazgo* in the family, pointing to historical urban mansions associated with it, verbalizing the quantity and antiquity of entailed property, and so on.

Second, of all kinship institutions, marriage is inherently the most determinant source for the realization of expression. The symbolic and expressive constitution of *confarreatio*, as the patrician form of marriage in ancient Rome, remains the model for aristocratic marriage today. The baroque elaboration of the aristocratic Mexican wedding is a domain of expression explicitly designed to emphasize social differences from all other segments of society while implicitly asserting the right to an ancient rite which no other group can claim. It is equally significant that contracting a proper alliance spawns many specific domains of expression. Endogamously, searching for a spouse of equal standing, with the right aristocratic pedigree, and with similar forms of behavior constitutes an extensive expressive domain. Either avoiding exogamous marriage or, if this is impossible, devising the best strategy to preserve aristocratic integrity in exogenous environments is another expressive domain, which has acquired significant proportions in the precipitous decline of the past generation. Thus the marriage domain of expression may be regarded as a mechanism for both preserving aristocratic identity and alleviating loss of economic affluence. The basic configuration of this form of aristocratic expression, *vis-à-vis* the plutocracy, is one of survival: if you cannot beat them, join them.

Third, the patronymic an individual bears is a determinant emblem of aristocratic membership. Properly contextualized in terms of place and circumstance, in order to discriminate them from their usage among common folk, aristocratic patronymics are endogenous marks of standing and exogenous signs of status. Endogenously, patronymics entail a wide range of expressive behavior: remembering illustrious patronymics; focusing on the deeds that their bearers accomplished since their inception in New Spain or independent Mexico; writing family genealogies and documenting how various patronymics are related to one another as marks of aristocratic standing; manipulating patronymics in the marriage game to demonstrate illustrious lineage; and so on. Exogenously, the gestalt of fifteen or so patronymics through which the aristocracy is perceived by the plutocracy, the upper-middle class, and educated Mexicans is extended to the entire group. This results in much behavior centered on aristocrats' presenting a united expressive image and generating an aura of exaltedness, with exogenous results that no longer resonate the way they used to a generation ago. This is yet another subterfuge that demonstrates the impotence of the aristocracy as playing a last card in the game of expressive survival.

Fourth, downward mobility has been the hallmark of the Mexican aristocracy in this century; and this process has engendered many new forms of expression. Great loss of wealth has rather radically changed the configuration of the exclusive expressive array of the aristocracy; domains that were once central have been discontinued or are marginally realized by a few remaining affluent families, such as those centered on the horse culture (polo, equitation, *charrería*) and philanthropic activities (engaging in *obras pías*, endowing *capellanías*). Loss of power has had the same effect, and the rather large complex of ceremonial public display that was so diagnostic of aristocratic dominance as a ruling class is entirely gone. What remains of this conglomerate of expressive manifestation, so central to the traditional aristocratic image, is the occasional wedding reported in the press. This elicits consternation among the educated public as to why such an event merits reporting: aristocrats are regarded as a relic of the past—the sooner forgotten the better. The rich and powerful plutocrats react rather condescendingly, implying that in terms of ostentation and display they can do better. Indeed, many of the new forms of expression since the increasing decline of the aristocracy for two generations are underlined by *embourgeoisement*. This means that most of the new domains of expression generated since the late 1940s are really emulation of nonaristocratic forms of expression. This inclusive complex is shared by all sectors of the superordinate class; it contains many domains ranging from fashion and entertainment to personal demeanor and participation in sports, all too extensive to be discussed here.

Fifth, the self-image of being the best of the best, *vis-à-vis* all other classes of society, is directly related to the organization of kinship as an extended system encompassing the entire aristocratic group. This is another fertile source of expressive realization, which again has endogenous and exogonous implications. With respect to superior self-image, the belief that aristocracy is in the blood, with multiple ties of kinship and marriage, bolsters the notion of the group as a unit and reinforces the "us versus them" syndrome. The reality of this position may be consciously questioned by many aristocrats; but unconsciously it translates into much alleviating expressive behavior, focused essentially on the proposition that they were the undisputed dominant class of the country for more than four centuries, which belies their present downward mobility. The inconsistency of this position does not deter most aristocrats from thinking, feeling, and conceiving of themselves as the best of the best. Aristocrats encourage a perception of themselves as an integrated group, minimizing differences, and belonging to a lineage extending to the Spanish Conquest, which most know to be a false claim. This rather large domain is indubitably the most unrealistic of the entire aristocratic expressive array.

In conclusion, kinship and its extensions are the most diagnostic structural domain generating conflict and survival forms of expression. From the wider societal perspective, however, aristocrats have become relics of the past—a great change from four generations ago, when they were the undisputed purveyors of superordinate expression. During the past two generations (a precipitous period of decline), aristocrats have become emulators of plutocratic expression; and their inclusive array includes many domains that are shared by the affluent middle and upper-middle classes. Moreover, the aristocratic exclusive array, which until the 1910 Revolution was a blend of public and private domains, has been entirely privatized and centered mostly on the household, the last bastion of aristocratic expression. In other words, aristocrats have ceased being structural innovators in Pareto's terms, but they are also not expressively creative; they are no longer the model of superordinate expression, a function that plutocrats have been increasingly appropriating. Thus aristocrats have played their last card in the game of survival: this reversal of roles signals the imminent demise of the aristocracy as a functional, distinctly perceived social class in the Mexican stratification system.

CHAPTER 8

INTERNAL STRATIFICATION AND
ORGANIZATION OF THE GROUP

As I have indicated in Chapter 7, the gestalt of the Mexican aristocracy and the monolithic image its members project are significantly different from the actual organization of the group. The aristocracy is a mildly ranked social class in which the standing of individuals and families depends on several factors: mainly, antiquity of lineage in the country, degree of contemporary and traditional wealth, and achievements and notable deeds of illustrious ancestors. In this chapter I analyze these and other factors in order to give the real — as contrasted with the ideal — view of the group, which (in a large variety of contexts and occasions) aristocrats manipulate in order to enhance endogenous aims and exogenous perceptions.

Factors and Considerations in the Ranking of
the Mexican Aristocracy Today

•

Antiquity of Lineage in the Land and Titles of Nobility

Antiquity of lineage (embodied in titles of nobility, membership in military orders, possession of landed estates, and ancient office-holding) has always been the primary determinant of aristocratic rank in Western society. In most European aristocracies an individual holding an ancient title of baron may outrank many a duke of seventeenth- or eighteenth-century creation. In Britain a mere squire who has been in possession of his landed estate since the

Domesday Book (1086) is more aristocratic than most earls and dukes of the realm (Montagu of Beaulieu 1970:98–105). The same obtains in the case of the Mexican aristocracy: descendants of conquistadors and original *encomenderos* in the sixteenth century, regardless of whether they had titles in the family, are the most aristocratic. The situation, of course, is more complex, and other factors must be considered.

Let us first consider antiquity of lineage by itself. As stated in Chapter 1, in terms of lineage and tradition, there are four recognized categories of aristocrats (see the section Strength and Demographic Configuration of the Aristocracy Today in Chapter 1). These are the recognized segments of the aristocracy today—the framework, if you will, that broadly determines aristocratic status, which in a variety of contexts is manipulated in the game of enhancing aristocratic standing.

Proof of descent from apical ancestors ascending to the foregoing periods comes from various sources: ancestral portraiture, private and publicly published genealogies (see Ortega y Pérez Gallardo 1908), family memoirs, historical accounts, *encomienda* documentation, hacienda records, association with a landed estate, and urban mansions (now invariably in the public domain). For an individual, family, or kin group having *pergaminos* means possessing variegated combinations of documentary evidence and visual attestation proving antiquity and illustriousness of lineage. For the most illustrious families and name groups (perhaps fifteen or so), the evidence and attestation are well known to most aristocrats and constitute the gestalt by which the group is perceived. About half of them trace descent to the sixteenth century: two of them to original conquistadors and the rest to large *encomenderos* and prominent settlers, founders of cities and towns.[1] The other half trace descent to the seventeenth century; almost all these apical ancestors were great landed magnates.

A few families and name groups can trace descent to the sixteenth century, thereby having high aristocratic standing. They are well known to the group as a whole, but they are not part of the gestalt by which the aristocracy is endogenously known and exogenously perceived. Conversely, there are three or four families and name groups of eighteenth-century extraction, all of them descendants of the great miner-entrepreneurs that dominated the economic life of the colony until the wars of Independence. These families and name groups belong to the gestalt elite with the highest aristocratic standing by virtue of former great wealth and/or outstanding achievement of some of its members. Thus antiquity of lineage is the most salient determinant of aristocratic rank but not a necessary condition for inclusion in the gestalt elite. Other factors such as economic power and individual accomplishments in the more recent past (usually between the French Intervention and the end of the Díaz regime) play a role in assigning aristocratic standing, particularly at the top.

The majority of aristocratic families and name groups trace descent to the eighteenth century, roughly from 1720 to 1810. This is the period when most titles of nobility were awarded to rich Creoles and *peninsulares*, who made great fortunes in mining. Titles of nobility were also awarded to landed and commercial magnates of seventeenth- and sixteenth-century extraction. Of the roughly 108 titles of nobility (there is no exact extant account of how many were awarded by the Spanish Crown in colonial times), three-fourths were awarded during this period. This is an important consideration in assessing contemporary aristocratic status which merits some discussion.

The traditional ground for awarding titles of nobility was distinguished military or administrative service to the Spanish Crown. This changed greatly in the eighteenth century. Almost all titles of nobility in the eighteenth century until Independence were granted for economic reasons. Landed aristocratic magnates and newly rich plutocratic miners vied for titles of nobility, which the Crown liberally granted because it generated revenue through the payment of two taxes (*lanzas* and *media annata*, privileges of the Crown going back to medieval times). Indeed, late colonial and early republican scholars maintained that most of the titles granted by the Crown throughout the eighteenth century until Independence did not reflect the true principles of Spanish ennoblement and that rich parvenus purchased them outright to satisfy their own desire for vulgar ostentation. It should be realized that this was not peculiar to a colonial version of the Spanish nobiliary system. On the contrary, this was a universal aspect of all Western European nobiliary systems, which began in England during the reign of James I when the title of baronet was created to generate revenues for the Crown. This practice has precedents in most European nobiliary systems going back to the early sixteenth century; and by the end of the seventeenth century it had become quite generalized and increasingly abused, including middle-range titles and the titles of count and marquess. To this day the European nobility frets about titles that were awarded for excellence in warfare and outstanding services to the Crown and those granted for economic reasons devised to enrich the Crown.

Most Mexican aristocrats today are not aware of this distinction concerning titles of nobility. All they know is that many titles were granted, in which they take great pride, especially when there were titles in the family or associated with the name group; and with rare exceptions (at least in this century) they generally do not try to activate them.[2] The mere awareness of having had a title in the family is sufficient to satisfy aristocratic pride and enhance standing in the group. While aristocrats associated with seventeenth-century titles know the inherent difference between them and subsequent titles and the prestige this entails, those associated with the later titles do not. Differences are minimized, leading to much manipulation. Discrimination between the grounds for ennoblement may be seen as irrelevant, as is the allegation that some of them were "bought," given that most of the new rich magnates to whom they were awarded in the eighteenth century were the architects of the boom that made New Spain a thriving economy. It should be realized that this arcane, scholastic arguing about aristocratic standing goes on among members of the older, more historically minded generations; the social significance of titles and other symbols of distinction is somewhat lost among the younger generations (the recently married and those approaching middle age).

About one-fourth of the group's families acquired aristocratic status after Independence, the last of them at about the end of the Díaz dictatorship. Most of this segment are at the periphery of the group in terms of inherent rank; but a few individuals rose to prominence, and their descendants today are distinguished aristocrats. These were the great plutocrats who made large fortunes and became powerful and influential between the late 1840s (when Mexico began to recuperate from the economic depression that ensued after Independence) and the early 1870s (a period of relative economic well-being that characterized the years after the expulsion of the French from the country). These upwardly mobile plutocrats had three provenances. One group was composed of Spaniards who had escaped the expulsion from Mexico in 1827 and their sons as well as others who migrated from Spain and its former colonies after the initial xenophobia had died down. The most successful among them became prime candidates for aristocratic incorporation. Most of their fortunes were made in trade, some in manufacturing, but almost all led to the acquisition of landed estates. Another group boasted foreigners, primarily English and French, who had become enfranchised in several Mexican cities in the pursuit of trading, manufacturing, and banking during the four decades after Independence. This group also included several highly placed personnel who came to Mexico with Maximilian during the French Intervention. Many second-generation families had become rich and influential by the onset of the Porfiriato, both in the capital and in provincial cities; several acquired aristocratic status. A third group included exclusively traditional, mostly provincial families of Spanish-Creole extraction who had accumulated land and urban property after two generations of independent life. The richest and most successful of these families were able to carve a prominent place in the ruling class of the country, but their descendants today are no more than four or five families that count among aristocrats of first rank.

Aristocrats as a group are well acquainted with titles of nobility, and the average adult over forty knows by name at least thirty of the more than one hundred that were granted in colonial times, most distinctly those awarded at the beginning of the seventeenth century and four or five associated with the great miners of the eighteenth century. More significantly, aristocrats are very conscious of the value of titles of nobility as the most ostensible symbols of aristocratic visibility. They also realize, however, that by themselves titles do not constitute a sufficient condition for determining aristocratic prominence and rank; antiquity of lineage, demonstrated by the various means mentioned above, does. Antiquity of lineage itself is not a necessary condition for aristocratic prominence. The best way to explain this quandary is to specify that Mexican aristocrats do make a distinction between prominence and rank, which is manifested as follows. Tracing descent to a sixteenth-century *encomendero* or founder of a town confirms an aristocrat today as being of high rank but not necessarily as being prominent. Today descent from a rich titled magnate of eighteenth-century extraction and being relatively wealthy make an aristocrat prominent but not necessarily high ranking.

The Effect of Wealth, Past and Present

At the end of colonial times the wealth of the established Mexican aristocracy as a class, together with that of the recently ennobled mining plutocracy, was one of the greatest in the world. Probably fifteen of the wealthiest aristocratic and plutocratic magnates in New Spain had fortunes (combining mining, manufacturing, trading, and land) ranging from three to seven million gold pesos (Ladd 1976:184–186), which would be roughly equivalent to 400 to 1,000 million dollars today. These fortunes dwindled rapidly after Independence, as mining in Mexico declined dramatically and the effects of the industrial revolution did not really become established until after the aristocracy had ceased to be the ruling class of the country. Nonetheless, at the end of the Díaz dictatorship, the landed and commercial wealth of the aristocracy was sufficient for most aristocrats to lead a privileged, seigneurial existence.

The Mexican Revolution of 1910 terminated the ruling functions of aristocrats locally and nationally; but considerable numbers of aristocrats—particularly those who had large urban holdings and a more diversified economy (hacienda land combined with various commercial enterprises and banking)—were still comparatively rich until the early 1940s, when the great plutocratic fortunes of the twentieth century began to develop. Until then aristocratic wealth was sufficient to perpetuate the group as the undisputed social class of Mexico City, where most aristocrats had concentrated by then. In this virtual mini-revival of the aristocracy as a social class, the richest among them played an important role by providing the material and economic means that a brilliant social life demands. What was the source of their wealth, and how was it instrumental in enhancing their aristocratic rank?

The source of wealth for rich aristocrats by the middle of the eighteenth century has been indicated above. On the one hand, the economic acumen of the eighteenth-century mining magnates—and of the last group of plutocrats in the nineteenth century who acquired aristocratic status—made these individuals the most progressive in adapting to changing times. On the other hand, the mixed economy they pursued (land, commerce, and banking) made it possible to survive the worst effects of the Revolution, especially the devastating land reform of the 1930s. Particularly instrumental in the survival of their moderate wealth in the twentieth century was the possession of urban property, which was never subject to the devastating effects of land reform. The socio-psychological profile of this group is apparent: a quite unaristocratic orientation that was not aimed at acquiring land as the main or sole source of wealth, as had traditionally characterized the Mexican aristocracy, which entry into the machine age in nineteenth-century Mexico did not essentially change.

The most affluent aristocratic families became the center of social life for the group and supplied the leaders for various "cultural" activities that are so much an aspect of a social class. The social life of the group was a brilliant round of balls and other less elaborate affairs. Aristocratic weddings once again became vicarious attractions, and the comings and goings of aristocrats were prominently reported in the press. It also helped that many of these activities took place in the palatial mansions in the old quarter of the city. Incidentally, this was the last time that aristocrats occupied these mansions, since by the late 1940s almost all of them had been acquired by the city or sold to business concerns. This was the ambiance in which the aristocratic group functioned as the social class of the capital. Concentrated in Mexico city, the aristocracy was reinvigorated; and for nearly two decades (roughly from the early 1930s to the early 1950s), it recaptured some of the social dominance and exaltedness of prerevolutionary days. The budding postrevolutionary plutocracy (not yet rich enough and socially inexperienced) together with the traditional upper-middle class of Porfirian extraction avidly emulated the aristocracy and constituted, as it had traditionally, the larger framework of superordinate expression and display.

This social renaissance is a veritable case of terminal expression, which—despite the demise of the aristocracy as a dominant class—was made possible largely by the vicariousness that always accompanies the formation of a new superordinate class with only one social model to emulate, namely, the aristocracy. From then on, the great power and wealth that the plutocracy achieved was the main cause for the steady decline and ultimate demise of the aristocracy as a social class. It is in this context that the comparatively rich aristocratic plutocrats identified above became highly visible and prominent; in the perception of the group, however, they did not necessarily increase in aristocratic rank. The prominence that wealth conferred did not come to these aristocrats overnight; rather, it took more than a century to gather sufficient aristocratic shine. Two examples illustrate how the process took place.

The first example concerns a very successful eighteenth-century miner who was ultimately ennobled. He was a *peninsular* who arrived in New Spain in 1727; forty years later he was one of the most prosperous mining entrepreneurs of the colony; and he was awarded the title of count in 1768. He is described by contemporary aristocratic informants as *un minero de pico y pala* (a pick and shovel miner), a college graduate of rather humble origins but with great vision and entrepreneurial skills. In the traditional pattern of plutocratic magnates in New Spain, he acquired landed estates, a process that was facilitated by the many haciendas that became available for purchase with the expulsion of the Jesuits from the Spanish possessions in the New World. Before he died in 1781, he founded El Monte de Piedad (the National Pawn Shop), a landmark institution in the history of Mexico City. His patronymic became widely known and remains so today among a wide spectrum of society. His diversified economy in mining, land, and commerce made him one of the seven richest men in the colony (Ladd 1976:184). His descendants prospered after Independence, even during the difficult generation that followed. The fourth count and his family played a prominent role during Maximilian's reign (1864–1867), when titles of nobility were briefly reinstated, and he was made a duke. During the unprecedented growth of the hacienda system and the pinnacle of eminence of the aristocracy following the French Intervention and throughout the Díaz regime, the duke's descendants were at the economic and social forefront of the group, a position that they were able to maintain until after the 1934 land reform.

The second example concerns the ennoblement of a landed magnate during the last decade of colonial rule, when the Spanish Crown granted titles of nobility. The apical ancestor of this magnate's family had arrived from Spain in the middle of the seventeenth century; by the middle of the eighteenth century, his descendants had acquired aristocratic status. The family was rich in land and engaged in diversified commercial enterprises. In overall wealth the family ranked among the twenty-five richest in the colony by the time one of its members was awarded the title of marquess in 1810 (Ladd 1976:184). After Independence, the family prospered more economically than most, particularly compared to those who had made fortunes in mining. (Most of these aristocratic families lost the majority of their wealth with the decline of mining after Independence, and several of them were no longer aristocrats by the end of the Porfiriato.) The third marquess also played a distinguished role in Maximilian's court, and his family was one of the important foci in the social life of the capital. By the end of the Porfiriato, the descendants of the marquess were among the leading *hacendados* in the country, in terms of both the extent of their holdings and the quality of agrarian operations. The visibility and prestige that this aristocratic family (or rather name group) continued to have until well after the 1934 land reform have a peculiar source. By the last two decades of the nineteenth century members of the family had become intensely interested in the culture of the horse. They imported several breeds for thoroughbred racing, equestrian events, and polo ponies. Indeed a member of the family is credited with having introduced competitive polo to Mexico. More significantly, in the aftermath of the armed phase of the Revolution, another member of the family was highly instrumental in reviving *charrería* (the practice and craft of the *charro* [cowboy], an extensive complex including equestrian skills).

This aspect of Mexican horse culture had traditionally brought together, however superficially, *hacendado* and *caporal* (cowboy hand), rich and poor, in a pursuit that until the Revolution had been the essence of being rural Mexican. Rescuing this aspect of Mexican culture, which had been decaying since before the end of the Díaz dictatorship, greatly endeared this aristocrat to a wide spectrum of Mexican society. The family's patronymic became a byword among diverse sectors of the Mexican population; in fact, this is the last time an aristocrat and his family were widely known beyond the narrow confines of the superordinate class.

These are two of probably a dozen rich aristocratic families—which include several of nineteenth-century banking-plutocratic extraction—that largely framed the last episode of aristocratic saliency as a social class. What can be deduced from these examples (which, although not quite typical, illustrate wealth as a factor in determining aristocratic visibility and prestige)?

First, despite being titled, both families were regarded as parvenus by the old established aristocracy that traced descent to the sixteenth century and certainly by the descendants of those who were titled in the seventeenth century. Having recently acquired aristocratic status, the families were on the periphery of the group, particularly the first-generation descendants of the founder of the National Pawn Shop. Three generations later, during the French Intervention, the two families had gained sufficient prominence to acquire a rather central position in the national aristocracy. These families continued to prosper economically. In three more generations, by the time of the 1934 land reform, they were among the most prominent and part of the elite gestalt of the aristocracy, particularly visible among various sectors of society by virtue of their ancestors' accomplishments that had affected other sectors of the population.[3]

Second, prominence and visibility did not confer on these rich, significantly newer families a higher rank in the unanimous view of dozens of informants. This is exclusively a function of antiquity of lineage. This aspect of aristocratic ideology (which is an invariant trait of all Western aristocracies), together with its patent irrationality, is strikingly expressed by an old informant:

> Since I was able to reason, I have heard my parents and kinsmen affirm that aristocracy is defined by the antiquity of *pergaminos* that you may have: the older they are, the more aristocratic you are. I have always thought this attitude unjust and somewhat absurd. And what is worse is that people like my family, with *pergaminos* not among the oldest and most illustrious [the family of this informant is of early-nineteenth-century extraction], believe all this and, when our children are about to marry, unconsciously think of *pergaminos*. This is the way we are, and until we disappear we are not going to change.

Thus prominent and visible families today are universally accepted as part of the elite gestalt of the aristocracy despite their lower rank, by virtue of having performed valuable services that benefit the entire group. The most exalted aristocrats, those with a proven history among the oldest in the land, are not above expressing in private that "there are others with more money, but we are the true aristocrats." Such is the implicit pecking order that characterizes ranking in this moribund social class.

Third, it may sound like splitting hairs to distinguish between aristocratic rank determined by antiquity of lineage and prestige and visibility based on wealth, but it makes sense sociologically. On the one hand, it endogenously safeguards the purity of aristocratic affiliation and provides members of the group with the illusion that they still are what they were in colonial times. On the other hand, it exogenously enhances the perception of the group as more than simply a fossilized social class with no apparent functions. At any rate, symbolic gymnastics of this kind have characterized the life of aristocrats during the past three generations.

The Effect of Illustrious Ancestors and Other Factors

There are other factors that confer aristocratic prestige and visibility, most notably, family ancestors that are regarded as illustrious by virtue of having been well known locally (provincially) or nationally for outstanding performance in endeavors such as administration, public service, scholarship, literature, the law, and so on. In fact, in the case of the two examples given above, the prestige and visibility of the two families were not so much based on wealth but on an ancestor's having founded the National Pawn Shop in one case and the promotion of *charrería* in the other. In every one of these categories, there are long lines of aristocrats who did outstanding work in the nearly 400 years as the dominant class of the country. Let us discuss how it affected families with differential antiquity of lineage.

There are at least ten families today with proven descent from founders of cities and towns in the sixteenth and seventeenth centuries, most notably, the founding of the city of Puebla in 1531, the second most important city of the country until the middle of the twentieth century. These families acquired great prominence locally, and their preeminence was recognized nationally before the aristocracy concentrated in Mexico City by mid-twentieth century. The descendants of these families today are among the most aristocratic, particularly those of sixteenth-century extraction. Under the rubric of administration, there were many aristocrats who occupied important positions throughout colonial times, extensively in local-level politics and occasionally at the viceregal level. At least seven families today can trace descent to viceroys of New Spain, the most notable example being the ninth viceroy, who was also the first Creole in the New World to have been titled. Less important positions were those of *adelantado* (captain general), *alcalde mayor* (provincial governor), *alguacil mayor* (constable in charge of Indian justice and affairs), and *oidor* (royal justice). In provincial cities aristocrats throughout colonial times dominated local-level politics by practically monopolizing the positions of *alcalde* (mayor) and *regidor* (councilman, alderman). The civil architecture of many provincial cities today is a visible testimony of this dominance. Beyond the excellence of their former mansions, numerous buildings gracing these cities are silent witnesses to the role aristocrats played during 300 years of provincial urban evolution. Perception of this aristocratic achievement was once locally prevalent; now it is fading from the local visual consciousness, and only a small educated minority associates the architectural geography of the city with those who transformed it. To aristocrats today, regardless of rank and antiquity of lineage, their ancestors' accomplishments in the cities of the country are a great source of pride and a validation of endogenous prestige.

Another administrative niche occupied by aristocrats was their near-monopoly of the high clergy throughout colonial times, which to some extent continued until 1910. It included archbishops, bishops, deans, and heads of convent and monastic orders, particularly the former. Given the disproportionate number of aristocratic women in convent seclusion, especially before Independence, convents were invariably veritable aristocratic fiefdoms.[4] This is another source of prestige, and aristocrats today take pride in ancestors who occupied these religious offices, as evidenced by the portraits of religious personages that are displayed in many aristocratic households.

In the same vein, but not always directly related to administration or public service, was membership in military orders. In traditional Spanish fashion, Creole and *peninsular* aristocrats were knighted throughout colonial times. The three main military orders were Santiago, Calatrava, and Alcántara; two others, Montesa and San Juan de Jerusalén (also known as Malta), were not as prestigious. From 1525 (when Cortés was made a knight of Santiago) until the end of colonial rule in New Spain, the Crown knighted more than 600 Creoles and *peninsulares:* 426 knights of Santiago, 121 of Calatrava, 66 of Alcántara, 6 of Montesa, and 11 of San Juan de Jerusalén. As in the case of titles of nobility, for the first 180 years after the Conquest most knighthoods were awarded for military and public service to the Crown; after the onset of the eighteenth century, however, most of the knighthoods were "bought" by the rich and powerful, thereby debasing the original grounds of awarding this dignity.

Again, this distinction of the grounds for awarding knighthood has been lost to contemporary aristocrats. Membership in military orders is validated by documentary evidence and ostensibly by portraits of the original knight (most of them dating back to the second half of the seventeenth and eighteenth centuries). It should be realized that, strictly speaking, knighthood was not hereditary; it was conferred for the life of the recipient, much like the contemporary British knighthood. In the Spanish system all *hidalgos a fuero de España* (members of the lower nobility according to Spanish nobiliary law) were *caballeros* (knights), *de facto* and *de jure;* and knighthood in military orders was an extra dignity reflecting the merits of an individual that did not need to be perpetuated. In practice, at least in New Spain, knighthood was remembered by descendants of the recipient and became a badge of honor and prestige. This tradition has survived the demise of military orders for more than a century and a half, and families still point with great pride to their knightly ancestors.

Intellectual achievement is another factor that contributes to contemporary aristocratic prestige, focused mainly on scholarship, literature, and the law. From the last quarter of the sixteenth century to the Porfiriato, there were aristocrats that excelled in these intellectual endeavors. From Gonzalo Gómez de Cervantes (1944) in the sixteenth century, Baltasar Dorantes de Carranza (1970) in the seventeenth century, Lucas Alamán (1942) and Alfredo Chavero (1901) in the eighteenth century, Joaquín García Icazbalceta (1947, 1954) and José Ramírez (1949) in the nineteenth century, to Ignacio Bernal (1962, 1980), Pablo Martínez del Río (1938, 1954), and Francisco Icaza (1969) in the twentieth century, aristocratic scholars made a significant intellectual contribution. This is particularly the case in provincial scholarship, in that much of the local social history and folklore was written by aristocrats until they ceased to be the local ruling class. In the eighteenth and nineteenth centuries there were prominent aristocratic naturalists, historians, physicians, judges, and authors; in the twentieth century, continuing in this tradition despite their precipitous decline, there are a significant number of first-rate aristocratic anthropologists, archaeologists, historians, and art historians.[5] Mexican aristocrats of all extractions are justifiably proud of the intellectual achievements of their ancestors and do not pass up the opportunity to parade them when the occasion requires them to bolster aristocratic rank. Aristocrats as a group are well aware of the exploitation they exerted when they were the ruling class, accept that this is a true assessment of the past, but are incensed when they are depicted as leeches on the body politic who never made any significant contribution to society.

There are finally idiosyncratic and personal factors that contribute to aristocratic prestige and visibility. Among the former are the two examples given above; many others that I have identified are most commonly associated with the provincial setting, before the aristocracy concentrated in Mexico City. The historical tradition of at least a dozen provincial cities associated with aristocratic nuclei is rich in accounts (occasionally going back to the sixteenth century) of specific individuals and families who were benefactors of the community, had a hand in urban development, and were examples of the genuine interest of aristocrats in the urban centers that they controlled. Personal factors refer essentially to the excellence of expressive behavior of particular families—so much praised and desired by all aristocrats—that made them stand out. I most tellingly identified this among provincial families that migrated to Mexico City in the 1930s and 1940s. Many of them, unsure of themselves and not that well known in the capital, made extra efforts to ingratiate themselves with the core aristocracy, with positive results in generating prestige and visibility. This is clearly expressed by a most distinguished aristocrat:

> This is an old family from Guadalajara, with a well-known name but without references in Mexico City. Since they settled in the capital at the end of the 1930s, they began to stand out in the social life of the group. Not because they had money, but because of the attractiveness and grace of their women and the courtesy and good manners of all of them. Fifteen years later, they were among the most appreciated and sought after families in the city's aristocratic circles.

The Interdigitation of Factors and the Behavioral and Ideological Significance of Rank

Fundamentally, aristocratic ideology stipulates that rank is essentially fixed by antiquity of lineage. Therefore, the factors which generate prestige and visibility do not entail any changes in the position of individuals and families in the hierarchy of the group. Perceptions of excellence (having amassed a great fortune, having had individually illustrious ancestors, and having performed noteworthy public deeds)—properly manipulated—give the impression of higher rank and loom larger in the conduct of everyday affairs and expressive realization than in the fixed nature of rank. This is a feature shared by all Western aristocracies and has been at work since classical times; together with the belief that aristocracy is in the blood, it constitutes the foundation of estate stratification that continues to configure much behavior in what remains of the aristocracy in the context of class stratification.[6] What does the confluence of factors that modify the perception of intrinsic aristocratic rank mean? What is the effect of this perception on the ranking of aristocrats into fairly distinct operational groups?

Let us first analyze the situation in terms of intrinsic aristocratic rank and what this means operationally and perceptually. Antiquity of lineage is the unequivocal standard of rank: the longer one's ancestors have been in the land, the more aristocratic one is. Thus descendants of conquistadors and founders of cities and towns are the epitome of rank and the model of manipulation. In the game of enhancing aristocratic rank, individuals and families of more recent extraction would claim *pergaminos* (genealogical connections, *mayorazgo* affiliations, membership in military orders, hacienda ownership), relating them to the descendants of this exalted segment or indirectly to conquistadors and founders of cities and towns who today do not have descendants constituting a name group.[7] Moreover, this original set of ancestors, endogenously and exogenously, constitutes the emblem of aristocratic distinction and at all times fosters this image; hence the pronounced proclivity to manipulate aristocratic rank among those of more recent (late-eighteenth- and nineteenth-century) extraction.

Descendants of seventeenth- and eighteenth-century extraction constitute, so to speak, the second and third ranks of the aristocracy today; those who achieved aristocratic status in the nineteenth century are a poor fourth and, behind their backs, are occasionally regarded as parvenus. This aristocratic ranking is the fundamental perception that the Mexican aristocracy has of itself, which behaviorally and operationally is modified by the various factors specified above. Before analyzing this juncture, we may ask: what does this ranking mean by itself, and does it have any function? The question has already been answered. To put it in a different perspective, ranking obsession is an expression of aristocratic concern everywhere. Forged in the feudal Middle Ages (in which the ranks of the superordinate estate, from knight to king, were kept neatly compartmentalized), it atavistically continues to configure the aristocracy in its terminal stage as a functioning class of Western superordinate stratification. It is as if, aware of their imminent demise as a group, aristocrats cling to arcane practices to assure themselves that they are still relevant.

Returning to the effect of other factors on antiquity of lineage, the structural entailments that generate visibility and prestige are the following. All four ranks are affected by the factors specified above (mainly wealth and illustrious ancestors in administration and public service) in structuring the relative standing of aristocrats as they are endogenously and exogenously perceived. Thus membership in the gestalt elite, as I have called the most prominent and visible families, includes aristocrats of sixteenth-, seventeenth-, and eighteenth-century (and in one exceptional case nineteenth-century) extraction who were also wealthy and/or had illustrious ancestors. By contrast, there are descendants of sixteenth-century conquistadors and settlers who are not so included because they cannot boast illustrious ancestors. The aristocratic group as a whole recognizes the high rank of these families even though they may live in relative obscurity, some of them even in dire economic circumstances. We may ask again: what does the distinction among ranks mean endogenously, and are there any behavioral entailments? The distinction means nothing more than the atavistic concern with old lineage that compels aristocrats to pay homage to those who possess it and to make their social life as appealing as possible. The behavior entailed means nothing except that families with *pergaminos* are cultivated as sources of possible spouses by the diminishing number of average aristocrats for whom old lineage is more important than wealth.[8]

Exogenously, no such distinction obtains: for plutocrats, the upper-middle class, and a few others still aware that aristocrats exist, visibility and prestige are their only perceptions of this now almost invisible social class. Finally, it should be noted that among members of the gestalt elite (families of eighteenth-century extraction with much public service and overall visibility) there is a degree of veiled resentment toward families of sixteenth-century origin with the most *pergaminos* but little public service, at least since Independence. An elder informant in the former category has the following to say about the ranking aristocratic family:

> [They] consider themselves to be the group's royalty. The truth is that they are undoubtedly the most distinguished family, with *pergaminos* to squander, but it is also true that since the end of colonial times none of them has excelled in the world of business or in some enterprise that would have given us luster as a group. Rather, they have managed to use their past [implying success in contracting matrimonial alliances and generating economic standing] but have created nothing new. The aristocratic spirit demands that a person's rank be reinforced with concrete facts and achievements so that it is not based merely on the past.

This, of course, is a self-serving statement that emphasizes the achieved aspects of aristocratic position and sour grapes at not having as many *pergaminos*. It also illustrates the ambivalence that most aristocrats exhibit concerning rank and prestige: the more conservative usually emphasize the former, whereas the majority favor the latter. This is one more trick in the perennial game of the aristocratic pecking order, which perhaps is irrelevant but no more so than much of the behavioral baggage of all classes in highly stratified societies.

Finally, what are the referential rank-prestige categories framing the social and cultural life of the Mexican aristocracy in its period of terminal decline? There are basically four. First are the gestalt elite as analyzed above (mostly composed of families of sixteenth- and seventeenth-century extraction with a sprinkling of prestigious families dating back to the eighteenth century). To reiterate, this small group (constituted by roughly sixty families) may be regarded as the ideal endogenous image of the group; but it is also the perception that aristocrats as a whole exogenously strive to project. The second category is constituted by some ninety families, descendants of seventeenth-century *encomenderos* and *hacendado*-entrepreneurs, and a few obscure families of sixteenth-century extraction. These families are rich in *pergaminos*, are sought after, but play a passive role in the life of the group. The third category includes the great majority of families (about five hundred) which can trace descent to individuals who achieved aristocratic status in the eighteenth century and a few of early-nineteenth-century extraction. They are the most ubiquitous in the overall life of the aristocratic group and the most active in manipulating evidence of antiquity of lineage for purposes of social standing and in the matrimonial game. The fourth and last category is comparatively small, consisting of probably no more than one hundred families, mostly of nineteenth-century extraction in addition to a few families that acquired aristocratic status between the end of the Porfiriato and 1940 or so. They are, so to speak, at the fringes of the aristocracy. They are recognized as bona fide members of the group but with the least rank and prestige.

To conclude, we may ask: do these categories have any operational significance in the social, economic, and religious lives of aristocrats? The answer is: very little. This is a function of various kinds of relationships among name groups, in which rank and prestige play a small role, as discussed in the following section.

Constitution of the Functional, Operational Segments in Aristocratic Life Today

The social, economic, and religious interaction among aristocrats has to a large extent been described and analyzed in terms of kinship in Chapters 7.

What remains to be clarified is the identification and configuration of the extra-kinship dimensions of the segments that complement aristocratic social and cultural life. The expressive life and ideology of the Mexican aristocracy have always had a monolithic configuration, but the group has been operationally fragmented. Since the seventeenth century the ruling class of the country has been structured in terms of fairly discrete segments, primarily because it was enfranchised in the capital and several provincial cities. Other factors instrumental in the aristocracy's fragmentation have varied throughout the last three centuries. With the aristocracy's concentration in Mexico City after the Revolution, aristocratic fragmentation continued, caused by other factors peculiar to twentieth-century conditions.

As far I have been able to ascertain, there are roughly a dozen identifiable segments that constitute the aristocracy today, each composed of six to ten family groups, with an average membership of eight nuclear families apiece. It was obviously impossible to arrive at an accurate estimate of group membership, mostly because at the fringes there is disagreement about whether a considerable number of families are accorded aristocratic status. These are almost invariably plutocratic families of Porfirian extraction that, in the perception of mainline aristocrats, have not entirely passed the expressive and behavioral gate-keeping requirements. For practical purposes, however, I estimate the membership of the group at about 5,500, including adults and children, which gives an approximate size of the operational segments as ranging from 200 to 600 people. The size of the segments depends largely on the factors that caused fragmentation, which are the following: dispersion in Mexico City, friendship and matrimonial alliances of long standing, occupational differentiation, place of origin before concentrating in the capital, and size of the name group.

As I have demonstrated in Chapter 7, dispersion in the megalopolis is an important factor in the configuration of the name group, the exocentric kindred, and the nonresidential extended family. The same obtains in the case of the operational segments whose kinship units play a complementary role. By the end of the Porfiriato the aristocracy was permanently enfranchised in the capital; and many provincial families that kept mansions in Mexico City resided in fairly close proximity in the colonial section of the city and three adjacent *colonias*. By 1950 this settlement pattern had come to an end. Aristocratic mansions in the historical section and nearby boroughs had been abandoned, and provincial aristocrats settled in the new upscale boroughs that accompanied the tremendous growth of the city from the mid-1930s onward. Thus by the late 1950s several segments of diverse name group composition had come into existence in several broad sections of the city but with a modicum of residential integrity, as they straddled two or at most three boroughs. Residential proximity, then, was the main factor in configuring eight of the operational segments into which aristocrats are grouped today.

Friendship and matrimonial alliances of long standing represent the second most important factor in accounting for fragmentation. There are at least a dozen name groups that have maintained close ties since the second half of the eighteenth century because of multiple marriages, claiming the same illustrious ancestors (holders of noble titles, knights in military orders, related *mayorazgos*), and continued social interaction. These are the most tightly knit segments and include the majority of the most prominent and visible name groups today. A variant of this pattern is that of the largest name group, which has a membership of nearly 300 people. So interactively close-knit is this name group that it amounts to an independent segment. Members of the four segments in this category do not exhibit any residential propinquity; they are dispersed throughout the megalopolis. Old ties of kinship and friendship bind them together.

Straddling dispersion in the megalopolis and friendship and matrimonial alliances which serve as the main factors of fragmentation stands occupational differentiation. Before their demise as the dominant class of the country, the great majority of aristocrats were landowners, whose economies frequently included business and banking operations. This situation changed greatly after 1910, and the aristocrats most affected were provincial aristocrats whose wealth was almost exclusively in land. While there were aristocratic lawyers, physicians, and members of other professions before 1910, these professions were almost hobbies and not means of subsistence. By 1950, however, many aristocrats had become professionals as their main or sole means of subsistence. A small percentage of aristocratic "plutocrats" engaged in business, manufacturing, and banking, constituting the richest families in the group (see Chapter 5). In a nutshell, occupational differentiation affects the two main factors of fragmentation by making aristocratic families gravitate to those with whom they have the most interests in common. Thus two of the segments entailed by old friendships and matrimonial alliances are composed primarily of the richest families in the aristocratic group, whereas all five segments constituted by residential propinquity include a large number of members of the same profession or subsidiary business activity.

Finally, what is the operational structure of the aristocratic segment that is different from the kinship units described and analyzed in Chapter 7, and what are its functions within the overall configuration of the group? With respect to structure, the segment is a quantitative extension of the name group but, in the alignment of personnel, is quite similar to the exocentric kindred. The only discernible difference is that the segment includes a considerably larger number of nonkin personnel. Moreover, it is a more fluid and less organically organized unit than both the exocentric kindred and nonresidential extended family. However, the segment is made up of exocentric kindreds and non-residential extended families of the various name groups that constitute the segments. In other words, it is a quantitative extension of the major kinship units but is qualitatively somewhat different in that it includes nonkin person-nel. With respect to function, the segment is operationally the same as the kinship units that discharge social, economic, religious, and other functions. In this respect, nothing more needs to be said about the segment than has already been described in Chapter 7: it constitutes the maximal institutional extension of aristocratic behavior and action. The organic configuration of the Mexican aristocracy until as late as the mid-1940s is gone but to a large extent is perpetuated in the segment, given dispersion in the megalopolis, di-versification of interests, and the economic constraints that the aristocracy has undergone in this century.

Evolution of the Aristocracy in the Twentieth Century and Its Terminal Position within the *Haute Bourgeoisie*

The evolution of the Mexican aristocracy from the 1910 Revolution to 1990 is discussed in *The Wages of Conquest*. The demise of the aristocracy as a ruling class and its transformation for most of the century are placed in the con-text of the new Mexico that economically and socially came into being as the result of the first successful popular revolution of the twentieth century. In the following section the focus is narrowed. The aristocracy is analyzed from the standpoint of the role it played in the formation of the country's new superordinate class, the stages of its interaction with the plutocracy, and its terminal position within the *haute bourgeoisie*.

Demise of the Aristocracy as a Ruling Class: 1910–1934

The overthrow of Porfirio Díaz at the end of 1910 was devastating for the aristocracy. The aristocracy's influence in formulating and executing govern-ment policy disappeared almost overnight. Although there was some physical violence, *hacendados* did not suffer unduly: the Mexican Revolution did not entail the violence and execution of aristocrats of the French Revolution. Many country mansions were sacked and destroyed, but most *hacendados* retained legal possession of the land until the massive land reform a generation later. Haciendas were abandoned, and landowners took refuge in large provincial cities and the capital. The loss of agrarian income dealt a deathblow to the aristocracy as a dominant class; the majority of aristocrats lost practically all landed wealth. This most severely affected provincial aristocrats, who, on the whole, did not have a diversified economy. Meanwhile, deep-seated antagonism of both a social and political nature prevented aristocratic participation at all levels of government and administration. Only at the local level, once revolutionary activity ebbed, did *hacendados* regain a modicum of control. In the cities aristocrats succeeded in protecting their mansions, but they lost the determinant influence that they had enjoyed during the Porfiriato. Significant numbers of aristocrats, in both the country and the city, were mistreated. Perhaps a few were killed; but these acts of violence generally resulted from immediate individual or mob action and not from a concerted effort on the part of responsible revolutionaries.

The reluctance of revolutionary leaders after the armed phase of the Revolution (1910–1919) to dismantle the great landed states and the return to some level of peaceful prosperity led *hacendados* to hope that the appropriation and redistribution of land would stop and that the hacienda system, though modified, would survive. The years from 1920 to 1934 were a period of relative recuperation for the aristocracy, whose expectation of retaining their landed estates fueled a relative improvement as a social class. Upwardly mobile elements of the political and social sectors sought rapport with the aristocracy as a legitimating mechanism, which many aristocrats welcomed as a survival strategy. Although a few aristocrats were able to retain a foothold in the new, still incipient plutocracy by virtue of converting agrarian and urban property into banking and manufacturing operations, the overwhelming majority of aristocrats languished in the expectation that the land problem would ultimately be resolved in their favor.

The hacienda system survived in its overall configuration until 1934 and, though crippled by violence, continued to produce some income. As an instrument of expression and as a focal point of the aristocratic worldview, however, it had been mortally wounded by 1920. The destruction and pillage of *cascos* were too extensive to allow the hacienda to recuperate its former expressive preeminence. Those haciendas that survived the fury of the Revolution or that could be repaired and refurbished continued to play a role in the expressive life of aristocratic families even after the massive land reform; but by then most families did not have enough money to undertake the massive job of reconstruction. In fact, as early as 1930, many aristocratic families began to acquire country residences, if they did not already have them, within relatively short distances of Mexico City and a few other urban centers. After 1940 most hacienda *cascos* lay in ruins or had been badly damaged, and many had been bought by members of the new political and ruling classes. Only a few were still occupied by aristocrats.

As a social class the aristocracy not only survived but relatively prospered, both as a clearly discernible group and as the collective carrier of superordinate expressive behavior. Simply put, as the model of upwardly mobile aspirations, aristocrats provided a unique commodity; and this expressive component alone made the aristocracy a viable social group for another two generations. Until the beginning of the Cárdenas administration, most of the great aristocratic mansions in Mexico City and important provincial cities were still inhabited by their original owners. Not until after the massive land reform were almost all of these mansions either expropriated or sold by their owners for economic reasons. In the old colonial mansions and in the new, nearly suburban residential areas established during the Porfiriato, many aristocratic families played leading roles in homogenizing the disparate elements of the evolving political and ruling classes. Some aristocrats managed to play a role in business, and their visibility enhanced the desirability of aristocratic expression for those vying for a place in the emerging superordinate stratification of the country. For the upwardly mobile people of the time, the aristocratic aura was still strong, and this was perhaps the main expressive attribute that sustained the aristocracy for another sixty years or so.

Terminal Aristocratic Renaissance (1935–1960)

These twenty-six years were probably the most critical for the aristocracy in this century, in the sense that for the last time there was a strong feeling among aristocrats of being an organic group indisputably at the top of the social scale. Ironically, this came about despite having been stripped of their land and losing social and economic control of the provincial cities traditionally associated with the hacienda, which precipitated the migration to Mexico City. The ambiance of the capital had always promised security in violent and uncertain times; and there, in the security of numbers, the aristocracy experienced one last moment of social saliency and visibility. Though the Revolution did not directly cause the obliteration of the aristocracy, the massive land reform most certainly launched this social class into a final process of disintegration.

The land reform was a shock of cataclysmic proportions for the aristocracy. In the short period of six years the hacienda system had come to an end. Whatever hopes the *hacendado* aristocracy cherished of retaining its landed estates dissolved, and its residual inputs vanished overnight. Expressive constraints conspired against aristocrats' becoming successful plutocrats, and most aristocratic families were reduced to relative poverty. A small number, however, made the transition successfully; and between the end of the Cárdenas administration and the late 1960s they could be counted among the rich and powerful. These exceptions may be explained in two ways. First, throughout the nineteenth century there had always been aristocrats who successfully combined agrarian operations with banking and industry; when these families lost their landed estates, they were not totally ruined. Second, another small *hacendado* group was realistic enough to realize that the hacienda would not survive, despite the reluctance of presidents Alvaro Obregón and Plutarco Elías Calles to break up the great landed estates. Thus between 1920 and 1933 members of this group sold most of their land to small farmers, individual peasants, and even Indian communities, investing the profit in urban property and the manufacturing industry. By the 1960s perhaps 10 percent of aristocratic families had survived economically and had established a plutocratic basis in the new *haute bourgeoisie*. The great majority of aristocrats, however, were devastated by the land reform and forced into the liberal professions.

Massive migration to Mexico City began in 1936, as I have indicated, triggered not only by the total loss of haciendas and a drastic decrease in income but by a new awareness of middle-class action and revolutionary assertion that made provincial life uncomfortable for aristocrats accustomed to undisputed control. The upwardly mobile elements of provincial cities were asserting themselves as never before and were no longer willing to accept passively the haughtiness and paternalism of aristocrats. With their haciendas gone and their local business in shambles, most aristocratic families opted for migration to Mexico City, a process that was completed by the early 1950s. Within the next two generations those aristocratic families that remained in provincial cities became downwardly mobile, and most of them lost aristocratic affiliation; they became part of local elites of politicians, new business leaders, and small-scale industrialists that in time developed into local plutocrats. These former aristocratic families are known as *familias venidas a menos*, as I have noted. Bona fide aristocrats regard them today as no longer part of the group but still accord them minimal recognition. Only in Guadalajara, Querétaro, and perhaps one or two more cities do there remain small nuclei of aristocratic families that are recognized as an integral part of the Mexican aristocracy.

In Mexico City provincial arrivals found a much larger, more congenial environment than in the rapidly changing cities that they had once so thoroughly controlled. In the capital aristocrats not only found a measure of security in numbers but were able to present a fairly united front against what they regarded as a hostile world developing around them. For *hacendado* aristocrats who did not have any other source of income, migration to Mexico City was simply a matter of survival. For a considerable number of aristocrats, however, the demise of the hacienda system was not a crushing blow, for they possessed a diversified economy in banking, industry, and urban property. Thus, during the two and a half decades following the massive land reform, the Mexican aristocracy concentrated in the capital included rich aristocrats, prosperous aristocrats, and those who had to start pretty much at the bottom, representing the majority. Their main economic survival strategy was to become professionals, as I have indicated, from physicians and lawyers, to architects and engineers, to chemists and business administrators. In a generation the aristocracy had made the transition from a rich landed base to a fairly comfortable economic position by engaging in the professions and an array of business and industrial enterprises.

Ideologically and expressively, the aristocracy remained unified and unchanged, supportive of its members, and quite close until the late 1940s. Even before 1940, however, diversification and the growing formation of small networks (segments) were apparent. In pursuing new means of economic survival, once cohesive aristocratic networks grew somewhat apart in establishing new social and economic connections forced upon them by the changing times. Nonetheless, even during the most difficult and insecure times in the 1930s, aristocrats were the undisputed social leaders in the capital, while in provincial cities this position of superordination was lost. Aristocratic life experienced a renaissance in Mexico City. Their ranks increased by migration, and aristocrats dominated social and religious events. Despite their loss of wealth, a rather large number of aristocratic families were sufficiently affluent to be in the limelight, constantly reported in the press, and still universally recognized by the middle and even lower classes of a city nearing 4 million people. This state of affairs continued until the late 1950s. A decade and a half later the aristocracy had lost this position, and the population at large had lost the ability to discriminate between traditional aristocrats and new plutocrats. The phenomenal demographic growth of the city, the growth and assertion of the middle classes, and the final formation of a rich and powerful plutocracy caused this terminal transformation. While the renaissance lasted, the aristocracy remained an integrated social class: its social life admired, and its expressive culture envied.

Aristocratic Withdrawal and Plutocratic Ascendance (1960–1980)

By the late 1950s only a few isolated pockets of aristocrats were still present in provincial cities; but from this time onward the Mexican aristocracy must be regarded as a social class enfranchised in Mexico City. This period marks the economic decline of the aristocracy (in contrast with the plutocracy), characterized by a significant lowering of living standards and a discontinuity in many domains of expression that had always been centered on this social class. Thenceforth, at most 5 percent of aristocrats were plutocrats as well—that is, had fortunes of several million dollars. The traditional recognition of aristocratic membership rapidly began to blur; the lower and middle classes were unable to discriminate between social standing and power and wealth, and only at the highest rungs of the stratification system were aristocrats recognized as a distinct social class or group.

Three rather distinct classes had come into existence: a political class embodied in the ruling party (at the end of undisputed hegemony in 1997); a ruling class of plutocrats; and a social class constituted by aristocrats. This superordinate segment of the Mexican stratification system is what I have called the *haute bourgeoisie*. The aristocracy remained for generations the preeminent social class by virtue of expressive and behavioral attributes that were desirable to political and plutocratic elites in their quest to validate social standing. Slightly different forms and mixtures of the political-ruling-social triad have been the basic model of superordinate stratification and upward mobility in Western stratification in modern times. As the aristocracy declined, the model paradoxically acquired renewed importance in shaping new political and ruling classes in superordinate positions. The model, with the aristocracy as an essential element, ultimately falters when ruling and political classes begin to create new expressive arrays independent of the aristocratic model.

As I have stated, there is little if any continuity between the membership of the political and ruling classes from the Porfiriato to the second half of the twentieth century. The aristocracy remained in a kind of precarious balancing act with the plutocracy. An already powerful plutocracy constituted the majority of the country's ruling class in close social and economic interaction with the political class. The political class constituted a strong minority of the ruling class and provided the undisputed leaders of the country. Thus the political class developed a close relationship with the ruling class, because of both overlapping memberships and the economic interests they had in common. The aristocracy had only a minor foothold in the ruling class, as aristocratic plutocrats were not among the magnates of the ruling class. Roughly four decades ago, then, the Mexican *haute bourgeoisie* achieved a constitution that has remained rather constant, composed of distinct classes that significantly overlapped each other, particularly along economic boundaries. The political class as such had no significant interaction with the aristocracy; and only as plutocrats, after discharging high office, did members of the political class have an input in the development of the aristocracy.

I have described and analyzed the formation of the Mexican plutocracy in the twentieth century and its configuration today (Chapter 1). Suffice it here to recapitulate and emphasize the most salient points. Although there were plutocratic nuclei in many of the largest cities of the country, by the late 1970s nearly 50 percent of the richest and most powerful plutocrats were concentrated in Mexico City. Together with some members of the political class, plutocratic magnates dominated the social life of the city and certainly occupied the limelight. Plutocratic mansions proliferated in the most fashionable quarters of the city, their activities were prominently reported in the press, and their economic success made them as talked about as prominent politicians. Mexico City already had more than 9 million people, and in this environment the aristocracy had little or no visibility.

Throughout these twenty years social interaction between aristocrats and plutocrats was generalized, no longer consisting of aristocratic condescension toward upstart plutocrats. In these two decades the plutocracy came into its own. As its power and wealth vastly surpassed that of the dwindling aristocracy, the plutocracy no longer accepted a passive role in its upwardly mobile aspirations. Aristocrats and plutocrats came into rather continuous and occasionally close contact in a wide array of social, economic, and "cultural" contexts and situations that tended to homogenize the two classes. The entire aristocracy and plutocracy, however, did not participate in this process of rapprochement; rather, the process was dominated by the interaction of the most forward-looking, liberal segment of the aristocracy and the most upwardly mobile and powerful segment of the plutocracy. As these segments constituted perhaps the majority of the two classes, the overall social and expressive rapprochement of a single superordinate group was strengthened. This, in fact, was the period of most intensive aristocratic-plutocratic expressive acculturation.

What dynamic propelled this interaction? The answer is twofold. First, in the time-honored fashion of the four renewals that the Mexican aristocracy has undergone since the Spanish Conquest, aristocratic-plutocratic interaction was configured in terms of needs: the plutocrats' desire to validate social standing in the game of upward mobility after reaching a high level of power and wealth, and the aristocrats' desire to gain or consolidate economic assets or to make new economic allies in order to preserve their social predominance. Second, though need configured aristocratic-plutocratic rapprochement in a fairly balanced manner, compromise established the guidelines of the process; and the give and take of aristocrats and plutocrats culminated in a reversal of fortune. For the first time aristocrats were incorporated into a budding social class of plutocrats, while the majority of aristocrats retreated, socially and expressively unable to surrender their traditionally undisputed role. As long as the acculturative role survived, however, aristocrats remained an active social class, still visible, and grudgingly accepted as a superordinate segment.

A New Superordinate System Comes into Being:
Plutocratic Predominance and Aristocratic Retreat
(1980–2000)

This period witnesses the divergent paths of the aristocracy and plutocracy and the near demise of the former as a distinct social class in the Mexican stratification system. By the mid-1990s the aristocracy had become little more than a self-defined and self-recognized group, although it continues to be somewhat vaguely recognized by the political and ruling sectors and the upper-middle class. The plutocracy, meanwhile, has asserted itself overwhelmingly, pursuing its own social and expressive course, and—insofar as the aristocracy has retreated—has become the social class. The situation is more complex than this characterization (see Chapters 1, 2, 4, and 5), for some aristocrats have become rather plutocratized, while some plutocrats have become aristocratized. The essential consideration of this terminal period, however, is that the aristocracy is losing its last asset, the expressive component, and no longer plays a significant role in the emerging superordinate system.

By the middle of this period the Mexican plutocracy residing in the capital and a few of the largest provincial cities reached a plateau of power and wealth unparalleled since the mining boom of the second half of the eighteenth century. About two thousand millionaire and billionaire families constituted the ruling class of the country, with an important political class component, and had virtually become the new social class. The plutocracy had come of age, dominated most aspects of public life, achieved a high level of recognition, and acquired a wide network of international connections. With close ties to the political class, the plutocracy was second only to the highest holders of political office in directly and indirectly formulating policy, managing its implementation, and supporting the status quo engendered by the ruling party. (It should be noted that this has not changed during the past ten years, since opposition parties, particularly the conservative Partido de Acción Nacional [PAN], have seriously challenged PRI, the ruling party for nearly seventy years. Indeed, since PAN won the presidency in 2000, there is even a closer relationship between the ruling and political classes of the country.)

Throughout this period the plutocracy acquired extensive international connections, and its economy extended beyond the domestic operations of a generation before. This multinational tie enriched the plutocracy not only economically but socially and expressively as well, giving it a new maturity and confidence. The plutocracy has become the overwhelmingly predominant class of the superordinate system. The majority of plutocrats no longer feel the attraction that in the early years of upward mobility had so impelled them to seek alliances with the aristocracy. The plutocracy has become an independent social class, no longer in awe of aristocratic lineage and expression, and has created its own expressive domains. At least since the late 1980s the plutocracy has been interacting with the aristocracy on the basis of social equality; indeed, this lapse of aristocratic-plutocratic interaction may be characterized as studied indifference, despite the significant increment of intermarriage between the two groups.

Finally, let me outline the aristocratic-plutocratic processes of expressive transmission and acculturation that have taken place since the postrevolutionary plutocracy began to coalesce in the late 1930s. It may be summarized into three developmental stages. First, during the early 1940s the new plutocracy made its appearance as a group to be reckoned with economically. Its social recognition by the aristocracy came fairly slowly, and it was not until the mid-1950s that its presence was generally established. This period was characterized by tentative, groping advances on the part of the plutocracy, and cautious appraisal and grudging acceptance on the part of the aristocracy. Within fifteen years the majority of plutocrats had shed their outward middle-class trappings and acquired the trappings of aristocrats. Most of the social interaction of the two sectors occurred in the context of business and banking, and on the whole remained quite formal.

Second, from the mid-1950s until about the mid-1970s the plutocracy became well versed in the details of upper-class genteel behavior. It took a more forceful social position, making its wealth and economic power an explicit instrument of assertive mobility. The aristocracy became increasingly willing to extend social recognition; some aristocrats opened themselves completely, as the manners and mores of the plutocracy came to resemble their own. Social interaction was extended to the home, though it was still somewhat asymmetrical in that plutocrats extended themselves willingly and lavishly whereas aristocrats largely retained the home as a last bastion of endogenous expression.

Third, since the late 1970s the acculturative cycle of expressive transference from the aristocracy to the plutocracy has ended, and a significant homogenization of expressive and behavioral patterns has been achieved (including the incorporation of plutocratic attitudes in the aristocracy). Most plutocrats have been sufficiently transformed to pass for upper-class, while aristocrats have publicly toned down their ancient claims so as to interact as equals with those who have most of the wealth and economic power. The center of social interaction has now significantly shifted to the almost sacred preserve of the aristocratic household, and only the most conservative and recalcitrant aristocrats do not extend social recognition to average plutocrats.

Intermarriage between aristocrats and plutocrats has taken place in all three acculturative stages; but only since the early 1980s has it become common, mostly as the result of the revolt of the young, who during the past decade and a half have been increasingly unwilling to toe the aristocratic line. There is no doubt that intermarriage will soon become generalized. When it does, and the cherished endogamy of the aristocracy comes to an end, it will certainly accelerate the conclusion of the final stage: the last gasp of the aristocracy as a self-defined, highly conscious, and well-delineated group.

The Aristocracy's Residual Social and Expressive Position as a Superordinate Group

Throughout this study I have used the term "aristocracy" with some hesitation to characterize the descendants of the old ruling class of Mexico. My justification for using the term is largely taxonomic, in that it discriminates properly between the three main sectors of the *haute bourgeoisie* extant since the Mexican Revolution. Despite their self-awareness as a class and pride in their illustrious past, most aristocrats acknowledge their anomalous position: they are the holders of social prestige, grudgingly acknowledged by many plutocrats; but aristocrats cannot buttress their position with the kind of wealth that had traditionally accompanied it. When asked to define their social class, most aristocrats today respond: "We were aristocrats but now we belong to the upper class." Even the decreasing number who quixotically maintain that they are still aristocrats by virtue of lineage and tradition qualify the answer by adding: "though today money is the only thing that counts and we shall soon pass into oblivion." Ninety years of hardship and dwindling wealth have made aristocrats realize that social status and prestige without adequate wealth can carry them only so far. They have reached a stage at which they will be unable to maintain a collective consciousness and self-awareness.

Members of the younger married generation express this final transformation well when they say that their children will grow up in a different world: they will no longer be able to guide their interaction with youngsters of the plutocracy or of any attractively rich and powerful segment of society; and as a result many of the customs and manners that were exclusively theirs will disappear. The consequences of this predicament are exemplified by the revolt of the young that has been going on for the past decade and by the correlate attitude of sensible parents who in subtle ways are preparing the young for the change. Most young married couples view the transformation not altogether negatively; they see a kind of release from the past, representing a more realistic attitude consonant with their present economic position. The older generations are despairing; and, for most of them, the future promises only the painful experience of witnessing the demise of centuries of dominance.

It is more difficult to gauge the ideology and general attitude of the plutocrats toward the aristocracy. It is clear, however, that they have not gloated over their overwhelming economic dominance. The average plutocrat has learned from aristocrats not to flaunt wealth and to discourage public ostentatious displays. Their wealth and economic power are enough to sustain them as the dominant sector of the *haute bourgeoisie* and to dismiss the slights of the most snobbish aristocrats. Plutocrats know that the future is theirs and that in the end social status, prestige, and the material symbols that accompany them cannot contend against wealth and economic power. Even more than aristocrats, plutocrats know their history well: lineage, social manners, and expressive components are essential, but they persist only when buttressed by appropriate power and wealth.

The aristocratic-plutocratic synthesis or amalgamation that was taking place and heading for a resolution in the early 1970s has not been realized. From the early 1980s onward, in fact, the aristocracy and plutocracy began to diverge. On the one hand, most aristocrats are either withdrawing or no longer seeking social interaction with plutocrats. The main reason for this attitude is the perception that, if their survival as a class is nearing an end, they should perish true to their aristocratic ideology. Here again, the cleavage between the younger and older generations has the aristocrats in a state of disarray that accelerates their own disappearance. On the other hand, the majority of plutocrats no longer consciously seek rapport with aristocrats—they have learned all they desire from aristocrats and are no longer drawn to the aristocratic worldview. In the emerging *imago mundi* of plutocrats, achievement, power, and wealth supplant lineage and tradition; and this independent realization sustains recent plutocratic assurance. Plutocrats know that if they are going to survive and prosper as a social and ruling class, however, they must create their own "lineage" and tradition. The younger generation of aristocrats will be the purveyors of these commodities that many plutocrats are still eager to acquire, as the rapidly increasing rate of intermarriage indicates. From this standpoint a sort of acculturative synthesis may perhaps emerge in the near future.

In *The Wages of Conquest* I chronicle the four major renewals (transformations) that the Creole and Mexican aristocracies have undergone since the Spanish Conquest. Although these renewals differed from one another with respect to the circumstances that provoked them and the economic and political circumstances that configured them, they all had one fundamental element in common: the aristocracy remained the preeminent social and ruling class. It was never threatened, and the aristocracy recognized and accepted upwardly mobile plutocrats on its own terms. Implicitly, this book deals with the aristocracy's last transformation, which departs radically from all previous ones. Strictly speaking it is not a renewal but a permanent transformation entailing the ultimate demise of the aristocracy, first as a dominant class and then as a social class, as outlined in this section.

The Mexican Revolution is the sufficient but not necessary cause of the aristocracy's political, economic, and social decline over the past ninety years. It would have taken longer, and the aristocracy would have survived with a greater social role, had the Revolution not taken place. In short, the aristocracy would not have been able to compete economically with the plutocracy: agrarian-generated wealth since the early nineteenth century has never been able to compete with industrial wealth. As Pareto (1980:31–93) brilliantly states, elites come to an end and are superseded by newer elites because they cannot adapt themselves to new constraints and are not able to innovate sufficiently to prevail. The Mexican aristocracy was not able to adapt to an economic world in which land was no longer the main wealth-producing mechanism. Though a few aristocrats became successful business leaders, the great majority were constrained by an *imago mundi* that even dire economic necessity could not totally overcome.

The Mexican aristocracy survived because of the unusual ethnic and colonial conditions that existed in Mexico until the turn of the century. With these conditions gone or greatly altered since 1910, the aristocracy is now reduced to an almost subterranean social group. Still, with an expressive commodity no longer marketable, the aristocracy survives as a marriage market, as an almost atavistic symbol of the past. By contrast, Western European aristocracies have survived somewhat better, perhaps because — for the past 130 years at least — revolutions have not accelerated their demise; and their symbolic and physical presence (as embodied in titles of nobility, the ritual roles that aristocrats may occasionally play, and the palaces still in their possession) is more physically imprinted in the societal consciousness. In Mexico lack of awareness of the aristocracy has been a negative factor for its survival as a distinct social class, as its former palaces and titles are beyond the perception of the overwhelming majority of the population.

The plutocracy, in contrast, still ascends socially and as a ruling class and — barring a major upheaval — will reach maturity within a generation. The continuing democratization of society will undoubtedly preclude the configuration of a social class approaching the position of the aristocracy ninety years ago, for it was the *de facto* estate-like configuration of Mexican society until the 1910 Revolution that allowed the aristocracy to constitute an endogenous, largely endogamous, and quite tightly knit social class. It is in this sense that aristocracies have come to an end in the twentieth century: the last 150 years have witnessed the thorough transition to a class system. The last vestiges of estate privilege and the implicit and explicit constraints that it imposes on the development of society have been largely eliminated. The Mexican plutocracy today is a fluid social class with none of the characteristics of a possible aristocracy of the future. This is not to suggest that the plutocracy is so fluid and unstructured that it would entail renewal every generation or so. Indeed, as the superordinate class in the stratification system, the Mexican plutocracy has developed along quite similar lines as those of the established plutocracies (ruling classes) of the United States and Western Europe.

Expressive Analysis

Expressively, there is nothing ethnographically or historically distinct in this chapter beyond specific domains that have not been analyzed in previous chapters, except for the cumulative effect of domains that appropriately exemplify the context of terminal expression. Throughout the expressive analyses of the foregoing chapters, this form of expression looms outwardly large as having affected much of the culture of the aristocracy during the past ninety years. After describing the most salient domains of this chapter's ethnography, I discuss how palliative expression in the context of terminal expression has underlined much of the behavior and action of the aristocracy in this century. This is a fitting conclusion to the study, given that terminal expression is the least known of the main forms of expression; furthermore, some generalizations are in order.

Titles of nobility are a rewarding domain for the analysis of the relationship between structure and expression. Titles of nobility today have no structural significance exogenously and by themselves are nothing more than an atavistic survival; they are more of an embarrassing liability than a social asset. Endogenously, however, the situation is different, as titles of nobility entail various social ends. Directly and by themselves they also have no structural significance, but their expressive manipulation does acquire such characteristics: that is, they are used for utilitarian ends. This is the case when aristocrats adduce titles of nobility to validate *pergaminos* in order to make an advantageous marriage or simply enhance one's rank in the group. Indeed, the same obtains for all other *pergaminos*-enhancing mechanisms, from membership in military orders and parading illustrious ancestors to hacienda ownership and flaunting memorable public deeds of the family. This example illustrates the contextual nature of specific domains of expression: at one level they may be strictly structural-utilitarian and at another expressive-nonutilitarian. Of all forms of expression analyzed in this book, the various domains of terminal expression have this contextual characteristic to the highest degree.

As an expressive domain, aristocratic ranking obsession is the counterpart to titles of nobility. The primary characteristic of ranking obsession is structural, but it leads to expressive entailments and works as follows. Keeping a strict pecking order has been a fundamental characteristic of Western aristocracy since feudal times; it had become more central by modern times, particularly after the demise of the *ancien régime* in Europe and in Mexico after the Revolution. For Mexican aristocrats, ranking has become a palliative for the loss of power and wealth, and this is now its main structural-utilitarian value (as I have demonstrated in several contexts). The various situations in which ranking is manipulated, however, unquestionably entail primary expressive activities, though they may have residual psychological value. Thus the strategies that individuals employ to manipulate rank are essentially idiosyncratic but entail collective dimensions based on economic means and social circumstances.

The same interpretation applies to all expressive domains analyzed in this book that have a primary or derived palliative function in the context of aristocratic decline. This form of expression merits identification as palliative, in addition to the three main forms of expression that I identified in the context of my study of magic and religion in rural Tlaxcala (Nutini 1988:377–397): natural (inherent), conflictual, and terminal. Palliative expression is quite common; it is associated with social groups that are undergoing rapid change or are on the verge of drastic transformation and with individuals in situations of pain and suffering. It is closely related to terminal expression, to which we turn now, as exemplified by an individual and collective example.

The revival of *charrería* in the aftermath of the armed phase of the Revolution by a prominent aristocrat is a telling example of terminal expression, motivated by the great concern that the aristocracy traditionally had for the equestrian arts. This was facilitated by the still considerable wealth of this man's family, which was beyond the means of most aristocrats, who in fact were by then giving up most of the expressive domains that had been so dear to them. As one 90-year-old informant put it in 1980, "Carlos had the intuition that we [the aristocratic group] were in the last stage of our monopoly of the equestrian arts, and he turned body and soul to the most Mexican of them, which had always been an integral part of hacienda life. Thus with a flourish we said farewell to something that had always been very dear to us, and at the same time we revived a moribund aspect of Mexico's popular culture." Notice that this informant takes collective credit for the revival of *charrería* — a common practice that (particularly in this century's decline) accentuates aristocratic consciousness of kind. More significantly, this quotation is a clear statement of terminal expression: a last outburst of excellence or creativity concerning the impending termination of a traditional institution or valuable practice of a social group.

As I have indicated, the social renaissance of the Mexican aristocracy from the early 1930s to the early 1950s is a collective case of terminal expression. It also exemplifies the necessary structural conditions (in this case, the relative economic affluence of the waning aristocracy *vis-à-vis* the new emerging plutocracy and the social inexperience of the latter) that make possible the sufficient realization of expression. In reconstructing this episode from male and female informants in 1980–1982, who were young and middle-aged at the time of the renaissance, it was evident that they took great pride in the social and expressive environment that they managed to create despite the adverse, and to some extent hostile, ambiance of the time. To be in the limelight again was collectively soothing, and aristocrats enjoyed every minute of it; it was almost like fifty years before, when they were the undisputed social class of the country. Centered on a dozen or so of the most affluent families, the social and to some extent religious life of aristocrats was (for the last time) a vicarious attraction for the capital's masses and a magnet for the budding plutocracy. This period coincided with the massive migration of provincial aristocrats to Mexico City, which also helped to the extent that the outstanding ambiance of the renaissance was for them an excellent introduction to a new, wider world of aristocratic expression. More than any other factor, the social brilliance of this period is due to the concentration in the capital of practically the entire Mexican aristocracy, which, for a rather evanescent moment, became terminally united into an organic whole. From then on, everything was anticlimactic for this vanishing class.

As in the foregoing example, the same collective claim and expressive ambiance obtained, as poignantly stated by a female informant who was in her early twenties by the middle of the renaissance:

From the time that we settled in Mexico City in 1939 [this family came from Puebla; its apical ancestor was the founder of the city in 1531] until the end of the 1940s were the happiest days of my life. We had an incredible social life, we were the center of attraction of the affluent classes, our activities were reported in the dailies' front pages, and the new rich assiduously sought us out. It was as if the revolution had not happened, given that everybody recognized who we were. I believe that by the end of the 1950s was the last time we felt like true aristocrats. Since then, people have slowly forgotten us and we count less and less; we are now, in 1990, like a shadow that fades in the penumbra.

To conclude, I briefly explore the relationship between terminal and palliative expression. Basically, they are configurationally the two faces of the same coin. Whereas one can conceive of palliative expression as an aspect of various situations of conflict, irrespective of the impending demise of a social system or institution, it is my empirical claim that palliative expression most often accompanies terminal expression as a well-specified context of behavior. In the context of the present book, certain kinds of expressive behavior are palliatives for the pain of seeing one's social group decline on the way to disintegration. Essentially, terminal expression is a context that generates palliative expression under particular circumstances determined by several factors: aristocratic rank and prestige, degree of *embourgeoisement*, wealth, and idiosyncratic characteristics. Thus the kind of palliative expression engaged in by the wealthy and more plutocratic aristocrats is different from that of conservative aristocrats, even though idiosyncratic characteristics play a variant role. This aspect of palliative expression has been extensively dealt with in Chapters 4, 5, and 7. Suffice it to emphasize here that all ranks and categories of aristocrats, as specified in this chapter, have slightly different models of palliative expression as determined by particular structural constraints.

Perhaps more significant is the configuration of collective palliative expression in extreme contexts of terminal expression, or, if you will, situations in which a practice, institution, or entire social group is in imminent danger of disappearing. The fate of the Mexican aristocracy during the past generation, as illustrated throughout this book, is a case in point. Another case that I have studied in depth is the demise of the traditional cult of the dead in Tlaxcala in 1965–1985, as manifested in the decoration of the graves in the cemetery and the offerings to the dead on the household altar (Nutini 1988). These cases exhibit remarkably similar collective expressive manifestations beyond individual, idiosyncratic realizations. In other words, individuals may emphasize different domains in the entire spectrum of the expressive array in question, but the palliative effect is collectively manifested. The terminal-palliative complex of the Mexican aristocracy that has been going on since the onset of the renaissance described above exhibits the same configuration as that of the exquisitely elaborate complex of the cult of the dead in Tlaxcala (particularly the decoration of graves in the cemetery) between 1950 and 1970, before it quickly deteriorated and nearly disappeared as perhaps the most spectacular expressive domains of Tlaxcalan religiosity.

In the same fashion, phenomena from the great outburst of social life until the late 1950s to practically all domains of expression of postrevolutionary origin (such as manipulating antiquity of lineage, parading distinguished ancestors, and, in general, exaggerated concern with *pergaminos*, which before the Revolution were important expressive domains but were taken as a matter of course) are manifestations of palliative expression in the ambiance of what most aristocrats expect: the imminent demise of their social group as endogenously self-defined with a modicum of organic integrity and exogenously identifiable by significant segments of the superordinate class.

Palliative expression may be regarded as an individual psychological mechanism that generates group solidarity under conditions of extreme social stress. The analogy that comes to mind is the common human proclivity to huddle, embrace, and seek close physical contact when disaster strikes and the integrity or security of the group is threatened. This, of course, is the essence of terminal expression; and that is why these two forms of expression are so often realized jointly or are causally linked to one another.

CONCLUSIONS

With different degrees of intensity and elaboration, the most salient issues and themes of the expressive ethnography presented in this book may be summarized as follows.

First, this study chronicles aristocratic decline in the twentieth century from the Mexican Revolution of 1910 to the present, including loss of economic power due mainly to the 1934–1940 land reform, the rise of a powerful plutocracy, and expressive constraints to emulate plutocratic ways.

Second, a new, postrevolutionary plutocracy (which includes a large segment of the political class) arose that supplanted the aristocracy as a ruling class. Due to the accumulation of great wealth in the last quarter of the twentieth century, it has become a social class independently of the aristocracy largely by creating its own expressive array.

Third, the superordinate class is composed of the aristocracy, plutocracy, and the upper-middle class, which are analyzed here in their structural (stratificational) and expressive interaction as well as in the ethnic, somatic (racial), and interactive (perceptual) context of the nation.

Fourth, the aristocracy has played a structural and expressive role in the formation of the plutocracy, from its inception in the early 1930s until the mid-1980s. On the one hand, marriage between aristocrats and plutocrats, which has been increasing over the past fifty years, serves to legitimize social position for the plutocrats and gain economic advantage for the aristocrats. On the other hand, the aristocracy functions as the expressive model for the plutocracy, a process of expressive displacement or acculturation which marks much of their social interaction.

Fifth, the aristocratic class has undergone a structural and expressive withdrawal and a change from the public to the private realization of expression. After losing its dominance of the cities it had controlled during the last years of the Porfiriato (including the capital and a dozen other important cities), the aristocracy had gone underground by the last third of the century, and its expressive life became centered in the household.

Sixth, the social and psychological functions of expression and their entailed consequences have played a role in the process of aristocratic withdrawal and survival. Specific domains of the various forms of expression serve as a mechanism of adaptation, as an index of change, and as a means of validating social status and rank.

Seventh, the ethnography of the aristocracy is a vehicle for understanding a number of structural characteristics of the Mexican stratification system and shared but differently realized expressive components. The cross-class analysis of such disparate domains as religious belief and practices, attitudes toward marriage, food preparation, and somatic perceptions illustrates some of the underlying themes of Mexico's pluriethnic society.

I conclude this book by addressing three major topics. First, I evaluate the analytical significance of studying the Mexican aristocracy as a part of the superordinate class in particular and in the context of the stratification system of the country in general. Second, I assess what has been accomplished and what remains to be done to generate an operational definition of expressive behavior in developing a general theory of expression. Particular stress is placed on the psychological component of expression in differential social settings and on an expansion of the discussion on the interrelationship between the psychological and social aspects of expressive behavior. Third, I elaborate on the expressive ethnography both as a case of urban ethnography and as a model for future ethnographies. The concept of expression as an index of acculturation illustrates the form and character of ethnicity and exemplifies the changes that Mexican social stratification underwent in the twentieth century.

The Psychological Components of Expression: Toward the Operationalization of Expressive Behavior

·

What Has Been Accomplished and What Still Must Be Done

Let us briefly recapitulate what has been accomplished expressively throughout this monograph. In chapters 3 through 8 I have discussed the contextual nature of expression and its manifold functions. The expressive array is viewed as a reflection of the changing fortunes of the aristocracy in the twentieth century as it moved from being the undisputed social and dominant class (1900–1910), to a sort of renaissance (1930–1950), to near demise (1950–2000). The environments in which new domains of expression have been created by aristocrats as a consequence of loss of power and wealth and *vis-à-vis* the social assertion and maturity of the plutocracy are specified in terms of social retreat and endogenous involvements.

Basically, five forms of expressive behavior have been identified with respect to individual and collective consequences: natural, conflictual, terminal, palliative, and vicarious. I have analyzed each of them endogenously in the context of aristocratic decline, exogenously as a reaction to plutocratic ascendance, or with respect to some general encompassing aspect of expression.

Natural expression, as a universal attribute of the cultural system of all classes and social groups, is defined with respect to the characteristic domains of Mexican aristocrats in particular and what they share with all Western aristocracies in general. I examine specific forms of expression in the social, religious, and economic contexts of the Mexican stratification system, particularly the plutocracy, the upper-middle class, and folk people. The main domains of the exclusive expressive array of the aristocracy are discussed in the ambiance of aristocratic decline, whereas the inclusive array exemplified the most salient domains that it shares with other sectors of the class-ethnic system of the country. This exercise demonstrates the most characteristic attribute of expressive behavior—namely, that the socio-psychological motivation for expressive realization is the same regardless of social class or ethnic affiliation.

Conflictual expression, as a special kind of behavior tied to changes in the social structure of such groups, is often associated with revolutions and individually with changes in socioeconomic standing and illustrates the overall transformation of the aristocratic array after the 1910 Revolution. Making use of Roberts and Sutton-Smith's (1962) "conflict-enculturation theory of model involvement," I describe this form of expression in terms of the loss of wealth and economic power and more recently of social prestige and position as a role model for the rising plutocracy that the aristocracy underwent in the twentieth century.

Terminal expression, perhaps more appropriately labeled "the calm before the storm," is more elusive to pinpoint and the least known. It takes place when a salient institution or entrenched social group stands at the threshold of rapid change or impending demise; the actors in the system, seeming to anticipate the eventual result, may exaggerate some customary structural discharge, which betrays a much more expressive than instrumental component. As construed in this book, terminal expression is really a syndrome that manifests itself as follows. Sensing that their group was in the last stage of social prominence and rapidly moving into irrelevance, aristocrats engaged in one last outburst of expressive realization, a renaissance of brilliant social activity (from the early 1930s to the early 1950s), ending forever their undisputed social dominance. As analyzed throughout the book, however, terminal expression is realized in several social contexts.

Palliative expression most often takes place in social groups that are undergoing drastic transformations and is consequently closely related to terminal expression. Individually, palliative expression often manifests itself when people are in difficult and painful predicaments. As applied to the Mexican aristocracy in its last stage before ceasing to be a functional group, palliative and terminal expression may be regarded as contextually complementary but performing basically the same function: assuaging the individual and collective pain of contemplating ultimate demise. Thus palliative expression embodies the individual mechanisms for the assuagement of pain, whereas terminal expression generates the social context of its realization.

Vicarious expression is a form of natural expression, certainly one of its most universal variations and particularly associated (at least in Western civilization) with social stratification and mobility, straddling the estate and class system. On the one hand, as a concept vicarious expression is the centerpiece in understanding the survival of the Mexican aristocracy as a social class in the twentieth century *vis-à-vis* the plutocracy. On the other hand, I am suggesting that vicarious expression is an explanation of the long-lasting trajectory of estate stratification from the dawn of Western civilization to the French and American Revolutions in the second half of the eighteenth century. Vicarious expression is tentatively explored in the contexts of estate and class stratification; and its two main aspects, vicarious perception and vicarious attraction, are identified. The main consequence of all forms of vicariousness is a relationship of power and control of superordinately over subordinately placed individuals and groups.

These forms of expression occur in manifold social, religious, economic, demographic, and political contexts. The contextual realization of expressive behavior involves the circumstances in which structural factors entail expressive consequences and, conversely, when the latter affect the former in creating new domains of expressive realization.

In summary, this book is the only extant ethnography undertaken from an expressive focus and strategy. Descriptively, the identified forms of expression are concretely embedded in a substantial body of data on a social class and placed in the context of a global stratification system. Analytically, several ad hoc explanations are generated, posited on the constraints that expressive behavior puts on individual and collective realization of structural potential. As I struggled with the sociological aspects of expression, I became painfully aware of my inability to bring psychological variables to bear upon the conceptualization of expressive behavior, a *sine qua non* for the study of this universal phenomenon. This was consistently the main impediment in achieving a more analytically sophisticated and theoretically adequate account of expression throughout the study.

In the remainder of this section I endeavor to clarify the relationship between the social and psychological components of expression and how the source of and motivation for the realization of expressive behavior are necessarily conditioned by antecedent psychological states as well as socially determined conditions.

The Individual (Psychological) and Collective (Social) Entailments of Expressive Behavior

As one of our immediate common ancestors at the turn of the century, Emile Durkheim (1947, 1951) was very effective in converting anthropologists and sociologists to the position that social phenomena must be conceptualized on the basis of social facts alone, totally disregarding psychology and biology. When a budding discipline reaches the threshold of the conceptualizing stage (that is, the earliest attempts to impose order on empirical data by subsuming them under the general rubric of theory), there is a strong tendency to assert its independence from all other disciplines. Almost from the beginning, however, Durkheim's strategy proved difficult to implement; and many anthropologists in the twentieth century strove to transcend this position and determine the role of psychology and biology in conceptualizing social phenomena. No anthropologist has ever contemplated total psychological reductionism, or "methodological individualism" as Ernest Nagel (1961:504–545) puts it; but as early as the 1920s, with the advent of culture and personality studies (see Bourguignon 1973:1093–1101) and subsequently psychological anthropology (see Spindler 1980), it became increasingly evident that "collective terms" (embodying social groups) alone cannot suffice to generate an adequate understanding of social phenomena; and "individual terms" (psychological factors) must be brought to bear on the situation at hand. As Nagel (1961:536) maintains, if adequate explanations are to be forthcoming, collective terms must to some extent be defined or based on individual terms. The same reasoning applies to biology: in explaining significant aspects of social phenomena, biological evolution must not be ignored. Sciences progress by cooperation and interaction with other sciences, not by isolationism and disciplinary tribalism.

This, of course, is the position of Edward Wilson (1998) in discussing the unity of knowledge and embodied in the concept of "consilience": "Units and processes of a discipline that conform with solidly verified knowledge in another discipline have proved consistently superior in theory and practice to units and processes that do not conform" (Wilson 1998:198). More specifically: "To infuse psychology and biology into economics and other social theory, which can only be to its advantage, means teasing out and examining microscopically the delicate concept of utility, by asking why people ultimately lean toward certain choices, and being so predisposed, why and under what circumstances they act upon them" (Wilson 1998:204).

Consilience, then, is the key strategy to propel anthropology into a mature stage of conceptualization; and what Wilson proposes is very much to the point in dealing with expression, as probably the most universal of human proclivities, in which choice and utility are so interrelated. How does an anthropologist like myself, so steeped in the Durkheimian tradition and consequently without any psychological training, go about teasing social utility out of the expressive choices that are made? This is a quandary confronted by all anthropologists who realize that there are many domains of inquiry that do not yield explanations, or even understanding, strictly on the basis of sociological analysis.

The plight of anthropologists searching for psychological consilience is essentially that whenever explanations are not forthcoming they must drastically modify Durkheim's dictum that "social facts must be exclusively explained by antecedent social facts" historically and culturally created to "social facts must be explained by antecedent psychological states." This is the predicament of the student of expression, given that beyond its natural manifestation (an invariant aspect of the psychic unity of humankind) expressive behavior is entailed by psychological factors, which, to be sure, are socially molded but individually manifested. Thus, as they have been conceived in this book, social stratification and mobility are molded by expressive vicariousness; vicarious attraction constitutes the social milieu in which individual vicarious perception is realized. I have descriptively specified how this form of expression is realized in various social milieux, but I do not have a theory to account for it. The same can be said about the other three identified forms of expression (terminal, conflictual, and palliative). Fundamentally, then, the explanation of all forms of expressive behavior must be contingent upon psychological theories congruent with the sociocultural conditions in which expressive behavior is realized.

Another perspective is that any form of expression concerning social stratification has a biological component: the apparently inherent proclivity that humans share with their immediate animal ancestors—namely, a pecking order that must be assumed in order to explain institutionalized status differences in hunting-gathering and folk societies and social classes in complex societies. Sociobiologists (Hamilton 1964a, 1964b; Trivers 1971; Wilson 1998; Maynard Smith 1999; Gaulin and McBurney 2001) have addressed this and related problems convincingly, and I have nothing to add.

However descriptively and analytically adequate this study of expression may be, it has not explained the phenomena because it does not entail theory: that is, the explanations that have been generated are lateral (functional) not vertical (causal). Bereft of consilience, most anthropologists stop short of generating causal explanations. At this point I turn to Wilson's concept that "behavior is guided by epigenetic rules"; as he specifies: "Epigenesis, originally a biological concept, means the development of an organism under the joint influence of heredity and environment. Epigenetic rules . . . are rules of thumb that allow organisms to find solutions to problems encountered in the environment. They predispose individuals to view the world in a particular innate way and automatically to make certain choices as opposed to others" (Wilson 1998:193). A logical extension of this position is that social behavior is molded by "epipsychological rules": that is, individual choices require collective representations in situations in which antecedent social facts do not explain institutions or manifold bundles of activities.

Epipsychological rules are fundamental to the study of expression. The choices that individuals make very often have a significant expressive component, above and beyond social antecedents. For example, activities as varied as choosing a profession, becoming a political activist, running for political office, and joining a street gang involve definite psychological factors that, although conditioned by the boundaries and constraints of the social structure in operation, become wholly intelligible only in terms of expressive choices. Many politicians, religious seers, and captains of industry in their manifestly utilitarian (social), goal-directed political, religious, or economic aims are often strongly motivated by expressive elements—that is, by that most human of desires: to assert one's individuality and to be noticed as contributing something, positive or negative, to the social system. From this perspective, seemingly instrumental but expressively laden contexts and practices are extremely important to study, for they are the crux of explaining how psychological inputs affect socially determined outcomes; they have practical importance that we would be well advised to harness. Perhaps if we understood well how expression and expressive behavior affect political, religious, and economic decisions and actions, we could cope more successfully with war, terrorism, famine, and other serious maladies of the twentieth-first century.

Expressive motivation and choice are fundamental not only individually but collectively as well. The cumulative mass of individual proclivities and choices of members of a social group constitutes the ensemble that has been denoted as its expressive array. In other words, the conceptualization of the passage from individual to collective expression means ascertaining the social, historical, and environmental circumstances and conditions under which it takes place. This is the primary assumption that structures the exclusive array as the diagnostic characteristic of a social class or any historically constituted group. The conceptualization of estate stratification in Western society as detailed in *The Wages of Conquest* (1995) is built on this assumption: namely, the perpetuation of a superordinate group (the aristocracy) motivated by the divine right of the king to rule. The collective choice of members of the aristocracy to rule over the commonality constitutes the motivation that lasts until estate stratification is replaced by the modern class system due to the naturalization of Western European society from the Renaissance onward, culminating in the French and American Revolutions. Psychological consilience, then, is not just epistatic (molding immediate individual behavior) but also "epidynamic" (to coin a neologism) in that it shapes collective behavior through time.

The general strategy for the study of expressive culture in terms of consilience outlined above entails more than adducing psychological factors that explain specific expressive behaviors; for example, the conflict-enculturation theory of model involvement developed by Roberts and Sutton-Smith (1962) to a large extent explains conflictual expression. Rather, what I envisage is a systematically integrated body of psychological theory that would invariantly explain the realization of expressive behavior throughout the entire spectrum of contexts in time and space (the gamut of societies from "primitive," to folk, to complex) and account for choice, motivation, and forms of realization. This conceptual aim is within reach, given the significant advances in cognitive and evolutionary psychology directly applicable to the analysis of cultural phenomena. The same is likely to occur in many traditional domains of anthropological inquiry: Durkheimian sociologizing is nearly dead, and both psychological consilience and biological consilience appear to be gaining acceptance.

In the remainder of this section I expand on a few points that need further elaboration: mainly, the role of vicariousness in most forms of expression and its relation to culture change and innovation. I also address the concept of altruism and its significance for the realization of expression.

Irrespective of the role it plays in expressive behavior, vicariousness is a determinant concept in the study of social organization. The term has three main denotations; in my opinion, the most dynamic and processual is "the state experienced or realized through imaginative or sympathetic participation in the experience of another [person]" (*Webster's Third New International Dictionary*, 1969). Vicariousness, so defined, has hardly been noticed by students of social behavior; yet it plays a most important role in the structure and dynamics of many groups and social contexts, ranging from stratification and mobility to economic behavior (as in the expressive analyses of Chapters 4 and 6). This by no means exhausts the significance of vicariousness, which underlies collective forms of behavior as diverse as parents' encouraging—nay, literally forcing—their children to excel in sports and creating a fantasy world, most often among disadvantaged groups, on the basis of perceived behavior of the rich, famous, or powerful. Vicariousness is a most potent factor motivating social action; indeed, in very few cultural domains is the passage from individual behavior to collective manifestation more pristinely realized. Moreover, most of its manifold domains of realization do not yield understanding and explanations based on the exclusive analysis of social facts. For example, I do not think that it is possible to explain many aspects of social stratification without assuming individual vicariousness (see the Expressive Analysis in Chapter 4). In other words, employing the awe generated by movie stars or famous athletes to induce people to buy commercial products cannot be understood by the confluence of social factors alone, and the psychological proclivity of vicarious perception must be invoked to explain vicarious attraction as a motivating agent (see the Expressive Analysis in Chapter 6).

To reiterate: vicariousness, as an explanatory factor of expressive behavior, is a psychological concept that can never be conceived as a product of the social structure of the group. Without belaboring the point, the fact that expressive vicariousness, or any other manifestation of the concept, is realized in concrete social settings should not be confused with its source in individual behavior, that is, as a residual aspect of the social structure in operation. Thus vicariousness as a central aspect of expression to a high degree exemplifies the socio-psychological strategy best suited to the explanation of much social action and, more specifically, of how expressive styles are realized in concrete social settings. It is in this hitherto uncharted area of socio-psychological research that the study of expression is expected to contribute and to answer a wide range of practical questions. What are the behavioral and expressive strategies that people and groups employ in the struggle for power and the acquisition of wealth? What are the psychological profiles of winners and losers in the stratification game? How does the realization of various expressive styles affect invention and innovation?

The relationship between vicariousness and expressive behavior has already been established, but it should be added that its various forms constitute the broad parameters in which emulation and the proclivity to be different are most effectively realized. Emulation is essentially the concretization of vicariousness (that is, the former is entailed by the latter)—or, if you will, it is in the context of vicarious perception that vicarious attraction is realized. Emulation, however, has a much broader range of entailments, as it independently structures many expressive domains ranging from class affiliation and mobility and religious ceremonialism to fashions of all kinds and the broad domain of art and entertainment. It is an integral part of all five identified forms of expression, and I am reasonably certain that the same will obtain in others that have not yet been identified. The syndrome of "being different" has a wide range of realizations, given that choice and motivation are at the heart of its dynamic psychological concerns.

In summary, cultural replication (or cultural transmission, if you will), in both its structural and expressive forms, is a concept that needs to be operationalized in a variety of diachronic and synchronic contexts. One of the recurring themes in this study is the relationship of expression to culture change. The basic notion I envisage is that changes in the social structure and overall organization of society are mirrored in the development of new domains of expression in a group or social class; this correspondence often provides significant inputs into the origin of the transformation and the reorganization of the group and society at large. Indeed, changes in the expressive array of the Mexican aristocracy after the Revolution of 1910 clarify the rise of a new plutocracy, the reorganization of the superordinate class, and the transformation of the global stratification system. More specifically, expressive acculturation is a key concept in understanding aristocratic decline, the configuration of the new plutocracy, and the redefinition of superordinate stratification.

Although this book deals with expressive innovation in several domains, let me briefly extend the role of expression in the context of innovation (creativity) across the sociocultural spectrum. Innovation is a phenomenon that is not simply an objectivization of the maxim that "necessity is the mother of invention." On the contrary, it obeys complex motivational factors determined primarily by psychological antecedents, which, to be sure, are realized in specified cultural contexts. (This is a good example of confusing psychological motivation with social realization.) A few examples illustrate the range of expressive innovation and creativity.

In an article on machine-shop production, Garry Chick and John Roberts (1987) discovered that despite the practice of providing lathe operators with a blueprint for the parts they crafted there was a significant expressive component in the final product; creativity was expressed in the tooling process, small nuances of feel and touch, and perception of the product as an aesthetic object. Teenagers in the United States dress almost in uniform; yet there is almost always something individually different in their attire (the cut of the pants, the shape of the shirt or jacket) that indicates creativity born out of expression. Similarly, of course, the same could be said about the dictates of fashion. This is an important aspect in the psychology of expressive motivation that has not received enough attention from social scientists and psychologists.

Although the necessary conditions for innovation (including every imaginable form of social, institutional, and ideological invention) are determined by cultural need at a given time, the sufficient conditions are mostly expressive. That is, innovators (inventors) may be stimulated by need; but the motivation and the choices they make to create are to a large extent determined by antecedent expressive-psychological conditions. From a slightly different perspective, the innovators' expressive behavior to a large extent molds what they create. What no one has yet been able to determine is the origin of motivating factors, which again are at the crux of establishing exactly how the individual creates culture and the latter molds the former.

Finally, let me add a few remarks about altruism, a few decades ago the bane of classic Darwinism, at least as perceived by most cultural anthropologists. Rational choice is one of the fundamental assumptions of much contemporary social science, most clearly evidenced in economics but implicitly underlying much of the theorizing of anthropology and sociology. Rational choice is basically selfish, but as Wilson (1998:205) points out: "Rational calculation is often unselfish. For complex, still poorly understood reasons, some of the most powerful emotions are patriotism and altruism. It remains a surprising fact that a substantial percentage of people are willing at a moment's notice to risk their lives to save those of strangers." Similarly, expression is not always rational (selfish); and, oddly enough, expressive behavior falls into the same category as patriotism and altruism. By this I mean that expression as an emotion is part of the fabric of society everywhere, but no one has yet given a explanation of its existence. Moreover, expression, like altruism, is fundamentally a psychological phenomenon that cannot be explained by antecedent sociological facts. Perhaps one could go a step further and link expression to similar behavior that has been observed in humans' closest animal ancestors, such as patterns of courtship and other forms of interaction, as they have been studied by primatologists (Packer 1975:209-220). In fact, I would maintain that expression, like altruism, is an innate human characteristic—the product of tens of thousands of years of biological evolution—like the many traits and proclivities that sociobiologists are increasingly elucidating.

Sociobiologists have explained altruism by invoking epigenetic rules in terms of both kin selection (Hamilton 1964a, 1964b) and reciprocity (Trivers 1971). Altruism in kin selection ultimately benefits all individuals in the altruist's kin group. Reciprocity is a system in which reciprocal behavior benefits the altruist as well as the recipient of the altruistic action. Epipsychological rules can be invoked to explain the nature of expression and expressive behavior, which, like altruism, entail elements of choice and consequences that include positive and negative results for the individual and the collectivity. It is difficult to envisage what these epipsychological rules will be; but intuition tells me that they should have pretty much the same epistemological form as the epigenetic rules that sociobiologists have formulated to explain such varied human categories of behavior as "kin selection," "parental investment," "mating strategies," "status and rank," "territorial expansion and defense," and "contractual agreement" (Wilson 1998:168–172). To say more would be pure speculation, but I think I have made a concrete suggestion.

Admittedly, I have not theoretically advanced the explanation of the universal phenomenon of expression; but the foregoing programmatic remarks do point toward a resolution. To reiterate, I do think that cultural anthropology will remain Ptolemaic for much longer, both in the mold advocated by postmodernism and as a more sophisticated kind of Durkheimianism. I would like to think that what I have suggested would be heeded by better minds than mine to generate "real" explanations for expression and other domains of cultural phenomena.

The Expressive Ethnography as a Case of Urban Anthropology and as a Model for Future Expressive Ethnographies

Substantively, this book is primarily a study of the Mexican aristocracy, centered predominantly on the second half of the twentieth century, at the end of which the aristocracy was on the verge of disappearing as a functional social class. As it is set within the confines of Mexico City, however, it is also a study in urban anthropology: the aristocracy, conceived as a "folk" group, is analyzed with reference to other classes and sectors of the Mexican stratification system. There is no descriptive model for expression; consequently, this book may be regarded as a standard ethnography focused on the expressive life and behavior of the aristocracy and proximate groups. In the remainder of these conclusions, I would like to address two problems. First, it is necessary to establish the relationship between standard and expressive ethnography; my intention is to discuss some methodological points that may be useful for studies of expressive culture. Second, I contrast urban and folk, traditional studies; the aim of the exercise is to determine some of the differences and similarities with respect to fieldwork and units of analysis.

Interrelationship of Standard and Expressive Ethnography

As I have indicated, there is no model for structuring the expressive ethnography of a social class or group or for placing it in proximate relationship to comparable social classes or groups. The following discussion, then, is the general *modus operandi* that guided the structure and analysis of this study, based essentially on the proposition that it is best to present the expressive array of a social class after a standard ethnography has been generated. This methodological approach is conceived as entailing optimal conditions for the analysis of the expressive culture (array) of a class or group, which, in turn, is the necessary step for the formal analysis of domains (the subject matter of the third volume in the series).

The presentation by chapters follows essentially the standard ethnographic format with some adaptations to the exigencies of the expressive description and analysis. The standard ethnography emphasizes the ideational order of the aristocracy centered on stratification and class consciousness, kinship and the organization of the household, ritualism and religion, exhibition and display, manners and mores, and concern with the past. All classic ethnographic domains, from material culture and economic organization to political participation and network relationships, receive significant attention. The expressive analysis is undertaken in Chapter 3; chapters 4 to 8 are self-contained to the extent that (on the basis of the standard ethnography) the most salient expressive domains are analyzed in a separate section.

Substantively, the standard ethnography of the aristocracy constitutes the bulk of the description, while the ethnographic outlines of the plutocracy, upper-middle class, and other sectors of the Mexican stratification system place the expressive domains of these various interacting sectors in perspective (that is, establishing common elements, significant departures, and convergence). From a different standpoint, these limited ethnographic forages made it possible to configure the exclusive and inclusive arrays in interaction, simplifying the task of pinpointing the process of expressive acculturation. In terms of amounts of both ethnographic and expressive information, the plutocracy receives the most attention, followed by the upper-middle class, the political sector, and some domains of the Indian, folk sector of the population, with which the aristocracy shares several expressive traits.

Throughout the book, the description and analysis of the expressive and structural contexts represent a process of zigzagging to ascertain what is exclusive to the aristocracy and proximate classes and what is shared by them. Thus, structurally, the standard ethnography was designed to isolate sociocultural elements and classes in interaction and then determine how they are configured in terms in networks of social, economic, political, and personal action. The expressive ethnography, in turn, was designed to establish the exclusive and inclusive array of the classes in interaction and specify the key junctures that are likely to coalesce in new acculturative domains.

I wish to expand on the discussion in Chapter 3 concerning the analysis of the global array of the aristocracy and by extrapolation that of the plutocracy as the dominant sector of the superordinate class. Based on the ethnographic data collected between 1979 and 1992 and additional information elicited from a sample of sixty male and female informants (ranging from teenagers to old people), the aristocratic expressive array constitutes a specific, self-contained body of data. Following closely the major categories of standard ethnography, the generated array contains these primary sectors of expressive realization:

1. *Demography and Race* (21 domains);
2. *Territorial Organization* (35 domains);
3. *Economy and Economic Life* (37 domains);
4. *Material Culture and Recreation* (87 domains);
5. *Political Organization and the State* (13 domains);
6. *Religious Organization* (41 domains);
7. *Social Organization and Stratification* (58 domains);
8. *The Life Cycle* (36 domains);
9. *History, Language, and Sociocultural Change* (43 domains);
10. *Hobbies and Sports* (34 domains);
11. *Etiquette and Protocol* (56 domains).

The total number of domains is 461, many of which can be constructed into several subdomains. Thus the global aristocratic array, which I have not yet entirely analyzed, comes to more than 1,500 domains and subdomains. A few more details may give a better idea of this corpus of information.

The expressive domains were elicited from informants in terms of six variables:

1. *Age* (child, teenager, young adult, middle-aged, and old);
2. *Sex* (male, female);
3. *Incidence of Realization* (on a scale of 1 to 5);
4. *Aristocratic Significance* (on a scale of 1 to 5);
5. *Costliness of Realization* (prohibitive, very, medium, none);
6. *Time of Realization* (1990, 1960, 1940, 1910).

Variables 1 and 2 are straightforward; but information on variables 3, 4, 5, and 6 was not forthcoming for all domains, and they need to be clarified. "Incidence of realization" refers to how common and widespread the domain is, which of course varies greatly in the substantive nature of the domain and the behavior or action it entails. "Aristocratic significance" refers to how important the domain is for the social and ideological configuration of the group and the role it plays in the aristocratic *imago mundi*; needless to say, elicited meaningful information here is limited and does not include more than 15 percent of all domains, though they are the most critically important. "Costliness of realization" includes monetary as well social cost: how much it taxes the economy of the individual and/or the family and the social reward or penalty associated with the domain's discharge. "Time of realization" applies to a limited number of domains, and the eliciting framework was designed to provide information on the changes that domains underwent throughout the twentieth century. For most domains, but particularly for that critical 15 percent, I recorded not only the quantitative information but a considerable amount of qualitative information as well.

To give the reader an idea of the magnitude and extent of the expressive array of the Mexican aristocracy, a few diagnostic examples of domains are pertinent. With respect to complexity and number of subdomains, the following are significant. "Remembrance of family coats of arms and heraldic rings" is a rather self-contained, easily handled domain operating in a wide spectrum of male and female aristocratic society. "The practice of sports" is a complex domain involving dozens of subdomains that could be scaled up to be an array in its own right; the same applies to other complex domains such as "dressing," "patterns of etiquette," "art exhibition and display," and several others. The composition of the domain "social and 'cultural' entertaining" is so extensive that in the third volume of the series it will be handled as an array in its own right.

This methodology for gathering and organizing quantitative and qualitative data warrants being replicated. In fact, I have already employed it in a folk context in an ongoing study of the cult of the dead in rural Tlaxcala; part of it has already been published (Nutini 1988), but most of it awaits quantitative analysis. Can the expressive ethnography of the aristocracy and its expressive array, as outlined above, be replicated in expressive studies of other social classes and groups? The answer is yes, and in basically in the same form. This provides me with the opportunity to say something about investigation of the expressive culture of other segments of Mexican society, which are mentioned only in passing in the text.

First, I envisage the same strategy discussed in this book, with some differences in emphasis. The five identified forms of expression are realized in every class and sector of the Mexican stratification and ethnic system, as I have partially confirmed in a study of social class and mobility in the Córdoba-

Orizaba region. Natural, vicarious, and conflictual forms of expression, for example, are realized across the entire spectrum of society (namely, urban social classes and rural ethnic sectors that can be properly isolated), whereas terminal and palliative forms of expression are most common among Indian-folk and transitional groups, almost entirely rural, in the process of becoming mestizo.

Second, in my fieldwork (in the states of Tlaxcala, Puebla, Veracruz, Mexico, and Hidalgo) and personal experience in central Mexico (in the states of Morelos, Oaxaca, San Luis Potosí, Guerrero, Michoacán, Guanajuato, Jalisco, and Aguas Calientes), expressive information on the twenty-five or so urban classes (from upper-middle to lower) and rural ethnic groups (from Indian to mestizo-secularized) indicates that each of these groups has a quite distinct exclusive array. This is particularly the case among rural ethnic groups — a quite understandable phenomenon since they are basically different societies or subsocieties. What is surprising is that the inclusive array of all these urban classes and rural ethnic groups shares a high common denominator. This may be explained by two factors: the overwhelming majority of rural and urban contemporary Mexicans are no more than four generations removed from their Indian-folk roots; and Mexico has been undergoing a rather homogeneous process of sociocultural change and modernization since World War II, despite the great differences in social status and economic differences that still persist in most sectors of society.

Third, most of the shared expressive domains of these various classes and ethnic groups are concerned with food preparation and consumption, ritualism and religion, kinship and social organization, manners and mores, and worldview. There are differences, of course, in the overall size of the expressive array; but it is not necessarily the case that the higher the ranking of these classes and ethnic groups, the larger the expressive array. For example, the expressive array of Indian-folk peoples is significantly larger than that of lower- and middle-class urbanites: these two populations share many ethnographic patterns and traits, but the urbanites have lost much of the ritualism, ceremonialism, and other traits associated with the folk tradition.

Urban Ethnography: Differences from and Similarities to Traditional Anthropological Ethnography

This book characterizes the Mexican aristocracy enfranchised in Mexico City as a "folk" group or community; by this term I wish essentially to denote that the aristocracy is basically studied here in the same fashion as a rural Mexican folk community, ranging from Indian-traditional to mestizo-secularized. The ethnography, in other words, is the same in design and execution; and, with a few exceptions, the issues are no different from investigating a traditional Indian community in the Sierra de Puebla or a secularized mestizo community in the Córdoba-Orizaba region. Despite dispersion in the urban context of the megalopolis, the aristocracy is sufficiently small and well bounded to warrant an ethnography employing traditional data-collection methods and techniques in the contextual ambiance of participant observation: structured, semistructured, and unstructured interviewing; administration of questionnaires (face-to-face interviews, self-administered); survey techniques (individually focused, group focused); direct, interactive observation (including self-awareness and attitudinal tests, clustering tasks, card-sorting tasks, and identification and correlation tasks); and indirect, unintrusive observation (archival research, contextual analysis) (Bernard 1988).

This strategy can be extended to the plutocracy, a more open-ended group than the aristocracy but sufficiently circumscribed and homogeneously structured. Moreover, within the boundaries of Mexico City and other large cities in the country are enclaves that in every respect are folk communities. These virtual urban villages have two origins. First, independent communities were engulfed by the enormous urban growth of the past fifty years. In Mexico City, for example, I am personally acquainted with about a dozen such cases, and I am sure there are many more. Second, quite often permanent migrants to urban centers from the same region congregate in certain urban neighborhoods, and it does not take long (sometimes as few as ten years) before a full-fledged community in the image of what was left behind comes into existence. I have been acquainted with this phenomenon during the past forty-five years in Mexico City as well as in smaller urban centers such as Puebla, Guadalajara, Córdoba, and Orizaba. Urban folk communities are either a continuation of what they were before being surrounded by the city or a faithful representation of the regional culture from which migrants came. This is most strikingly manifested in the continuation of practices that urbanites find quaint and that vaguely remind them of what their parents or grandparents practiced before settling in the city: a well-structured *mayordomía* (stewardship) system, a ritualistic *compadrazgo* system, distinct marriage and kinship practices, an organized cycle of religious and secular celebrations, and so on.

Most interestingly, almost as a rule urban folk communities are conservative; they are self-contained and actively isolate themselves from the surrounding city, occasionally to the extent of erecting a kind of social *cordon sanitaire*. This conscious effort to remain faithful to their folk traditions has paid off, and many communities remain conservative—some of them after two generations of existence. This is the case, for example, with San Juanico Ixtacuistla, a sizable community of more than 3,000 people in the midst of a fairly commercial area less than three miles (a short distance in the megalopolis) from the civic center of Mexico City. Astonishingly, it remains today as traditionally folk as many communities that I have studied in the rural Tlaxcala-Pueblan Valley.

Beyond these rather restricted social groups, the traditional ethnographic method is not sufficient and must be used as a supplement to network techniques, specialized surveys, and other sociological methods of data-collection. Generating adequate ethnographies of urban groups and domains is always useful, but one cannot adequately investigate, say, class stratification without quantitative techniques (as I found out in my ongoing study of class formation and mobility in the Córdoba-Orizaba region). Ethnography is important in interpreting quantitative data, and it is my considered opinion that many sociological studies suffer for lack of an adequate ethnographic base. I mean, of course, descriptive ethnography; for what I would call "analytical" ethnography entails explanatory dimensions independently of quantitative analysis. Thus, although the investigation of a social class—a collective too numerous and diverse—cannot be encapsulated in an ethnography, without it the quantitative explanation of class formation and mobility would be diminished.

Having acknowledged the limitations of urban ethnography, how can we specifically make use of it in the study of manifold urban groups and problems? I believe the present book exemplifies the various uses of ethnographic analysis in several contexts: first and foremost, as a tool for isolating and investigating social groups that have historically coalesced as the interaction of class, race, and ethnicity. This is particularly exemplified in the case of Mexico City (a macrocosm of the nation, in which within the span of three generations one can identify all meaningful social groups of Mexican society); purely quantitative techniques would not tell us the effect of these three factors in structuring the functional, interactive segment of society. From this standpoint, ethnographies of urban ethnic groups, specialized occupations, or perhaps even subclasses of society would give us greater understanding of urban society than the quantitative recitation of statistical facts. It is not an either/or question. Ethnography in the urban environment may be conceived as a receptacle in which quantitative research is interpreted; this, of course, applies to most domains of social and anthropological research.

Second, both descriptive and analytic urban ethnographies are a *sine qua non* for understanding ethnicity and its evolution in the twentieth century and explaining interethnic relations as a factor in class formation. These are problem areas which have not received sufficient attention, and urban areas are the ideal setting to study them. The large urban centers, especially Mexico City, have attracted the most varied populations from all over the nation for more than fifty years; they range from Indian-traditional to secularized mestizo communities. In fact, more than 35 percent of Mexico City's inhabitants today were not born in the city. Many of these populations—two and occasionally three generations removed from their folk roots—maintain active ties with their ancestral communities and return periodically, especially for Holy Week and All Souls'–All Saints' Day. An example should make clear what I have in mind by studying ethnicity ethnographically. Permanent migrants to urban areas from Tlaxcala, mostly to Mexico City and Puebla, return annually to their native communities for All Souls'–All Saints' Day for as much as two generations. As long as they do so, they are regarded as bona fide community members who can be relied upon socially, religiously, and economically. If they fail to return for three consecutive years, they are no longer so regarded: they cease to be considered active members of kin groups and participants in the religious organization of the community. This cutting of the ethnic umbilical cord means essentially that migrants have made the transition from folk to urban culture. This and many other examples that could be adduced demonstrate the use of ethnography for understanding the mechanisms of ethnicity.

Third, one cannot entirely understand the spectacular growth of urbanization in the second half of the century without thoroughly delving into the motivating factors that generated it. Moreover, the cultural baggage that migrants bring to the city from their ancestral communities and regions must be assessed in order to gauge their adaptation to the city, particularly economic factors that play an important role in class formation and mobility. This requires complementing traditional village ethnography and urban ethnography (which, with an ethnohistorical component, I have been doing for more than a generation, first in the Tlaxcala-Pueblan Valley and more recently in the Córdoba-Orizaba region).

Perhaps two examples focused on Mexico City would give a better idea of what is involved. The first is concerned with tailors and barbers from more than a dozen communities in central Tlaxcala. Since the turn of the century villagers from this region have migrated to Mexico City to practice these occupations; today they number about 2,000 barbers and nearly as many tailors. In time most of them have settled permanently in the city, but some continue to shuttle once a week between community and place of work, doing piecework for tailor shops in the city (that is, picking up garments on weekends, doing the work at home in the community, and returning for more work the following weekend). The second example concerns cart ice-cream vendors in Mexico City from three communities in southern Jalisco. Since the late 1940s villagers from these communities have monopolized this occupation, to the extent that more than 3,000 of them are now active in the busiest *colonias* of the city. In both cases, permanent migration to the city has led to the establishment of folk urban communities occupying well-bounded social and economic niches. I have identified similar examples in the cities of Puebla, Veracruz, Córdoba, and Orizaba involving occupations such as store clerks, butchers, bakers, masons, carpenters, and several others; these are smaller in scale but entail basically the same social, economic, and residential factors.

Urban ethnography, as it has been practiced in the United States since the 1960s, has been focused on specific problems and groups such as drug addiction and street gangs (Agar 1973; Bourgois 1995; Fleisher 1995). This is a limited view that I have tried to expand in the foregoing remarks as applying to Mexico as well as to most pluriethnic societies. The complementary use of ethnography in the quantitative study of ethnicity, urban group formation, and economic mobility is perhaps the best strategy for understanding and explaining social class formation, sociocultural change (secularization and modernization), and rampant urban growth. These are important themes that are not entirely understood and problems that afflict developing countries everywhere.

In conclusion I wish to emphasize that, although this book is an expressive ethnography of the Mexican aristocracy, it contains a significant amount of information about several sectors of society. I would like to think that it presents a fair description and analysis of the main sectors of Mexican society in social, religious, and economic interaction in the context of class, race, and ethnicity. It draws on more than twelve years of intensive fieldwork, ranging from Indian-folk peoples to the superordinate classes of society, and on forty-five years of personal experience with diverse social, demographic, and rural-urban environments in central Mexico. One of the basic premises on which this book is based is that, in order to understand the restructuring of Mexican society after the Revolution of 1910, the rich and powerful and the socially exalted must be put in structural, ideological, and expressive interaction with the middle and lower and folk sectors of society. Here my overwhelming concern with sectors of the superordinate class is solely justified by the fact that we know so little about them, but it should be assessed and balanced with respect to my ethnographic work in central Mexico.

NOTES

Chapter 2. The Relationship of Class and Ethnicity

1. To a certain extent this is corroborated by the following example. In the late 1880s the government of Porfirio Díaz engaged in a limited policy of European "colonization." In the words of the dictator himself, he wanted Europeans to come to Mexico "para mejorar la raza" (to improve the race) (Zilli 1980:15–19). His idea was to establish a series of "colonies" in various regions of Mexico, so that the colonists would intermarry with local Mexican populations. The best-known example is that of Italians imported in the early 1890s. Díaz apparently wanted immigrants from Latin countries in Europe but not from Spain, so he settled for northern Italians from the Veneto area (he pointedly specified that he did not want southern Italians because they were all mafiosi). Nearly 2,000 immigrants arrived in Mexico and were settled in three communities: Nueva Italia, in the state of Michoacán; Chipilo, in the state of Puebla; and in Manuel González, in the state of Veracruz. They were given land and the means to get started; and by the early 1930s these were prosperous communities, as they are today (Domingo Nanni, personal communication, 1979). Two generations later, many had left their communities and became successful professionals, and a few came to occupy important positions in government and the private sector. But Díaz's expectation did not come true, for neither in their communities nor in the wider world did they intermarry with Mexicans; they remained highly endogamous. It was not until about twenty-five years ago that they began to intermarry with Mexicans. In the summer of 1958, during a survey of the Nahuatl-speaking peoples in the states of Tlaxcala and Puebla, I visited Chipilo: an oasis of blond, Germanic-looking peasant phenotypes in startling contrast to a sea of communities of typical Mexican Indian phenotypes.

Chapter 3. The Realization of Expression
in the Ethnographic Context

1. Notice that I have consistently used the term "European" and avoided the term "white," which is not used in Mexico as a racial category with the same meaning as in the United States. The exceptions are contextual: occasionally to denote a culturally non-Indian individual at the local or regional level, or in the national urban and rural contexts to indicate fairness but not a somatic category.

Chapter 4. The Organization of Urban Living

1. The palaces and mansions of the aristocracy were generally two- or three-story structures with an exterior and interior courtyard. The first story of the exterior courtyard was a place of business, where the offices of the various agrarian and other enterprises of the owner were located. The second (and occasionally the third) story of the exterior courtyard served as the living quarters of the aristocratic family: the drawing rooms, dining rooms, and ballroom for social entertainment and display; and the bedchambers and other rooms of individual family members. These two spaces were clearly demarcated, which has survived in the contemporary aristocratic household. The first and second stories of the interior courtyards were the quarters of servants and personnel attached to the household; this interior space also included stables, utility rooms, and storage areas.

2. Throughout most of the Middle Ages castles and manors were the main rural residences of the aristocracy; not until modern times (roughly at the onset of the sixteenth century) was the classical rural-urban pattern resumed. This came about by the demise of seigneurialism and the increasing urbanization of the higher and lower nobility. By the end of the eighteenth century (with perhaps the exception of England) the great majority of aristocrats had their main residence in the city but invariably kept a country place.

Chapter 5. Economy, Material Culture,
and Political Participation

1. In fact, the origins of Mexican *haute cuisine* go back to pre-Hispanic times. For example, Bernal Díaz del Castillo (the main eyewitness source for the history of the Conquest of Mexico) says that more than 100 different dishes were prepared daily for the table of Motehcuzoma Xocoyotzin, the last ruler of Tenochtitlan (Mexico City) (Díaz del Castillo 1967:125). Throughout colonial times Mexican cuisine developed a distinctive character by combining pre-Hispanic and Spanish ingredients, condiments, forms of cooking, and presentation of food (Miranda 1987). In the nineteenth century, after the French Intervention, Mexican cuisine was enriched by French and Italian elements; and by the turn of the century it had achieved a degree of sophistication that warrants the appellation of *haute cuisine* (Ovando 1983).

2. I have not provided a list of the most outstanding and commonly prepared recipes for different occasions because one of my informants (a 75-year-old lady) and I are collaborating on a book on aristocratic cuisine and the sociological implications it

entails. The volume also deals with the etiquette of food consumption and dressing and associated practices, which are not included in the present book.

3. To define "elegance," "sobriety," and similar expressively loaded terms used in this book is difficult but not intractable. There are obviously no absolute definitions for these expressive terms; but as discussed in Chapter 4, the task is contextually simplified and made manageable when confined to specific cultural domains or subdomains. In the context of the *haute bourgeoisie*, the situation is further simplified; for, as in the context of color combinations in Western European society, aristocratic standards are still the benchmark for defining these expressively loaded terms.

4. In the name of maintaining an illusory aristocratic identity, families do not use assets that can easily be liquidated for investing in or capitalizing business enterprises. This expressive commitment is, in feedback fashion, rationalized on the grounds either that aristocrats are incompetent at making money or that this is an endeavor beneath them. This quandary captures perfectly the conjunction of expressive commitment, structural conditions, and the feedback effect that obtains between them.

5. This difference in the U.S. and Mexican political systems of patronage, I believe, rests on the fact that Mexican society (at least the more educated sectors of the population) does not exhibit the anti-intellectualism so patently present in U.S. society. Admittedly, I may be wrong. I believe, however, that the average U.S. voter would accept without objection the nomination of the CEO of a great corporation as ambassador to a key foreign nation but would have great reservations about a famous writer, a great artist, or even a Nobel laureate in science being appointed to the same position.

6. Here I have in mind many ethnographic descriptions of tribal and folk peoples' magico-religious and social events, when the slightest deviation from sacred, or even secular, formulas and incantations detracts from or cancels the intended purpose of rites and ceremonies. This also obtains in the superordinate estate (and after 1800 the ruling classes) of Western civilization from classical times to the present, albeit in attenuated form. The ritualism and exaggerated ceremonialism of the Romans are well known. An example is the traditional marriage by *confarreatio* (the traditional form of marriage among patricians through which the wife passed into the hands of the husband's *familia* [family], lineage [*stirps*], and clan [*gens*], from which plebeians were totally barred), centered on the gods of the household (*lares* and *penates*). It was the most complex event in the ritual and ceremonial life of the superordinate estate, executed with the benefit of extremely elaborated and exacting formulae. The life of the medieval feudal aristocracy was fraught with an excessive concern with ritualism and ceremonialism, so exacting and monotonic that it is difficult to understand today. An example is the investiture of a knight by a higher personage in the feudal order, again done with the most exacting ritualism—any slight deviation from it rendered the investiture invalid.

Chapter 6. Religion

1. At the wedding of the daughter of one of the richest men in Mexico (worth more than $2 billion) in 1990, one of my best aristocratic informants said that he had been

told by the wedding "director" that about $800,000 had been spent in liquor for the affair, attended by more than 2,000 guests. The list included 100 cases of 1956 Dom Perignon champagne, 150 cases of 1959 Château Lafite and 1957 Château Margaux red and white Bordeaux wine, and many cases of the finest liqueurs (cognacs, cordials, and so on). It had all been imported from France, as my informant ironically remarked, "and without paying a cent in import duty." Then he added, "Those incredible wines merited infinitely better food."

2. It is not known with certainty when Epiphany acquired its present form. The first attestation, more or less as it is celebrated today, is from the end of the seventeenth century (Zamora Plowes 1945:457). It is likely, however, that it dates back to the sixteenth century, as part of the elaborate array of ritual and ceremonial subterfuges that the mendicant friars used for purposes of conversion and catechization.

3. The *casa chica* (setting up a smaller house for a concubine) is a very old phenomenon in Mexican society, going back to the sixteenth century. It is practiced by all classes of society and was probably influenced by Indian polygyny when this form of marriage was abolished by the advent of Catholicism. The *casa chica* is still found, but its incidence has greatly declined since it was legislated some twenty years ago that offspring of a *casa chica* inherit equally with legitimate children.

4. Since abortion in Mexico is illegal, I did not ask how it was performed. Nor did I go on to ask for the details of the three cases of sending the daughter away to give birth and then having the baby adopted. Although the elicitations generally took place in a relaxed ambiance, there was a latent tension that made me realize that I had gone far enough. Only in four cases were the conditions such that I was able to elicit more detailed information.

5. All that I know about the Spanish aristocracy historically supports this assertion. Of more immediate significance, when the Convent of Santa Clara in the city of Puebla in 1932 was exposed by the civil authorities to have been operating illegally for many decades, about 150 fetuses were found in the crypt of a chapel. Authorities speculated that the fetuses belonged to young girls of elite families of the city who had been sent there to abort (Fausto Marín Tamayo, personal communication, 1961).

6. As far as I am aware, the moment at which a new soul comes into existence has not been fixed dogmatically in Catholicism, and there are apparently competing theological theories: at the moment of sexual intercourse; when the sperm fertilizes the egg; at the end of the journey in the fallopian tube; and possibly other opinions. So it seems to me that this informant's opinion is just as logically possible as any of the above.

Chapter 7. Social Organization

1. This is the essence of asymmetrical social acculturation, in which one of the groups in interaction has dominance of some sort over the other. When the Mexican aristocracy was the ruling class of the country, plutocrats became aristocrats; since the Revolution the reverse has been taking place by virtue of the plutocrats' great wealth. Thus the process goes on in creating a new ruling class.

2. This information was elicited from fifteen plutocratic and upper-middle-class informants with close social and affinal ties to prominent aristocrats. It was supplemented with information elicited randomly, but not systematically, among sporadic middle-class informants with an interest in aristocratic matters. Throughout this book I have consistently avoided the personalization of ethnographic information and the identification of individuals, families, and groups in order to avoid invidious comparisons. This is one juncture, however, at which I could not avoid mentioning specific names.

3. I arrived at this figure based on the fact that during the past two generations the number of children per nuclear family has seldom been more than three. Indeed, among younger married couples one or two children is the rule.

4. It has been estimated (Peter Corsi, personal communication, 1989) that more than two thousand folk people a week settle in Mexico City. And I know, firsthand, that they bring with them many of their social and cultural traditions and institutions, which not infrequently persist for more than a generation. It usually takes twenty to thirty years before these populations, from all regions of the country, divest themselves of most of their folk roots; even then, a significant substratum remains.

5. Notice that I am using "cousin" in the standard use of the term in the U.S. kinship system. In other words it includes male and female cousins (*primos* and *primas*) and uncles and aunts (*tíos* and *tías*) at the parental and grandparental generations in the Spanish kinship system. The Spanish terms *primo* and *prima* apply to members of ego's own generation—that is, they cannot be used cross-generationally.

6. This statement, however, needs clarification. By traditionally arranged marriage I do not necessarily mean that the parents of the bride and groom get together and plot the union of their offspring for some clear social or economic advantage. This strategy stopped before the turn of the century. Arranged marriage as it was practiced until recently involved social pressures, veiled threats of withholding heirlooms, and insinuations of disinheritance.

7. Particularly in baptism and marriage there is a special bond established between *padrinos* and *ahijados* that definitely goes beyond the real kinship relationship that binds them. This is the exception that confirms the rule that *compadrazgo* is at best an extension of kinship but not an independent system.

Chapter 8. Internal Stratification and Organization of the Group

1. In *The Wages of Conquest* I note that the survival and adaptability of the descendants of distinguished conquistadors were very low. They were superior warriors but mediocre managers. Public and private genealogical information indicates that only a handful of conquistadors were members of the Creole aristocracy by 1600. This explains how few individuals and families today can trace descent to original conquistadors.

2. To revalidate or reactivate a title of nobility in Mexico today would be nothing more than an exercise in customary futility, since titles of nobility were abolished after In-

dependence. The main reason why aristocrats are disinterested in revalidating titles, however, is that it is considered *cursi*. Moreover, most aristocrats consider it snobbish when occasionally the rightful possessors of titles are referred to, or refer to themselves, as the count and countess or marquess and marchioness of such and such.

3. This reconstruction is based on historical material in private archives, genealogical information, and interviews with male and female informants over eighty in the late 1970s. The interviews included aristocrats of various ranks, among which were members of the two examples' name groups.

4. One of the main reasons for this situation is that quite often parents forced daughters into convent life: it was cheaper to pay a convent dowry than a marriage dowry. I have extensive documentary and anecdotal evidence for this practice.

5. This is the same as the contributions that European aristocrats made to the development of science and scholarship in these centuries. The Baron de Montesquieu, the Marquis de Condorcet, Comte de Buffon, Chevalier de Lamarck, Lord Monboddo, Charles Darwin, Sir Francis Galton, and many others were titled nobles or belonged to the gentry. Proportionally, there were by far more aristocratic than commoner scientists and scholars in modern times (1500 to 1900). This is easy to explain. The superordinate class (probably never more than 10 percent of the total population) was the only sector of society that had the economic means and leisure time to dedicate to research and scholarly pursuits, given that there was little or no government support.

6. While the emphasis on bloodlines is understandable in a system in which status is ascribed, the emphasis on antiquity of lineage is rather difficult to explain as taking overwhelming precedence over achievement. For example, why is it that some obscure noblewoman in Sicily whose family may trace descent to the tenth century or a mere squire in Britain who has been in possession of his land since the Norman conquest ranks as intrinsically more aristocratic than many a titled noble of more recent extraction but with a distinguished record of public service to the Crown? No easy explanation comes to mind, but it is a deeply ingrained principle. Of course, this is only ideologically true; structurally the situation is quite different.

7. By the end of the seventeenth century the direct line of descent of many conquistadors and founders of cities and towns had come to an end (that is, did not survive as patronymic name groups). Contemporary aristocrats, however, may legitimately trace descent to them by adducing matronymic genealogical connections. The same can be achieved by other means, involving some creative tampering with *pergaminos*.

8. This is as close as I can get to explaining the subtle, arcane, and somewhat irrational distinction between aristocratic rank and prestige to which the moribund Mexican aristocracy still adheres. I have observed this phenomenon in several aristocratic settings in Europe and the New World.

Notes to pages 290–296

GLOSSARIES

General Glossary

Spanish, French, Latin, Nahuatl, and Hispanicized Nahuatl terms used in the text are explained when they first occur; but for the convenience of the reader, terms that are used twice or more have been compiled here. Proper nouns are capitalized.

acasillado: Resident laborer on a landed state during the Porfiriato; debt peon.

ahijada: Goddaughter.

ahijado: Godson.

ancien régime: Old political and ruling system; in France, and all Western countries, the old estate system.

antojitos (mexicanos): Mexican treats or snacks.

apadrinar: To ritually sponsor an individual, object, or occasion.

buena facha: To have a good appearance; to look phenotypically European.

caciquismo: Strong attachment to a leader as a patron and as a source of economic and social well-being.

capellanía(s): Chaplaincy; a salient domain of expression among aristocrats until the Mexican Revolution of 1910, which has marginally survived.

casa porfiriana: Architectural style, based on some French features, developed during the last two decades of the Porfirio Díaz regime.

casco(s): Mansion or manor of a landed estate; after the Mexican Revolution of 1910, mostly the gutted framework of a mansion or manor.

castas: Racial mixtures of Indians, whites, and blacks; an elaborate system of racial classification in eighteenth-century Mexico.

catrín (catrines): City slicker; mestizo; urbanite.

charrería: The practice and craft of the *charro* (cowboy); an extensive complex including rodeos, shows of equestrian skill, and a variety of ancillary activities.

colonia(s): Neighborhoods, boroughs, sections of Mexico City.

compadrazgo: Ritual kinship; the complex of personal, social, religious, and symbolic attributes that accompanies kinship.

confarreatio: The patrician form of marriage in ancient Rome, which continues as the model of aristocratic marriage.

criollo: Creole; Spaniard born in Mexico; originally in the sixteenth century, a strictly racial, somatic category; it subsequently acquired cultural definitional characteristics.

criollos güeros: Blondish Creoles; one of several terms that refer to whites.

cursi: Tacky; kitschy; pretentious.

despedidas de soltera: Bridal showers that take place in the homes of the bride's relatives and intimate friends several weeks before the wedding.

despedidas de soltero: Bachelor parties, usually in public venues, that take place several weeks before the wedding.

encomendero: Spanish or Creole grantee of Indian labor; until roughly the middle of the seventeenth century, *latifundia* owner.

encomienda: Indians granted as tributaries to individual Spaniards or Creoles during the sixteenth and seventeenth centuries.

equites: Knights; in early Roman times, those who fought on horseback; from the first Punic War onward, capitalists, business owners, and tax collectors; by the late Republic organized as an intermediate social order between patrician and plebeians.

familias venidas a menos: Downwardly mobile families; dropout aristocratic families.

gente blanca: White people.

gente decente: Decent or proper people; a rather ambivalent term used from the middle of the seventeenth century onward, referring primarily to affluent Creole and Spanish populations standing below the aristocracy; in the twentieth century, the mostly white upper-middle class.

gente de razón: Mestizos; urbanites; non-Indians.

gente güera: Light-skinned people; white people.

gentes propias: Proper people; in the twentieth century, primarily upper-middle class families with whom the aristocracy interacts on a slightly superordinate foot of equality.

güero(a): Light-skinned male or female.

hacendado: Latifundia owner from the middle of the seventeenth century until the Mexican Revolution of 1910.

hacienda: *Latifundia;* the form of land tenure that predominated in Mexico from the middle of the seventeenth century until the Mexican Revolution of 1910.

haute bourgeois: Member of the *haute bourgeoisie;* a rich and powerful plutocrat.

hidalgo: Member of the lower nobility or gentry; individual entitled to a coat of arms with access to other nobiliary privileges.

hidalgo a fuero de España: Member of the lower nobility according to Spanish nobiliary law.

hidalguía: Lower, lesser, or nontitled nobility; gentry; the second rank of the Spanish aristocracy, with counterparts in all Western aristocracies.

la indiada: "That mob of Indians"; deprecatory term used to refer to the majority of Mexicans by essentially white populations.

madrina: Godmother; female ritual sponsor; term of reference for female ritual sponsor.

mayorazgo: Entailed property; primogeniture; until well into the nineteenth century, perhaps the main institution perpetuating titles of nobility and aristocratic status; since then, while no longer a legal institution, it has continued to affect the unequal distribution of property among siblings until the present.

mayordomía: Sponsorship of a religious fiesta in honor of a particular saint, together with a complex of ritual, ceremonial, administrative, and economic functions.

mestizo: Individual of mixed Indian and Spanish ancestry; originally in the sixteenth century a strictly racial, somatic category; by the onset of the nineteenth century, it had become essentially a cultural category and remains so today.

metiche: Meddlesome people in general.

la naquiza: "That herd of *nacos,*" a corruption of Totonaco, the name of an

Indian group on the Gulf coast; deprecatory term used to refer to the majority of Mexicans by essentially white populations.

noviazgo: Courtship; going steady; formal engagement leading to marriage.

obras pías: Endowed charities; any philanthropic or charitable activity.

padrinazgo: Ritual sponsorship; but unlike *compadrazgo*, entailing no permanent duties and obligations.

padrino: Godfather; male ritual sponsor; term of reference for ritual sponsor.

peninsular: Spaniard born in Spain; a Spaniard who resided in Mexico during colonial times in an official or private capacity.

pergaminos: Documentary evidence and visual attestation proving antiquity and illustriousness of lineage.

petite histoire: Minor history; personal history; family, genealogical, topical, and regional history written by aristocrats.

Porfiriato: The dictatorship of Porfirio Díaz (1876–1910).

raza cósmica: "Cosmic race"; a denotative term, created by intellectuals, to refer to the Indian-mestizo society that they conceive Mexico to be.

raza de bronce: "Race of bronze"; a denotative term, created by intellectuals, to refer to the Indian-mestizo society that they conceive Mexico to be.

rosca: A round or oblong kind of cake covered with sugar and candied fruit, eaten communally for Epiphany (January 6, Día de Reyes).

santo: Name day; usually coincides with a person's birthday.

separación de bienes: Essentially, the Mexican version of the prenuptial agreement in the United States.

tecuhtli: Member of the upper nobility or lordly class in pre-Hispanic times.

tlatoani: King or a member of the kingly class in pre-Hispanic times.

velorio: Wake.

weekendismo: The practice of aristocratic families and families of the superordinate ranks of society spending weekends in a country place or refurbished hacienda.

zócalo: Mexico City's central square.

Analytical Glossary

Several analytical terms in this book have no standardized usage or are generally not used in the anthropological literature. In order to help the reader, the terms are briefly defined as I employ them throughout the book.

The Mexican Aristocracy

acculturation: One of the main forms of culture change. When two groups (aristocracy and plutocracy) with different social traditions come into direct contact in a variety of contexts that may include selective adoption and social, economic, and political pressures, a resultant group comes into being that partakes of the original groups in interaction; the difference results from the inequalities of borrowing and transmission, which are internalized and reinterpreted according to a process of action and reaction in the resultant group.

aristocratic-plutocratic acculturation: In the twentieth century, the superordinate realignment of classes through which a new plutocracy becomes aristocratized as the ruling class of the country, and the traditional aristocracy becomes plutocratized on the way to terminal decline.

bourgeoisie: In the late Middle Ages (1200–1500), the highest ranking class of the commoner estate. Since the onset of modern times, the middle classes of the stratification system. In contemporary Mexico, *burguesía* commonly denotes bureaucrats, business leaders, and generally those who do not do manual work, whereas intellectuals indiscriminately and derogatorily extend the use of the term to the rich and powerful.

class: In Western civilization, during the *ancien régime*, the subdivisions of the noble and common estates. The major subdivisions of society since the establishment of equality before the law brought about by the American and French Revolutions. There is no agreement among sociologists and anthropologists about the nature and definition of class, and the concept remains rather vague. This book deals mainly with superordinate stratification, and in this respect I follow Raymond Aron (1966:201–210) and Digby Baltzell (1966) in distinguishing social class (elite), political class, and ruling class.

conflict expression: See the section What Has Been Accomplished and What Still Must Be Done in the Conclusions.

embourgeoisement: Literally, becoming bourgeois; after the onset of the nineteenth century, the changes undergone by Western aristocracies due to their loss of wealth and political power.

expression (expressive culture): One of the ideational (superstructural in Marxist terms) components of culture, together with ideology, worldview, belief system, custom, and values. Although expression is based on a structural, material context, it is not part of the superstructure. Expression is a contextual and contextually created entity: that is, it may take place in any contextualized time and space. To put it differently, expression, as the concept is used in this book, is an aspect of individual action but always within specific social milieux. Expression may thus be defined as a necessary component of culture that conditions behavior regardless of cultural content.

expressive acculturation: In Mexico, the process that has molded the interaction of aristocrats and plutocrats since the early 1930s, which has resulted in the maturation of the plutocracy as the superordinate social class of the country and accelerated the terminal demise of the aristocracy.

expressive array: The total of all patterns and contexts in a given social group that entirely or partially realize expression. Every group has an expressive array that is peculiar to itself, in terms of both intensity and the contexts in which expression is realized.

expressive behavior: Contextual and contextually created behavior socially, economically, religiously, and phenotypically constituted. Although expressive behavior is psychologically motivated and individual, it nonetheless has a collective, structured manifestation closely related to the social structure. Thus expressive behavior may be nominally defined as the individual and collective choices that the members of a group can make. By themselves they do not necessarily alter the group, but they signify whatever changing conditions the group is experiencing. The motivation of expressive behavior makes it nonutilitarian or noninstrumental. In functional terms, however, expressive behavior is an integral part of the social structure, as it manifests or exhibits certain diagnostic aspects of the social structure.

expressive domain: The basic component of the expressive array. It may be defined as any cultural context in which expressive behavior is realized with some degree of semantic unity. The domain is not a fixed unit or entity of expressive realization; it can aggregate to higher levels or narrow levels according to the needs of the analysis.

expressive manipulation: Emphasizing, deemphasizing, and/or transposing individual and/or collective material, social, economic, phenotypical, and any other traits or characteristics in order to enhance expressive status.

haute bourgeoisie: High bourgeoisie; rich and powerful plutocracy. Social class that had its inception in the fifteenth and sixteenth centuries, competed with the aristocracy in the seventeenth and eighteenth centuries, and asserted itself in the nineteenth and twentieth centuries.

natural expression: See the section What Has Been Accomplished and What Still Must Be Done in the Conclusions.

palliative expression: See the section What Has Been Accomplished and What Still Must Be Done in the Conclusions.

political class: The small minority who actually exercise the functions of government. Of the three main subclasses of superordinate stratification, it is the least permanent but has sufficient structural continuity to merit the denotation of class.

renewal of elites: The four realignments of personnel undergone by the Mexican aristocracy since its inception in the sixteenth century: 1550–1630, 1730–1810, 1850–1900, and 1940–1990. In all four renewals rich and powerful plutocrats join the ranks of the aristocracy by acquiring the exclusive expressive array of the latter. In the first three renewals the aristocracy remains dominant as the ruling and social class of the country, whereas in the last renewal the aristocracy ceases to be the ruling class and faces impending extinction as a social class. This is essentially Pareto's (1935) concept of the circulation of elites.

ruling class: This class includes those privileged people who, without exercising actual political functions, influence those who govern and those who obey, either because of the moral authority they hold or because of the economic or financial power they possess. While ruling classes are more structured and have more continuity than political classes, they are the most difficult to identify.

seigneurialism: Fundamentally, feudalism without vassalage and military service. The terms for these institutions are quite often confused in the historical literature. Feudalism was the law of the land in Europe until the beginning of the fourteenth century. From then on, due to the political and administrative assertion of the centralized monarchy, seigneurialism gradually replaced feudalism;

and by the beginning of the sixteenth century the transformation
had been accomplished. The *encomienda* system (which gave rise to
the hacienda system) that the Spaniards introduced in the New
World was thus seigneurialism, not feudalism, as many historians
have characterized it. Seigneurialism was a slight improvement
over feudalism, but the common folk continued to be oppressed
and exploited.

social class (elite): All those who (in diverse activities) are high in the
hierarchy, who occupy any important privileged position, whether
in terms of wealth or prestige. This is Aron's definition of "elite,"
but I prefer the term "social class" because the former is too
impermanent and does not include the essentially expressive
attributes of the aristocracy as it survived until the twentieth
century—namely, lineage, heredity, and social exaltedness. By
contrast, the other two definitions of class ("political," "ruling")
are underlain primarily by structural attributes.

structural-expressive stratification: The combined structural and expressive
study of social stratification (class formation, mobility, and
persistence). The basic assumption of this book is that structural
variables alone give an incomplete account of stratification. The
complementarity of so-called objective, structural variables (such
as wealth, power, education, residence, etc.) and expressive
variables is a *sine qua non*. Otherwise it would not make sense to
regard the Mexican aristocracy as a functional social class after it
lost all power and most of its wealth.

terminal expression: See the section What Has Been Accomplished and
What Still Must Be Done in the Conclusions.

terminal expressive exclusivity: The decline of the aristocracy as the exclusive
purveyor of superordinate vicariousness. The aristocratic
distinctness of dress, personal presentation, and public behavior is
acquired by plutocrats and the upper-middle class. As a result the
aristocracy loses visibility, and the plutocracy becomes the
subclass to emulate expressively.

upper-middle class: As used in this book, the term does not have the
denotation that it has in U.S. sociology. I use "upper-middle class"
as a combination of structural, mostly economic attributes plus a
large expressive component but significantly modified by ethnic
phenotypical considerations. This thin veneer of society in Mexico

City is the milieu where the aristocracy is proximately embedded as a complementary group, constituting, so to speak, the fringe boundaries of aristocratic social interaction.

vicarious expression: See the section What Has Been Accomplished and What Still Must Be Done in the Conclusions.

BIBLIOGRAPHY

Adams, Brooks
1896   *The Law of Civilization and Decay*. New York: Macmillan.
Agar, Michael H.
1973   *Ripping and Running: A Formal Ethnography of Heroin Addicts*. New York: Seminar Press.
Alamán, Lucas
1942   *Disertaciones sobre la historia de la República Mexicana*. Mexico City: Editorial Jus.
Allen, Frederick L.
1935   *The Lords of Creation*. New York: E. P. Dutton.
Alvarez, Alejandro, Jr.
1990   *La ciudad antigua de México, siglos XVI–XVII*. Mexico City: Publicaciones de Bancomer.
Amory, Cleveland
1947   *The Proper Bostonians*. New York: E. P. Dutton.
Aron, Raymond
1966   "Social Class, Political Class, Ruling Class." In *Class, Status, and Power: Social Stratification in Comparative Perspective*, ed. Reinhardt Bendix and Seymour Martin Lipset. New York: Free Press.
Ashburn, Frank D.
1944   *Peabody of Groton*. New York: Coward McCahn.
Baltzell, Digby E.
1966   "'Who's Who in America' and 'The Social Register': Elite Upper Class Indexes in Metropolitan America." In *Class, Status, and Power: Social*

Stratification in Comparative Perspective, ed. Reinhardt Bendix and Seymour Martin Lipset. New York: Free Press.

Baudot, George

1977   *Utopie et histoire au Mexique*. Paris: Privat.

Bazancourt, Claude L. de

1931   *Le Mexique contemporain*. Paris: La Rochelle.

Beals, Carleton

1954   *Porfirio Díaz*. Mexico City: Editorial Sánchez.

Ben-David, Joseph

1966   "The Growth of the Professions and the Class System." In *Class, Status, and Power: Social Stratification in Comparative Perspective*, ed. Reinhardt Bendix and Seymour Martin Lipset. New York: Free Press.

Bendix, Reinhardt, and Seymour Martin Lipset, eds.

1966   *Class, Status, and Power: Social Stratification in Comparative Perspective*. New York: Free Press.

Bernal, Ignacio

1962   *Bibliografía de arqueología y etnografía: Mesoamérica y Norte de Mexico, 1514– 1960*. Memoria 7. Mexico City: Instituto Nacional de Antropología e Historia.

1980   *A History of Mexican Archeology*. London: Thames and Hudson.

Bernard, Russell H.

1988   *Research Methods in Cultural Anthropology*. Newbury Park: Sage Publications.

Beteta, Ramón

1935   *Economic and Social Progress in Mexico*. San Francisco: Johnson and Sons.

Bonfil Batalla, Gillermo

1994   *México profundo: Una civilización negada*. Mexico City: Editorial Grigalbo, S.A. de C.V.

Boster, James S.

1986   "Exchange of Varieties and Information between Aguaruna Manioc Cultivators." *American Anthropologist* 88: 428–436.

Bourgois, Philippe

1995   *In Search of Respect: Selling Crack in the Barrio*. Cambridge: Cambridge University Press.

Bourguignon, Erika

1973   "Psychological Anthropology." In *Handbook of Social and Cultural Anthropology*, ed. John J. Honingmann. Chicago: Rand McNally and Company.

Buchler, Ira R., and Henry A. Selby

1968   *Kinship and Social Organization: An Introduction to Theory and Method*. New York: Macmillan Co.

Buelna, Alejandro, Jr.

1940   *México: Historia, turismo, y costumbres*. Mexico City: Litografía Moderna.

Bulnes, Francisco
1916   *The Whole Truth about Mexico.* Detroit: Blaine Ethridge Books.
Bush, Michael L.
1984   *The English Aristocracy: A Comparative Synthesis.* Manchester: Manchester University Press.
Chavero, Alfredo
1901   *Pinturas jeroglíficas.* Mexico City: Editorial Pablo del Campo.
Chick, Garry, and John M. Roberts
1987   "Lathe Craft: A Study in Part Appreciation." *Human Organization* 46: 305–317.
Covarrubias, Diego de
1953   *Opera.* Madrid: Imprenta de la Luz.
Crawford, Michael H.
1975   "Historical-Demographic Analysis of Indian Populations in Tlaxcala, Mexico." *Social Biology* 230: 40–50.
Davis, Kingsley, and Wilbert E. Moore
1945   "Some Principles of Stratification." *American Sociological Review* 10 (2): 242–249.
Dawkins, Richard
1989   *The Selfish Gene.* London: Oxford University Press.
Dennet, Daniel C.
1995   *Darwin's Dangerous Idea: Evolution and the Meaning of Life.* New York: Simon and Schuster.
DeWalt, Billie, and Martha C. Reese
1994   *The End of Agrarian Reform in Mexico.* La Jolla, Calif.: University of California at San Diego Center for U.S.-Mexican Studies.
Díaz del Castillo, Bernal
1967   *Historia verdadera de la conquista de la Nueva España.* Mexico City: Editorial Porrúa, S.A.
Dorantes de Carranza, Baltasar
1970   *Sumaria relación de las cosas de la Nueva España.* Mexico City: Jesús Medina, Editor.
Durand, José
1953   *La transformación social del conquistador.* 2 vols. Mexico City: Porrúa y Obregón, S.A.
Durkheim, Emile
1947   *The Division of Labor in Society.* Chicago: Free Press of Glencoe.
1951   *Suicide: A Study of Sociology.* Chicago: Free Press of Glencoe.
Evans-Pritchard, E. E.
1949   *The Sanusi of Cyrenaica.* London: Oxford University Press.
Fernández de Recas, Guillermo
1931   *Mayorazgos de la Nueva España.* Mexico City: Biblioteca Nacional.

Flandrau, Claude M.

1908   *Viva México*. México City: Imprenta Flores.

Fleisher, Mark S.

1995   *Beggars and Thieves: Lives of Urban Street Criminals*. Madison: University of Wisconsin Press.

Fortes, Meyer

1959   "Descent, Filiation, and Affinity." *Man* 52: 193–197, 206–212.

Fox, Robin

1967   *Kinship and Marriage: An Anthropological Perspective*. Cambridge: Cambridge University Press.

Galván, Mariano

1984   *Ordenanzas de tierras y agua*. Mexico City: Imprenta del Gobierno.

Gamio, Manuel

1922   *La población del Valle de Teotihuacán*. Mexico City: Secretaría de Agricultura y Fomento, Dirección de Antropología.

García Icazbalceta, Joaquín

1947   *Don Fray Juan de Zumárraga: Primer obispo y arzobispo de México*. Mexico City: Colección de Escritores Mexicanos.

1954   *Bibliografía mexicana del siglo XVI*. Mexico City: Agustín Millares Carlo Editores.

García Pimentel, Juan

1978   "La terminología de parentesco en América Latina." *Revista de Estudios Sociológicos* 15: 120–145.

García Purón, Manuel

1964   *México y sus gobernantes: Biografías*. Mexico City: M. Porrúa.

Gaulin, Steven J. C., and Donald H. McBurney

2001   *Psychology: An Evolutionary Approach*. Upper Saddle River, N.J.: Prentice Hall.

Gellner, Ernst

1987   *The Concept of Kinship and Other Essays*. London: Oxford University Press.

Gibson, Charles

1952   *Tlaxcala in the Sixteenth Century*. New Haven, Conn.: Yale University Press.

Gómez de Cervantes, Gonzalo

1944   *La vida económica y social de la Nueva España al finalizar el siglo XVI*. Mexico City: José Porrúa e Hijos.

González Navarro, Moisés

1957   "El Porfiriato: La vida social." In *Historia moderna de México*, ed. D. Cosío Villegas. Buenos Aires: Editorial Hermes.

Goodenough, Ward H.

1964   "A Problem in Malyo-Polynesian Social Organization." *American Anthropologist* 57: 76.

Goodwin, William K.

1953   *Decline and Survival of the Aristocracy*. Liverpool: Landon Brothers.

Hall, Frederic
1937   *The Laws of Mexico.* San Francisco: A. L. Bancroft.
Hamilton, William D.
1964a   "The Genetical Evolution of Social Behavior." *Journal of Theoretical Biology*
        7: 1–16.
1964b   "The Genetic Evolution of Social Behavior II." *Journal of Theoretical Biology*
        7: 17–52.
Herodotus
1965   *History.* London: Routledge and Kegan Paul.
Homans, George C., and Charles P. Curtis, Jr.
1934   *An Introduction to Pareto: His Sociology.* New York: Alfred A. Knopf.
Humboldt, Alexander von
1966   *Ensayo político sobre el reino de la Nueva España.* Mexico City: Editorial
        Porrúa, S.A.
Hymann, Herbert H.
1966   "Value Systems of Different Classses." In *Class, Status, and Power: Social
        Stratification in Perspective,* ed. Reinhardt Bendix and Seymour Marin Lipset.
        New York: Free Press.
Icaza, Francisco A.
1969   *Diccionario autobiográfico de conquistadores y pobladores de Nueva España.*
        Guadalajara, Mexico: Edmundo Aviha Levy.
Kessing, Roger M.
1975   *Kin Groups and Social Structure.* Philadelphia: Harcourt Brace.
Kirchhoff, Paul
1959   "The Principles of Clanship in Human Societies." In *Readings in
        Anthropology,* ed. Morton Fried. Chicago: University of Chicago Press.
Ladd, Doris M.
1976   *The Mexican Nobility at Independence, 1780–1826.* Austin: University of Texas
        Press.
Laurin-Frenette, Nicole
1976   *Las teorías funcionalistas de las classes sociales: Sociología e ideología burguesa.*
        Madrid: Siglo Veintiuno Editores, S.A.
Linton, Ralph, and Adelin Linton
1950   *Halloween through Twenty Centuries.* New York: Henry Schuman.
Lynd, Robert S., and Helen M. Lynd
1937   *Middletown in Transition.* New York: Harcourt Brace.
Malinowski, Bronislaw
1922   *Argonauts of the Western Pacific.* New York: E. P. Dutton.
Martínez de Cosío, Leopoldo
1946   *Los caballeros de las ordenes militares en México.* Mexico City:: Editorial
        Santiago.

Martínez del Río, Pablo

1938   *El suplicio de los hacendados y otros temas agrarios.* Mexico City: Ediciones Polis.

1954   *La comarca lagunera a fines del siglo XVI y a principios del XVII.* Publicación No. 30 del Instituto de Historia. Mexico City: Universidad Autónoma de México.

Mauss, Marcel

1923   "Essai dur le Don." *L'Année Sociologique* (second série).

Maynard Smith, John

1976   "Group Selection." *Quarterly Review of Biology* 51: 277–283.

1999   *The Origins of Life: From the Birth of Life to the Origin of Language.* New York: Oxford University Press.

Mendieta y Núñez, Lucio

1966   *El problema agrario de México.* Mexico City: Porrúa Hermanos.

Meyer, Jean A.

1976   *The Cristero Rebellion: The Mexican People between Church and State, 1926–1929.* New York: Cambridge University Press.

Miranda, José

1987   *La formación económica del encomendero en los orígenes del régimen colonial.* Mexico City: Stylo.

Montagu of Beaulieu, Lord

1970   *More Equal Than Others: The Changing Fortunes of the British and European Aristocracies.* London: Michael Joseph.

Murdock, George Peter

1972   "Anthropology's Mythology." *Journal of the Royal Anthropological Institute* (1972): 17–24.

Nagel, Ernest

1961   *The Structure of Science.* New York: Harcourt Brace.

Nickel, Herbert J.

1988   *Morfología social de la hacienda mexicana.* Mexico City: Fondo de Cultura Económica.

Nutini, Hugo G.

1968   *San Bernardino Contla: Marriage and Family Structure in a Tlaxcalan Municipio.* Pittsburgh: Pittsburgh University Press.

1984   *Ritual Kinship: Ideological and Structural Integration of the Compadrazgo System in Rural Tlaxcala.* Princeton: Princeton University Press.

1988   *Todos Santos in Rural Tlaxcala: A Syncretic, Expressive, and Symbolic Analysis of the Cult of the Dead.* Princeton: Princeton University Press.

1995   *The Wages of Conquest: The Mexican Aristocracy in the Context of Western Aristocracies.* Ann Arbor: University of Michigan Press.

1997   "Class and Ethnicity in Mexico: Somatic and Racial Considerations." *Ethnology* 36 (3): 227–238.

Nutini, Hugo G., and John M. Roberts

1993   *Bloodsucking Witchcraft: An Epistemological Study of Anthropomorphic Supernaturalism in Rural Tlaxcala.* Tucson: University of Arizona Press.

Nutini, Hugo G., with Douglas R. White

1977   "Community Variations and Network Structure in the Social Functions of *Compadrazgo* in Rural Tlaxcala, Mexico." *Ethnology* 16: 353–384.

Olavarría, Roberto

1945   *México en el tiempo: Fisonomía de una ciudad.* Mexico City: Litografía Moderna.

Ortega y Pérez Gallardo, Ricardo

1908   *Historia genealógica de las familias más antiguas de México.* Mexico City: A. Carranza Editores.

Ovando, Carlos de

1983   *Documentos misceláneos del Archivo Pérez de Salazar de Ovando.* N.p.

Packer, Charles

1975   "Male Transfer in Olive Baboons." *Nature* 255: 209–220.

Pareto, Vilfredo

1935   *The Mind and Society.* New York: Harcourt Brace.

1980   *Trattato di sociologia generale.* Milan: Edizioni di Comunitá.

Pérez de Salazar, Francisco

n.d.   *Documentos varios del Archivo de Don Francisco Pérez de Salazar.* N.p.

Perrot, Roy

1968   *The Aristocrats: A Portrait of Britain's Nobility and Their Way of Life Today.* New York: Macmillan.

Powis, Jonathan K.

1984   *Aristocracy.* New York: Basil Blackwell.

Quintana, Manuel

n.d.   *Colección de documentos genealógicos.* N.p.

Rábago, Daniel

n.d.   *Documentos inéditos sobre la familia Rábago.* N.p.

Radcliffe-Brown, Alfred Reginald

1933   *The Andaman Islanders.* Cambridge: Cambridge University Press.

1952   *Structure and Function in Primitive Society.* London: Oxford University Press.

1956   "Introduction." In *African Systems of Kinship and Marriage,* ed. A. R. Radcliffe-Brown and Daryll Forde. Oxford: Oxford University Press.

Ramírez, José F.

1949   *Noticias sacadas de un manuscrito intitulado Relaciones de todas las cosas que es en el Nuevo México desde el año 1538 hasta el de 1626.* Mexico City: Editorial Jus.

Redfield, Robert

1930   *Tepoztlan, a Mexican Village.* Chicago: University of Chicago Press.

Ridley, Matt

1996   *The Origin of Virtue.* London: Viking Press.

Roberts, John M.

1976   "Belief in the Evil Eye in World Perspective." In *The Evil Eye*, ed. Clarence Maloney. New York: Columbia University Press.

Roberts, John M., Chen Chiao, and Triloki N. Pandey

1975   "Meaningful God Sets from a Chinese Personal Pantheon and a Hindu Personal Pantheon." *Ethnology* 14 (2): 121–148.

Roberts, John M., and Garry E. Chick

1979   "Butler County Eight Ball: A Behavioral Space Analysis." In *Sports, Games and Play: Social and Psychological Viewpoints*, ed. Jeffrey H. Goldstein. Hillsdale, Ill.: Lawrence Erlbaum.

1987   "Human Views of Machines: Expression and Machine Shop Syncretism." In *Technology and Social Change*, ed. H. Russell Bernard and Perti Pelto. Prospect Heights, Ill.: Waveland Press.

Roberts, John M., and Thomas V. Golder

1970   "Navy and Polity: A 1963 Baseline." *Naval War College Review* 23: 30–41.

Roberts, John M., and Susan M. Nattrass

1980   "Women and Trapshooting: Competence and Expression in a Game of Physical Skill with Chance." In *Play and Culture*, ed. Helen B. Schwartman. West Point: Leisure Press.

Roberts, John M., and Brian Sutton-Smith

1962   "Child Training and Game Involvement." *Ethnology* (1) 2: 166–185.

Robichaux, David L.

1995   "Le mode de perpétuation des groupes de parenté: La residence et l'héritage a Tlaxcala (Mexique), suivi d'un modèle pour la Mesoamérique." Doctoral diss., University of Paris.

Romero de Terreros, Manuel

1956   *Antiguas haciendas de México*. Mexico City: Editorial Patria.

Romney, Kimbal A., S. C. Weller, and W. H. Bachelder

1986   "Cultural Consensus: A Theory of Culture and Informant Accuracy." *American Anthropologist* 88:313–338.

Russell, Bertrand

1945   *A History of Western Philosophy*. New York: Simon and Schuster.

Sahagún, Fray Bernardino de

1956   *Historia general de las cosas de la Nueva España*. 4 vols. Mexico City: Editorial Porrúa, S.A.

Schama, Simon

1989   *Citizens: A Chronicle of the French Revolution*. New York: Alfred A. Knopf.

Schneider, David M.

1980   *American Kinship: A Cultural Account*. Chicago: University of Chicago Press.

Slade, Doren L.

1990   *Making the World Safe for Existence: Celebration of the Saints among the Sierra Nahuat of Chignautla, Mexico*. Ann Arbor: University of Michigan Press.

Sodi Pallares, Ernesto
1968   *Casonas antiguas de la Ciudad de México*. Mexico City: La Prensa.
Spindler, George M., ed.
1980   *The Making of Psychological Anthropology*. Berkeley: University of California Press.
Sugiyama Lebra, Takie
1993   *Above the Clouds: Status Culture of the Modern Japanese Nobility*. Berkeley: University of California Press.
Tacitus
1948   *Tacitus on Britain and Germany*. London: Penguin.
Tannenbaum, Frank
1910   *Peace by Revolution: Mexico after 1910*. New York: Cambridge University Press.
Tovar y de Teresa, Guillermo
1990   *La ciudad de los palacios: Crónicas de un patrimonio perdido*. Mexico City: Imprenta de la Ciudad de México.
Trivers, Robert L.
1971   "The Evolution of Reciprocal Altruism." *Quarterly Review of Biology* 46: 35–57.
1985   *Social Evolution*. Menlo Park: Benjamin/Cummungs Publishing Co.
Turner, John K.
1914   *Barbarous Mexico*. Austin: University of Texas Press.
Vargas Martínez, Ubaldo
1971   *La Ciudad de México (1325–1960)*. Mexico City: Editorial Siglo Veintiuno.
Vasconcelos, José
1966   *La raza cósmica: Misión de la raza iberoamericana*. Mexico City: Molina Enrique.
Voget, Fred E.
1975   *A History of Ethnology*. New York: Holt, Rinehart, and Winston.
Warner, Arthur R.
1960   *English Genealogy*. Oxford: Oxford University Press.
Warner, W. Lloyd
1942   *The Social Life of a Modern Community*. New Haven: Yale University Press.
1957   *American Life: Dream and Reality*. Chicago: University of Chicago Press.
1959   *The Living and the Dead: A Study of the Symbolic Life of Americans*. New Haven: Yale University Press.
1960   *Social Class in America: A Manual of Procedures for the Measurement of Social Status*. New York: Harcourt Brace.
1961   *The Family of Gods: A Symbolic Study of Christian Life in America*. New Haven: Yale University Press.
1963   *Yankee City*. New Haven: Hartcourt Brace.
Weckmann, Luis
1984   *La herencia medieval de México*. 2 vols. Mexico City: El Colegio de México.

Whetten, Nathan L.

1972   "Factores históricos de la clase media en México." In *Las clases sociales en México*, ed. M. O. de Mendizábal. Mexico City: Editorial Nuestro Tiempo.

Wilson, Edward O.

1998   *Consilience: The Unity of Knowledge*. New York: Alfred A. Knopf.

Wright, Marie Robinson

1955   *Picturesque Mexico*. Philadelphia: Alsop Press.

Zamora Plowes, Leopoldo

1945   *Quince uñas y Casanova aventureros: Novela histórica picaresca*. Mexico City: Talleres Gráficos de la Nación.

Zilli, Alfredo

1980   *Historia de la Colonia Manuel Gonzales*. Jalapa, Veracruz: Imprente de la Universidad Veracruzana.

INDEX

12, 18, 30, 282–283, 312, 346n5, 346n8; configuration of social and ruling class in context of final renewal, 10–15; decline of, 7, 8, 9, 10–15, 17–18, 134–135, 300–302, 305–313; demise of aristocracy as ruling class from 1910 to 1934, 300–302; demographic composition and contextual definition of, 30–50; differential efficacy or expressive behavior, social mobility and class affiliation in terminal decline, 4–10; downward mobility of, 224–229, 280, 303–304; economic position and occupations and professions of, 16–17, 19, 35, 36, 42, 126, 153–160, 162, 225, 286, 287, 288–289, 299, 303–304; and education, 156–157, 160, 258; *embourgeoisement* of, 19, 73, 78, 117, 145, 151, 167, 280, 351; and entertainment and display, 21–22, 116, 117; evolution of, in twentieth century and its terminal position within *haute bourgeoisie*, 300–313; exclusivity and consciousness of kind among, 90–94, 100–109, 115–118; expressive acculturation of, with and without dominance, 4–10; expressive array of, 26–28; expressive ethnography of, 2–4, 9–10, 77–94, 320–322, 330, 338–339; fragmentation of, 42, 99–100, 235–236, 298–300; gestalt elite of, 296–297; goals of study of, 9–10; as government officials, 16, 160–163; group realignment and concentration in Mexico City, 32–37, 39, 95, 287–288, 298; and household, 20–21; impact of Mexican Revolution on, 5–6, 7, 12, 33–34, 158–159, 160, 185, 192, 286–287, 300–303, 311; Indian ancestry of, 56–60, 63–65; interaction, acceptance, and rejection between plutocrats and, 16–18, 19, 31–32, 40–42, 45, 65–69, 144, 158, 225, 226–227, 238, 296, 305–311; and kinship, 20; material culture of, 139–153, 163–167; and mutual perceptions

and self-image of superordinate and subordinate classes, 69–74; name recognition for, 37, 39, 40–41; negative reactions to, 18, 41, 144; network analysis of, 3; personal behavior and demeanor of, 19–20; phenotypical reality and ideal self-image of, 58–65; plutocratic predominance and aristocratic retreat from 1980 to 2000, 307–309; political participation of, 160–163, 244; position of, in context of *haute bourgeoisie*, 15–22; in provincial cities, 33–37, 39–40, 98, 99, 227, 294, 305; racial composition of, 51–58; relationship between political class and, 11, 16, 160–163; relationship between upper-middle class and, 31, 40–41, 65–69, 84–85, 296; and renewal of elites, 3–5, 8–15, 311, 353; residual social and expressive position of, as superordinate group, 309–313; self-identification and self-image of, 30–32, 38–40, 58–65, 83, 280–281; as social class, 11–12, 15, 17–18, 30–31, 42, 305; statistics on, 3, 11, 28, 31, 32–34, 37, 95, 112, 149–150, 226, 227, 298, 305; summary of themes and issues on, 318–319; symmetrical and asymmetrical transfer and incorporation between plutocrats and, 18–22; as term, 309–310; terminal aristocratic renaissance from 1935 to 1960, 302–305, 315; wealth of, 36, 109, 149–150, 153–154, 159–160, 225, 226, 227, 236–237, 260, 286–291, 305, 343n4; withdrawal of, and plutocratic ascendance from 1960 to 1980, 305–307. *See also* Catholicism; Kinship; Marriage; Stratification and internal organization; Urban living

Aristocracy in Western Europe, 2, 8–12, 18, 30, 82, 135, 168, 219–220, 225, 226, 282–283, 312, 346n8

Aristocratic-plutocratic acculturation, 9–10, 13, 78–79, 120, 145, 167–168, 225, 351

Aron, Raymond, 351, 354
Arts and crafts: in aristocrats' residences, 103, 104–109, 113, 229, 260; inheritance of, 260; and plutocrats, 152, 168; pre-Hispanic art, 103, 121; public display of, 120–121, 125, 244; religious art, 203
Augustine, Saint, 129
Automobiles, 151
Ayuda (economic help), 243–244, 251, 254–255

Bachelor parties, 180, 181, 348
BAE (Bureau of American Ethnology), 23
Baltzell, Digby, 351
Banco de Comercio de México, 120
Banco Nacional de México, 96, 120
Banker clubs, 120
Banking and finance, 14, 17, 19, 42–44, 46, 120–121, 153, 157–160, 287, 299, 303, 304
Baptism (sacrament), 224, 243, 244, 251, 273, 274, 275, 345n7
Barbers, 337–338
Batanes (fulling-mills), 112
Beauty. *See* Physical appearance and beauty
Bendición de casa (blessing of new home), 273
Bernal, Ignacio, 293
Birth control, 187, 253–254
Birthday celebrations, 123, 143, 146
Blacks, 51, 52
Blanco (white), 51, 53
Boas, Franz, 23
Body, culture of, 127–128
Body adornment, culture of, 127–128
Bolo (coins thrown at children after baptism), 275
Bourgeoisie, 351. *See also* Embourgeoisement
Bridal showers, 180–181, 348
Britain, 282–283, 284, 293, 346n6
Buena facha (to have a good appearance), 60, 347

Buffon, Comte de, 346n5
Bureau of American Ethnology (BAE), 23
Business. *See* Industry and commerce
Business administration, 156, 157, 158, 304

Caballeros (knights), 293
Caciques, 65
Caciquismo (strong attachment to leader as patron), 347
Calles, Plutarco Elías, 14, 43, 303
Candlemas, 183
Capellanía (chaplaincy), 185, 192–193, 280, 347
Caporal (cowboy hand), 289
Cárdenas, Lázaro, 6, 159, 272, 302, 303
Casa chica (house of concubine), 188, 344n3
Casa de los Azulejos, 96
Casa porfiriana (architectural style), 97, 98, 101, 132, 347
Cascos (mansions or manors), 154, 301–302, 348
Castas (racial classification system), 57, 58, 64, 348
Catering services, 123, 124, 142–143, 177
Catholicism: and abortion, 189–191, 344nn4–5; and annulment of marriages, 268; of aristocracy of Mexico, 21–22, 184–208; and baptism, 224, 243, 244, 251, 274, 275, 345n7; and birth control, 187, 253–254; Candlemas, 183; characteristics of Mexican Catholicism, 169–175; and clergy, 192–193, 208–210, 292; contravention of customary beliefs and practices for social reasons, 186–193; and convents, 292, 346n4; deviations from dogma and reconfiguration of the cult, 193–208; and devil, 198–199; devotional activities and cult of the saints, 210–217; and divorce, 187–189, 268–270; dogma of, 186, 198; Epiphany, 175, 181–184, 218–219, 344n2; in Europe, 169, 197–198, 201;

expressive analysis of, 217–220; and
heaven, 202–203; and hell, 201–202;
and Holy Trinity, 215–216; ideological and pragmatic characteristics of
aristocratic Catholicism, 21–22, 184–
208; and Jesus Christ, 210, 211, 215;
and kindred network, 243; liturgy,
clergy, and local congregation,
208–210; loss of respect for clergy,
192–193, 209; magical component
of Mexican Catholicism, 173–174,
204–207; and Mass attendance, 209,
216; and miracles, 206, 207; and
monolatry, 171, 195–198; and nannies, 211–212; and novenas, 213; and
nuclear family, 259; philosophical
transformation of, at expense of
orthodox beliefs, 207–208, 216–217;
and pilgrimages, 212–213; and plutocrats, 21–22; pragmatic nature of
Mexican Catholicism, 171–173, 184–
208; and processions, 212–213; and
purgatory, 203–204, 210, 211; realization of worship and organization
of the cult, 208–217; relationship
between aristocracy and church,
191–193, 209, 219–220; ritualism
and ceremonialism in, 146, 175–185,
194–195, 202–203, 207, 208, 217; and
rosary, 213, 243; and sacraments, 199,
209, 224, 273–276; and saints, 170,
171, 183, 195–196, 203, 210, 211, 213,
214–216; and sin and guilt, 199–201;
in Spain, 171, 192; teleology of, 201–
204; and theories on inception of
new soul, 344n6; in United States,
194; as validation of aristocratic
rank, 184–186, 219–220; and Virgin
Mary, 171, 183, 186, 195, 196, 203,
210–211, 213, 214–216; and wakes and
responsories, 213–214, 243; and wedding celebrations, 123–125, 145, 146,
175–181, 209–210, 273, 343–344n1;
and young people, 259
Catrines (city slickers; mestizos), 53, 348
Celibacy, 268, 270

Ceremonialism. *See* Ritualism and ceremonialism
Chaperoning, 256
Charrería (Mexican-style horseback
riding), 125, 280, 289, 291, 314, 348
Charro (cowboy), 289, 348
Chavero, Alfredo, 293
Chick, Garry, 328
Chihuahua, 33, 35, 153
Children and youth: custody of, fol-
lowing divorce, 270; employment
of young people before marriage,
257–258; enculturation of, 241, 255,
256, 264; friction over, in kindred
network, 240–241; number of, in
nuclear families, 252–254, 345n3;
parental authority over, 255–257; and
religion, 259; shift in kindred affiliation by, 232. *See also* Households;
Kinship
Chipilo, Puebla, 341n1
Christ. *See* Jesus Christ
Christianity. *See* Catholicism
Christmas, 182, 183, 242
Churches. *See* Catholicism; Protestantism
Ciudad Juárez, 46
Class: definition of, 351; and dynamics
of interaction of aristocracy with
plutocracy and upper-middle class,
65–69; expressive analysis of, 79–
94; and expressive arrays, 26–27;
interclass and interethnic relations
and reinterpretation of cultural and
racial perceptions, 74–76; and "juntos pero no revueltos" syndrome,
85–86, 127, 158; mutual perceptions
and self-image of superordinate and
subordinate classes, 69–74; relationship of ethnicity and, 51–76; in
United States, 85. *See also* Political
class; Ruling class; Social class (elite)
Clergy, 192–193, 208–210, 292. *See also*
Catholicism
Clothing: and clothing stores, 122–123;
and *embourgeoisement*, 280; men's

and acceptance, 39–40; genealogical connections between capital and
provincial aristocrats, 40; group
realignment and concentration in
Mexico City, 32–37, 39, 95, 287–288,
298; and haciendas previously owned
by families, 40; ideological self-
identification and structural reality,
30–32, 38–40; name recognition, 37,
39, 40–41; strength and demographic
configuration currently, 37–42
Demographic composition of plutocracy, 42–50
Descriptive ethnography, 24–25, 337
Despedidas de soltera (bridal showers),
180–181, 348
Despedidas de soltero (bachelor parties),
180, 181, 348
Devil, 198–199
Díaz, Porfirio, 14, 32, 33, 42, 96–97, 110,
115, 160, 223, 225–226, 285, 286, 288,
289, 300–301, 341n1, 350
Díaz del Castillo, Bernal, 342n1
Díaz Ordáz, Gustavo, 160
Dinner parties. *See* Cocktail and dinner
parties
Diplomatic service, 16, 160, 162
Discrimination, 63–64
Divorce, 187–189, 268–270
Dorantes de Carranza, Baltasar, 293
Downward mobility of aristocrats,
224–229, 280, 303–304
Dowry, 259, 267, 346n4
Dressing. *See* Clothing
Duendes (fairies), 206, 207
Dulia (honoring saints), 171, 195–196,
210, 215
Durango, 33, 35
Durkheim, Emile, 322–324, 330

Economy: agrarian enterprises and
land tenure, 153–155, 286, 287; aristocracy's economic position and
involvement in occupations and professions, 16–17, 19, 35, 36, 42, 126,
153–160, 162, 225, 286, 287, 288–289,

299, 303–304; banking and finance,
14, 17, 19, 42, 43, 44, 46, 120–121,
153, 157, 158–160, 287, 299, 303, 304;
economic interaction between aristocracy and plutocracy, 16–17, 19;
expressive analysis of, 163, 168; and
hacendados, 38, 41, 42; and manufacturing, 17, 19, 35, 43, 44, 153, 157, 159,
286, 299, 303; and mining, 14, 38, 225,
286, 288, 289; and multinationals,
308; plutocrats' commercial interests, 42, 43, 44, 225, 226–227. *See also*
specific commercial interests
Education: of aristocrats, 156–157, 160,
258; continuing education, 128, 137;
of *haute bourgeoisie*, 157; of middle
class, 41, 46–47; of plutocrats, 46–
47; of upper-middle class, 46–47, 73;
of women, 157
Ego-focus kinship, 231
Elite. *See* Social class (elite)
Embourgeoisement: compared with passage from Indian to mestizo status,
73; definition of, 226, 351; and downward mobility of aristocrats, 280; of
marriage, 267; and material culture,
145, 151; of nuclear family, 257, 258;
and political participation, 167; and
realignment of aristocrats' inclusive
array, 19, 78; and terminal expression, 316; and urban environment,
117–118; of Western aristocracies, 8,
117–118, 225
Employment. *See* Economy
Emulation, 327
Encomenderos (Spanish or Creole
grantees of Indian labor), 5, 37, 38,
56, 57, 224, 283, 286, 297, 348
Encomienda (Indians granted as tributaries to Spaniards or Creoles), 224,
348
Encomienda system, 5, 8, 184, 224, 354
Endogamy, 31, 39, 57, 222, 262–264, 279,
309, 341n1. *See also* Marriage
Endogenous ethnography, 22–23, 25
Engineering, 17, 46, 156, 157, 304

England. *See* Britain

Entertainment and display, 21–22, 116, 117, 118, 121–122, 125–127, 280. *See also* social events, such as Cocktail and dinner parties

Epigenesis, 324, 329

Epiphany, 175, 181–184, 218–219, 344n2

Epipsychological rules, 39–330, 324–325

Equestrian clubs, 119–120

Equitation and equitation clubs, 119–120, 125, 152, 280

Equites (knights), 73, 348

Escuela Médico-Militar, 157

Espanto (fright), 206

Ethnicity and race: cultural whitening syndrome, 66, 84, 87–89; and discrimination, 63–64; and dynamics of interaction of aristocracy with plutocracy and upper-middle class, 65–69; expressive analysis of, 79–94; Indian ancestry of aristocracy, 56–60, 63–65; interclass and interethnic relations and reinterpretation of cultural and racial perceptions, 74–76; and miscegenation in colonial Mexico, 52–53; mutual perceptions and self-image of superordinate and subordinate classes, 69–74; phenotypical reality and ideal self-image of aristocracy, 58–65; and physical appearance and beauty, 55, 58–65, 82, 84; of plutocrats, 66–67; racial categories, 51–53, 55–57, 74–75; racial composition of aristocracy and its ideational and physical underpinnings, 51–58; relationship of class and, 51–76; statistics on, 56–57; of upper-middle class, 67; and upward mobility, 54, 63, 66–69

Ethnography: analytical (or in-depth) ethnography, 25, 336, 337; definition and development of, 22–25; descriptive ethnography, 24–25, 337; endogenous ethnography, 22–23, 25; exogenous ethnography, 22–23, 25; expressive analysis of race, class, and

ethnicity, 79–94; interrelationship of standard and expressive ethnography, 330–334; methodological considerations for, 77–79; "salvage ethnography," 23; sources of qualitative and quantitative data for, 28–29, 335; systematic ethnography, 22, 23; urban ethnography compared with traditional anthropological ethnography, 334–339. *See also* Expressive ethnography

Etiquette and protocol, 146–148, 240

Europeans: and aristocratic plutocratic acculturation, 168; and Catholicism, 169, 197–198, 201; Italian immigrants to Mexico, 341n1; and kinship, 221; marriage between aristocrats and foreigners of European extraction, 263; and nobility, 284; phenotypic traits of, 54–55, 58–65, 66–69; plutocracies in Western Europe, 313; as term, 342n1; and wedding celebrations, 176, 179; Western European aristocracies, 2, 8–12, 18, 30, 82, 135, 168, 225, 226, 282–283, 312, 346n5, 346n8

Europeo (European), 51

Evans-Pritchard, E. E., 23

Exclusive array of aristocracy, 78, 81–85

Exclusivity and consciousness of kind, 90–94, 100–109, 115–122, 118, 119

Exocentric kindred. *See* Kindred network

Exogamy, 238–239, 256, 257, 265–266, 279, 309. *See also* Marriage

Exogenous ethnography, 22–23, 25

Expression (expressive culture): aristocratic realization of expression in declining and changing urban context, 132–138; as changing aspect of culture, 219; and culture change, 327–329; definition of, 25–26, 129–132, 351; and encompassing domains of race, class, and ethnicity, 79–94; and epipsychological rules, 324–325; forms of, 28, 130, 314, 315–317, 320–322; individual (psychological) and collective (social) entailments of expressive behavior, 322–330; and kinship, 278–281; and material culture, 163–167; methodological considerations for, 77–79, 129–132; operationalization of expressive behavior, 320–322; and religion, 217–220; and stratification and internal organization, 313–317; and study of Mexican aristocracy, 2–4, 77–94, 318–322; and urban living, 129–138

Expressive acculturation: definition of, 352; and etiquette, 148; and interaction, acceptance, and rejection between aristocrats and plutocrats, 16–18; marriage between aristocrats and plutocrats, 18–19, 20; of Mexican aristocracy with and without dominance, 4–10; of plutocrats, 18–22, 47–49, 78; process of, 15

Expressive array, 9–10, 26–28, 78–79, 81–94, 168, 352

Expressive behavior: as contextual, 27; definition of, 25–26, 352; individual (psychological) and collective (social) entailments of, 322–330; operationalization of, 320–322; types of, 28, 130, 314–317, 320–322

Expressive domains: definition of, 27–28, 352; marriage between aristocrats and plutocrats, 18–19; of phenotypic considerations, 82; of race, class, and ethnicity, 79–94

Expressive ethnography: as case of urban anthropology, 330; definition of, 25–28; individual (psychological) and collective (social) entailments of expressive behavior, 322–330; interrelationship of standard ethnography and, 330–334; of kinship, 278–281; of material culture, 163–167; methodological considerations for, 77–79, 129–132; of Mexican aristocracy, 2–4, 9–10, 77–94, 318–322, 330, 338–339; operationalization of expressive behavior, 320–322; of race, class,

and ethnicity, 79–94; of religion, 217–220; sources of qualitative and quantitative data for, 28–29, 335; of stratification and internal organization of aristocracy, 313–317; urban ethnography compared with traditional anthropological ethnography, 334–339; of urban living, 129–138

Expressive manipulation, 352–353

Expressive vicariousness, 137–138

Extended family (nonresidential), 246–252

Familias venidas a menos (downwardly mobile families), 227–228, 303–304, 348

Families. *See* Kinship; Marriage

Family planning. *See* Birth control

Farming and ranching, 17, 153–155

Fashion. *See* Clothing

Fashion shows, 126

Ferdinand and Isabella, 220

Feudalism, 343n6, 353–354

Fiesta de guardar (canonical holiday in Catholic annual calendar), 183

Finance. *See* Banking and finance

Firearms, 51, 128

First communion, 273, 274, 276

Food: and catering services, 123, 124, 142–143; distinction between festive and daily consumption of food and drink, 143–144; for Epiphany, 183–184, 350; after first communion, 276; and food stores, 123; hot and cold qualities of, 206; Mexican *haute cuisine*, 140–143, 164, 165, 342n1; at wakes, 213–214; for wedding celebrations, 124, 177–178

Food stores, 123

Foreign plutocrats, 14, 43, 44–45, 47, 49, 285

Fox, Robin, 231

Fragmentation of aristocracy, 42, 99–100, 235–236, 298–300

French Intervention, 60, 96, 102, 285, 288, 289, 290, 342n1

French Revolution, 8, 10, 12, 164, 321, 325
Funeral homes, 213, 214
Furniture, 101-102, 105-109, 113, 260

Galton, Sir Francis, 346n5
Gamio, Manuel, 23
García Icazbalceta, Joaquín, 293
Geertz, Clifford, 25
Genealogical name group (GNG), 223
Gente blanca (white people), 348
Gente decente (decent or proper people), 348
Gente de razón (Mestizos; urbanites; non-Indians), 349
Gente güera (light-skinned people; white people), 61, 349
Gente propias (proper people; upper-middle-class families), 73, 349
Gestalt elite, 296-297. See also Aristocracy in Mexico
Ghosts, 206, 207
Gift giving, 146, 181, 183, 243
GNG (genealogical name group), 223
Golf, 125
Gómez de Cervantes, Gonzalo, 293
Gómez de Cervantes family, 96
Goodenough, Ward, 231
Government officials, 160-163
Graduación (graduation from primary or secondary school), 273
Gravitas, 144
Great Britain. See Britain
Greeks, 82, 109-110
Guadalajara, 33, 36, 37, 46, 96, 153, 294, 335
Guanajuato, 33, 96
Güeros (light-skinned people), 53, 89, 349
Guilt and sin, 199-201

Hacendado cities, 33-35, 38
Hacendados (latifundia owners): as aristocrats, 5, 35-36, 38, 91, 289; and compadrazgo (ritual kinship), 271-272; definition of, 349; descendants of, 297; economic interests of, 38, 41, 42, 289; and Epiphany, 182; and horse culture, 289; land of, 154, 159, 301, 303; memory and awareness of, by middle and lower classes, 41, 114; and Mexican Revolution, 72, 301; migration to Mexico City by, 304; peons taking names of, 224; and religion, 182, 192, 197, 208-209, 212, 213; and Spanish political class in colonial period, 56; and witchcraft and sorcery, 197

Haciendas (latifundias): and country retreats, 110, 111, 113-114, 132, 154-155, 302; definition of, 349; demise of, 33-34, 212; and extended families, 262; after Mexican Revolution, 301-302; name of formerly owned hacienda for aristocratic recognition, 40; nannies from, 211-212; religious practices on, 197, 208-209, 212, 213; sale of, as pequeña propiedad (parcel of land less than 100 hectares), 158-159; size of, 153. See also Hacendados (latifundia owners); Hacienda system

Hacienda system, 5, 8, 33-34, 115, 116, 153, 155, 184, 197, 212, 224, 272, 288, 301-302, 304

Haute bourgeoisie (rich and powerful plutocrats): composition of, 12-15; and culture of body and body adornment, 127-128; definition of, 305, 349, 353; and democratic state, 74; economic interaction between aristocrats and, 16-17, 19; education of, 157; and entertainment and display, 21-22, 117; evolution of aristocracy in twentieth century and its terminal position within, 300-313; and expressive acculturation, 15, 78-79; and household, 21; interaction, acceptance, and rejection between aristocrats and, 16-18, 19, 31-32, 40-42, 45, 65-69; and kinship, 20; marriage between aristocrats and, 17, 18-19, 20; and material culture, 149-153; and personal behavior and demeanor, 19-20; phenotypes of, 66–67; position of aristocracy in context of, 15–22, 225; symmetrical and asymmetrical transfer and incorporation between aristocrats and, 18–22; and traveling abroad, 128; and urban living from 1960 to 1995, 117–122. *See also* Plutocracy

Haute cuisine, 140–143, 164, 165, 342n1. *See also* Food

Heaven, 202–203

Heirlooms, 101–109, 133–134, 179–180, 229, 254, 260, 261, 267, 276

Hell, 201–202

Heredity. *See* Lineage and heredity

Hermandades (brotherhoods), 212

Herodotus, 22, 23

Hidalgos (members of lower nobility or gentry), 5, 220, 349

Hidalgos a fuero de España (members of lower nobility according to Spanish law), 293, 349

Hidalguía (lower, lesser, on nontitled nobility), 5, 39, 170, 349

Hijas de familia (family wards), 257

Holy Trinity, 215–216

Homes. *See* Residences

Honeymoon, 267

Hong Kong, 171

Horses and horse culture, 119–120, 125, 152, 280, 289, 314

Households: ancestral household and nonresidential extended family, 248, 249–250; and aristocracy in Mexico generally, 20–21; colors for household decoration, 107, 136; and country retreats, 98, 109–114, 132, 151, 154–155, 242, 243, 260, 262, 302, 342n2; decoration and arrangement of public domain of, 97, 101–103, 105–109, 136, 342n1; furniture of, 101–102, 105–109, 113, 260; heirlooms in, 101–109, 133–134, 179–180, 229, 254, 260, 261, 267, 276; of Japan, 101; and kindred networks, 235–236, 244–246; as last bastion of aristocratic exclusivity and self-identity, 100–109; of pluto-

crats, 21, 119, 151; pre-Hispanic art in, 103; as shrine to ancestors, 100–105, 132–133. *See also* Kinship; Marriage; Nuclear family household

Housing. *See* Residences

Hunting, 128, 151, 152, 153

Icaza, Francisco, 293

Illegitimacy, 344n4

Inclusive array of aristocracy, 78–79, 85–94

Income. *See* Wealth

La indiada (deprecatory term for Mexicans), 70, 349

Indians: aristocrats' attitude toward, 71–72; aristocrats' Indian ancestry, 56–60, 63–65; Catholicism of, 171–172, 174, 184, 223–224; community structure of, 92–93; and *compadrazgo* (ritual kinship), 271; conversion of, to Catholicism, 184, 223–224; and cultural whitening syndrome, 89; culture of, 54, 71–72; and *encomienda* system, 5, 8, 184, 224, 354; on hell, 201; and interclass and interethnic relations, 76; and kinship, 246; marriage between Spanish and, in colonial period, 57–58, 64–65, 263; middle-class attitudes toward, 72; naming of, by missionaries, 223–224; passage of, to mestizo status, 73, 76; phenotypic traits of, 59–60, 63–65, 69–74, 89; plutocrats' knowledge of culture of, 72; as racial category, 51, 52, 74, 75; and ritualism and ceremonialism, 144–145, 165–166; upper-middle-class attitudes toward, 72; and witchcraft and sorcery, 197

Indígenas, 89

Indio (Indian), 51, 52

Inditos, 89

Industrial Revolution, 8

Industry and commerce, 14, 17, 35, 42, 43, 44, 288, 299, 303, 304

Inherent (or natural) expression, 28, 130, 314, 320

Living name group (LNG), 223
LNG (living name group), 223
Lower classes: aristocrats' attitude toward, 71–72; attitude toward aristocracy by, 70; Catholicism of, 173–174; and cultural whitening syndrome, 89; on hell, 201–202. *See also* Working class

Machines and electronic implements, 151–152, 167–168
Madrina (godmother), 271, 274–275, 349
Magical supernaturalism, 173–174, 204–207
Mal aire (evil air), 206
Mal de ojo (evil eye), 206
Malinowski, Bronislaw, 23
Mandas (promises made to God, Virgins, or saints), 215
Mansions. *See* Residences
Manuel González, Veracruz, 341n1
Manufacturing, 17, 19, 35, 43, 44, 153, 157, 159, 286, 299, 303
Marianism. *See* Virgin Mary
Marriage: age of, 254, 264; annulment of, 268; between aristocrats and plutocrats, 17, 18–19, 20, 92, 227, 237–240, 256, 257, 265–266, 279, 309; arranged marriages and matchmaking, 254, 265, 345n6; in colonial period, 52, 57–58; of consanguines or affines, 264; and courtship, 266, 350; and divorce, 187–189, 268–270; and dowry, 259, 267, 346n4; and endogamy, 31, 39, 57–58, 222, 262–264, 279, 309; of European colonists in Mexico in 1890s, 341n1; and exogamy, 238–240, 256, 257, 265–266, 279, 309; factors affecting initiation of, 264–265; first-cousin marriage, 262; between foreigners of European extraction and aristocrats, 263; and honeymoon, 267; ideal form of, among partners of equal social standing, 263–264; between Indian nobles and Spanish, 57–58, 64–65, 263; of Italian

immigrants, 341n1; and kinship system, 222, 231, 234, 241, 262–270; and nonresidential extended family, 247–248; and prenuptial agreement, 270, 350; of provincial aristocrats, 35, 36, 40; between provincial and capital aristocrats, 36, 40; in Roman society, 176, 218, 279, 343n6, 348; and separation, 268–270; of U.S. plutocrats and European aristocrats, 168; virginity before, 267; and wedding celebrations, 123–125, 145, 146, 147, 175–181, 209–210, 218, 242, 244, 273, 274, 276–277, 279, 343–344n1
Martínez del Río, Pablo, 293
Material culture: clothing, 122–123, 127–128, 148; of different classes generally, 139; distinction between festive and daily consumption of food and drink, 143–144; distinctive traditional and idiosyncratic character of aristocratic material array, 140–149; expressive analysis of, 163–167; machines and electronic implements, 151–152, 167–168; Mexican *haute cuisine*, 140–143, 164, 165, 342n1; protocol and etiquette, 146–148; reciprocity and exchange, 145–146, 181, 243; ritualism and ceremonialism, 144–145, 165–166, 175–185, 194–195, 202–203, 207, 208, 217, 343n6; shared and diminished material culture of aristocrats and plutocratic dominance, 149–153, 165, 167–168; sports, 121, 125, 148, 152, 153; travel, 128, 148; wedding celebrations, 123–125, 145, 146, 147, 175–181, 209–210, 242, 244, 343–344n1
Maximilian, 285, 288, 289
Mayorazgo (entailed property; primogeniture), 81, 225, 236, 251, 259–262, 278–279, 349
Mayordomía (sponsorship of religious fiesta), 170, 212, 335, 349
Media annata (taxes), 284
Medicine, 17, 156, 157, 159, 293, 304

The Mexican Aristocracy

Men: beauty standards for, 62; and
Catholicism, 196; and child custody
following divorce, 270; clothing
and personal adornment for, 128;
division of labor in nuclear family
households, 255, 258; employment
of young men before marriage,
257–258; inheritance of, 259–262;
punctiliousness of, 144; religious
practices of, 211, 215–216. *See also*
Aristocracy in Mexico; Economy;
Households; Kinship; Marriage;
Plutocracy
Mérida, 33, 35
Mestizos: aristocratic pride in mestizo
ancestry, 64–65; Catholicism of,
173, 174; and class membership, 75–
76; community structure of, 92–93;
and *compadrazgo* (ritual kinship), 271;
Creoles as, 11, 56, 74; and cultural
whitening syndrome, 89; definition
of, as racial category, 51, 52–53, 74,
75, 349; on hell, 201; and kinship,
246; names of, 224; passage from
Indian to mestizo status, 73, 76;
peasants as, 76; phenotypes of, 60,
67, 69–74, 89; as political class, 11,
12; statistics on, 56; upper-middle
class as, 67
Methodological individualism, 323
Metiche (meddlesome people), 349
Mexican aristocracy. *See* Aristocracy in
Mexico
Mexican Independence, 11, 84, 223, 225,
239, 285, 288, 289
Mexican Revolution (1910), 5–7, 11–
13, 32–34, 42–43, 54, 72, 102, 115,
158–160, 185, 192, 218, 224, 225, 278,
286–287, 300–303, 311
Mexico City: *colonias* of, 96–99, 235,
236, 298–299, 338; concentration of
aristocracy in, 32–37, 39, 95, 235–236,
287–288, 298; directory of prominent families of, 90–91; dispersion of
aristocrats in, 235–236, 298, 335; kindred networks in, 235–236; migration

of folk people to, 345n4; migration of plutocrats to, 47; migration
of provincial aristocrats to, 34–37,
39, 98, 99, 235, 247, 294, 302–304,
315; plutocracy in, 47, 49–50, 306;
population of, 116, 304, 306, 337; in
Porfirian period, 115; residences of
aristocrats in, 95–100, 287, 298–299;
tailors and barbers in, 337–338; *zócalo*
of, 95, 96, 350. *See also* Urban living
Middle Ages, 73, 219–220, 223, 342n2,
343n6
Middle class: and art exhibits, 121; attitudes toward aristocracy by, 41, 70,
116–117; Catholicism of, 173, 174; and
compadrazgo (ritual kinship), 271; and
cultural whitening syndrome, 88–89;
education of, 41; exclusivity and consciousness of kind among, 93; and
food, 141; and knowledge of Indian
culture, 72; origin of plutocrats in,
46; recognition of social status by,
31; statistics on, 174; workplace interaction between aristocrats and, 158.
See also Upper-middle class
Migration: of folk people to Mexico
City, 345n4; of foreign entrepre-
neurs to Mexico, 14, 44–45; of
plutocrats to Mexico City, 47; of
provincial aristocrats to Mexico
City, 34–37, 39, 98, 99, 235, 247, 294,
302–304, 315
Military, 11, 292–293, 313
Mining, 14, 38, 225, 286, 288, 289
Miracles, 206, 207
Miscegenation, 52–53
Mobility. *See* Downward mobility;
Upward mobility
Monboddo, Lord, 346n5
Monolatry, 171, 195–198
Monotheism, 171
El Monte de Piedad (National Pawn
Shop), 288, 290, 291
Monterrey, 46
Montesquieu, Baron de, 346n5
Morelia, 33

Morgan, Lewis Henry, 23
Mulato (white and black heritage), 51
Multinationals, 308
Muñeco (small hidden figure in Epiphany cake), 183
Murdock, George Peter, 24
Museo de la Ciudad de México, 96
Museums, 118, 120–121, 125, 158
Music, 125, 127, 151

NAFTA, 161
Nagel, Ernest, 323
Name groups: definition, origins, and strengths of, 222–224, 279–280; downward mobility and aristocratic identity, 224–229; endogenous and exogenous implication of, 229–230; and kindred networks, 234
Name recognition for aristocracy, 37, 39, 40–41
Nannies, 211–212
La naquiza (deprecatory term for Mexicans), 70, 71, 349–350
National Archives, 158
National Autonomous University of Mexico, 46, 160
National Institute of Anthropology and History, 158
National Museum of Anthropology, 158
National Museum of Fine Arts, 158
Natural (or inherent) expression, 28, 130, 314, 320
Negro (black), 51, 52
Network analysis, 3
New Spain. *See* Colonial period
Nightclubbing, 126
Nobility, titles of, 284–286, 288, 289, 313, 345–346n2
Nonresidential extended family: and ancestral household, 248, 249–250; definition, structural elements, and composition of, 246–250; functions and household strength of, 250–252; and marriage, 247–248; and patrilineal bias, 249–250; *troncal* pattern of, 248; types of, 248–249. *See also* Kinship

North American Free Trade Agreement (NAFTA), 161
Notarías (notary public offices), 156
Notaries public, 156, 157
Nouveaux riches (*los nuevos ricos*), 5, 45, 48, 108, 149
Novenas, 213
Noviazgo (courtship), 266, 350
Nuclear family household: age of marriage, 254, 264; authority, social control, and changing perspective of, 254–262; constitution and numerical strength of, 252–254; division of labor in, 255, 258; finances of, 254–255, 257–258; inheritance and lingering effects of *mayorazgo*, 225, 236, 259–262, 278–279; number of children in, 252–254, 345n3; parental control over children and young people in, 255–257; religious functions of, 259; social functions of, 257–259. *See also* Households; Kinship; Marriage
Nueva Italia, Michoacán, 341n1

Oaxaca, 33, 35, 96, 153
Obras pías (endowed charities), 280, 350
Obregón, Alvaro, 303
Oidor (royal justice), 292
Oil industry, 13, 14, 43
Orizaba, 335, 338

Padrinazgo (ritual sponsorship, entailing no permanent duties and obligations), 273–277, 345n7, 350
Padrinos (godfathers, godparents), 86, 224, 271, 273–277, 345n7, 350
Padrinos de casamiento (wedding godparents), 179
Pajes de honor (pages of honor at weddings), 179
El Palacio de Iturbide, 95–96
Palliative expression, 28, 314, 315–317, 321
PAN (Partido de Acción Nacional), 161, 308
Parada de cruz (erection of cross), 273

ruling class, 44–45, 305–307; and self-identification of aristocracy, 31–32; as social class, 15, 308, 312–313; and sports, 125, 148, 152, 153; statistics on, 44, 49–50; summary of themes and issues on, 318–319; symmetrical and asymmetrical transfer and incorporation between aristocrats and plutocrats, 18–22; in United States, 168, 313; upper-middle-class origins of, 47, 49; upwardly mobile plutocrats, 48–49, 306–309; and urban living from 1960 to 1995, 117–122; wealth of, 43, 44–49, 87, 116, 145, 149–150, 226–227, 285, 286, 308. *See also Haute bourgeoisie* (rich and powerful plutocrats); Ruling class

Political class, 9–16, 40–41, 43–44, 158–159, 160–163, 305–306, 308, 353

Political participation of aristocracy, 160–163, 244

Polo, 120, 125, 148, 152, 280, 289

Pompas fúnebres (funeral homes), 213, 214

Poor. *See* Poverty

Porfiriato, 96–97, 110, 115, 125, 160, 223, 225–226, 261, 285, 286, 289, 297, 298, 300–301, 350. *See also* Díaz, Porfirio

Postal system, 43

Poverty: and aristocratic-plutocratic marriage, 239; and *compadrazgo* (ritual kinship), 271, 277; and cultural whitening syndrome, 89; downward mobility of aristocrats, 224–229, 303–304; within kinship networks, 236–237, 239

Powell, John Wesley, 23

Prenuptial agreement, 270, 350

PRI (Partido Revolucionario Institucional), 12, 13, 14, 161, 162, 308

Primera piedra (setting foundations of house), 273

Primogeniture (*mayorazgo*), 81, 225, 236, 251, 259–262, 278–279, 349

Primos, primas (male and female cousins), 345n5

Processions, 212–213

Professions and scholarship, 14, 17, 35, 155–158, 162, 293, 299, 303, 304, 346n5

Protestantism, 199, 201–202

Protocol and etiquette, 146–148, 240

Provincial aristocracy, 33–37, 39–40, 98, 99, 227, 235, 247, 294, 302–305, 315

Public administration, 157–158, 160–163

Puebla, 33, 35, 36, 37, 46, 96, 291, 315, 335, 337, 338, 344n5

Pulque, 154

Purgatory, 203–204, 210, 211

Quéretaro, 33, 96

Race. *See* Ethnicity and race

Radcliffe-Brown, Alfred Reginald, 23, 24

Railroads, 13, 43

Ramírez, José, 293

Ranching. *See* Farming and ranching

Ranks of aristocracy, 184–186, 219–220, 282–297, 313–314

Raza cósmica ("cosmic race" of Indian-mestizo society), 350

Raza de bronce ("race of bronze" of Indian-mestizo society), 350

Reciprocity and exchange, 145–146, 181, 243

Reconquest, 184

Redfield, Robert, 23

Reforma Laws (1857), 12

Regidor (councilman, alderman), 292

Religion. *See* Catholicism; Protestantism

Renewal of elites, 3–5, 8–15, 38, 311, 353

Residences: apartments as, 99; architecture of, 97, 98–99, 347; colors for household decoration, 107, 136; country retreats, 98, 109–114, 132, 151, 154–155, 242, 243, 260, 262, 302, 342n2; decoration and arrangement of household public domain, 97, 101–103, 105–109, 136, 342n1; of European aristocrats, 342n2; furniture of, 101–102, 105–109, 113, 260; heirlooms in, 101–109, 133–134, 179–180, 229, 254,

260, 261, 267, 276; household as last bastion of aristocratic exclusivity and self-identity, 100–109; households as shrine to ancestors, 100–105, 132–133; of plutocrats, 21, 119, 151; pre-Hispanic art in, 103; prerevolutionary residential patterns and changes from 1910 to 1990, 95–100, 132, 287–288

Restaurants, 141, 177

Retail businesses, 122–123, 125–128, 159

Ritualism and ceremonialism, 144–145, 146, 165–166, 175–185, 194–195, 202–203, 207, 208, 217, 271, 343n6. *See also* specific ceremonies, such as Wedding celebrations

Roberts, John, 129, 132–133, 218–219, 321, 326, 328

Robichaux, David, 246, 252

Roman society, 73, 109–110, 176, 218, 221, 279, 343n6, 348

Rosaries, 213, 243

Rosca (cake eaten for Epiphany), 183, 184, 350

Ruling class: configuration of social and ruling class in context of final renewal, 10–15; definition of, 353; demographic configuration of plutocracy today, 42–50; interaction, acceptance, and rejection between aristocrats and, 16–18, 19, 31–32, 40–42, 45, 65–69; plutocracy in Mexico as, 44–45, 305–309; position of aristocracy in context of, 15–22; relationship between political class and, 14–15, 16, 43–44, 308; symmetrical and asymmetrical transfer and incorporation between aristocrats and, 18–22; and symmetrical social acculturation, 344n1; and Western aristocracies, 10. *See also* Plutocracy

Sacraments, 199, 209, 224, 273–276

Sahagún, Bernardino de, 22, 23

Saints, 170, 171, 183, 195–196, 203, 210, 211, 213, 214–216. *See also* Catholicism

Salinas de Gortari, Carlos, 160, 161

Salon México, 127

"Salvage ethnography," 23

San Juanico Ixtacuistla, 336

San Luis Potosí, 33

San Mateo de Valparaiso, marquesses of, 95–96

Santiago de Calimaya, counts of, 96

Santos (name days), 114, 275, 350

Scapular, 204

Scholarship. *See* Professions and scholarship

Schoolcraft, Henry, 23

Seances, 207

Seigneurialism, 5, 6, 7, 8, 39, 342n2, 353–354

Self-identification and self-image of aristocracy, 30–32, 38–40, 58–65, 83, 280–281

Separación de bienes (prenuptial agreement), 270, 350

Shopping, 122–123, 125–126

Sicily, 171, 197, 346n6

Sin and guilt, 199–201

Slaves, 52

Slumming, 126–127, 136–137

Social class (elite): configuration of social and ruling class in context of final renewal, 10–15; definition of, 354; exclusive array of, 78; Mexican aristocracy as, 11–12, 15, 17–18, 30–31, 42, 305; plutocracy as, 15, 308, 312–313; and Western aristocracies, 10

Social function of kinship, 242–243, 257–259. *See also* specific social functions, such as Wedding celebrations

Social mobility. *See* Downward mobility; Upward mobility

Social organization. *See* Kinship; Stratification and internal organization

Social stratification. *See* Stratification and internal organization

Sociedades anónimas (corporations), 159

Sorcery. *See* Witchcraft and sorcery

Spain: aristocracy in, 4, 220, 221;

Catholicism in, 171, 192; kinship system of, 345n5; nobiliary system of, 284; and *peninsulares*, 11, 55–57, 284, 288, 292, 350
Spanish Conquest, 52, 65, 81, 83, 220
Sports, 121, 125, 148, 152, 153, 280
Stores, 122–123, 125–126, 159
Stratification and internal organization: antiquity of lineage, 282–286, 288–296, 313; aristocracy's residual social and expressive position as superordinate group, 309–313; aristocratic withdrawal and plutocratic ascendance from 1960 to 1980, 305–307; constitution of functional, operational segments in aristocratic life today, 297–300; demise of aristocracy as ruling class from 1910 to 1934, 300–302; evolution of aristocracy in twentieth century and its terminal position within *haute bourgeoisie*, 300–313; expressive analysis of, 313–317; and illustrious ancestors, 291–294; and intellectual achievement, 293; plutocratic predominance and aristocratic retreat from 1980 to 2000, 307–309; ranking of aristocracy today, 282–297, 313–314; structural-expressive stratification, 9, 354; terminal aristocratic renaissance from 1935 to 1960, 302–305, 315; titles of nobility, 284–286, 288, 289, 313, 345–346n2; wealth of aristocrats, 286–291
Structural-expressive stratification, 9, 354
Superordinate class. *See* Aristocracy in Mexico; Plutocracy; Upper-middle class
Supreme Court of Mexico, 160
Sutton-Smith, Brian, 129, 132–133, 218–219, 321, 326
Systematic ethnography, 22, 23

Tacitus, 22
Tailors, 337–338

Tampico, 33, 35
Tecuhtli (member of upper nobility), 57, 65, 350
Teleology of Mexican Catholicism, 201–204
Terminal expression, 28, 130, 314, 315–316, 321
Terminal expressive exclusivity, 115–118, 354
Testigos (witnesses at weddings), 179, 276–277
Theaters, 118, 125
Titles of nobility, 284–286, 288, 289, 313, 345–346n1
Tlatoani (member of kingly class), 57, 65
Tlaxcala, 314, 316, 333, 334, 336, 337–338
Travel, 128, 148
Troncal extended family, 248

United States: Catholicism in, 194; class and upward mobility in, 85; cousins in kinship system of, 345n5; divorce in, 270; fundamentalism in, 199, 202; honeymoons in, 267; plutocracy in, 168, 313; teenagers in, 328; urban ethnography in, 338
Universidad Anahuac, 156–157
Universidad Iberoamericana, 156
Universidad Nacional Autónoma de México, 156
Upper-middle class: and business ownership, 126; and *compadrazgo* (ritual kinship), 271; and culture of body and body adornment, 127–128; definition of, 73, 354–355; and divorce, 188; education of, 73; and *familias venidas a menos* (downwardly mobile families), 227–228; and food and drink, 141, 143–144; and gift giving, 181; and knowledge of Indian culture, 72; lineage and heredity of, 84–85; and mutual perceptions and self-image of superordinate and subordinate classes, 69–74; phenotypes of, 67; plutocrats as, 47, 49;

relationship between aristocracy
and, 31, 40–41, 65–69, 84–85, 144,
296; and sports, 125; wealth of, 73,
118. *See also* Middle class; Plutocracy
Upward mobility: and cultural whitening syndrome, 66, 84, 87–89; and
ethnicity, 54, 63, 66–69; and expressive vicariousness, 138; of plutocrats,
48–49, 306–309; in United States,
85
Urban anthropology, 330
Urban ethnography, 334–339
Urban living: aristocratic realization of
expression in declining and changing urban context, 132–138; and
clubs, 119–120; and country retreats,
98, 109–114, 132, 151, 154–155, 242,
243, 260, 262, 302, 342n2; expressive analysis of, 129–138; expressive
value of material establishments
of, 122–129; household as last bastion of aristocratic exclusivity and
self-identity, 100–109, 342n1; plutocratic, *haute bourgeois* exclusive urban
environment from 1960 to 1995, 117–
122; prerevolutionary residential
patterns and changes from 1910 to
1990, 95–100, 342n1; social and material adaptation to, with restricted
economic means, 115–129; terminal
expressive exclusivity of aristocratic
urban environment from 1910 to
1960, 115–118

Valle de Orizaba, counts of, 96
Velorio (wake), 350
Veracruz, 338
Vicarious attraction, 137–138
Vicarious expression, 28, 321–322
Vicariousness, 326–327
Vicarious perception, 137–138
Virginity, 267
Virgin Mary, 171, 183, 186, 195, 196,
203, 210–211, 213, 214–216. *See also*
Catholicism

Wages of Conquest (Nutini), vii, viii, 1, 77,
300, 311, 325, 345n1
Wakes and responsories, 213–214, 243
Warner, W. Lloyd, 129
Wealth: of aristocrats, 36, 109, 149–150,
153–154, 159–160, 225, 226, 227, 236–
237, 260, 286–291, 305, 343n4; and
migration of foreign entrepreneurs
to Mexico, 14, 44–45; of *nouveaux
riches*, 5, 45, 48, 149; of plutocrats,
43, 44–49, 116, 145, 149–150, 226–
227, 285, 286, 287, 308; and political
class, 13; of provincial aristocrats, 36;
of upper-middle class, 73, 118; varying degrees of, in kindred network,
236–237
Wedding anniversaries, 146, 272
Wedding celebrations, 123–125, 145, 146,
147, 175–181, 209, 218, 242, 244, 273,
274, 276–277, 279, 343–344n1
Weekendismo (weekends in the country
for aristocratic families), 111, 114, 350
Western European aristocracies, 2, 8–12,
18, 30, 82, 135, 168, 219–220, 225, 226,
282–283, 312, 346n5, 346n8
Whites, 51, 53–54, 74–75, 89, 342n1,
348, 349. *See also* Cultural whitening
syndrome
Widows, 251
Wilson, Edward, 323, 324, 329–330
Witchcraft and sorcery, 173, 174, 197, 206
Women: beauty standards for, 62; and
child custody following divorce,
270; clothing and body adornment
for, 123, 127–128, 148; continuing
education of, 128, 137; in convents,
292, 346n4; culinary expertise of,
142, 164; division of labor in nuclear
family households, 255, 258; education of, 157; employment of young
women before marriage, 257; inheritance of, 259–262; in professions,
157; religious practices of, 195–196,
211, 213, 214–216; and separation
from husband, 268–270; shift in
kindred affiliation by, 232; virginity